CREDITOR PRIORITY IN EUROPEAN BANK INSOLVENCY LAW

This book provides the first comprehensive treatment of creditor priority in European bank insolvency law.

Following reform in the wake of the global financial crisis, EU law requires that Member States have in place bank-specific insolvency frameworks. Creditor priority – the order in which different creditors bear losses should a bank fail – differs substantially between bank-specific and general insolvency law. The bank-specific creditor priority framework aims to ensure that banks can enter insolvency proceedings without disrupting financial stability.

The book provides a systematic and thorough account of the Bank Recovery and Resolution Directive and other EU legislation that governs creditor priority in bank resolution and liquidation proceedings, and their interaction with national law. The framework is analysed from several perspectives, including comparison with creditor priority in English, German and Norwegian general insolvency law. Moreover, the book places the evolution of the framework and its justifications within the broader post-crisis shifts in bank regulation, and critically examines the assumptions that underlie these developments. Finally, the book discusses how this area of law could evolve in the future.

Hart Studies in Commercial and Financial Law: Volume 10

Hart Studies in Commercial and Financial Law

Series Editors: John Linarelli and Teresa Rodríguez de las Heras Ballell

This series offers a venue for publishing works on commercial law as well as on the regulation of banking and finance and the law on insolvency and bankruptcy. It publishes works on the law on secured credit, the regulatory and transactional aspects of banking and finance, the transactional and regulatory institutions for financial markets, legal and policy aspects associated with access to commercial and consumer credit, new generation subjects having to do with the institutional architecture associated with innovation and the digital economy including works on blockchain technology, work on the relationship of law to economic growth, the harmonisation or unification of commercial law, transnational commercial law, and the global financial order. The series promotes interdisciplinary work. It publishes research on the law using the methods of empirical legal studies, behavioural economics, political economy, normative welfare economics, law and society inquiry, socio-legal studies, political theory, and historical methods. Its coverage includes international and comparative investigations of areas of law within its remit.

Volume 1: The Financialisation of the Citizen: Social and Financial Inclusion through European Private Law
Guido Comparato

Volume 2: MiFID II and Private Law: Enforcing EU Conduct of Business Rules
Federico Della Negra

Volume 3: Reforming Corporate Retail Investor Protection: Regulating to Avert Mis-Selling
Diane Bugeja

Volume 4: The Future of Commercial Law: Ways Forward for Change and Reform
Edited by Orkun Akseli and John Linarelli

Volume 5: The Cape Town Convention: A Documentary History
Anton Didenko

Volume 6: Regulating the Crypto Economy: Business Transformations and Financialisation
Iris H-Y Chiu

Volume 7: The Future of High-Cost Credit: Rethinking Payday Lending
Jodi Gardner

Volume 8: The Enforcement of EU Financial Law
Edited by Jan Crijns, Matthias Haentjens and Rijnhard Haentjens

Volume 9: International Bank Crisis Management: A Transatlantic Perspective
Marco Bodellini

Volume 10: Creditor Priority in European Bank Insolvency Law: Financial Stability and the Hierarchy of Claims
Sjur Swensen Ellingsæter

Creditor Priority in European Bank Insolvency Law

Financial Stability and the Hierarchy of Claims

Sjur Swensen Ellingsæter

•HART•

OXFORD • LONDON • NEW YORK • NEW DELHI • SYDNEY

HART PUBLISHING

Bloomsbury Publishing Plc

Kemp House, Chawley Park, Cumnor Hill, Oxford, OX2 9PH, UK

1385 Broadway, New York, NY 10018, USA

29 Earlsfort Terrace, Dublin 2, Ireland

First published in Great Britain 2022

A catalogue record for this book is available from the British Library.

A catalogue record for this book is available from the Library of Congress.

Library of Congress Control Number: 2022946909

ISBN: HB: 978-1-50995-365-3
ePDF: 978-1-50995-367-7
ePub: 978-1-50995-366-0

Typeset by Compuscript Ltd, Shannon

ACKNOWLEDGEMENTS

The foundations of this book were laid in my doctoral thesis which I defended at the University of Oslo, Faculty of Law, in February 2020. The process of turning the thesis into a book manuscript has required substantial work, and the book differs from the thesis in several respects: First, the book employs a new comprehensive analytical framework. Secondly, the book deals with creditor priority in resolution and the winding up of banks to a greater extent than the thesis does. Thirdly, through the process, several chapters from the thesis have been significantly compressed, while some chapters have been discarded.

The book has benefited from the help of several people, and I would like to express my gratitude. During my work with the thesis I received excellent supervision from Professor emeritus Kåre Lilleholt and dr.juris Knut Bergo. My thesis was assessed by a highly competent committee consisting of Professor Wolf-Georg Ringe, Professor Michael Schillig and Professor Inger Berg Ørstavik. Their thorough assessment and the discussion during the doctoral defence gave very helpful feedback. Michael also kindly offered me advice in the process of drafting the proposal for what would eventually become this book.

I also wish to thank the Department of Private Law at the University of Oslo for providing me with a four-year position as a doctoral research fellow during my doctoral studies. My employment coincided with that of several researchers who have become my friends. While I have been working on the book, I have been employed as an associate professor at the Department of Law and Governance at BI Norwegian Business School. I wish to thank all my colleagues for their contributions to a friendly and intellectually stimulating environment.

I am greatly indebted to my parents, Anne Lise and Anders. Thank you for your enduring encouragement and support in connection with the research, as well as in life more generally.

The winter of 2020 is a period of special significance to me. I defended my doctoral thesis, but more importantly, I then met Agnes, who has made the subsequent years fantastic. Thank you for all the encouragement and support.

Finally, I am grateful that Hart offered to publish the book. I wish to thank Hart's commissioning and production teams for all their help and Hart's anonymous reviewers for their valuable feedback.

TABLE OF CONTENTS

LIST OF ABBREVIATIONS

AT1	Additional Tier 1
BCBS	Basel Committee on Banking Supervision
BER	Bail-in Exclusion Regulation, Commission Delegated Regulation (EU) 2016/860
BRRD	Bank Recovery and Resolution Directive, Directive 2014/59/EU (as amended)
BRRD II	Directive (EU) 2019/879
CBD	Covered Bonds Directive, Directive (EU) 2019/2162
CET1	Common Equity Tier 1
CIWUD	Credit Institutions Winding Up Directive, Directive 2001/24/EC (as amended)
CRD I	Capital Requirements Directive I, Directive 2006/48/EC
CRD IV	Capital Requirements Directive IV, Directive 2013/36/EU (as amended)
CRR	Capital Requirements Regulation, Regulation (EU) No 575/2013 (as amended)
DGS	Deposit Guarantee Scheme
DGSD	Deposit Guarantee Scheme Directive, Directive 2014/49/EU (as amended)
ECB	European Central Bank
ECJ	European Court of Justice
ESCB	European System of Central Banks
ELA	Emergency Liquidity Assistance
EMIR	European Market Infrastructure Regulation, Regulation (EU) No 648/2012 (as amended)
ESRB	European Systemic Risk Board
FCD	Financial Collateral Directive, Directive 2002/47/EC (as amended)

FSB	Financial Stability Board
GFC	Global Financial Crisis
G-SII	Global Systemically Important Institution
InsO	Insolvenzordnung
KWG	Kreditwesengesetz
LCRR	Liquidity Coverage Requirement Regulation, Commission Delegated Regulation (EU) 2015/61 (as amended)
MREL	Minimum Requirement for Own Funds and Eligible Liabilities
RWA	Risk-weighted Assets
SFD	Settlement Finality Directive, Directive 98/28/EC (as amended)
SRB	Single Resolution Board
SRM	Single Resolution Mechanism
SRMR	Single Resolution Mechanism Regulation, Regulation (EU) No 806/2014 (as amended)
SSM	Single Supervisory Mechanism
SSMR	Single Supervisory Mechanism Regulation, Regulation (EU) No 1024/2013
TLAC	Total Loss-Absorbing Capacity

TABLE OF CASES

EFTA Court

European Union

Germany

Norway

UK

TABLE OF LEGISLATION AND TREATIES

Germany

Norway

Legislation

Regulations

UK

Legislation

Statutory instruments

European Union

Primary legislation

Regulations

Directives

Other

1

Introduction

1.1. Nature of the Subject

This book analyses three questions. First, to what extent is there a difference between EU bank insolvency law and general insolvency law in terms of creditor priority? Secondly, what are the rationales that best explain the existence of creditor priority rules specific to bank failures? Thirdly, has the approach to creditor priority in bank insolvency law changed over time and, if so, how does this development fit with broader trends in banking regulation?

The book explores the above questions against the background of the exponential growth in EU legal acts concerning the insolvency of banks in the aftermath of the global financial crisis (the GFC) of 2007–2009. The crisis caused several jurisdictions to introduce bank-specific insolvency frameworks.[1] This, in turn, resulted in the EU adopting the Bank Recovery and Resolution Directive (BRRD),[2] which requires Member States to give public authorities the power to place credit institutions, investment firms and affiliated entities under a sector-specific insolvency procedure termed *resolution*.

Resolution involves public authorities taking control of a failing financial institution or affiliated company and possibly recapitalising the institution by varying the rights of shareholders and creditors. In essence, resolution serves as a means for ensuring that the business of financial institutions is carried on insofar as the public interest requires. An essential prerequisite to this end is that the business again turns solvent, which necessitates that it be relieved of at least parts of the financial burdens that contributed to its financial distress. One power, or *resolution tool* in the terminology employed in BRRD, that may be employed to reach this

[1] M Haentjens, B Wessels and L Janssen, *New Bank Insolvency Law for China and Europe, Volume 2: European Union* (The Hague, Eleven International, 2017) 20–21.

[2] Directive 2014/59/EU of the European Parliament and of the Council of 15 May 2014 establishing a framework for the recovery and resolution of credit institutions and investment firms and amending Council Directive 82/891/EEC, and Directives 2001/24/EC, 2002/47/EC, 2004/25/EC, 2005/56/EC, 2007/36/EC, 2011/35/EU, 2012/30/EU and 2013/36/EU, and Regulations (EU) No 1093/2010 and (EU) No 648/2012, of the European Parliament and of the Council [2014] OJ L173/190. The directive has been amended by Directive (EU) 2017/2399 of the European Parliament and of the Council of 12 December 2017 amending Directive 2014/59/EU as regards the ranking of unsecured debt instruments in insolvency hierarchy [2017] OJ L345/96 and Directive 2019/879 (EU) of the European Parliament and of the Council amending Directive 2014/59/EU as regards the loss-absorbing and recapitalisation capacity of credit institutions and investment firms and Directive 98/26/EC [2019] OJ L150/296 (BRRD II).

result is to write down the debt of the institution subject to resolution. The directive terms this power the *bail-in tool*. Resolution authorities are also empowered to transfer assets and liabilities to a third party, which may be either another bank or a government-controlled bank established to assume the assets and liabilities in question. BRRD terms these powers the *sale of business tool* and the *bridge institution tool*, respectively.[3]

Despite their differences, all the resolution tools involve some creditors not being paid in full. A bail-in involves reducing the creditors' claims against the institution. The transfer tools envisage a transfer of the institution's assets to a third party while leaving all or some liabilities in the residual entity. Accordingly, such measures must be accompanied by rules that determine how the losses are to be distributed among the creditors. Such rules govern the priority among creditors of the entities under resolution.

There are numerous differences between the resolution proceeding set out in BRRD and general insolvency proceedings in terms of institutional, procedural and substantive matters. Importantly, the resolution regime does not distribute losses among creditors by duplicating the priority rules found in the general insolvency law of the resolved entity's home state. The bail-in tool explicitly requires resolution authorities to observe a priority hierarchy that deviates from that found in general insolvency law. The transfer tools also permit forms of loss distribution that deviate from that mandated by the priority rules found in general insolvency law.

Not all institutions are to be resolved in the event of failure. The main rule under BRRD is that banks are to be wound up under 'normal insolvency proceedings' and that the resolution powers are only to be invoked in cases where necessary to safeguard certain public interest objectives. It follows from the directive's definition of normal insolvency proceedings that this term essentially refers to whatever proceedings that the relevant Member State employs for winding up banks.[4] Member States may choose between employing the same winding-up proceedings as are applicable to any company or a sector-specific variant modified to account for concerns specific to bank failures. While Member States generally remain free to determine how banks are to be wound up, BRRD contains requirements concerning the priority of certain depositors and other creditors.[5]

BRRD is complemented by other pieces of EU legislation that seek to influence which creditors bear the losses of resolving or liquidating a bank. BRRD itself provides the resolution authorities with the power to require that a given percentage of a bank's financing stems from equity or debt that has priority below its other debts in resolution and winding up. Moreover, the implementation of the Commission's Financial Services Action Plan during the turn of the millennium

[3] We will refer to the two powers together as the *transfer tools* or the *transfer powers*.
[4] See BRRD art 2(1)(47).
[5] See 5.3.

saw the adoption of directives that require Member States to give financial market participants preferential treatment in insolvency proceedings, whether bank-specific or general.[6] Together with the BRRD's provisions on resolution and creditor priority, these legal acts give rise to a bank-specific creditor priority framework.

Naturally, the question of creditor priority is not unique to resolution and the winding up of banks. The question of priority arises whenever a company is insolvent or is on the brink of becoming so.[7] As the debtor's resources are scarce, the legal order must determine how the available means are to be distributed or which creditors must forgo their claims. Most legal orders respond to this problem through general insolvency procedures that involve the appointment of an insolvency professional who assumes the power to sell the assets of the debtor company and distribute the proceeds among its creditors. States are also increasingly adopting legislation that allows for the restructuring of company debts without necessitating the consent of all creditors thereby affected, thereby facilitating insolvent companies' return to solvency and struggling companies avoiding becoming insolvent. Save for a small number of exceptions, general insolvency proceedings are applicable to insolvent companies regardless of the economic sector in which they operate. There is not a specific procedure for, say, companies operating in the shipping sector or companies that operate airlines. The financial sector is thus one of few exceptions to how the legal order generally approaches the problem of insolvency.

As stated previously, the first objective of this book is to analyse how EU bank insolvency procedures differ from general insolvency law in terms of creditor priority. The strategy for achieving this end is as follows. We will first identify the priority rules in general insolvency proceedings of a sample of European legal systems – one of an EU and euro area jurisdiction (German law), one of a European Economic Area jurisdiction (Norwegian law) and one of an ex-EU jurisdiction (English law). English and German law are chosen because they represent two influential legal traditions and economies, while Norwegian insolvency law is chosen because it is widely regarded as representative of the insolvency law of the Scandinavian countries. The starting point for this analysis is the liquidation proceedings that we will discuss at 3.1.3,[8] as these form the backbone of insolvency law, both in general and in terms of priority. We conduct a comparative study of the two most important questions of priority that arise in the context of this type of proceedings. The first of these concerns the extent to which it is possible for a company to grant security interests that remain effective

[6] Directive 98/26/EC of the European Parliament and of the Council on settlement finality in payment and securities settlement systems [1998] OJ L166/45 (the Settlement Finality Directive or SFD); Directive 2002/47/EC of the European Parliament and of the Council on financial collateral arrangements [2002] OJ L168/43 (the Financial Collateral Directive or FCD).

[7] E Hüpkes, 'Allocating Costs of Failure Resolution' in RM Lastra (ed), *Cross-Border Bank Insolvency* (Oxford, Oxford University Press, 2011) para 5.13.

[8] We will use the terms 'liquidation' and 'winding up' interchangeably.

following the commencement of liquidation proceedings. In other words, this is a question of to what extent it is possible for a company and specific creditors to contract for priority over other creditors. The second question concerns the priority rules that apply in liquidation proceedings for the distribution of whatever value is available for sharing among the unsecured creditors. An analysis of the extent to which it is possible to use restructuring proceedings to upend the priority scheme of liquidation proceedings completes our discussion of priority in general insolvency law.

Against this backdrop, we move on to analyse the priority regime that applies in bank insolvency proceedings. For reasons explored in chapter seven, the priority regime of bank insolvency proceedings is a modified version of that applicable in generally applicable liquidation proceedings. As a result, an analysis of the sector-specific legislation implicitly answers the question of the extent to which there are differences between the general and bank-specific frameworks in terms of priority. We also explore a feature that lacks a counterpart in general insolvency law: regulatory requirements for how banks use their freedom to contract with specific counterparties for priority above or below that of general unsecured creditors. While such requirements are not priority rules in the strictest sense, they have the potential to exercise great influence on how creditors ultimately share losses in a bank failure.

The second objective of the book is to identify the rationales that best explain why bank-specific priority rules differ from those that apply in general insolvency law. To this end, we will consult legal and economic theory on creditor priority in general and bank-specific insolvency proceedings, identify the policy implications of the different strands of the theory and examine the extent to which the general and sector-specific frameworks conform to the prescriptions of the different normative views.

A third objective of the book is to investigate whether the approach to creditor priority in bank insolvency law has changed over time and, if so, how this development fits with broader trends in banking regulation. It shall be argued that such a development has occurred, and that this parallels the evolution of EU banking regulation from a paradigm of meta-regulation to one of technocratic fine-tuning (TFT).

1.2. From Meta-Regulation to Technocratic Fine-Tuning

1.2.1. What Is Regulation?

While chapter nine shall elaborate upon the argument that banking regulation has evolved towards a TFT approach, reference is made to this development throughout the book. It is therefore at this point necessary to define what is meant by meta-regulation and TFT regulation, respectively. Before we go on to do so at 1.2.2 and 1.2.3, we first need to discuss what we refer to as regulation.

Following Baldwin et al, it might be useful to distinguish between the three conceptions of regulation.[9] The first conception sees regulation as commands by a regulator. A statute that requires banks to disclose certain financial information to the public is thus regulation under this definition. The same definition applies where a statute prohibits the taking of deposits from the public without a public authorisation. This is perhaps the most intuitive conception of regulation.[10] When contrasted to broader conceptions of regulation, this first conception is often termed *command-and-control* regulation.[11] The second conception sees regulation as 'deliberate state influence'. This conception includes command-and-control regulation, but also what may be termed *economic regulation* – that is, the use of economic instruments to induce certain behaviour (subsidies, tax deductions) or to deter unwanted actions (taxes on activities that generate pollution). The third – and broadest – conception of regulation that Baldwin et al describe defines regulation as 'all mechanisms affecting behaviour'.[12] By contrast to the other two conceptions this does not treat regulation as necessarily involving the state. Moreover, it is not required that the mechanism is intended to affect behaviour.

Coglianese and Mendelson propose that regulation is defined by four attributes: *target, regulator, command* and *consequences*. Accordingly, to constitute regulation something must involve a *regulator* – eg a legislative body – *commanding* a *target* – eg a bank – to do or abstain from doing something.[13] Moreover, the command must be backed by a *consequence*. The consequence may either be a negative in the case of non-compliance – eg a fine – or a positive in the case of compliance – eg a subsidy. This definition seems to overlap with Baldwin et al's second conception of regulation except that Coglianese and Mendelson do not explicitly make deliberate state influence a part of regulation.

Coglianese and Mendelson's definition is useful for categorising different forms of regulation. We will therefore employ this definition in this book. However, it is for present purposes necessary to make certain adjustments to the definition. The first is that the consequences must either involve the use of coercion that requires a statutory basis or the use of public funds. The second is that the command must concern the exercise of an economic activity.

[9] R Baldwin, M Cave and M Lodge, *Understanding Regulation: Theory, Strategy, and Practice*, 2nd edn (Oxford, Oxford University Press, 2012) 2–3.

[10] P Drahos and M Krygier, 'Regulation, institutions and networks' in P Drahos (ed), *Regulatory Theory: Foundations and Applications* (Acton, ANU Press, 2017) 12–13.

[11] J Black, 'Decentring Regulation: Understanding the Role of Regulation and Self-Regulation in a "Post-Regulatory" World' (2001) 54 *Current Legal Problems* 103, 105.

[12] Baldwin, Cave and Lodge (n 9) 3.

[13] C Coglianese and E Mendelson, 'Meta-Regulation and Self-Regulation' in R Baldwin, M Cave and M Lodge (eds), *The Oxford Handbook of Regulation* (Oxford, Oxford University Press, 2010) 148.

1.2.2. Command-and-Control Regulation, Self-Regulation and Meta-Regulation

Regulation can take on several forms. As discussed above, one such form is command-and-control regulation. However, states often employ other forms of regulation to induce or discourage certain forms of behaviour. Regulatory scholars sometimes present *self-regulation* and *meta-regulation* as opposites of command-and-control regulation. However, the usage of these terms is not consistent.[14] It is therefore useful to discuss the meanings that scholars have attached to these terms and how these fit into the definition of regulation that we adopted at 1.2.1.

Baldwin et al argue that '[s]elf-regulation can be seen as taking place when a group of firms or individuals exerts control over its own membership and their behaviour'.[15] In other words, 'self-regulation' for these authors comprises rules promulgated by private actors that bind other private actors. However, the literature offers a variety of sub-groups of self-regulation, some of which involve the state.[16] As argued by Black, regulatory systems frequently include approaches that do not fit easily on either side of a state-/self-regulation divide.[17]

Meta-regulation is related to some of the conceptions of self-regulation. For Baldwin et al, meta-regulation 'refers to processes in which the regulatory authority oversees a control or risk management system, rather than carries out regulation directly'.[18] Coglianese and Mendelson understand the term as referring to how outside regulators seek to induce targets to develop self-regulatory responses to public problems.[19] The Capital Requirements Directive IV Article 74(1) is an example of meta-regulation: The provision establishes an obligation for Member States to require that banks have in place 'robust governance arrangements', which includes 'adequate internal control mechanisms, including sound administration and accounting procedures'.[20] Upon closer inspection, one may argue that the provision actually envisages two regulatory instruments: First, the Member State (the regulator) shall require the bank (the target) to establish 'robust governance arrangements' (the command). Failure to do so may result in a penalty (a consequence). Secondly, the bank (the target) shall comply with the 'robust governance

[14] Black (n 11) 115–21; P Grabosky, 'Meta-regulation' in P Drahos (ed), *Regulatory Theory: Foundations and Applications* (Acton, ANU Press, 2017) 149.

[15] Baldwin, Cave and Lodge (n 9) 137.

[16] ST Omarova, 'Rethinking the Future of Self-Regulation in the Financial Industry' (2010) 35 *Brooklyn Journal of International Law* 665, 675–77.

[17] J Black, 'Mapping the Contours of Contemporary Financial Services Regulation' (2002) 2 *Journal of Corporate Law Studies* 253.

[18] Baldwin, Cave and Lodge (n 9) 147.

[19] Coglianese and Mendelson (n 13) 150.

[20] Directive 2013/36/EU of the European Parliament and of the Council on access to the activity of credit institutions and the prudential supervision of credit institutions and investment firms, amending Directive 2002/87/EC and repealing Directives 2006/48/EC and 2006/49/EC [2013] OJ L176/338 (CRD IV).

arrangement' (the command) that the bank has drawn up (as regulator). Failure to do so may result in a penalty (a consequence).

As we will discuss at 2.3, capital requirements are a central element of contemporary banking regulation. In short, capital requirements constitute limits on the extent to which banks can finance their operations with debt. Banks must thus ensure that their equity – ie the difference between their assets and liabilities – stays above applicable minimum levels. Some scholars describe the capital requirements framework as an instance of meta-regulation.[21] This conclusion is not intuitive, as these requirements at first glance appear as archetypes of command-and-control regulation. However, the framework provides that banks may exercise influence over the determination of the minimum level of equity that they must maintain. This is because some of the minimum levels are determined by reference to a 'total risk exposure amount', which is a measure that seeks to capture the riskiness of bank assets.[22] Supervisors may allow banks with sufficiently advanced risk-management systems to use their own models for calculating the total risk exposure amount.[23]

When the bank itself determines its total risk exposure amount, the obligation to maintain capital in an amount that exceeds the applicable threshold (the command) is a product of both state and bank input. This means that the bank is not only the target of the regulation, but also a co-regulator. Accordingly, the capital requirements framework in this regard differs from command-and-control regulation where commands are exclusively issued by the legislature, the government or other entities external to the regulatory target.

1.2.3. Technocratic Fine-Tuning

This book will argue that both EU banking regulation and creditor priority in bank insolvency law have become increasingly complex in the aftermath of the GFC. With respect to financial regulation, this is a widely held view.[24] However, as is also acknowledged, there is no single definition as to what regulatory complexity entails or how it is measured.[25]

[21] M Andenas and IH-Y Chiu, *The Foundations and Future of Financial Regulation* (London, Routledge, 2014) 102; J Black, 'Paradoxes and Failures: "New Governance" Techniques and the Financial Crisis' (2012) 75 *Modern Law Review* 1037, 1046; M Ojo, 'Risk management by the Basel Committee: Evaluating progress made from the 1988 Basel Accord to recent developments' (2010) 18 *Journal of Financial Regulation and Compliance* 305, 310.

[22] CRR art 92(2).

[23] CRR art 143.

[24] D Aikman et al, 'Taking uncertainty seriously: simplicity versus complexity in financial regulation' (2021) 30 *Industrial and Corporate Change* 317; D Awrey and K Judge, 'Why Financial Regulation Keeps Falling Short' (2020) 61 *Boston College Law Review* 2295; P Gai et al, 'Regulatory complexity and the quest for robust regulation' (2019) European Systemic Risk Board Reports of the Advisory Scientific Committee No 8.

[25] See eg J-E Colliard and C-P Georg, 'Measuring Regulatory Complexity' (2020) CEPR Discussion Paper 14377; Z Amadxarif et al, 'The language of rules: textual complexity in banking reforms' (2019) Bank of England Staff Working Paper No 834.

In this book, the complexity of a regulatory framework refers to the degree to which the content of the legal obligations it imposes differs between the individual targets of the regulation.[26] As regulatory obligations of banks are increasingly tailored to the specific characteristics of individual entities, and requirements are intended to vary over time, EU banking regulation has become increasingly complex in this sense. In the context of creditor priority, complexity increases with the differentiation in treatment between different categories of creditors.

An argument that will be developed is that the increasing complexity can be understood as part of a *technocratic fine-tuning* (TFT) approach that has emerged following the GFC. TFT regulation has three attributes, the first being complexity. The second attribute is that regulatory output is determined through case-by-case decisions by bank supervisors and other agencies, as opposed to through legislation adopted by legislatures. The third attribute is that the exercise of the powers to regulate is – at least ostensibly – constrained by numerous conditions.

TFT regulation gives rise to certain tensions and trade-offs. The rationale for TFT regulation is proportionality: to achieve the objective of banking regulation – chiefly financial stability – without placing unnecessary restrictions on bank business models. However, an approach of individual requirements tailored by agencies is potentially in conflict with ideals such as the rule of law and democratic legitimacy. Placing conditions on the powers to regulate is a potential fix to these issues, but whether such conditions in practice bind administrative regulators depends on how they are worded and the intensity with which courts are willing to review regulatory decisions should they be subject to legal challenge. These tensions and trade-offs will be discussed in chapter nine.

1.3. Terminology

This book analyses EU law requirements for creditor priority under the resolution framework set out in BRRD and national frameworks for winding up banks that do not qualify for resolution on public interest grounds. The reason for considering creditor priority under both frameworks is two-fold. First, the priority regime applicable in resolution is in part determined by priority in winding up proceedings applicable to banks. Secondly, juxtaposing the two regimes could reveal whether the public interests involved have led the creditor priority framework applicable in resolution to depart from general insolvency law principles to a greater extent than that applicable in the winding up of banks.

It is useful to have a collective term for the legal frameworks governing resolution and winding up of banks, respectively. To this end, the book uses the term 'bank insolvency law'. It should be noted that some use bank insolvency law to

[26] *cf* P Krishnamurthy, 'Rules, Standards, and Complexity in Capital Regulation' (2014) 43 *The Journal of Legal Studies* S273, S274–S275.

refer to the latter of the two frameworks; when used in this narrow sense, references to bank insolvency law do not include resolution.[27]

EU law uses terminology that some may perceive as awkward. To increase the readability of the book, we will attempt to do away with some of these terms where permissible. We will generally speak of banks when discussing the entities that may be resolved. BRRD applies to 'institutions', which in turn comprise 'credit institutions' and 'investment firms', and certain financial holding companies. Banks – ie entities that accept deposits from the public and lend to physical persons and corporations – are a subset of credit institutions: the Capital Requirements Regulation (CRR) Article 4(1)(1) defines a credit institution as 'an undertaking the business of which is to take deposits or other repayable funds from the public and to grant credits for its own account'. A bank issues deposits, whereas an entity can constitute a credit institution even if its funding consists of other forms of finance from the public, such as bonds. In other words, all banks are credit institutions, but not all credit institutions are banks.

Banks are subject to supervision. When speaking of authorities tasked with supervising whether banks, other credit institutions and investment firms comply with capital requirements, liquidity requirements and other prudential rules, EU law generally uses the term 'competent authorities'. For convenience, we will use the term 'bank supervisor' when discussing the authority that is the competent authority for banks.

Norway is not a member of the European Union. However, through the Agreement on the European Economic Area of 1992 (the EEA Agreement), Norway is required to transpose into Norwegian law most of the EU legal acts discussed in this book. We will at times refer to how Norway has satisfied its obligations in this respect. For convenience, we will refer collectively to legal obligations that arise under both EU law and EEA law as EU law, save where EEA law differs from EU law.

1.4. The Structure of the Book

The structure of this book is as follows. Chapters two and three set the scene for the analysis of priority in subsequent chapters. Chapter two reviews the arguments for society's concern with bank failures and discusses the means employed for preventing these, namely prudential regulation and the legal framework for the public backing of struggling banks. Thereafter, chapter three introduces the main features of the general insolvency proceedings of the sample jurisdictions and bank insolvency proceedings. Moreover, this chapter discusses the emergence of bank-specific insolvency procedures by seeking to identify why general insolvency proceedings are considered to be inappropriate for banks.

[27] See eg M Schillig, 'EU bank insolvency law harmonisation: What next?' (2021) 30 *International Insolvency Review* 239.

Chapter four discusses the priority framework for general insolvency proceedings in English, German and Norwegian law. The chapter analyses the extent to which it is possible for companies in these jurisdictions to give specific creditors priority by granting security interests, as well as the extent to which mandatory priority rules differentiate among unsecured creditors. Against this background, the chapter attempts to unearth the underlying logic of the generally applicable creditor priority frameworks.

Chapters five to eight move on to creditor priority in bank insolvency law. The structure follows a two-tracked system for bank insolvency procedures implicit in BRRD. Chapter five thus discusses the bank-specific priority rules that apply when a bank is wound up, while chapter six does the same in the context of a resolution. Chapter seven identifies the rationales that best fit with the bank-specific priority framework. Chapter eight analyses the extent to which public authorities can require banks to issue debt that ranks below general unsecured debt in a winding up or resolution.

Chapters nine and ten conclude the book. Chapter nine elaborates upon the technocratic fine-tuning approach (TFT) to regulation in current banking regulation and argues that the creditor priority framework now contains elements that reflect a TFT approach. Chapter ten considers the future of bank-specific creditor priority rules.

2

Why and How Society Seeks to Limit Bank Failures

2.1. Society's Concern with Bank Failures

2.1.1. Introduction

Bank-specific insolvency procedures form part of a wider institutional set-up that seeks to prevent bank failures that could potentially imperil financial stability. The other constituent parts of this set-up are discussed in subsequent parts of this chapter. The purpose of the following sections is to introduce some of the fundamental ideas that underpin society's concern with bank failures. To this end, 2.1.2 and 2.1.3 discuss the different activities in which banks engage and their distinct financial structure. Thereafter, 2.1.4 seeks to identify the rationales that explain society's current concern with preventing bank failures.

2.1.2. What Banks Do

At its core, a bank possesses two characteristics. The first is that it makes loans, which are often long term. The second is that it accepts deposits from the public. Large European banks do not, however, restrict their services to such 'core banking'. They supplement these activities with what we may term investment banking. The investment banking services offered by banks include underwriting share issuances, advisory services and brokerage. Recently, banks have increasingly engaged in trading in securities for their own account. Nevertheless, deposit-taking and lending remain a bank's core functions. In the following paragraphs, we will discuss how theory explains the prevalence of institutions that combine lending with deposit-taking.

The classic narrative of banking is that banks act as intermediaries between persons with surplus funds to invest and borrowers with capital needs. Banks engage in *maturity transformation* by financing long-term lending such as mortgages and corporate loans with short-term deposits. The activity also involves *liquidity transformation* – the liabilities that a bank has towards depositors are liquid, even though the bank's assets are illiquid. The banking sector's lending activity gives borrowers with financial needs an alternative to obtaining funds directly from investors in the capital markets by issuing shares or bonds. Accordingly, banking brings about the benefit of increased access to capital. It is worth posing the question of exactly how maturity and liquidity transformation bring about benefits. It is not apparent that there is a need to supplement the capital markets. In principle, persons and entities with excess capital could lend directly to firms, in which case there would be no element of intermediation.[1]

What is it about the link between the taking of deposits and the extension of loans that seemingly allow banks to perform functions that capital markets cannot? One rationale is that banks invest on behalf of their depositors. Under this conception, banks function as *delegated monitors*.[2] The need for a delegated monitor arises when the ultimate lenders (ie depositors) are small. Given such circumstances and an absence of banks, borrowers would have to borrow directly from more than one lender. Each lender needs to incur costs to acquire information about prospective borrowers' investment projects before lending and to verify the outcome of a borrower's investments after extending the loan so that the borrower does not keep all profits to itself without remunerating the lenders for their investment. Given that there is more than one lender, this would lead to each lender performing the same monitoring, thus wastefully duplicating one another's efforts. A financial intermediary improves upon this situation by performing the monitoring functions on behalf of all lenders, thus eliminating duplication and reducing costs.

This does not suffice to explain why banks combine lending with deposit-taking, however. The ultimate lenders could continue to lend directly to borrowers and hire a person to collectivise their monitoring efforts. The answer that the delegated monitor theory offers is that the issuance of deposits functions as a measure for ensuring that the monitor (ie the bank) will diligently perform its mandate. The need for such a measure arises because depositors otherwise have no assurance that banks are doing this. Accordingly, we face a variation of what economists term *agency problems* – where a principal cannot be sure that its agent will perform its duties. This is where the combination of deposit-taking and lending comes in: by committing to repay its depositors (ie the ultimate lenders), a bank also commits itself to monitor, as it would otherwise not be able to make the repayments. In other words, the deposit contract aligns a self-interested bank's incentives with the interests of the depositors. As banks now have a device for committing themselves to perform the monitoring task, savers are willing to extend funds to banks. This, in turn, reduces the cost of lending. One implication of the monitoring function

[1] G Gorton and A Winton, 'Financial Intermediation' in GM Constantinides, M Harris and RM Stulz (eds), *Handbook of the Economics of Finance*, vol 1A (Amsterdam, Elsevier, 2003) 437.

[2] The seminal work is DW Diamond, 'Financial Intermediation and Delegated Monitoring' (1984) 51 *Review of Economic Studies* 393. For a concise explanation of the article's insights, see F Allen, E Carletti and X Gu, 'The Roles of Banks in Financial Systems' in AN Berger, P Molyneux and JOS Wilson (eds), *The Oxford Handbook of Banking*, 2nd edn (Oxford, Oxford University Press, 2014) 30–31 and Gorton and Winton (n 1) 440–42.

performed by banks is that the banks make more financing available to the real economy. Reducing the costs associated with lending money should lead to an increase in profitable projects. This would also mean that an increase in the financing available directly from savers in the capital market would not necessarily be available to offset any reduction in the overall financing capacity of the banking sector. In other words, if the banking sector decreases its lending, the aggregate availability of financing decreases.

Under the delegated monitor view, depositors do not attach any particular value to holding deposits as opposed to other instruments. Their holding of deposits is merely an efficient investment. Other strands of banking theory hold that deposits have characteristics valued by depositors. In contrast to the lending-centred orientation of the delegated monitor theory, the starting point of this approach to a theory of banking is the issuance of deposits.[3] Deposit-taking solves private parties' problem of being unable to predict when they will require liquidity in the future. It is better for a large body of depositors to hold deposits in a bank than individually engaging in 'self-insurance' by putting together portfolios of risky assets and liquidity. Moreover, and perhaps partly owing to the existence of deposit insurance and other constituent parts of the 'safety net' that we discuss at 2.4, deposits are viewed as so safe that they function as currency.[4] In fact, most currency takes the form of bank deposits, as the aggregate sum of deposits dwarfs that of banknotes and coins.

Assuming that this premise is correct, it does not necessarily explain the existence of the core business models of modern banks. Why are long-term loans the asset of choice for backing liquid deposits? History shows that deposit-taking institutions will not inevitably invest in long-term assets – until the start of the twentieth century, US and UK banks would seldom extend credit with a maturity beyond a few months.[5] Numerous reform proposals have questioned the need to combine deposit-taking with long-term lending. One view is that it would be possible to create *narrow banks* that back deposits with ultra-safe assets such as US treasury bonds.[6] As we shall see at 2.3.7, some jurisdictions have recently placed restrictions on the assets that banks may hold. These reforms, however, are not as radical as the narrow bank proposal, as banks may still lend long term to at least some private parties in all jurisdictions concerned.

While it may be difficult to provide an account of the rise of banks as we currently know them, it remains clear that banks are a dominant factor in the financial system. Naturally, the mere existence of such a state does not prove that this state is desirable. The relative importance of the banking sector to capital markets

[3] DW Diamond and PH Dybvig, 'Bank Runs, Deposit Insurance, and Liquidity' (1983) 91 *Journal of Political Economy* 401.

[4] GB Gorton, *Slapped by the Invisible Hand: The Panic of 2007* (Oxford, Oxford University Press, 2010) 19.

[5] G Pennacchi, 'Narrow Banking' (2012) 4 *Annual Review of Financial Economics* 141, 142–43.

[6] See Pennacchi (n 5) for an overview of different versions of this idea.

varies across economies. For instance, banks play a larger role in European economies than in the US economy.[7] Some will say that European economies rely too much on banks: for instance, the Commission is currently seeking to strengthen Europe's economy by making it less dependent upon bank financing.[8] Some view the banks' dominance as a result of public subsidies that ultimately boost their profitability. These subsidies are what we at 2.4 term the *safety net* – a set of explicit and implicit public guarantees for the liquidity and solvency of banks.

As mentioned above, some banks are engaged in activities beyond deposit-taking and lending. In some jurisdictions, banks have long combined 'core' banking functions with *investment banking* – or, in EU law parlance, investment services and activities.[9] This consists of underwriting securities offerings and providing advice in connection with mergers and acquisitions. Banks that combine core and investment banking are known as *universal banks*.[10] In recent times, banks have increasingly held assets other than loans to households and corporations. First, they increasingly lend to each other. Secondly, larger banks have commenced substantial trading operations. The relative importance of lending was on the decline for a long time,[11] but the post-crisis era has seen the reversal of this trend as large banks have generally reduced their ratios of trading assets to total assets.[12]

2.1.3. How Banks Fund Themselves

The business model of today's banks involves a level of equity financing that is much lower than that common outside the financial sector. A bank's equity typically equals around 5 per cent of its assets,[13] while sound non-financial corporations' equity ratio is usually at least 30–40 per cent. While banks maintained even lower equity levels in the period leading up to the financial crisis, it is safe to say they remain exceptionally highly leveraged. In the following, we will look more closely at the various forms of debt financing employed by banks.

As discussed at 2.1.2, the taking of deposits is a defining feature of banks. In relative terms, deposits may constitute a less dominant part of bank liabilities than

[7] Allen, Carletti and Gu (n 2) 27–29.

[8] Commission, 'A Capital Markets Union for people and businesses-new action plan' COM (2020) 590 final.

[9] See the list in Directive 2014/65/EU of the European Parliament and of the Council of 15 May 2014 on markets in financial instruments and amending Directive 2002/92/EC and Directive 2011/61/EU [2014] OJ L173/349 (MiFID II), annex I.

[10] AD Morrison, 'Universal Banking' in Berger, Molyneux and Wilson (n 2).

[11] See High-level Expert Group on reforming the structure of the EU banking sector, 'Final Report' (2 October 2012) (the Liikanen Report) 15 for developments in bank lending in the euro area between March 1998 and March 2012.

[12] Committee on the Global Financial System, 'Structural changes in banking after the crisis' (2018) CGFS Papers No 60, 19.

[13] See eg European Banking Authority, '2021 EU-wide Stress Test: Results' (30 July 2021) 10. Note that the figures reported in EBA's report concern the *leverage ratio*. As we will revisit at 2.3.5, the leverage ratio metric is similar, but not identical, to an equity-to-assets ratio.

what was earlier the case, but this form of liabilities remains a dominant feature on bank balance sheets.[14]

In the period leading up to the financial crisis, banks increasingly funded themselves with short-term *wholesale funding*, funding that comes from other banks and money market funds. These creditors are very sensitive to changes in credit risk, as many banks discovered during the financial crisis when their short-term creditors increased their demanded rate of interest and even withdrew funding altogether. Since 2009, this trend has been somewhat reversed, as banks are increasingly relying more on household and corporate deposits than on wholesale funding.[15] In particular, the borrowing of eurozone banks from US money market funds fell over the course of the global financial crisis and the Eurozone crisis.[16]

Several developments indicate that wholesale investors are less willing to take credit exposures towards (other) banks. One such development is that wholesale funding is increasingly made on a secured basis. Secondly, wholesale funding is lent at shorter maturities than before. A third development is banks taking further steps to reduce (or even eliminate) credit risk towards other banks by clearing repos through clearing houses.[17] In doing so, the clearing house steps into the contractual relationship by assuming the respective rights and obligations of the original parties, thereby transforming their credit exposure against the original counterparty to one against the clearing house.

Banks also fund themselves with long-term debt by issuing bonds and other debt instruments. Capital markets currently offer bank bonds that carry different risks. First, there are general unsecured bonds. These rank *pari passu* with the general unsecured debt of the bank. Secondly, there are covered bonds. While the legal structure employed differs from jurisdiction to jurisdiction, investors in such bonds generally obtain recourse to a pool of assets ahead of the issuer's other creditors. The issuer is obliged to ensure that the value of the assets in the pool exceeds a given threshold during the term of the bonds. Investors typically regard such bonds as very safe. Thirdly, banks issue bonds for regulatory purposes. These bonds rank behind general unsecured debt. Viewed as a whole, the relative importance of bond financing reportedly declined for eurozone banks from 2005 to 2015.[18] As far as the relative importance of different bonds is concerned, covered bonds have supplanted general unsecured bonds as a source of financing in recent years.[19] In Norway, the issuance of covered bonds has gone from being non-existent in 2007 to making up well over 60 per cent of Norwegian banks' aggregate bond issuances in 2020.[20]

[14] European Central Bank, 'Report on financial structures' (October 2017) 37.

[15] European Central Bank (n 14); Bank of England, 'Financial Stability Report' (July 2019) 32.

[16] A van Rixtel and G Gasperini, 'Financial crises and bank funding: recent experience in the euro area' (2013) BIS Working Papers No 406, 13–15.

[17] European Central Bank, 'Recent developments in the composition of bank funding in the euro area' (2016) ECB Economic Bulletin 32.

[18] European Central Bank (n 17) 34.

[19] van Rixtel and Gasperini (n 16) 16.

[20] Norges Bank, 'Det norske finansielle systemet' (2021) 31.

2.1.4. Why Do Bank Failures Cause Concern?

Left to the devices of general insolvency law, a struggling bank could see itself subject to liquidation, which in turn could lead to the cessation of its activities and its creditors not recovering their claims in full. The emergence of a special bank insolvency framework signals that this outcome is not always desirable. This special concern contradicts the logic of the market economy, as firms are generally subject to the vagaries of the market and cease to operate when they can no longer obtain financing. Bank resolution proceedings constitute a contrast to the general trend for handling the distress of larger companies addressed at 3.1.4, as the restructuring of such companies increasingly confines itself to involving a bargain between the company's shareholders and its financial creditors, either through informal negotiations or in restructuring proceedings that involves judicial supervision and sanction rather than intervention.[21]

The emergence of bank-specific insolvency procedures thus clearly reflects a perceived public interest in preserving the business operations of certain banks. In the following text we will seek to identify the rationales that suggest that bank failures could imperil the provision of services of importance to society. An intuitive starting point for inquiry is what policymakers themselves are saying about the matter. Accordingly, our analysis revolves around three key concepts in BRRD and EU financial regulation: critical functions, financial stability and systemic risk.

BRRD Article 31(2) sets out five resolution objectives. The objectives are:

(a) to ensure the continuity of critical functions;
(b) to avoid a significant adverse effect on the financial system, in particular by preventing contagion, including to market infrastructures, and by maintaining market discipline;
(c) to protect public funds by minimising reliance on extraordinary public financial support;
(d) to protect depositors covered by Directive 2014/49/EU [DGSD] and investors covered by Directive 97/9/EC; and
(e) to protect client funds and client assets.

Of the five objectives, only the first two may potentially explain the interventionist approach that is resolution. Non-intervention could achieve the third objective of preventing the use of public funds. Moreover, the protection of retail depositors, retail investors and clients turns on whether these persons recover their funds, not whether the legal response to the bank's failure is resolution or a winding up under the applicable 'normal insolvency proceedings'. It is true that depositors, investors and clients could have an interest in their bank continuing to provide services. As we shall see below, however, deciding on whether such an interest merits public

[21] S Paterson, 'Rethinking Corporate Bankruptcy in the Twenty-First Century' (2016) 36 *OJLS* 697, 708.

efforts to continue the bank's operations is little more than a question of determining whether a bank's deposit-taking is a critical function. Accordingly, both the fourth and fifth objectives fail to explain an independent concern with how banks fail. We will therefore restrict our attention to the first and the second resolution objectives.

The first resolution objective is 'to ensure the continuity of critical functions'.[22] 'Critical functions' is a defined term that refers to

> activities, services or operations the discontinuance of which is likely in one or more Member States, to lead to the disruption of services that are essential to the real economy or to disrupt financial stability due to the size, market share, external and internal interconnectedness, complexity or cross-border activities of an institution or group, with particular regard to the substitutability of those activities, services or operations.[23]

Pursuant to this definition, two qualities may qualify a function as critical. First, a function is critical when it is of essential importance for the real economy. Secondly, a bank's activities can also constitute a critical function if their disruption could impair financial stability. There appears to be some overlap between the resolution objective of protecting critical services and that of avoiding 'a significant adverse effect on the financial system'. In the following section, we will first discuss how a bank's failure could lead to the disruption of services essential to the real economy. Thereafter, we will examine the link between bank failures and financial stability.

One rationale for preventing the failure of banks is that banks maintain the availability of credit for households and non-financial companies.[24] The underlying rationale is closely related to the view that banks act as 'delegated monitors'. As discussed at 2.1.2, this view holds that banks solve information asymmetry and agency problems to a greater extent than do non-intermediated financial markets. By acting as intermediaries between those with excess liquidity (depositors) and those in need of it (borrowers), banks contribute to increasing the amount of credit available to those in need. In turn, the realisation of profitable projects fosters growth.

Even if one accepts that banks serve as delegated monitors, it does not necessarily follow that society should be concerned with bank failures. If the banking sector as a whole provides an adequate amount of credit, it does not matter if the sector comprises, say, 99 or 100 banks. This assumes that the other 99 banks will respond to the failure by increasing their lending, thereby picking up the slack left by the demise of the 100th bank. This assumption may not hold, however.

[22] BRRD art 31(2)(a).

[23] BRRD art 2(1)(35). BRRD is supplemented by a Commission Delegated Regulation, which contains its own definition of critical functions. We will limit our attention to BRRD's definition for present purposes.

[24] Commission, 'Proposal for a Directive of the European Parliament and of the Council establishing a framework for the recovery and resolution of credit institutions and investment firms and amending Council Directives 77/91/EEC and 82/891/EC, Directives 2001/24/EC, 2002/47/EC, 2004/25/EC, 2005/56/EC, 2007/36/EC and 2011/35/EC and Regulation (EU) No 1093/2010' COM (2012) 280 final 4.

As we will revisit subsequently, the failure of one bank may leave a gap in the credit available. This, again, should be a case of concern if one subscribes to the delegated-monitors view. Since this view holds that the credit offered by banks contributes to increasing the amount of profitable projects realised, the reverse implication must be that a reduction in available credit reduces this number.

A firm's demise is generally a good thing for its competitors, who are then able to expand their market shares. It is therefore somewhat counterintuitive that a bank's failure could reduce overall credit availability. Economic theory offers several explanations for why bank failures may have this effect. One explanation is that a bank failure could signal to other banks that the failed bank's loan portfolio is below average.[25] If other banks hold this belief, they could be reluctant to assume lending relationships with borrowers that formed a part of that portfolio, since those borrowers, on average, are sub-par. Even if other banks wish to take on the borrowers in question as clients, they would have to increase their lending. It is not certain that banks have the capacity to do this. One reason is that banks are required to maintain a certain minimum ratio of equity to assets.[26] Extending loans involves a decrease in this ratio. The failure of one bank could coincide with financial distress among other banks in the same market. Distressed banks will often try to *increase* their amount of equity. Taking on the borrowers of a failed bank is counterproductive to this end.

We have now fleshed out one account of the case for why society should seek to prevent bank failures. Some might be troubled by the implication that we should go to extreme lengths to prevent the exit of failed banks, as the state's commitment to save banks in difficulties enables them to reap undue benefits.[27] Such concerns could be due to a rejection of the basic premise of the delegated monitors view, namely that banks only fund profitable enterprises. While it is possible for banks to fail even under such a lending policy, experience shows that banks encountering financial problems often do so because they finance asset bubbles. Given that the financing of asset bubbles is not desirable, it must surely be the case that a reduction in credit availability is not always a bad thing? If we answer this question in the affirmative, we face the difficult problem of identifying criteria for disentangling financing of profitable enterprises from financing that fuels asset bubbles. This means that it can be difficult to determine when a reduction in credit availability is a 'good' or 'bad' thing.[28]

Another potential rationale for preventing bank failures is that a failure may cause problems for depositors. As we shall discuss further at 2.4, there are specific

[25] Gorton and Winton (n 1) 463, 467 and the research described therein.

[26] See 2.3.

[27] A Admati and M Hellwig, *The Banker's New Clothes: What's Wrong with Banking and What to Do about It* (Princeton, Princeton University Press, 2013) 136–39.

[28] DK Tarullo, 'Time-Varying Measures in Financial Regulation' (2020) 83 *Law and Contemporary Problems* 1, 4.

insurance schemes that seek to protect deposits of up to 100,000 euro. Whether deposit-taking meets BRRD's definition of a critical function depends on how one views the functioning of banks. Under the delegated monitors view, deposits are a firm-specific investment on par with a bond issued by an industrial company. That the claim takes the form of a deposit repayable on demand is merely an incidence of this being the most efficient way of ensuring that banks will indeed monitor on behalf of their depositors. The legal status of deposits is arguably consistent with this view, as deposits constitute a claim for repayment from the issuing bank rather than the depositor having a proprietary right to some asset held by the bank. Thus, even in the presence of regulation, deposit insurance schemes and priority rules, depositors remain exposed to the bank's solvency. Viewing depositors as investors does not rule out society's having a special concern with the safety of deposits. For instance, it is not uncommon to see commentators framing deposit insurance as a matter of consumer protection.[29] It does, however, seem that deposit insurance sits uneasily with the entire theory of banks as delegated monitors. This theory rationalises the bank business model of lending long against short-term liabilities as something banks do to commit themselves to lend diligently, as they will otherwise face repayment demands. Deposit insurance will, however, dampen the incentive of depositors to demand repayment in such a scenario. This, in turn, blunts the banks' incentive to act in the interest of the depositors.

What seems clear is that the protection of the interests of depositors *qua* investors does not necessarily imply a need to continue the operations of failing banks. Whether an individual institution performs a critical service by taking deposits is a different question from whether deposits should receive some form of special protection. Deposit insurance and priority rules make it possible to allow banks to fail under normal insolvency proceedings and still ensure that depositors recover in full. Accordingly, deposit-taking cannot constitute a critical service solely by reference to the interest of depositors in recovering whatever deposit balances they may have outstanding when a bank fails.

As discussed at 2.1, some theories of banking take deposit-taking as their starting point. From this perspective, banks exist because of a demand for a means to store liquidity by holding information-insensitive debt. This view implies that policy should ensure there are sufficient opportunities for storing value. This would mean that a bank's deposit-taking could constitute a critical service, but only insofar as the bank's depositors could not find other banks willing to accept deposits if the bank should cease its operations.

Finally, a service that banks offer is the access to payment systems. When a customer pays a wine merchant for a bottle of wine by using its payment card

[29] See A Campbell and P Cartwright, 'Deposit Insurance: Consumer Protection, Bank Safety and Moral Hazard' (1999) 10 *European Business Law Review* 96, 100, who stated that the primary aims of the 1994 predecessor to DGSD were 'protecting consumers and ensuring stability'.

at the merchant's shop, the ultimate result is that the customer's deposit balance with his bank decreases, while the merchant's balance increases in a corresponding amount (net of fees).[30] The contribution of payment systems is to ensure that this result is not only possible when the customer and the merchant have accounts with the same bank, but also when they have accounts with different banks. Payment systems contribute to the function of bank deposits as a means of exchange and make transactions more convenient which, in turn, increases economic activity. The customer is spared the inconvenience of having to carry banknotes. Payment systems also contribute to reducing more substantial transaction costs. Whereas settling the payment of goods and services previously required a physical meeting between the parties, claims can now be settled through the direct or indirect transfer of deposit balances.

When could an individual bank's provision of payment services constitute a critical function as defined by BRRD? Arguably, this will not often be the case. A breakdown of payment systems would undoubtedly impair the functioning of the economy. Barring the cases where a bank operates a payment system and clears transactions across its accounts, however, it is not apparent that an individual bank's failure would cause the collapse of a payment system. The more likely effect of a bank ceasing to operate would be its clients needing to find another bank to access payment systems.

To sum up, we have so far discussed when an individual bank's lending, deposit-taking and participation in payment systems may constitute 'critical functions' as defined in BRRD Article 2(1)(35). A bank's lending operations could fall under this definition insofar as its cessation would cause businesses with profit-generating projects to lose out on financing. A bank's deposit-taking would be deemed a critical function insofar as other banks would not be able to absorb the demand for deposits. Finally, an individual bank failure's potential to disrupt the payment system would likely require the bank to have had a central role in its technical operation.

The concern for the provision of critical functions is closely linked to the concern for *financial stability*. Theory and policy documents ascribe somewhat different definitions to this term.[31] In a survey, Allen and Wood note that the term can be used to describe two fundamentally different concepts.[32] Under the first conception, the term sometimes denotes *a state of affairs* – the functioning of the financial system at any given time. Under this notion, financial stability is present when savings are allocated towards productive projects. Financial instability is present where the system ceases to perform this function. The Bank of England's

[30] For the details of this process, see T Kokkola (ed), *The Payment System: Payments, Securities and Derivatives, and the Role of the Eurosystem* (Frankfurt am Main, European Central Bank, 2010) 55–59.

[31] For an overview, see GJ Schinasi, 'Defining Financial Stability' (2004) IMF Working Paper WP/04/187 13ff.

[32] WA Allen and G Wood, 'Defining and achieving financial stability' (2006) 2 *Journal of Financial Stability* 152, 154–55.

definition of financial stability is an example of this first conception. The definition reads as follows:

> Financial stability is the consistent supply of the vital services that the real economy demands from the financial system (which comprises financial institutions, markets and market infrastructures). Those services are:
>
> - providing the main mechanism for paying for goods, services and financial assets;
> - intermediating between savers and borrowers, and channelling savings into investment, via debt and equity instruments; and
> - insuring against and dispersing risk.[33]

Under its second conception, financial stability describes *a quality of a given financial system*. More specifically, this quality is its resilience against shocks. A definition recently used by ECB fits best within this category: Financial stability is defined as 'a state where the build-up of *systemic risk* is prevented' (emphasis added).[34] Systemic risk is described as 'the risk that the provision of necessary financial products and services by the financial system will be impaired to a point where economic growth and welfare may be materially affected'.[35] Under this definition, financial stability is not necessarily present even when excess savings are transmitted to investments in the real economy, as systemic risks may be looming.

The definition of financial stability adopted by the Norwegian legislature in finansforetaksloven § 1-1 straddles the dichotomy noted by Allen and Wood. This provision defines financial stability as entailing 'that the financial system is sufficiently robust to receive and repay deposits and other repayable funds from the public, channel funding, execute payments and redistribute risk in a satisfactory manner'. Essentially, financial stability entails that services are performed in a 'satisfactory manner' (which describes the system's output at a given time) and that the system is 'sufficiently robust' to continue to do so in the future (which describes the system's resilience).

All of the above definitions are vague. All embody the view that there exists some optimal level of the provision of financial services and that it is acceptable that the services offered over time can both exceed and fall short of this level. However, the definitions all leave open what this level is and what variance society will accept. It seems reasonably clear that society accepts a probability of financial crises above zero, and this gives rise to the difficult task of pinpointing exactly where the threshold for an unacceptable level of risk lies.[36]

The vague concept of financial stability and the associated difficulties in assessing the achievement of this goal stand in stark contrast to the trend in monetary policy to set numeric inflation targets, such as the ECB's target of an inflation rate

[33] Bank of England, 'Annual Report and Accounts: 1 March 2016–28 February 2017' (2017) 32.

[34] European Central Bank, 'Financial Stability Review' (May 2017) 3.

[35] European Central Bank (n 34) 3.

[36] M Andenas and IH-Y Chiu, *The Foundations and Future of Financial Regulation* (London, Routledge, 2014) 28.

'below, but close to, 2% over the medium term'.[37] Conversely, no official policy states that some measure of credit availability should hover around a given level at all times. The absence of a precisely defined objective has implications for the judicial review of acts made by supervisory and resolution authorities.[38] The Court of Justice of the European Union (CJEU) has dealt with questions in several recent cases on whether various measures have been necessary for protecting financial stability. In particular, the questions have emanated from litigation on the legality of *ad hoc* resolution measures taken by Member States prior to the adoption of BRRD.[39] For the most part, the merits of the CJEU's rulings have been somewhat opaque. The decisions have made it clear that the objective of financial stability can serve as an interpretative device to justify derogations from directive provisions that ostensibly are without exceptions, as well as an objective of general interest capable of legitimising limitations to the fundamental right to property. Strikingly, the Courts rarely elaborate on what they refer to by the term 'financial stability' or why the measures at hand were necessary for attaining the objectives in the cases. This can, perhaps, be said to conform to the 'pragmatic pattern' found more generally in the ECJ's handling of Eurozone crisis cases where the Court has readily accepted arguments at face value in considering the economic effects and rationales of measures made by the EU institutions and the Member States.[40]

Leaving the vague definitions of financial stability aside, one implication of this objective is to ensure the continuity of critical services as discussed above. However, given the interconnections between banks, bank insolvency policy could also involve measures aimed at preventing the problems of one bank from spreading to others. We will in the following discuss the risk of such contagion.

The objective of containing systemic risk has risen to prominence since the financial crisis. Among other initiatives, the EU has established a European Systemic Risk Board (ESRB), a body tasked with responsibility for 'the macro-prudential oversight of the financial system within the Union in order to contribute to the prevention or mitigation of systemic risks to financial stability in the Union'.[41]

[37] K Alexander, 'The European Central Bank and Banking Supervision: The Regulatory Limits of the Single Supervisory Mechanism' (2016) 13 *European Company & Financial Law Review* 467, 486.

[38] M Lamandini, D Ramos and J Solana, 'The European Central Bank (ECB) Powers As a Catalyst for Change in EU Law. Part 2: SSM, SRM and Fundamental Rights' (2017) 23 *Columbia Journal of European Law* 199, 214. See also G Lo Schiavo, *The Role of Financial Stability in EU Law and Policy* (Alphen aan den Rijn, Kluwer Law International, 2017) 61.

[39] See Case C-526/14 *Tadej Kotnik and Others v Državni zbor Republike Slovenije* ECLI:EU:C:2016:570; Case C-41/15 *Gerard Dowling and Others v Minister for Finance* ECLI:EU:C:2016:836; and Joined Cases C-8/15 P to C-10/15 P *Ledra Advertising Ltd and Others v European Commission and European Central Bank (ECB)* ECLI:EU:C:2016:701. See also the General Court's ruling in Case T-680/13 *Dr. K. Chrysostomides & Co. LLC and Others v Council of the European Union and Others* ECLI:EU:T:2018:486.

[40] Lamandini, Ramos and Solana (n 38) 215. See also M Dawson, A Maricut-Akbik and A Bobic, 'Reconciling Independence and accountability at the European Central Bank: The false promise of Proceduralism' (2019) 25 *European Law Journal* 75, 91; N de Boer and J van 't Klooster, 'The ECB, the courts and the issue of democratic legitimacy after Weiss' 57 *CML Rev* (2020) 1689, 1711–12.

[41] Regulation (EU) No 1092/2010 of the European Parliament and of the Council on European Union macro-prudential oversight of the financial system and establishing a European Systemic Risk Board [2010] OJ L331/1 (ESRBR) art 3(1).

The rationale for society's concern with bank failures is that banks are viewed as crucial for providing businesses and consumers with access to credit and payment services. Essentially, systemic risk denotes the risk that an event materially impairs the system's ability to perform these services. The ESRB Regulation defines the term as 'a risk of disruption in the financial system with the potential to have serious negative consequences for the internal market and the real economy'.[42] Likewise, BRRD defines the term *systemic crisis* as 'a disruption in the financial system with the potential to have serious negative consequences for the internal market and the real economy'.[43]

Until recently, as noted above, the ECB explicitly defined financial stability as 'a state where the build-up of systemic risk is prevented'.[44] Systemic risk is 'the risk that the provision of necessary financial products and services by the financial system will be impaired to a point where economic growth and welfare may be materially affected'.[45] According to the ECB's account, systemic risk derives from three sources: An endogenous build-up of financial imbalances, large aggregate shocks hitting the economy or the financial system and contagion effects across markets, intermediaries or infrastructures. This definition is oriented towards the ultimate effects on the real economy: The concept of systemic risk only comprises risks the materialisation of which could result in a material adverse effect on the real economy.

Economic literature has proposed various definitions of systemic risk. In an early contribution, de Bandt and Hartmann define systemic risk as the risk of experiencing certain *systemic events*.[46] Under this framework, there are two kinds of systemic events – systemic events in the narrow and the broad sense. A systemic event in the *narrow* sense is negative news about one financial institution or a market that subsequently leads to adverse effects on other institutions. A 'domino effect' thus occurs: the other institutions are not directly affected by the initial event but are affected nonetheless due either to links to the initially affected institution or simply to being a part of the same financial system. A systemic event in the *broad* sense is defined as a 'shock' that has simultaneous adverse effects on many institutions.

Importantly, only the risk of *strong* systemic events qualifies as systemic risk under de Bandt and Hartmann's framework. A systemic event in the narrow sense is only strong insofar as it causes the failure of other financial institutions as its effects ripple through the financial system. Likewise, a systemic event in the broad sense is only strong if it causes a significant part of the affected financial institutions or markets to fail or crash.

A definition that is much-cited in legal scholarship defines systemic risk as 'the risk that (i) an economic shock such as market or institutional failure triggers

[42] ESRBR art 2(c).
[43] BRRD art 2(1)(30).
[44] European Central Bank (n 34) 3.
[45] ibid.
[46] O de Bandt and P Hartmann, 'Systemic Risk: A Survey' (2000) ECB Working Paper No 35, 10–11.

(through a panic or otherwise) either (X) the failure of a chain of markets or institutions or (Y) a chain of significant losses to financial institutions, (ii) resulting in increases in the cost of capital or decreases in its availability, often evidenced by substantial financial-market price volatility'.[47] Like the ECB's definition, a necessary element of systemic risk is the potential for effects on the real economy, here described as worsening credit conditions.

How then, could the failure of a bank cause systemic risk to materialise? Under some of the above definitions, the cessation of a dominant bank's supply of critical functions could constitute such an event insofar as competitors replace these functions insufficiently. A large bank's ceasing to lend could thus constitute a systemic event. What most people likely have in mind when speaking about systemic risk is something else, namely contagion risk. This is the risk that the problems of one institution will spread across the financial system, thus decreasing the supply of financial services in the process.

Economic theory has conceptualised several forms of contagion.[48] The first form is caused by direct links between financial institutions.[49] Such links arise because banks lend to and trade with each other. When a bank has lent money to another bank, it suffers a loss if the other bank fails to repay the loan. In theory, a bank defaulting on a sufficiently large interbank loan could make the lending bank insolvent. However, even if the default does not make the lending bank insolvent, it could cause it to experience a *run* involving its creditors withdrawing deposits and other short-term funding. The source of this risk is that the lending bank's creditors could interpret the news about the insolvent bank's failure as an indication that the lending bank's asset portfolio was less valuable than the creditors assumed. In the extreme, the run could turn a bank balance-sheet insolvent as it sells off assets at 'fire sale' prices to obtain the cash necessary to satisfy the repayment demands, thereby depleting its equity.

The tendency of banks to own similar assets may cause a second type of contagion. This form of contagion does not require any direct contractual links between banks. One speaks of the mechanism at play as an *asset-side channel* for contagion. In their survey of the literature on the asset-side contagion mechanism, Brunnermeier and Oehmke distinguish between the *loss spiral* and the *margin spiral*.[50] Loss spiral theories are based on the following reasoning: as banks own similar types of assets, a sudden disruption in the market for the assets in question can lower solvency ratios across the sector. This could be triggered by a shock to one bank, which in turn sells off assets. In normal times, a sale does not necessarily

[47] SL Schwarcz, 'Systemic Risk' (2008) 97 *Georgetown Law Journal* 193, 204.

[48] For a survey of existing literature, see S Benoit et al, 'Where the Risks Lie: A Survey on Systemic Risk' (2017) 21 *Review of Finance* 109; de Bandt and Hartmann (n 46).

[49] MK Brunnermeier and M Oehmke, 'Bubbles, Financial Crises, and Systemic Risk' in GM Constantinides, M Harris and RM Stulz (eds), *Handbook of the Economics of Finance*, vol 2B (Amsterdam, Elsevier, 2013) 1264.

[50] Brunnermeier and Oehmke (n 49) 1253–54.

cause any problems: the seller receives the cash equivalent to the asset's fundamental value, and asset prices therefore remain unchanged. However, the market participants that assign the asset the highest value could potentially have liquidity issues and be unable to purchase the asset in question. The last thing banks facing liquidity issues want to do is use their cash to purchase illiquid assets. Under such circumstances, the asset could end up being sold to other market actors that do not value the asset as highly and are only willing to purchase the asset at a lower price.[51] This sale reduces the solvency ratio of banks holding the asset in question,[52] which could cause further withdrawals requiring yet another round of sales at distressed prices.

The risk of a *margin spiral* arises because banks provide collateral to obtain secured short-term funding from other banks and wholesale creditors.[53] The amount of cash that a bank can borrow against a given asset is the value of the asset less a given percentage – a *haircut* in finance jargon. This means that the loan a bank can obtain by offering a given asset as collateral is less than the asset's market value. If other market participants start to sell off assets in a volume sufficient to affect the prices of securities used as collateral, it becomes more difficult to fund positions in the assets in question.[54] This further reduces the demand for such assets, which in turn results in lower prices.[55] This decreases the amount of funding that can be borrowed against the asset in question, and so on.

Another form of contagion is informational contagion,[56] which occurs when imperfect information about Bank A's problems causes the creditors of Bank B to withdraw their funds. In this case, the withdrawals occur because creditors do not know if the failure of Bank A was caused by a risk peculiar to that institution or a risk all banks face. If Bank A's problems were specific to this bank, there would be no reason to run on Bank B. Conversely, if Bank A's troubles are caused by a risk to which also Bank B is exposed, it could be sensible for Bank B's creditors to run.

Imperfect information about the links between banks can also cause runs. The preceding example assumed that there were no links between Bank A and Bank B. Suppose instead that the links between different banks are not known in the market. Creditors do not know if Bank B is exposed to Bank A, which has become insolvent. If Bank B has a large enough exposure to Bank A, it is adversely affected by the failure, regardless of whether this failure was caused by the materialisation of a risk idiosyncratic to Bank A. If Bank B's creditors believe that such an exposure exists, it could be rational to run on Bank B. As the relationship and

[51] A Shleifer and R Vishny, 'Fire Sales in Finance and Macroeconomics' (2011) 25 *Journal of Economic Perspectives* 29, 30.

[52] Brunnermeier and Oehmke (n 49) 1260.

[53] ibid 1253.

[54] ibid 1258.

[55] ibid 1258.

[56] Benoit et al (n 48) 121; Gorton and Winton (n 1) 516.

exposures between different banks is not public information, bank creditors are, to some extent, left to guess. Even if its financial position is sound, Bank B could therefore have trouble obtaining financing following the collapse of another bank.

2.2. The Pre-Crisis Turn Towards Meta-Regulation

2.2.1. Introduction

This section argues that capital and liquidity requirements regulation – two of the most important elements of prudential banking regulation – increasingly developed towards a paradigm of meta-regulation in the decades preceding the GFC. As discussed at 1.2.2, meta-regulation involves requiring the targets of regulation to impose regulatory requirements on themselves, thereby making the State and regulatory subject co-regulators.

Our starting point is 1988, when the Basel Capital Accord was agreed. This accord set out an international standard for capital requirements regulation and was shortly thereafter made part of EU law. We will at 2.2.2 discuss the accord and subsequent reform of EU capital requirements regulation up to the GFC.

In contrast with the case of capital requirements, the important field of liquidity regulation was not subject to harmonisation in EU law prior to the GFC. We will therefore at 2.2.3 discuss the national approaches in place immediately before the GFC and how these fit within a trend towards meta-regulation.

2.2.2. Capital Requirements

Capital requirements constitute the most central part of the regulatory regime applicable to banks. In its most basic form, a capital requirement entails imposing an obligation on a bank to ensure that a minimum percentage of its funding stems from equity. Given that equity is the difference between a company's assets and its liabilities, equity requirements limit the amount of debt banks can assume. If regulatory requirements prescribe that a bank must finance its assets through at least five per cent equity, this means that a bank with assets equal to 100 billion can assume a maximum debt of 95 billion euro. However, as subsequent sections will show, this example is a mere approximation. The currently applicable capital adequacy framework is much more detailed.

Harmonised capital adequacy regulation has been part of EU law since the adoption of the Second Banking Directive in 1989.[57] The adoption of this and

[57] Second Council Directive 89/646/EEC on the coordination of laws, regulations and administrative provisions relating to the taking up and pursuit of the business of credit institutions and amending Directive 77/780/EEC [1989] OJ L386/1.

other directives setting out technical prudential rules[58] followed the adoption in 1988 of a framework by the Basel Committee on Banking Supervision (BCBS), often termed the Basel Capital Accord or Basel I.[59] BCBS was then – and remains – an informal forum comprising the central banks and supervisory authorities of jurisdictions with internationally important banks.[60] The committee develops standards for prudential regulation that are not legally binding on any state but that are widely observed nonetheless. Both the BCBS's standards and implementing EU legislation have subsequently undergone several rounds of revision.

The Basel I framework centred around a *risk-weighted* approach to capital requirements. The basic idea that underpins this approach is that two portfolios of assets may involve different levels of risk notwithstanding that they have the same accounting value: The accounting value of a claim against the German government that accrues a low interest rate may be the same as that of a claim against a highly leveraged company that accrues a high interest rate. However, the risk that the borrower defaults is higher in the latter case. This, in turn, makes a bank that lends to risky companies more likely to become insolvent than a bank that lends to highly creditworthy sovereigns. Accordingly, the riskier portfolio should lead to a higher capital requirement than the other.

There are different approaches to risk-weighted capital requirements. First, policymakers must decide upon the risks that the capital requirement is meant to reflect. Secondly, once policymakers have decided upon the risks against which banks must hold capital, the policymakers must establish the parameters for calculating the risk-weighted capital requirements of individual banks.

Basel I originally set out a framework for capital requirements that reflected *credit risk*. Credit risk is the risk that a party against which the bank has a claim, defaults on its payment obligation towards the bank.[61] The capital that banks would have to maintain given a certain level of credit risk was to be calculated by applying what has since become known as *the standardised* approach in EU capital requirements regulation. Under this approach, asset values are multiplied by statutorily determined *risk-weights*. For example, Basel I assigned a risk-weight of 50 per cent to '[l]oans fully secured by mortgage on residential property that is or will be occupied by the borrower or that is rented'.[62] This meant that if a bank were to provide

[58] See eg Council Directive 89/299/EEC of 17 April 1989 on the own funds of credit institutions [1989] OJ L124/16, which laid out criteria for what counted as regulatory capital, and Council Directive 89/647/EEC of 18 December 1989 on a solvency ratio for credit institutions [1989] OJ L386/14, which laid out the methodology for calculating the amount of regulatory capital banks must hold.

[59] Basle Committee on Banking Supervision, 'International Convergence of Capital Measurement and Capital Standards' (July 1988).

[60] The number of jurisdictions represented in the BCBS has increased following the adoption of Basel I. At that time, the committee comprised representatives from the Group of Ten countries (Belgium, Canada, France, Germany, Italy, Japan, the Netherlands, Sweden, Switzerland, the UK and the US) and Luxembourg.

[61] Basle Committee on Banking Supervision, 'International Convergence of Capital Measurement and Capital Standards' (July 1988) 8–9.

[62] ibid 22.

such a loan in an amount of one million euro, the loan would add 50 per cent of that amount – ie 500,000 euro – to the bank's total risk exposure amount. As the bank would have to maintain a total capital ratio of eight per cent of the total risk exposure amount, adding such a loan to the balance sheet would increase required capital by an amount equal to eight per cent of 500,000 euro, ie 40,000 euro.

The approach of Basel I attracted criticism for not being sufficiently risk sensitive. There were relatively few categories into which different exposures were to be divided. For instance, a secured loan to a healthy corporation would have to be backed by the same amount of capital as a defaulted unsecured loan notwithstanding that the former loan carries a much lower risk of loss than the latter.

The framework eventually permitted banks to use their own risk models for calculating capital requirements. In 1996 the so-called Market Risk Amendment incorporated *market risk* into the Basel framework. Market risk is 'the risk of losses in on and off-balance sheet positions arising from movements in market prices'.[63] This comprises the risk that banks will incur losses from making speculative investments in debt and equity instruments.[64] As regards the methods for measuring market risk, the Market Risk Amendment included a standardised approach that was in keeping with the standardised method for calculating credit risk. However, a novel feature was the inclusion of a second method: the *internal models approach*. The Basel Committee recommended that banks should be able to use their internal models for calculating capital requirements in respect of market risk insofar as their internal risk management practices were found satisfactory by their supervisor.[65]

Shortly after the publication of the Market Risk Amendment, the Basel Committee commenced its work on a comprehensive revision of the capital requirements framework. A new framework – dubbed Basel II – was published in 2004.[66] Importantly, the new framework allowed banks to use the internal models for calculating capital requirements in respect of credit risk: The *internal ratings-based approach* (IRB) would henceforth be an alternative to the standardised approach for banks with sufficiently sophisticated internal risk systems. Through the adoption of the first Capital Requirements Directive (CRD I), the EU subsequently adjusted its capital requirements framework accordingly.[67] In short, the framework provided that banks able to convince their supervisors that their internal models and systems were prudent would be allowed to use internal data in part or entirely as the input for calculating credit risk.[68] This was often a lucrative

[63] Basle Committee on Banking Supervision, 'Amendment to the Capital Accord to incorporate market risks' (January 1996) 1.

[64] ibid.

[65] ibid 38.

[66] Basel Committee on Banking Supervision, 'International convergence of capital measurement and capital standards: a revised framework' (June 2004).

[67] Directive 2006/48/EC of the European Parliament and of the Council relating to the taking up and pursuit of the business of credit institutions (recast) [2006] OJ L177/1 art 84ff.

[68] See also L Dragomir, *European Prudential Banking Regulation and Supervision: The legal dimension* (London, Routledge, 2010) 135–38.

option for the banks concerned, as the use of the IRB approach typically led to significantly lower capital requirements than those yielded by the standardised approach.[69]

The Basel accords and implementing EU directives set out to establish common *minimum* requirements for bank capital. Conversely, there were no attempts at curtailing capital requirements that went beyond the agreed upon minimum. Accordingly, Member States were free to impose higher capital requirements on domestic banks. Moreover, the Basel principles on banking supervision have from inception stated that supervisors should be able – but not obligated – to require that individual banks maintain more capital than the common minimum requirement.[70] In line with this, CRD I also contemplated such a power.[71] However, many supervisory authorities reportedly did not impose such requirements on the banks under their remit.[72]

In the UK the bank supervisor's policy was to set individual capital requirements that exceeded the eight per cent minimum requirement to capture risks that this requirement did not reflect.[73] It appears that large UK banks in the period between the adoption of Basel I and the implementation of CRD were on average required to hold capital equal to around nine per cent of risk-weighted assets, ie one percentage point more than the Basel I requirement.[74] The average requirement for smaller banks was slightly higher. Neither German nor Norwegian supervisory authorities appear to have adopted a practice of imposing binding requirements higher than the statutory minimum.[75]

It is important to note that the pre-crisis regulation of bank capital did not solely rely on quantitative requirements. First, qualitative requirements supplemented the obligation to observe the quantitative minimum requirements: Basel II stated that 'bank management [bears] responsibility for ensuring that the bank has adequate capital to support its risks beyond the core minimum requirements'.[76] Secondly, the framework required banks to develop self-regulatory responses to the risk of failure and thus employed such meta-regulatory strategies as discussed

[69] AG Haldane, 'Constraining Discretion in Bank Regulation' in C Goodhart et al (eds), *Central Banking at a Crossroads: Europe and Beyond* (London, Anthem Press, 2014) 25; V Le Leslé and S Avramova, 'Revisiting Risk-Weighted Assets: Why Do RWAs Differ Across Countries and What Can Be Done About It?' (2012) IMF Working Paper No 12/90.

[70] Basle Committee on Banking Supervision, 'Core Principles for Effective Banking Supervision' (1997) 24.

[71] CRD I art 136.

[72] GA Walker, 'Basel III market and regulatory compromise' (2011) 12 *Journal of Banking Regulation* 95, 96.

[73] Financial Services Authority, 'Individual Capital Ratios for Banks: Policy Statement' (2001) 3.

[74] SJA de-Ramon, WB Francis and K Milonas, 'An overview of the UK banking sector since the Basel Accord: insights from a new regulatory database' (2017) Bank of England Staff Working Paper No 652, 29.

[75] See Bundesanstalt für Finanzdienstleistungsaufsicht, 'Annual Report 2016' 92–93; Finanstilsynet, 'Annual Report 2016' 28.

[76] Basel Committee on Banking Supervision, 'International Convergence of Capital Measurement and Capital Standards' (June 2006) 204.

at 1.2.2. For example, Basel II established the following as one of four principles for of supervisory review: 'Banks should have a process for assessing their overall capital adequacy in relation to their risk profile and a strategy for maintaining their capital levels'.[77] In keeping with this standard, CRD I Article 123 provided that banks should

> have in place sound, effective and complete strategies and processes to assess and maintain on an ongoing basis the amounts, types and distribution of internal capital that they consider adequate to cover the nature and level of the risks to which they are or might be exposed.

Bank supervisors were to assess whether such strategies and processes were in place, and, if they were not, require the bank concerned to remedy the issue.[78] To this end, the supervisor could require banks to hold more capital than the minimum requirement.

The third pillar of the Basel II framework concerned disclosure obligations. Banks were to make public details of their levels of regulatory capital and their risk management systems. The idea was that financial markets participants would penalise banks with risky business models – eg bond markets requiring higher interest rates to lend to risky banks. In this manner public information about banks would foster *market discipline*. This approach was very much in keeping with the 'disclosure paradigm' that has long permeated financial market regulation, where regulation reflects the belief that capital markets are well functioning if sufficient information is available.[79] CRD I Article 145ff introduced disclosure requirements into EU banking regulation.

2.2.3. Liquidity Requirements

A defining feature of banks is that their assets are often illiquid – eg loans to households and companies – while a substantial portion of their liabilities, such as deposits, are short term. A bank that faces an unexpectedly high level of deposit withdrawals may have to sell illiquid assets to access the cash necessary to repay depositors. As discussed at 2.1.4 such sales may, in turn, have adverse effects on the bank itself and, potentially, other banks that have similar loans on their balance sheet. A regulatory response to this risk is to require that banks maintain a minimum amount of liquid assets such as cash.

Such *quantitative* liquidity requirements were not part of the Basel framework prior to the GFC. Nor did pre-crisis EU law harmonise the liquidity requirements

[77] ibid 205.

[78] CRD I art 136.

[79] See eg E Avgouleas, 'The Global Financial Crisis and the Disclosure Paradigm in European Financial Regulation: The Case of Reform' (2009) 6 *European Company and Financial Law Review* 440, 442–43; N Moloney, *EU Securities and Financial Markets Regulation*, 3rd edn (Oxford, Oxford University Press, 2014) 54.

of the Member States.[80] The lack of international coordination allowed for different national approaches.

In the UK pre-crisis regulation required banks to maintain 'adequate liquidity' enabling them to meet obligations as they fell due.[81] The Financial Services Authority (FSA) was tasked with producing guidelines for how individual banks should comply with the general requirement.[82] The FSA's policy was in many respects akin to command-and-control regulation. For instance, the policy statement quantified the discounts that banks were required to deduct from the value of marketable assets that count as liquidity. However, the policy also included elements of meta-regulation, one example being that banks could apply for permission to use their own models for estimating the extent to which deposits could be expected to be withdrawn.

German liquidity requirements were set out in a separate regulation, the *Liquiditätsverordnung* (LiqV). Under this regulation, banks were generally required to maintain a ratio of liquid assets – measured for an asset by applying by multiplying the asset's value by the applicable percentage – to liquid liabilities above one. However, LiqV § 10 authorised the supervisor to allow certain banks to use internal models. While the liquidity regulation entered into force on 1 January 2007, no banks had applied for and received permission by 1 January 2008.[83]

Norwegian law contained only qualitative requirements in the years immediately preceding the GFC.[84] Up until 2006, Norwegian banks had been subject to quantitative liquidity requirements.[85]

2.2.4. Conclusions

The introduction of the possibility of using internal models to determine capital and liquidity requirements represented a turn towards meta-regulation in banking regulation. While legislation required banks to maintain equity above a certain threshold, that threshold could potentially be a function of the individual bank's internal models. This meant that regulators and individual banks in a sense acted as co-regulators of capital requirements.

[80] A McKnight, 'Basel 2: the implementation in the UK of its capital requirements for banks' (2007) *Law and Financial Markets Review* 327, 336.

[81] FSA Handbook (as of January 2005) IPRU (BANK) 3.3.15R.

[82] ibid chs LM and LS.

[83] M Pohl, 'Die Öffnungsklausel der Liquiditätsverordnung – Entwicklung und praktische Umsetzung' (2008) 20 *Zeitschrift für Bankrecht und Bankwirtschaft* 423, 425.

[84] Finansieringsvirksomhetsloven § 2-17.

[85] Finansdepartementet, 'Om lov om endringer i lov 18. juni 1993 nr. 109 om autorisasjon av regnskapsførere (regnskapsførerloven), lov 15. januar 1999 nr. 2 om revisjon og revisorer (revisorloven), lov 10. juni 1988 nr. 40 om finansieringsvirksomhet og finansinstitusjoner (finansieringsvirksomhetsloven) og enkelte andre lover' Ot.prp. nr. 44 (2005–2006) 39–40.

2.3. The Reorientation Towards 'Technocratic Fine-Tuning' in Post-Crisis Banking Regulation

2.3.1. Introduction

The GFC resulted in wide-ranging reforms of banking regulation. Importantly, several aspects of the capital requirements framework were substantially overhauled.[86] Moreover, quantitative liquidity requirements were harmonised at EU level.[87] This section argues that many of the key reforms represent a trend towards the regulatory approach of technocratic fine-tuning (TFT) discussed at 1.2.3.

This was not a necessity when policymakers were searching for alternatives to the meta-regulatory approach of the pre-GFC era. Reform could instead conceivably have taken the form of more 'blunt' rules that would reduce some of the risks while also curtailing desired activities. However, reform proposals that involved more blunt regulation were largely eschewed.[88]

Given our objective, several pieces of important regulatory developments are not given separate discussion. These include the regulation of remuneration to bank employees,[89] the centralisation of bank supervision in the Banking Union through the establishment of the Single Supervisory Mechanism (SSM),[90] and the establishment of the European Banking Authority and the other parts of the European system of financial supervision. However, such developments are mentioned in passing when relevant.

2.3.2. The Minimum Own Funds Requirement and the Continued Use of the IRB-Approach

The own funds requirement obliges banks to ensure that their capital exceed certain minimum thresholds. These thresholds are calculated by reference to the applicable total risk exposure amount. As discussed at 2.2.2, a bank's total risk exposure amount is, somewhat simplified, a risk-weighted measure of its assets.

[86] See 2.3.3–2.3.5.

[87] See 2.3.6.

[88] See 2.3.7.

[89] Directive 2013/36/EU of the European Parliament and of the Council on access to the activity of credit institutions and the prudential supervision of credit institutions and investment firms, amending Directive 2002/87/EC and repealing Directives 2006/48/EC and 2006/49/EC [2013] OJ L176/338 (CRD IV) art 92ff.

[90] Council Regulation (EU) No 1024/2013 of 15 October 2013 conferring specific tasks on the European Central Bank concerning policies relating to the prudential supervision of credit institutions [2013] OJ L287/63.

More specifically, the own funds requirement means that a bank's *Common Equity Tier 1 capital ratio, Tier 1 capital ratio* and *total capital ratio* must exceed 4.5 per cent, six per cent and eight per cent of the total risk exposure amount, respectively.[91]

The Common Equity Tier 1 capital ratio requirement obliges banks to maintain Common Equity Tier 1 (CET1) capital in an amount of at least 4.5 per cent of the total risk exposure amount.[92] Essentially, CET1 comprises shares and other capital instruments that qualify as equity, as well as retained earnings.[93]

The Tier 1 capital ratio requirement stipulates that banks must maintain CET1 and Additional Tier 1 (AT1) capital of at least six per cent of the total risk exposure amount.[94] Additional Tier 1 capital comprises perpetual instruments.[95] While loans that never mature can qualify as AT1 capital, any instrument obliging the issuer to repay the paid-up amount at a future date cannot. The terms of an AT1 instrument may provide that the issuer shall make distributions or interest payments at future dates, but the issuer must have discretion to cancel any scheduled payments.[96]

The total capital ratio requirement provides that banks must maintain CET1, AT1 and Tier 2 capital in an aggregate amount of at least eight per cent of the total risk exposure amount.[97] Tier 2 instruments must be subordinated to ordinary debt. Tier 2 classification does not require that the instrument is perpetual, as it suffices that the instrument has an original maturity of at least five years.[98] It is not required that the issuer has discretion to cancel payments on the instruments, but the holders of the instruments cannot have the right to accelerate the loan under circumstances other than the issuer's insolvency or winding up.[99]

Current own funds requirements are stricter than those in force prior to the GFC. While the aggregate own funds requirement remains eight per cent of risk-weighted assets, the framework has undergone three changes of particular importance.[100] First, the minimum requirement for CET1 capital has increased from two per cent to 4.5 per cent. Secondly, fewer items count as CET1 capital. Thirdly, the overhauled regulations introduced stricter requirements for counting subordinated debt as own funds.

As discussed at 2.2.2, the pre-GFC framework opened for banks receiving permission to calculate the total risk exposure amount using their own models. This attracted criticism, as studies indicated that the output of the internal models

[91] CRR art 92(1).
[92] CRR art 92(1)(a).
[93] CRR art 26.
[94] CRR art 92(1)(b).
[95] CRR art 52(1)(g).
[96] CRR art 52(1)(l)(iii).
[97] CRR art 92(1)(c).
[98] CRR art 63(g).
[99] CRR art 63(l).
[100] P Davies, 'The Fall and Rise of Debt: Bank Capital Regulation After the Crisis' (2015) 16 *European Business Organization Law Review* 491, 494.

varied significantly from bank to bank and that this variation could not be explained solely by reference to differences in the riskiness of credit exposures.[101]

Post-crisis reform did not result in the repeal of the IRB framework. This approach to calculating capital requirements thus remains an option for banks with sufficiently sophisticated risk management systems. However, some restrictions were introduced into the Basel framework. Importantly, a recent addition to the Basel framework somewhat reduces the difference between employing the standardised approach and the IRB approach. This additional requirement – which is often referred to as an *output floor* – provides that a bank's capital requirements cannot be lower than 72.5 per cent of the capital requirement calculated under the standardised approach.[102] The Commission has recently put forward a proposal for amendments to the Capital Requirements Regulation – which sets out the currently applicable provisions for calculating the minimum capital requirements – that would introduce the output floor.[103]

2.3.3. Pillar 2 Requirements

The current capital requirements framework does not solely rely on the minimum own funds requirement to prevent banks from taking on unacceptable risks. Banks must conduct an 'internal capital adequacy assessment process' that involves an internal assessment of whether the bank should hold capital exceeding the minimum requirement. The bank supervisor reviews this process as part of a supervisory review and evaluation process (SREP) required under the Capital Requirements Directive IV (CRD IV), which replaced CRD I following the GFC.[104] While requirements for banks to conduct such internal assessments were already part of CRD I, a novel feature of CRD IV is that the supervisor shall carry out annual 'stress tests' of individual banks, that is, assess how the bank's capital levels would fare in adverse economic scenarios.[105]

The supervisor has the power to require that banks hold capital in excess of CRR's minimum requirements. In the extreme, a bank in breach of such a requirement, which is often referred to as a 'pillar 2 requirement', could have its authorisation withdrawn.[106] Importantly, supervisors shall require banks to hold additional own funds when the minimum capital requirements do not adequately

[101] Haldane (n 69) 19; Le Leslé and Avramova (n 69).

[102] Basel Committee on Banking Supervision, 'Basel III: Finalising post-crisis reforms' (December 2017) 137.

[103] Commission, 'Proposal for a Regulation of the European Parliament and of The Council amending Regulation (EU) No 575/2013 as regards requirements for credit risk, credit valuation adjustment risk, operational risk, market risk and the output floor' COM (2021) 664 final.

[104] CRD IV art 97(1).

[105] CRD IV art 100.

[106] CRD IV art 18(d).

reflect the risks to which the bank is exposed.[107] This means that supervisors shall make such requirements notwithstanding how the bank concerned approaches the relevant risks. By contrast, additional capital requirements under CRD I would require either a bank breaching regulatory requirements or the determination that the capital held by it – implicitly considered adequate by the bank itself – be insufficient to 'ensure a sound management and coverage of [its] risks'.[108] Pillar 2 requirements have thus become more of a proactive measure than they were in the pre-GFC framework. This development is also supported by CRD IV requiring bank supervisors to carry out stress tests, as a supervisor by so doing will form an independent view on some of the risks faced by the banks under its supervision.

How does one determine whether or not the amount of capital necessary to comply with the own funds requirement is sufficient to cover the risks faced by a given bank? CRD IV Article 104a(2) provides that

> risks or elements of risk shall only be considered as not covered or not sufficiently covered by the own funds requirements … where the amounts, types and distribution of capital considered adequate by the competent authority … are higher than the own funds requirements …

Read literally, additional capital is necessary if the competent authority – ie the bank supervisor – says that it is necessary. The discretion of the supervisor is somewhat constrained by the second subparagraph of Article 104a(1), which states that bank supervisors shall only impose a pillar 2 requirement 'to cover the risks incurred by individual institutions due to their activities, including those reflecting the impact of certain economic and market developments on the risk profile of an individual institution'. The requirement thus cannot be imposed to mitigate systemic risks.

EBA has published guidelines on the SREP process.[109] Among other things, the guidelines flesh out what bank supervisors should consider when determining whether and in what amount a bank should be required to hold capital in excess of the minimum own funds requirement. However, it remains the case that a supervisor will retain considerable discretion even if it carries out the assessment in line with the guidelines, as these are not particularly prescriptive with respect to delineating relevant risks.[110]

It is thus clear that bank supervisors are to have considerable discretion when determining whether to impose pillar 2 requirements. Many EU supervisors tend to impose pillar 2 requirements upon most banks. It is thus the exception rather than the rule that the CRR minimum requirement constitutes the binding capital requirement for a bank.

[107] CRD IV art 104a(1)(a).

[108] CRD I art 136 read in conjunction with art 124(3).

[109] European Banking Authority, 'Guidelines on common procedures and methodologies for the supervisory review and evaluation process (SREP) and supervisory stress testing under Directive 2013/36/EU' (18 March 2022) EBA/GL/2022/03.

[110] European Banking Authority (n 109) paras 365–401.

2.3.4. Capital Buffer Requirements

The implementation of the Basel III standard in EU law saw the inclusion of capital buffer requirements in CRD IV. The buffers require banks to hold capital in excess of their own funds requirement and any additional pillar 2 requirement.

While a breach of the capital requirements addressed in the previous sections could lead to a bank losing its authorisation or becoming subject to resolution, a breach of the capital buffer requirements merely leads to restrictions on the bank's distributions to holders of CET1 or AT1 instruments, and the bank awarding and paying out bonuses to its staff.[111] This allows a bank's capital to go below what is necessary to satisfy the buffer requirements for a period without prejudicing the bank's authorisation.

The buffers could be viewed as responses to various forms of criticism levelled at the Basel II framework both before and after the GFC. One problem was the failure to mitigate the *procyclicality* of bank leverage.[112] Procyclicality refers to how banks tend to have large, highly leveraged balance sheets in good times, but smaller balance sheets with higher relative amounts of equity financing in less favourable conditions. As prices rise in good times, banks are able to expand their asset holdings without breaching capital requirements. If asset prices subsequently decline, some banks may find their capital ratio below both regulatory capital ratios and what the funding market requires to continue extending credit. One strategy for increasing equity levels is to 'de-leverage' by selling assets and cutting back on lending. As noted at 2.1.4, problems could arise when many banks pursue such a strategy simultaneously.

A response to the problem of procyclicality is to subject banks to time-varying capital requirements that are stricter in times of benign economic conditions. Such an approach underlies the countercyclical capital buffer requirement. Under CRD IV Article 136, each Member State shall appoint a 'designated authority' that fixes a countercyclical capital buffer rate in the interval between zero and 2.5 per cent of the total risk exposure amount. The authority sets the level according to the economic conditions in the Member State concerned. In boom times, the requirement shall be set high.[113] Conversely, during an economic slump, the requirement shall be low to incentivise bank lending. An implicit premise of the

[111] CRD IV art 141.

[112] M Brunnermeier et al, 'The Fundamental Principles of Financial Regulation' (Geneva Reports on the World Economy, ICMB/CEPR 2009) 20–21. For arguments against variable capital buffer requirements as a solution to this issue, see J-C Rochet, 'The Future of Banking Regulation' in M Dewatripont, J-C Rochet and J Tirole, *Balancing the Banks: Global Lessons from the Financial Crisis* (Princeton, Princeton University Press, 2010) 97–98.

[113] J Armour et al, *Principles of Financial Regulation* (Oxford, Oxford University Press, 2016) 308; L Amorello, 'Europe Goes "Countercyclical": A Legal Assessment of the New Countercyclical Dimension of the CRR/CRD IV Package' (2016) 17 *European Business Organization Law Review* 137, 146 and the references contained therein.

buffer requirement is that banks shall raise equity when they are in breach of the requirement. However, there is nothing in the design of the requirement that prevents banks from instead adopting a strategy of deleveraging to restore equity levels.[114]

The adjustment of national countercyclical capital buffer requirements in March 2020 as COVID-19 spread throughout Europe provides an example of how authorities in charge respond to shocks to the economy: In the UK, the Financial Policy Committee reduced the rate to zero per cent. In Norway, the Ministry of Finance lowered the rate from two per cent to one per cent.[115]

The Basel II regime attracted criticism for its microprudential orientation where regulation aims at preventing the failure of individual institutions.[116] The ultimate aim is to protect depositors and, insofar as the state is the ultimate guarantor of deposits, the taxpayer.[117] According to the critics, the problem with a microprudential approach is that compliance with regulation that makes sense at the level of individual institutions could lead to aggregate behaviour that is prejudicial to the financial system as a whole. For instance, it is sensible for a bank that wishes to increase its capital ratio to sell assets and use the proceeds to pay off debt.[118] However, if all banks sell off assets at the same time, this could disturb the market for the assets in question. This involves the asset-side channel for contagion that we discussed at 2.1.4: the turmoil causes a drop in the value of the assets and, consequently, the capital ratios of banks that hold assets subject to a large-scale sell-off. Accordingly, individual attempts to increase capital ratios could, in some circumstances, result in decreasing capital ratios across the banking sector.

The prescription for this problem is *macro*prudential regulation. A macroprudential approach aims at safeguarding the financial system.[119] Some macroprudential measures have made their way into the current Basel framework and EU law implementing this framework. One measure is the capital conservation buffer requirement, which obligates all banks to maintain additional CET1 capital of 2.5 per cent of the bank's total risk exposure amount.[120]

The macroprudential rationale is also found in the additional buffers applicable to systemically important banks. There are two categories of systemically important banks: global systemically important institutions (G-SIIs) and other systemically important institutions (O-SIIs). CRD IV leaves the classification of a bank as a G-SII and O-SII to authorities designated by the Member States based on

[114] Armour et al (n 113) 307.

[115] The Norwegian Ministry of Finance has since then delegated the task of setting the countercyclical capital buffer requirement to Norges Bank.

[116] SG Hanson, AK Kashyap and JC Stein, 'A Macroprudential Approach to Financial Regulation' (2011) 25 *Journal of Economic Perspectives* 3, 3; Brunnermeier et al (n 112) 10.

[117] Hanson, Kashyap and Stein (n 116) 4; Brunnermeier et al (n 112) 3.

[118] Hanson, Kashyap and Stein (n 116) 5.

[119] Hanson, Kashyap and Stein (n 116) 3.

[120] CRD IV art 129.

several criteria.[121] It should, however, be noted that the Financial Stability Board publishes recommendations on which banks should be classified as G-SIIs and that EU Member States have so far aligned their G-SII classifications with these recommendations. At the time of writing, FSB classifies eight EU banks and three UK banks as G-SIIs.

When determining the G-SII buffer requirement, Member States shall place G-SIIs within one of five or more categories. The G-SIIs falling within the least risky category shall be assigned a buffer requirement of 1% of the institution's total risk exposure amount.[122] The O-SII buffer requirement is to be set between zero and three per cent of the O-SII's total risk exposure amount.[123]

Finally, CRD IV leaves room for Member States to apply a systemic risk buffer to the financial sector or a subset of that sector.[124] The buffer can only be set to 'prevent and mitigate macroprudential or systemic risks not covered by [CRR]'.[125] EU and EEA Member States have made use of this possibility to varying degrees. Norway has introduced such a buffer requirement and applies a buffer rate of 4.5 per cent in respect of exposures located in Norway,[126] while Germany applies a buffer rate of two per cent to exposures secured by residential property.

2.3.5. The Leverage Ratio

As mentioned, criticism has been levelled at the possibility of calculating capital requirements with the IRB approach. One perceived problem with this approach is that the use of historical internal data means that the models will likely indicate borrowers as less likely to default when the model is applied during a boom.[127] The models also failed to capture the risk of rare but extremely destructive events such as those that occurred during the GFC.[128] A third critique is that the process for determining capital requirements under the IRB approach is so complex that it is next to impossible for anyone other than the bank and its supervisor to comprehend.[129]

Beyond the increase of risk-weighted capital requirements, the BCBS has responded to this issue by introducing into the Basel framework a minimum

[121] CRD IV art 131.
[122] CRD IV art 131(9).
[123] CRD IV art 131(5). CRD IV art 131(5a) provides that the buffer requirement may be set higher following the Commission's approval.
[124] CRD IV art 133.
[125] CRD IV art 133(1).
[126] Finansforetaksloven (ffl.) § 14-3(2); Forskrift om kapitalkrav og nasjonal tilpasning av CRR/CRD IV § 27.
[127] Armour et al (n 113) 304.
[128] Armour et al (n 113) 302; Rochet (n 112) 93.
[129] Rochet (n 112) 84.

requirement for the ratio of a bank's capital to unweighted asset values.[130] As this requirement applies in parallel to the risk-weighted capital requirements, it effectively establishes a lower bound or 'floor' on bank capital levels. Following an amendment of CRR in 2019,[131] banks are now subject to a leverage ratio requirement that applies in parallel with the own funds requirement.[132] Generally, the requirement stipulates that banks must ensure that their ratio of Tier 1 capital – roughly speaking, equity (CET1 capital) and subordinated perpetual instruments (AT1 capital) – to their *total exposure measure* is at least three per cent. In brief, the total exposure measure is the sum of the accounting value of the bank's assets plus values that CRR ascribes to certain off-balance sheet items (such as a bank's contingent liabilities under a bank guarantee that it has issued in respect of the debts of a client).[133] Accordingly, the total exposure measure may exceed the value of the accounting value of the bank's assets.

In the years after the GFC, calls were made in academia for increasing own funds requirements by imposing an unweighted capital requirements on banks. While the leverage ratio requirement is an unweighted capital requirement, the proposal involved a substantially higher equity-ratio requirement than does the requirement adopted.[134]

In addition to the leverage ratio requirement, G-SIIs are subject to a *leverage ratio buffer requirement*, which obliges banks to maintain Tier 1 capital on top of the capital applied towards the leverage ratio requirement. The buffer rate shall be half of that applied when calculating the bank's G-SII buffer requirement discussed at 2.3.4.[135] If a bank's G-SII buffer requirement is one per cent of its risk-weighted assets, the G-SII's leverage ratio buffer requirement will thus be 0.5 per cent of the unweighted value of its assets. As with risk-weighted capital buffers, the sanction for noncompliance consists of dividend restrictions and other capital conservation measures.[136]

2.3.6. Liquidity Requirements

The funding structure of banks leaves them vulnerable to large aggregate repayment demands from depositors and other short-term creditors. As observed

[130] Basel Committee on Banking Supervision (n 102) 140ff.
[131] Regulation (EU) 2019/876 of the European Parliament and of the Council of 20 May 2019 amending Regulation (EU) No 575/2013 as regards the leverage ratio, the net stable funding ratio, requirements for own funds and eligible liabilities, counterparty credit risk, market risk, exposures to central counterparties, exposures to collective investment undertakings, large exposures, reporting and disclosure requirements, and Regulation (EU) No 648/2012 [2019] OJ L150/1.
[132] CRR art 92(1)(d).
[133] CRR art 429(4).
[134] Admati and Hellwig (n 27).
[135] CRR art 92(1a) (as in force from 1 January 2023).
[136] ibid.

at 2.1.4, the responses of individual banks to liquidity issues may cause problems at other banks. Accordingly, both micro- and macroprudential perspectives necessitate that banks maintain sufficient liquidity.[137] In contrast to what is the case for capital requirements, EU law has only recently harmonised liquidity requirements. This followed BCBS's publication of its liquidity coverage ratio standard in 2013.[138] The standard became a part of EU law through the adoption of CRR and a Delegated Commission Regulation that requires banks to comply with a liquidity coverage requirement (LCR).[139] To comply with this requirement, a bank must maintain liquid assets sufficient to service liquidity outflows (eg withdrawals of deposits) over a 30-day period under 'gravely stressed conditions'.[140]

The LCR Regulation (LCRR) sets out detailed requirements for the computation of net liquidity outflows. The regulation does not mandate that banks employ a specific mix of funding sources. However, as the liquidity requirement generally increases with a bank's reliance on short-term funding, the LCR effectively constrains its ability to rely on short-term funding. Moreover, the requirement limits the extent to which banks may obtain short-term financing by offering liquid securities as security, as only unencumbered assets count towards LCR.[141]

In addition to the LCR, banks must meet the net stable funding ratio (NSFR) requirement, which stipulates that the sum of a bank's *available stable funding* must exceed its *required stable funding*.[142] A bank's *available stable funding* is essentially the sum of the products resulting from multiplying its individual liabilities by a weight. Liabilities are assigned weights in the interval between zero and 100 per cent according to their term and other attributes. Generally, the underlying principle is that the shorter the term of the liability, the lower the weight. A bank that relies heavily on demand deposits will therefore have a lower amount of available stable funding than a bank that finances its operations with a higher amount of debt with a maturity of a year or more.

The methodology for determining a bank's *required stable funding* follows a similar approach. This measure equals the sum of the products resulting from multiplying individual assets and off-balance sheet items by weights. CRR assigns weights to assets based on the liquidity or the maturity of the asset. For instance, assets designated as highly liquid, such as bonds issued by Member States or certain covered bonds, will have a weight of zero per cent.[143] Accordingly, a bank can hold such assets without increasing the amount of available stable funding it

[137] J Tirole, 'Lessons from the Crisis' in M Dewatripont, J-C Rochet and J Tirole, *Balancing the Banks: Global Lessons from the Financial Crisis* (Princeton, Princeton University Press, 2010) 60.

[138] Basel Committee on Banking Supervision, 'Basel III: The Liquidity Coverage Ratio and the liquidity risk monitoring tools' (January 2013).

[139] Commission Delegated Regulation (EU) 2015/61 to supplement Regulation (EU) No 575/2013 of the European Parliament and the Council with regard to liquidity coverage requirement for Credit Institutions [2015] OJ L11/1 (LCRR).

[140] CRR art 412(1).

[141] LCRR art 7(2).

[142] CRR art 428b.

[143] CRR art 428r(1)(a).

must maintain to satisfy the NSFR. At the opposite end of the spectrum, certain long-term loans will have a weight of 100 per cent.[144]

As discussed at 2.3.3, the pillar 2 framework gives supervisors authority to require banks to maintain capital above the statutory minimum requirement. Likewise, CRD IV Article 105 provides that supervisors shall have a power to impose stricter liquidity requirements on individual institutions where this is deemed necessary.

2.3.7. Structural Reform and Central Counterparty Clearing

This chapter has so far argued that post-crisis reform in EU banking law fits within a regulatory approach of technocratic fine-tuning (TFT). It is reasonable to interpret this as a response to the GFC discrediting the reliance on meta-regulation in pre-crisis regulation. However, the shift towards the TFT approach was not the only option for moving away from the pre-crisis paradigm. Policymakers could instead have opted for blunt *risk elimination* rather than fine-tuned *risk reduction*. An example of the former is the US regulatory response to the bank failures during the Great Depression which, among other things, involved the enactment of legislation that prohibited banks from combining lending and deposit taking with investment banking. Such an approach differs from that of technocratic fine-tuning: rather than seeking to *reduce* the risk that losses from investment banking spill over to the banking business, the rationale underpinning such legislation is to *eliminate* this risk by ensuring that banks do not have an investment banking division from which losses may spill over.

There are examples of post-crisis legislation that prohibit banks from making certain transactions. This section will discuss the two most prominent examples of such legislation: so-called structural reform (sometimes also referred to as 'ring fencing') and requirements that derivatives trading are either cleared through a central counterparty or subject to robust collateral arrangements.

We will first examine structural reform. Banks have two core characteristics: They make long-term loans and take deposits. European states have traditionally not prohibited banks from combining these core activities with investment banking and securities trading. This regulatory environment has permitted the rise of large *universal banks* whose business involves not only lending and taking deposits, but also investment banking and proprietary trading. This attracted criticism in the aftermath of the financial crisis. A first critique proceeds from the perspective described at 2.1.2 where banks provide vital services to the economy by taking deposits and extending credit.[145] When a bank also performs investment services

[144] CRR art 428ah.

[145] Independent Commission on Banking, 'Final Report: Recommendations' (September 2011) 25; J-H Binder, 'Ring-Fencing: An Integrated Approach with Many Unknowns' (2015) 16 *European Business Organization Law Review* 97, 115.

and activities, this exposes its depositors and borrowers to the risk that such activities will cause the bank to fail, thus making the deposits unavailable and cutting off the borrowers' access to credit.

Another argument for structural separation can be made on the grounds of preventing state bailouts and the ensuing *moral hazard*, a theme we will address in more detail at 2.4.4.[146] Influenced by a wish to protect a failing bank's depositors and borrowers, states may 'bail out' the bank. Traditionally, bailouts have not only benefited depositors and borrowers. Government-funded recapitalisations and guarantees have most often made all creditors whole, including those that are more sophisticated than the common retail depositor. Anticipating the possibility of a bailout in the event of failure, creditors give banks access to credit on cheaper terms.[147] If the bank combines its deposit-taking and lending with trading activities, the government is, in effect, subsidising the trading. If the bank chooses to assume a higher amount of risk in its trading than it would in the absence of the bailout expectations, the end result is an increase in the risk that the trading activities will cause the bank to fail.

A potential policy fix for concerns over the combination of 'core' banking and trading activities is to separate the two. Reform along these lines was adopted by the UK in 2013, as the Financial Services (Banking Reform) Act 2013 introduced a ring-fencing regime through amendments of the Financial Services and Markets Act 2000.[148] The regime largely resembled the recommendations set out in a report authored by the government-appointed Independent Commission on Banking.[149] Certain activities are now off limits for larger deposit-taking entities.[150] First, subject to certain exemptions, such entities cannot deal in investments as a principal.[151] Secondly, these entities are subject to limits on assuming exposures against other financial institutions.[152]

The UK regime does not prohibit deposit-taking banks from forming part of the same group as an entity that engages in the prohibited activities. As put by Wetzer, one may describe the results of the reform as 'structured universal banking'.[153] Financial groups may constitute universal banks on a group level but must, in that case, comply with restraints on its group structure. In line with the

[146] Independent Commission on Banking (n 145) 25.

[147] Liikanen Report (n 11) 94.

[148] For an overview, see K Alexander, 'Regulating the Structure of the EU Banking Sector' (2015) 16 *European Business Organization Law Review* 227, 231–40.

[149] T Wetzer, 'In two minds: the governance of ring-fenced banks' (2019) 19 *Journal of Corporate Law Studies* 197, 203.

[150] Financial Services and Markets Act 2000 (Ring-fenced Bodies and Core Activities) Order 2014, SI 2014/1960, reg 11(d) provides that the regime does not apply to deposit-taking institutions that have 'core deposits' (roughly speaking, deposits held by individuals and small businesses) of less than £25 billion. In addition, the regime excludes certain types of deposit-taking institutions as such.

[151] Financial Services and Markets Act 2000, s 142D.

[152] Financial Services and Markets Act 2000 (Excluded Activities and Prohibitions) Order 2014, SI 2014/2080, reg 13ff.

[153] Wetzer (n 149) 203.

recommendations of the Independent Commission on Banking, measures must be taken to insulate the ring-fenced entity from other group entities that engage in activities off limits for that entity.[154] The UK regime has recently been subject to review by a government-appointed panel. Among other things, the panel concluded that the ring-fencing regime should stay in place but that the scope of banks to which it applies should be somewhat narrowed down.[155]

Efforts were made to introduce harmonised ring-fencing rules at EU level. An expert group chaired by Erkki Liikanen, then the governor of the Bank of Finland, was established in February 2012. In October 2012, the group delivered its final report, commonly known as the Liikanen report. The Liikanen report recommended that regulation should prohibit larger deposit-taking banks from engaging in business such as proprietary trading, extending credit to hedge funds and investing in private equity firms.[156] Such activities would have to be conducted in a separate entity.

In 2014, the Commission put forward a proposal for a regulation that would require G-SIIs and banks with substantial trading activities to separate banking and trading activities.[157] Importantly, the regulation would generally prohibit such banks, their parent companies and their subsidiaries from engaging in proprietary trading.[158]

The Commission's proposal failed to win sufficient backing in the EU's legislative bodies, however, and it was ultimately withdrawn.[159] Hardie and Maccartney report that the Commission faced resistance from France and Germany against EU rules stricter than the structural reform measures the two states had enacted between the publication of the Liikanen report and the Commission's proposal.[160] In the absence of legislation harmonising ring fencing obligations, Member States remain free to decide the extent to which their banks should be obligated to separate deposit-taking from various trading activities.

An initiative that culminated in the adoption of EU law is the reform of over-the-counter (OTC) derivatives trading, which is now subject to the European

[154] See Prudential Regulation Authority, Ring-fenced Bodies Instrument 2016, rr 3.5 and 12, which requires that the ring-fenced entity conducts dealings with other group members that are not themselves ring-fenced at arm's length terms, and r 4.4, which requires ring-fenced entities to ensure that no more than a one-third of the members of its board of directors are employees or directors of such other group members.

[155] Independent Panel on Ring-fencing and Proprietary Trading, 'Final Report' (March 2022).

[156] Liikanen Report (n 11) 101–102.

[157] Commission, 'Proposal for a Regulation of the European Parliament and of the Council on structural measures improving the resilience of EU credit institutions' COM (2014) 43 final. For discussions of the proposal, see Alexander (n 148) 240–46 and M Lehmann, 'Volcker Rule, Ring-Fencing or Separation of Bank Activities: Comparison of Structural Reform Acts Around the World' (2014) LSE Law, Society and Economy Working Papers 25/2014, 13–14.

[158] COM (2014) 43 final, 26 (proposed art 6(1)(a)).

[159] See Commission, 'Commission Work Programme 2018: An agenda for a more united, stronger and more democratic Europe' COM (2017) 650 final, annex 4.

[160] For an analysis of this process, see I Hardie and H Macartney, 'EU ring-fencing and the defence of too-big-to-fail banks' (2016) 39 *West European Politics* 503.

Market Infrastructure Regulation (EMIR).[161] EMIR requires banks to take measures to reduce counterparty risk when trading in derivatives. Unsecured derivatives trading between financial institutions has thus been consigned to the rubbish heap of history. Accordingly, EMIR embodies the same distrust as structural reform of the pre-crisis regulatory paradigm, where banks may take on all kinds of risk as long as they hold capital commensurate to the risks.

The risk-reducing measures that banks must take in relation to a derivatives contract vary according to the characteristics of the contract. Following a proposal from the European Securities and Markets Authority (ESMA), the Commission may declare that a class of derivatives is subject to a clearing obligation.[162] The clearing obligation requires parties with a certain level of derivatives exposure to clear the trade through a central counterparty (CCP) that assumes the rights and obligations that the parties have towards one another under the contract.[163] Suppose that two banks have entered into a foreign exchange swap involving an obligation to exchange US dollars against euros at some future date. The clearing of that swap would involve the CCP's assuming the first party's right to receive US dollars and obligation to pay euros and the second party's right to receive euros and an obligation to pay US dollars to the other party. The original parties' rights and obligations towards each other would cease once the CCP agreed to clear the trade. As a result of the clearing, what was initially an exposure towards the creditworthiness of another bank would become an exposure against the CCP.

Not all derivatives are subject to clearing. As a result, banks may still lawfully incur rights and obligations towards each other in respect of such trades. However, they must ensure that the ensuing exposures are subject to a security arrangement.[164] A Commission Delegated Regulation provides specific criteria that the security arrangements must satisfy.[165]

2.3.8. Conclusions

Several pieces of EU's regulatory reform represent a shift towards the TFT regulation discussed at 1.2.3: First, the framework often produces quantitative regulatory

[161] Regulation (EU) No 648/2012 of the European Parliament and of the Council on OTC derivatives, central counterparties and trade repositories [2012] OJ L201/1. EMIR was recently revised by Regulation (EU) 2019/834 of the European Parliament and of the Council of 20 May 2019 amending Regulation (EU) No 648/2012 as regards the clearing obligation, the suspension of the clearing obligation, the reporting requirements, the risk-mitigation techniques for OTC derivative contracts not cleared by a central counterparty, the registration and supervision of trade repositories and the requirements for trade repositories [2019] OJ L141/42.

[162] EMIR art 5(2).

[163] EMIR art 4.

[164] EMIR art 11(3).

[165] Commission Delegated Regulation (EU) 2016/2251 supplementing Regulation (EU) No 648/2012 of the European Parliament and of the Council on OTC derivatives, central counterparties and trade repositories with regard to regulatory technical standards for risk-mitigation techniques for OTC derivative contracts not cleared by a central counterparty [2016] OJ L340/9.

requirements intended to vary between different banks and over time, the most prominent examples being the pillar 2 requirements, and the countercyclical and G-SII/O-SII capital buffer requirements. Secondly, the power to determine such requirements is frequently delegated to agencies. Thirdly, the exercise of these powers is subject to numerous constraints.

The new leverage ratio framework is less easy to fit within a narrative of TFT regulation. The leverage ratio *requirement* – ie the requirement that applies to all banks – is an example of classic command-and-control regulation: First, it is set out in EU level 1 legislation and is as such a direct result of decisions made by the EU legislature. Secondly, it is straightforward to implement once the accounting values of a bank's assets have been determined. By contrast, the applicability of the leverage ratio *buffer requirement* depends on whether the bank is considered a G-SII, which, in turn, is a decision that results from a framework that involves technocratic fine-tuning.

The harmonisation of liquidity requirements contains some elements that are in keeping with pre-crisis national approaches, and some that diverge. As discussed at 2.2.3, quantitative liquidity requirements were already before the GFC part of both German and UK regulation. Accordingly, the fundamental approach remains the same. However, there are also differences. It is not possible for banks that follow requirements generated by internal models to be exempt from the requirements set out in LCRR and CRR. The regulatory framework thus embodies one mark of TFT regulation in that it produces detailed command-and-control regulation. Moreover, the power of supervisors to require liquidity in excess of the minimum requirements of CRR and LCRR creates the potential for even more fine-tuned liquidity requirements.

The perceived shortcomings of meta-regulation are thus remedied by measures that rely on the ability of expert bureaucrats to fine-tune the framework so that risks are reduced below a certain – although largely undefined – level. More blunt regulation – the compliance with which would be more onerous to banks – was proposed but such proposals were either largely watered down (leverage ratio) or failed to produce EU-level legislation (structural reform/ringfencing).

2.4. The Safety Net: Deposit Insurance, Central Bank Liquidity Support and Government Rescues

2.4.1. Introduction

Regulation and supervision do not rule out the possibility of bank failure. History provides numerous examples of governments providing financial support to ailing banks over concerns that a failure could disrupt the functioning of the banking sector. For reasons set out at 2.4.4, such public support can be controversial. EU law imposes certain constraints on the use of public support.

The approach is somewhat Janus-faced, as EU law both requires the establishment of support schemes through the Deposit Guarantee Scheme Directive (DGSD) while constraining the use of public funds through the State aid rules set out in the Treaty on the Functioning of the European Union (TFEU) and BRRD.[166] The following sections will explore this legal framework and how it solves the conflict between preventing the risk of potentially disruptive failures and the disadvantages associated with public support.

2.4.2. Deposit Insurance

We have on numerous occasions touched upon the risk of bank runs and their potential adverse effects on financial stability. A ubiquitous response to these risks is the establishment of deposit insurance schemes that guarantee parts of a bank's deposits. The harmonisation of national deposit guarantee schemes is a relatively long-lived feature of EU banking law. Since the adoption of the first Deposit Guarantee Scheme Directive in 1994, the approach to this issue has developed from one of minimum harmonisation to a regime that, barring a few national options, is fully harmonised as set out in DGSD.[167]

DGSD requires that Member States establish schemes that guarantee the repayment of 'covered deposits'.[168] A defining characteristic of a covered deposit is that the deposit constitutes an 'eligible deposit', that is, any deposit that does not fall within one of the 11 categories set out in DGSD Article 5(1).[169] These categories include deposits held by public authorities, other banks and other financial firms. Conversely, deposits held by natural persons and non-financial companies are generally eligible deposits. As a main rule, the deposit guarantee scheme guarantees eligible deposits of up to 100,000 euro. If a deposit exceeds this level, the guarantee only applies to the first 100,000 euro, and the excess is not a covered deposit. There are some exemptions to this coverage level. In some cases, DGSD requires coverage of balances exceeding 100,000 euro.[170] In other cases, it permits, but does not require, Member States to provide for more comprehensive coverage of certain deposits.[171]

The deposit-taking institutions authorised by a Member State finance the applicable DGS. DGSs are thus segregated along national borders. The Commission has proposed the establishment of a European Deposit Insurance Scheme (EDIS).[172]

[166] Treaty on the Functioning of the European Union [2012] OJ C326/47.
[167] Directive 2014/49/EU of the European Parliament and of the Council on deposit guarantee schemes [2014] OJ L173/149.
[168] DGSD arts 6(1) and 8(1).
[169] DGSD art 2(1)(5).
[170] DGSD art 6(2).
[171] DGSD art 6(3).
[172] Commission, 'Proposal for a Regulation of the European Parliament and of the Council amending Regulation (EU) 806/2014 in order to establish a European Deposit Insurance Scheme' COM (2015) 586 final.

This would create a joint deposit insurance fund for Member States partaking in the Banking Union. As we will return to at 10.3, the Commission's proposal has so far failed to gain traction, however.

If a failing bank is of a certain size, the funds available to the DGS could prove insufficient. As ruled by the EFTA Court in the *Icesave* case, and now set out in the recital of DGSD, Member States are not liable towards depositors in the event the applicable DGS fails to honour its payment obligations.[173] It is possible that covered deposits nonetheless are de facto state backed, as for many governments it would be unthinkable to leave holders of such deposits empty handed.

2.4.3. State Aid

As evidenced by recent experience, deposit guarantee schemes do not eliminate the risk that banks will fail. First, as discussed at 2.1.3, banks have short-term creditors who are not depositors covered under a DGS. In the absence of other assurances that they will recover their claims in full, such creditors have both the option and the incentive to demand repayment from struggling banks. Secondly, regardless of their liability structure, banks are entirely capable of becoming insolvent because of loss-making activities and investments.

Various forms of public financial support offer opportunities to prop up struggling banks and ensure they continue to provide their services. Currently, the general State aid rules and BRRD together make up the framework for the legality of the provision of financial support to banks.[174] In the following section we will discuss the State aid regime's limits and conditions for the granting of different forms of support to banks before we go on to analyse the additional limits for public support brought about by the adoption of BRRD.

The EU law State aid regime constrains governments' ability to use fiscal means to save ailing national banks. The definition of State aid is found in TFEU Article 107(1). The provision declares any measure as prima facie incompatible with the internal market if the measure: (i) confers an economic advantage on an undertaking, (ii) involves a transfer of public resources, (iii) is selective, (iv) distorts competition, and (v) has an effect on trade between Member States.[175]

Measures that constitute State aid are unlawful unless TFEU Article 107(2) provides that the aid is lawful or the Commission approves the aid pursuant to

[173] Case E-16/11 *EFTA Surveillance Authority v Iceland* [2013] EFTA Ct. Rep. 4, para 178; DGSD recital 45.

[174] In addition, the ECB's Governing Council can veto the provision of emergency liquidity assistance by a national central bank within the European System of Central Banks, see TFEU Protocol (No 4) on the Statute of the European System of Central Banks and of the ECB [2012] OJ C326/230 art 14.4. See also A Steinbach, 'The Lender of Last Resort in the Eurozone' (2016) 53 *CML Rev* 361, 371–75.

[175] See Commission, 'Commission Notice on the notion of State aid as referred to in Article 107(1) of the Treaty on the Functioning of the European Union' (Notice 2016) OJ C262/1 para 5 and MA Cyndecka, 'The problem of objectives pursued by the state under the application of the Market Economy Investor Principle (MEIP)' (2015) 128 *Tidsskrift for Rettsvitenskap* 263, 264–65.

TFEU Article 107(3) following a notification from the Member State concerned. In the present context, Article 107(3)(b) and (c) are of relevance. Article 107(3)(b) covers inter alia 'aid … to remedy a serious disturbance in the economy of a Member State', while Article 107(3)(c) covers 'aid to facilitate the development of certain economic activities or of certain economic areas, where such aid does not adversely affect trading conditions to an extent contrary to the common interest'.

Traditionally, the Commission has relied on Article 107(3)(c) when determining whether to approve aid to struggling firms, financial or non-financial alike. Based on its practice, the Commission has developed guidelines for handling such cases. Among other things, the guidelines require that the financing of the recipient's restructuring in part comes from private-sector resources and compensatory measures to offset the distortive effects of saving a failed firm. The 2014 Rescue and Restructuring Guidelines embody the Commission's current policy.[176] In the early stages of the financial crisis, the Commission relied on its power to approve solvency aid to failing banks pursuant to Article 107(3)(c), as it considered the problems to stem from the business models of the banks in question.[177]

However, as the financial crisis developed, the Commission began to use Article 107(3)(b) as the legal base for its decisions on aid to banks. Moreover, the Commission developed bank-specific guidelines setting out the terms the aid must satisfy to receive approval.[178] The most prominent guideline is currently the 2013 Banking Communication.[179] Public financial support may take different forms: governments may support banks through both liquidity and solvency assistance. Measures could aim at individual banks or be sector wide. The Commission's guidelines reflect this heterogeneity by making the approval of different forms of aid conditional upon different conditions. In the following paragraphs, we will provide an account of different forms of financial support that banks have received in recent times and the circumstances under which the Commission will accept various support measures.

One example of liquidity support aimed at individual banks is the provision of emergency liquidity assistance (ELA) by a central bank to solvent but illiquid banks. The Commission does not consider ELA to constitute State aid if certain conditions are satisfied.[180] First, it is required that the recipient is not insolvent.

[176] Commission, 'Guidelines on State aid for rescuing and restructuring non-financial undertakings in difficulty' (Communication 2014) OJ C249/1 (2014 Rescue and Restructuring Guidelines).

[177] C Ahlborn and D Piccinin, 'The Application of the Principles of Restructuring Aid to Banks during the Financial Crisis' (2010) 9 *European State Aid Law Quarterly* 47, 49–50.

[178] For an overview, see V Iftinchi, 'State aid and the financial sector' in F-C Laprévote, J Gray and F De Cecco (eds), *Research Handbook on State Aid in the Banking Sector* (Cheltenham, Edward Elgar, 2017) 55–56.

[179] Commission, 'Communication from the Commission on the application, from 1 August 2013, of State aid rules to support measures in favour of banks in the context of the financial crisis' (Communication 2013) OJ C216/1 (2013 Banking Communication). The Commission recently launched a consultation procedure aimed at 'gathering evidence and views on the effectiveness, efficiency, relevance, coherence and EU added value of these rules'.

[180] 2013 Banking Communication (n 179) point 62.

Secondly, the loan must be fully secured. Thirdly, the central bank must demand a penal interest rate for extending the loan. Fourthly, the measure must be taken at the central bank's initiative.

A state guarantee covering the debt of all or parts of its domestic banks achieves the same result as ELA. The difference is that while ELA involves transferring money to banks to enable them to repay their claims, a guarantee may either remove the incentive of bank creditors to demand repayment or incentivise other market actors to extend new funds to the bank when it needs to refinance maturing debt. If successful, a government guarantee prevents a run from occurring without necessitating money transfers. A measure commonly employed during the financial crisis was schemes where banks in need of liquidity could apply for government guarantees against paying a fee.

Even if made sector-wide, guarantee schemes easily constitute State aid.[181] During the crisis, the Commission was inclined to accept that such measures were a necessity in light of the prevailing conditions. Guarantee schemes could receive the Commission's blessing insofar as only solvent banks were eligible for support and the banks would pay the state 'adequate remuneration' for its exposure under any guarantees issued.[182] Approval of such aid was further conditional upon that the terms of the guarantee would prohibit banks from pursuing aggressive business expansion.[183] The guidelines have become more restrictive through several amendments that culminated in the currently applicable 2013 Banking Communication. In order to escape the requirement of a restructuring plan, banks benefiting from the guarantee must now have no 'capital shortfall', as opposed to merely being solvent.[184] The 2013 Banking Communication defines such a shortfall as 'a capital shortfall established in a capital exercise, stress-test, asset quality review or an equivalent exercise at Union, euro area or national level'.[185] Accordingly, identifying an individual bank's capital shortfall involves a bank supervisor's determination of a threshold that its capital should exceed in different projected scenarios and assessing whether its capital would exceed that threshold. If the bank suffers from a capital shortfall, the Commission will require the Member State to submit a restructuring or wind-down plan within two months unless the bank has reimbursed the aid by then.[186] As we will discuss below, both a restructuring plan and a liquidation plan involve the bank's subordinated creditors bearing losses.

[181] S Gebski, 'Competition First? Application of State Aid Rules in the Banking Sector' (2009) 6 *Competition Law Review* 89, 92–95.

[182] Commission, 'The application of State aid rules to measures taken in relation to financial institutions in the context of the current global financial crisis' (Communication 2008) OJ C270/8 (2008 Banking Communication) point 26.

[183] 2008 Banking Communication (n 182) point 27.

[184] 2013 Banking Communication (n 179) point 58.

[185] ibid point 28.

[186] ibid point 58.

ELA and state guarantees do not decrease a bank's debt or increase its net assets. In other words, the measures do not remedy any underlying solvency problems. To this end, a recapitalisation is necessary. A recapitalisation may involve the increase of a bank's assets, as is the case when a company makes a share issue for a cash consideration. Alternatively, a bank may be recapitalised by decreasing its liabilities, as in the case of a debt restructuring under general insolvency law or a bail-in of claims in resolution. In both cases, the bank's ability to repay its creditors is improved. Moreover, creditor incentives to run on the bank should cease when the bank's equity rises to a certain level.

Roughly speaking, a Member State's subscription for shares constitutes State aid if the issuer is unable to attract such funding from private parties.[187] Under the Commission's current guidelines, the approval of a bank recapitalisation that constitutes State aid is normally conditional upon agreement over a restructuring plan.[188] Such a plan shall provide for measures that will restore the bank's ability to compete in the market and will often involve the bank agreeing to scale down activities that caused its recapitalisation needs.[189] Moreover, based on the view that the recapitalisation of failing banks distorts competition, the Commission will frequently require that the bank agrees to execute measures that mitigate the distortion. Examples of such measures include the sale of assets or business lines as well as restrictions on how aggressively banks may compete for new business following the recapitalisation.[190]

The Commission will normally require that private parties bear parts of the recapitalisation costs. Shareholders and subordinated creditors will normally have to contribute through 'burden-sharing' measures.[191] Such measures normally involve the writing down of equity and subordinated debt instruments. Accordingly, the Commission's policy normally ensures that subordinated creditors do not benefit from a government-funded recapitalisation.

Several provisions of BRRD make it clear that the directive does not seek to rule out financial support to banks entirely. Rather, BRRD's approach to this issue is to regulate the extent to which the writing down of shares and debt must accompany aid measures. We have seen that in some cases the provision of support to struggling banks requires that the bank's subordinated creditors contribute to shoring up the bank by having their claims written down. In this section, we will analyse the extent to which BRRD increases the amount of losses creditors must bear in connection with a bank receiving government support.

[187] For an analysis of why this is the case, see G Lo Schiavo, 'State Aids and Credit Institutions in Europe: What Way Forward?' (2014) 25 *European Business Law Review* 427, 436–37.

[188] For analysis of when agreement over such a plan will be required prior to the approval of the aid measure, see Iftinchi (n 178) 71–72.

[189] See Iftinchi (n 178) 62ff.

[190] Iftinchi (n 178) 65–66; F-C Laprévote, 'Selected Issues Raised by Bank Restructuring Plans Under EU State Aid Rules' (2012) 11 *European State Aid Law Quarterly* 93, 101–105.

[191] 2013 Banking Communication (n 179) points 40–46.

A link between BRRD's resolution framework and the State aid regime lies in the conditions for resolution. As we will discuss at 3.4.2, one of the conditions for resolution is that a bank is 'failing or likely to fail'. Generally, a bank in need of 'extraordinary public financial support' is considered to satisfy this condition.[192] Such support comprises both State aid and aid provided at supranational level that would have been State aid if provided by a Member State, in both cases insofar as the purpose of the support is to 'preserve or restore the viability, liquidity or solvency of [the bank]'.[193] There are, however, exceptions to this rule. In the following paragraphs, we will discuss whether the receipt of various forms of public financial support qualifies a bank as failing or likely to fail.

Some of the support measures discussed above are not considered State aid at all, central bank emergency liquidity assistance (ELA) being a notable example. Accordingly, the receipt of such support does not as such qualify the recipient bank as failing or likely to fail. BRRD therefore permits banks to receive ELA without necessitating the resolution of the bank and the bailing-in of creditor claims.

Other forms of liquidity support often constitute State aid. As mentioned above, the 2013 Banking Communication provides that the Commission will approve these measures without making the approval conditional upon restructuring measures if the recipient bank does not suffer from a 'capital shortfall'. BRRD does not change this state of affairs, as the directive does not necessarily deem banks 'failing or likely to fail' by virtue of the receipt of liquidity support.[194] Even if BRRD was in force during the financial crisis, it would thus still have been possible to enact the liquidity schemes discussed above without necessitating resolution and creditors taking losses.

Save for an exception for 'precautionary recapitalisations' which we will address below, solvency support results in a bank's being deemed 'failing or likely to fail'. As discussed, the Commission's approval of solvency support to banks under the State aid framework comes with strings attached. The Commission has in the past made the approval of State aid taking the form of a bank's recapitalisation conditional upon commitments to restructure the bank's business. Such measures have included the eventual liquidation of the bank, sale of the business to another institution, sale of specific business lines or assets and limitations on business activities. This gives rise to the question of what additional limits, if any, resolution places on the use of State aid.

Under the Commission's general policy, it approves solvency aid to banks conditional upon the writing down of the bank's shares and subordinated debt. While the State aid guidelines do not make such a write-down an unconditional requirement,[195] BRRD does. The directive provides that any State aid other than

[192] BRRD art 32(4)(d).
[193] BRRD art 2(1)(28).
[194] BRRD art 32(4)(d)(ii).
[195] The writing down of the bank's shares and subordinated debt will not be required if this would 'endanger financial stability or lead to disproportionate results', see the 2013 Banking Communication (n 179) point 45.

a 'precautionary recapitalisation' will require that all own funds instruments are written down.[196]

The Commission's State aid policy does not make the approval of solvency support conditional upon the write-down of general unsecured debt. However, the grant of State aid could require that the institution is resolved, which in turn could affect general unsecured debt. When a bank is resolved, BRRD places additional constraints on the provision of state support. These requirements differ according to whether the resolution aims at preserving the legal entity (ie resolution involving the use of the bail-in tool) or continuing the business in another entity (ie resolution involving the sale of business tool or the bridge institution tool).

BRRD applies certain conditions to support accompanying the use of the 'bail-in tool'. The bail-in tool involves the resolution authority writing down claims against the bank under resolution. The lawfulness of support measures funded directly by the government requires the presence of a systemic crisis.[197] Moreover, the resolution authority may only – and to a limited extent – use the resolution fund for recapitalisation purposes.[198] Perhaps most importantly, both support from the government and the resolution fund require that the bank's liabilities are written down in an amount of at least eight per cent.[199]

Conversely, no additional requirements apply for solvency support in connection with the exercise of the transfer tools. The exercise of the transfer tools involves the resolution authority transferring all or parts of the failed bank's assets and liabilities to a private-sector purchaser or a government-controlled entity (a 'bridge bank'). BRRD does not contain any prohibition against a bridge bank assuming the general unsecured debt of the institution under resolution. Moreover, the directive does not appear to prohibit the state from granting a guarantee to a private-sector purchaser, which might be necessary for such a purchaser to assume general unsecured debt.

It should also be noted that BRRD's additional requirements for burden sharing with private creditors do not apply when a bank is wound up under liquidation proceedings rather than resolved under the resolution framework. This was exploited in the context of the recent liquidation of the failing Italian banks Veneto Banca and Banca Popolare di Vicenza. As the banks entered liquidation, another Italian bank assumed the banks' assets and non-subordinated debt. The sale followed a tender procedure that involved the Italian state providing a guarantee for the failing banks' assets to induce potential purchasers. The Commission approved the aid pursuant to TFEU Article 107(3)(b), subject to the write-down of the banks' own funds instruments. It was thus not necessary to write down non-subordinated debts, and creditors holding such claims escaped

[196] BRRD art 59(3)(e).
[197] BRRD art 37(10).
[198] BRRD art 101(1)(f).
[199] BRRD arts 37(10) and 44(5).

the failure unscathed as the purchaser assumed their claims. The framework for public support of banks has attracted criticism in the wake of this case.[200]

2.4.4. Problems Associated with the Safety Net

The use of public funds to save failing banks is controversial. Some argue that states should generally refuse to extend support to ailing banks. Although a policy of non-intervention may result in temporary pain should a crisis occur, this would force banks to become more prudent, which in turn would foster long-term stability in the financial system. As seen in the preceding section, the EU's current framework for public support of banks does not reflect this view. A more mainstream view is that it is not desirable for the state to commit to a policy of no support under any circumstances, but society should seek to minimise reliance on state support as a tool for managing financial crises. In this section, we will explore three arguments against the use of State aid: arguments revolving around moral hazard, competition and the so-called doom loop. We will also consider how EU law balances the need for states to be able to intervene with these three counterarguments.

One issue with public support of banks unable to attract private capital is that it gives rise to a so-called moral hazard problem. It is not always clear what users of the term 'moral hazard' mean and it is therefore useful to clarify how this term is understood in the present context. The related concept of 'market discipline' is a helpful starting point. The use of this term and moral hazard seems to indicate that the two are antonyms. For instance, the Commission's 2013 Banking Communication states that '[s]tate support can create moral hazard and undermine market discipline'.[201] Creditors exercise 'market discipline' when an increase in a bank's risk-taking results in an increase in its funding costs or, in extreme cases, cuts off its access to debt financing.[202]

Nier and Baumann implicitly define market discipline by listing three conditions that must be satisfied for it to materialise:

> First, investors in bank liabilities need to consider themselves at risk of loss if the bank defaults. Second, market responses to changes in the bank's risk profile need to have cost implications for the bank and its managers. Third, the market must have adequate information to gauge the riskiness of the bank.[203]

[200] MA Schillig, 'The (Il-)Legitimacy of the EU Post-Crisis Bailout System' (2020) 28 *American Bankruptcy Institute Law Review* 135, 196–98; IG Asimakopoulos, 'The Veneto Banks Resolution: It Shall Be Called 'Liquidation'' (2018) 15 *European Company Law* 156, 161.

[201] 2013 Banking Communication (n 179) point 40.

[202] See R Bliss, 'Market Discipline in Financial Markets: Theory, Evidence, and Obstacles' in Berger, Molyneux and Wilson (n 2) 569, who terms this form of market discipline 'direct market discipline'. 'Indirect market discipline' denotes the process whereby the market's assessment of a bank's risk of failure (as implied by price signals) informs the decisions of bank supervisors.

[203] E Nier and U Baumann, 'Market discipline, disclosure and moral hazard in banking' (2006) 15 *Journal of Financial Intermediation* 332, 333–34.

The first condition is of interest in this context: The operation of any insolvency framework means that some unsecured creditors will suffer losses if a company becomes insolvent. This condition is not satisfied if the same creditors benefit from explicit or implicit public guarantees.[204] If a bank creditor believes that the state will supply the funds necessary to save insolvent banks, it will naturally be less concerned with monitoring the risks undertaken by the bank. Likewise, expectations that a government guarantee or central bank ELA will be available for banks to refinance short-term funding could allow banks to maintain lower liquidity reserves than they would in the absence of such expectations. Some, therefore, view ELA as causing moral hazard and eroding market discipline.[205] Market discipline thus suffers in such circumstances, as the risk of having credit exposures towards a bank does not entirely reflect the risk of it failing.[206] In other words, the bank's increased risk-taking is not fully 'penalised' by higher funding costs.

In the present context, a feature particular to the moral hazard issue is that the state is seldom under a legal obligation to support national banks. However, critics argue that an implicit guarantee has risen nonetheless from the willingness of governments to support failing banks in the past. In other words, the underlying logic is that the state's support of a failing bank today strengthens the market's belief that the support will be forthcoming should the need arise tomorrow.[207] This, in turn, affects the willingness of creditors to extend loans to banks that benefit from implicit support. The problem was also highlighted in the Commission's Impact Assessment that accompanied its original proposal for BRRD:

> The management, senior executives and shareholders of systemic institutions could on the basis of past evidence reasonably expect that while they stand to gain from the upside risk (profits) of their actions, society would have to cover the downside risk (losses).[208]

A lack of market discipline does not necessarily imply that banks will increase their risk-taking to a level above what is optimal. It is, however, a conventional view that assuming risk is in the interest of the shareholders of banks and other companies, as shareholders are protected by limited liability.[209] Further, it is often assumed that bank management enjoys bonus schemes that incentivise such increased risk-taking. What is best for bank shareholders is not necessarily the optimal choice once all other effects are taken into account. For example, while systemic risk

[204] See also Armour et al (n 113) 342.
[205] Schillig (n 200) 192.
[206] See Bliss (n 202) 570.
[207] Armour et al (n 113) 342.
[208] Commission, 'Impact Assessment accompanying the document proposal for a directive of the European Parliament and of the Council establishing a framework for the recovery and resolution of credit institutions and investment firms and amending Council Directives 77/91/EEC and 82/891/EC, Directives 2001/24/EC, 2002/47/EC, 2004/25/EC, 2005/56/EC, 2007/36/EC and 2011/35/EC and Regulation (EU) No 1093/2010' (Commission staff working document) SWD (2012) 166 final, 10.
[209] See MC Jensen and WH Meckling, 'Theory of the Firm: Managerial Behavior, Agency Costs and Ownership Structure' (1976) 3 *Journal of Financial Economics* 305, 334–36.

increases when a sufficiently large share of the banking sector increases its risk-taking, this does not matter to the bank shareholders (in their capacity as such).[210] This is because they do not fully bear the costs when the systemic risk materialises, the capacity of the financial system to allocate investments is impaired and the real economy consequently suffers.[211]

How does the post-BRRD regime for public support reflect the concerns over market discipline? The approach is somewhat different for various forms of state support. First, liquidity support in the form of central bank ELA that satisfies the criteria established in the 2013 Banking Communication does not constitute State aid, and burden-sharing from the recipient bank's creditors is therefore not necessary. Insofar as the state implicitly guarantees covered deposits, this also constitutes a form of liquidity support. Neither of the two forms of support is entirely costless for beneficiary banks. Central banks must grant ELA at a 'penal interest rate' to steer such support clear of qualifying as State aid. Moreover, ELA must be fully secured. This means that banks must maintain a certain level of unencumbered assets that the central bank will accept as security, which in turn somewhat limits the risk they may take on. A bank's participation in a deposit guarantee scheme requires the making of contributions to the scheme. Since one of the inputs for determining an individual bank's required contribution to the DGS is the bank's risk of failure, the implicit guarantee is not costless.[212] Explicit government guarantees will most often constitute State aid. While the approval of the Commission to such support will require appropriate remuneration of the risk assumed by the government, no burden-sharing is necessary if the bank does not suffer from a capital shortfall, as discussed at 2.4.3.

The conditions for the approval of State aid are more onerous in the case of measures that support banks with a capital shortfall, whether in the form of liquidity or solvency support. Generally, approval will necessitate burden-sharing measures consisting of the write-down of shares and subordinated debt. Save for cases involving a 'precautionary recapitalisation', support will also lead to the recipient bank's being deemed failing or likely to fail under BRRD with the consequence that the bank shall be resolved or wound up. In a resolution involving the recapitalisation of the bank through a bail-in, shareholders and creditors must suffer losses of at least eight per cent of the bank's total liabilities to make support legal. If enforced, BRRD's requirements will partly establish market discipline, as the bailed-in creditors do not benefit from an implicit guarantee.

We now turn to a second issue surrounding public support to banks, namely the potential conflict between financial stability and competition. Rescuing

[210] For an analysis of how systemic risk may be harmful to bank shareholders that hold a diversified share portfolio, see J Armour and JN Gordon, 'Systemic Harms and Shareholder Value' (2014) 6 *Journal of Legal Analysis* 35.

[211] R Kraakman et al, *The Anatomy of Corporate Law: A Comparative and Functional Approach*, 3rd edn (Oxford, Oxford University Press, 2017) 100.

[212] DGSD art 13.

insolvent entities arguably contradicts the logic of the market economy. The Commission's 2014 Rescue and Restructuring Guidelines, which set out the conditions generally applicable to State aid to failing firms, stress how the elimination of insolvent actors from the market is conducive to market efficiency.[213] The underlying idea is that market actors have little incentive to invest effort into making their services more efficient if governments intervene to save less efficient competitors. Under this rationale, state support leads to a less efficient provision of services, a cost at least partly borne by end users. The interface between financial support to banks and competition concerns is not limited to support provided. An implicit guarantee also affects competition. As the banks viewed as implicitly guaranteed can raise debt financing at a lower cost, they enjoy an advantage over banks that are not viewed as likely to attract government support in the event of failure.[214]

Some challenge the appropriateness of applying principles of general State aid policy to the case of bank failures. What is questioned is the assumption that the banking sector's ability to meet the demand for banking services is unaffected by the exit of one participant. As discussed at 2.1.4, one reason why states are reluctant to let banks fail is the fear that other market participants are unable to assume its activities. The implication of this view negates the assumption that one bank's exit would not affect the sector's ability to meet the demand for banking services.[215]

The fact that the granting of State aid to banks is subject to a sector-specific regime could indicate that the Commission attaches less weight to promoting competition in its State aid policy for the financial sector. Certain differences between the 2013 Banking Communication and the 2014 Rescue and Restructuring Guidelines could be taken as evidence confirming this intuition. For instance, the current Rescue and Restructuring Guidelines apply the principle that at least half of the costs of restructuring a failing firm must come from the private sector,[216] while the Banking Communication requires the write-down of shares and subordinated debt without any corresponding quantitative requirement. On the other hand, it is not as if the Commission's general State aid policy effectively prohibits aid to non-financial firms. The Rescue and Restructuring Guidelines view the mitigation of a market failure as a legitimate justification for State aid.[217] An example of circumstances that justify support of a failing firm is 'a risk of disruption of an important service which is hard to replicate and where it would be difficult for any competitor to simply step in'.[218] These circumstances are arguably similar to those

[213] 2014 Rescue and Restructuring Guidelines (n 176) point 6.

[214] T Beck et al, *Bailing out the Banks: Reconciling Stability and Competition* (London, Centre for Economic Policy Research (CEPR), 2010) 51. See also SWD (2012) 166 final 10.

[215] See Beck et al (n 214) 55. In fact, everything else being equal, banks could benefit from the bailout of a competitor, as financial stability benefits all financial institutions, see I Angeloni and N Lenihan, 'Competition and state aid rules in the time of banking union' in E Faia et al (eds), *Financial Regulation: A Transatlantic Perspective* (Cambridge, Cambridge University Press, 2015) 95.

[216] 2014 Rescue and Restructuring Guidelines (n 176) point 64.

[217] ibid point 38.

[218] ibid point 44(b).

that could render a bank's services 'critical functions', as discussed at 2.1.4. One could argue that the disruption of critical functions and financial stability associated with bank failures is a particularly acute form of market failure. Accordingly, one could also interpret that the comparatively laxer conditions for support to banks reflect a view that the effects of market failures in this area are graver than the effects in other sectors.

A third issue with public support to banks is the creation of a 'doom loop' between governments and their banks, as illustrated by the Eurozone crisis. In brief, the doom loop works as follows: suppose that a large bank is struggling and that market participants anticipate that its home state will use public funds to save it. This creates an expectation that the state will have to increase its public spending. An increase in public spending makes the state's debt burden more difficult to carry and therefore causes the credit risk of its sovereign debt to rise. A rise in credit risk translates into increased funding costs for the state. Problems do not necessarily stop there. As lending to the state becomes riskier, the market value of its outstanding bonds falls. If the struggling bank has a large holding of the government bonds of its home state, as is common,[219] the decrease in the value of the bonds has a negative impact on its solvency. This, again, increases the risk that the state will have to intervene, thereby putting additional pressure on the value of its bonds.[220] The state and its banking sector thereby continue to pull each other down. The link between sovereigns and banks also causes problems in normal times, as the credit risk of banks becomes a function, in part, of the strength of their government. This distorts competition and contradicts the very idea of a single market for financial services.

The source of the 'doom loop' is the expectation that the state will bear the costs should a domestic bank fail. One solution to the doom loop is for states to make clear that they will not save their banks. Such a commitment could take the form of a constitutional provision prohibiting bank bailouts. It appears, however, that no states have taken this route. Within the eurozone, the solution to the doom loop issue has taken a different form. Rather than decoupling banks from public financial backstops, the solution is to provide banks with a financial backstop separate from their home state. The move towards the creation of a common deposit guarantee scheme reflects such a desire to make banks less run-prone and eliminate competitive distortions caused by the sovereign-bank nexus.[221] The eurozone states' creation of the European Stability Mechanism (ESM) also builds upon the idea that eurozone banks should have a supranational backstop, as the ESM may

[219] Brunnermeier and Oehmke (n 49) 1269. Current regulation encourages this. Under the standardised approach for calculating risk-weighted capital requirements, banks are not required to back holdings of bonds issued by EU Member States and denominated in the issuer's domestic currency with own funds, see CRR art 114(4).

[220] Brunnermeier and Oehmke (n 49) 1269; N Moloney, 'European Banking Union: Assessing its risks and resilience' (2014) 51 *CML Rev* 1609, 1622.

[221] COM (2015) 586 final 4.

use its funds not only to lend to participating states, but also to recapitalise directly banks established in these states.[222]

To conclude this section, our discussion shows that while there are issues surrounding government support to struggling banks, EU law still allows for liquidity and solvency support measures. While the granting of solvency support as a main rule requires that the bank's shareholders and some of its creditors take losses, states remain free to design general liquidity support schemes that allow creditors of struggling banks to escape losses. This renders salient the question of whether other measures could reduce the likelihood that governments find themselves forced to provide financial support to troubled domestic banks. The various forms of regulation that we discussed at 2.3 constitute one set of such measures. Another measure is the resolution framework. The adoption of this framework reflects the view that a tailor-made bank-specific insolvency procedure makes it more likely that bank failures do not cause unacceptable damage to the overarching objectives of financial regulation that we discussed at 2.1.4, namely the preservation of critical services and other aspects of financial stability. The next chapter will explore what separates bank-specific insolvency proceedings from general insolvency law, and what arguments that posit that BRRD's resolution procedure will serve these objectives better than general insolvency procedures.

[222] See Board of Governors of the European Stability Mechanism, 'Establishment of the instrument for the direct recapitalisation of institutions' (Resolution, 8 December 2014).

3

The Emergence of Bank-Specific Insolvency Proceedings

3.1. One Size Fits All: The General Approach to Corporate Financial Distress and Insolvency

3.1.1. Introduction

The objective of this chapter is to provide an account of the legal frameworks that constitute bank insolvency proceedings. Before we turn to the details of these frameworks, it is helpful to describe the background against which policymakers have drawn up the bank-specific regime. An understanding of what bank insolvency proceedings are not enriches both our understanding of what bank insolvency proceedings are and the subsequent analyses of the contributions such proceedings can provide to the broader objectives of financial regulation.

We will therefore start the chapter with an introduction to the general corporate insolvency proceedings of England, Germany and Norway, that is, those that apply to all companies save banks and certain other financial companies. This raises the question of which proceedings count as general insolvency proceedings for present purposes. We then move on to discuss why general insolvency proceedings are deemed as inappropriate for the specific challenges attached to bank failures. Thereafter, we discuss the emergence of bank-specific insolvency proceedings.

3.1.2. What are Insolvency Proceedings?

Concepts such as 'general insolvency proceedings' or 'general insolvency law' are difficult to define in the abstract. Within individual jurisdictions, one often surmises that a tacit understanding exists regarding what counts as insolvency law: To grasp which proceedings constitute insolvency law, one must consult books on general insolvency law and examine what proceedings such books address and thus implicitly categorise as part of this field of law. While both EU law and international law coordinate national insolvency laws by harmonising their approaches to the jurisdiction of courts in matters concerning insolvency proceedings,[1] such instruments have not produced a universal definition of which proceedings constitute insolvency proceedings. The use of such terms in legislation and treaties tends to be context specific.[2] In some cases, policymakers avoid the problem by drawing up an exhaustive list of the various national proceedings that shall constitute insolvency proceedings under a given legal instrument.[3]

There is general agreement that (insolvent) liquidation proceedings are insolvency proceedings. Liquidation proceedings may only commence once a company is or, in some jurisdictions, is likely to, become insolvent. In essence, such proceedings involve an insolvency professional, who is in some cases appointed by a court, taking control of the company's assets, selling the assets to the highest bidder and thereafter distributing the proceeds among the creditors in the order prescribed by statute.[4]

More controversy attaches to whether restructuring proceedings form part of insolvency law. A defining feature of a restructuring framework is that it provides for the possibility of amending the terms of a company's liabilities notwithstanding that not all affected creditors have consented thereto. However, there is great variation as regards the conditions for the adoption of a restructuring, and whether the initiation of such a process has ancillary effects such as the suspension of individual creditor enforcement rights while negotiations take place. Eidenmüller uses 'corporate insolvency law' as an umbrella term for 'proceedings that aim at a restructuring of corporate debtors and those that are directed toward liquidation'.[5] In a similar vein, Mevorach and Walters argue that insolvency and restructuring proceedings together constitute 'a comprehensive, unified body of law' that consist of proceedings that address 'coordination problems for which private ordering alone does not provide effective solutions, with the goal of maximising enterprise value across a sliding scale of situations ranging from anticipated to actual distress'.[6] Tollenaar argues that there is no 'principle difference' between restructuring and

[1] In EU law such rules are set out in the Insolvency Regulation, see Regulation (EU) 2015/848 of the European Parliament and of the Council of 20 May 2015 on insolvency proceedings (recast) [2015] OJ L141/19.

[2] H Eidenmüller, 'What is an insolvency proceeding?' (2018) 92 *American Bankruptcy Law Journal* 53, 66; H Anderson, 'What is the purpose of insolvency proceedings?' (2016) *Journal of Business Law* 670, 670.

[3] The Insolvency Regulation takes this approach, see recital 9; Case C-116/11 *Bank Handlowy w Warszawie SA and PPHU 'ADAX'/Ryszard Adamiak v Christianapol sp. z o.o.* ECLI:EU:C:2012:739 para 33; Case C-461/11 *Ulf Kazimierz Radziejewski v Kronofogdemyndigheten i Stockholm* ECLI:EU:C:2012:704 para 24; R Bork and R Mangano, *European Cross-Border Insolvency Law* (Oxford, Oxford University Press, 2016) paras 2.48–2.50.

[4] C Gerner-Beuerle and M Schillig, *Comparative Company Law* (Oxford, Oxford University Press, 2019) 978.

[5] H Eidenmüller, 'Comparative Corporate Insolvency Law' in JN Gordon and W-G Ringe (eds), *The Oxford Handbook of Corporate Law and Governance* (Oxford, Oxford University Press, 2018) 1006.

[6] I Mevorach and A Walters, 'The Characterization of Pre-insolvency Proceedings in Private International Law' (2020) 21 *European Business Organization Law Review* 855, 859.

liquidation and that 'a restructuring can be regarded as a form of credit bidding, where the business is sold and, upon majority resolution, acquired by the creditors in exchange for their claims'.[7]

Others adopt a narrower definition of insolvency law. Madaus defines insolvency law as the legal framework that governs 'statutory liquidation proceedings for insolvent debtors'.[8] This means that the legal framework that governs 'proceedings in which a restructuring contract (workout) is concluded with judicial assistance' is not part of insolvency law, and rather constitutes the distinct field of restructuring law. Part of Madaus' argument is that liquidation and restructuring proceedings address different questions. Liquidation proceedings 'respond to a common pool problem with collective effects … to address the needs following from this problem',[9] and the 'common pool problem' stems from the debtor having insufficient funds for paying all its creditors.[10] By contrast, restructuring proceedings 'only address the issue of concluding a contract'.

We have earlier defined bank insolvency proceedings as resolution and national winding-up proceedings applicable to banks.[11] Both frameworks apply creditor priority rules for determining how losses are distributed among creditors when the public interest and/or the interest of the creditors as a whole dictate that not all bank creditors can be paid in full. When selecting the generally applicable frameworks to compare with the bank-specific priority framework, it is generally of interest to include all legal frameworks that comprise rules concerning loss distribution among creditors in cases where at least some of them must forgo their claims in the interest of the creditors as a whole and/or securing the continuation of a profitable business. Therefore, we will consider creditor priority in both liquidation and restructuring frameworks. We will use the term 'general insolvency law' as shorthand for both proceedings without this implying the taking of a position on what is part of general insolvency law proper.

Before we embark upon assessing the relevant proceedings, a further note on terminology is due. The personal scope of the insolvency proceedings differs across the jurisdictions. English law contains separate insolvency proceedings for corporations and natural persons. Conversely, German and Norwegian insolvency proceedings apply, for the most part, to all persons, whether physical or not. The terminology employed in the legislation of these jurisdictions reflects this. The English corporate insolvency legislation speaks of 'the company' when referring to the entity whose affairs are wound up or whose debts are restructured. Conversely, German and Norwegian provisions speak of 'the debtor'

[7] NWA Tollenaar, 'The European Commission's Proposal for a Directive on Preventive Restructuring Proceedings' (2017) 30 *Insolvency Intelligence* 65, 71–72.

[8] S Madaus, 'Leaving the Shadows of US Bankruptcy Law: A Proposal to Divide the Realms of Insolvency and Restructuring Law' (2018) 19 *European Business Organization Law Review* 615, 641.

[9] Madaus (n 8) 631.

[10] Madaus (n 8) 623.

[11] See 1.3.

(*der Schuldner* and *skyldneren*, respectively). Since our concern is companies that fail, we will use 'the company' as the term that refers to the entity that is subject to insolvency proceedings.

3.1.3. Liquidation Proceedings

As defined above, the essence of a liquidation proceeding is that a (usually court-appointed) insolvency professional takes control of the company's assets, sells the assets and thereafter distributes the proceeds among the creditors. The jurisdictions differ in that English and Norwegian law contain liquidation proceedings that are separate from the restructuring proceedings, while German law contains one unitary insolvency proceeding governed by the *Insolvenzordnung* (InsO), the outcome of which can be both a liquidation and a restructuring. The default mode of a German insolvency proceeding is to liquidate the company. Accordingly, this section will discuss how the German insolvency proceeding operates in its default mode.

English law contains different modes of liquidations. For present purposes, we will ignore liquidation proceedings that do not imply that the company is insolvent (such as 'members' voluntary winding up') or that commence following other insolvency proceedings. This leaves us with two modes of liquidation: creditors' voluntary winding up and a winding up by the court (compulsory winding up). A key difference between these is that the power to commence a creditors' voluntary winding up lies with the members – ie the shareholders – of the company, while the courts have the power to commence a compulsory winding up following a petition from a person having standing to do so. Accordingly, while a voluntary winding up is a private form for distributing an insolvent company's assets, a compulsory winding up is a court-initiated and supervised proceeding.

Save for an English law creditors' voluntary winding up, liquidation proceedings usually commence following a court order. Typically, the court may only make such an order in respect of a company upon receiving a petition to do so from a person having standing and the court being satisfied that the company meets the applicable insolvency test. The insolvency test differs across the jurisdictions. In *English law*, the decision of a court to order a compulsory winding up requires the presence of one of the grounds set out in section 122 of the Insolvency Act 1986. One ground is that the company is unable to pay its debts.[12] A company is deemed to be unable to pay its debts when the company is unable to pay its debts as they fall due.[13] A company may be deemed unable to pay its debts not only when it is, in fact, unable to do so, but also when it suffers from so-called balance-sheet

[12] Insolvency Act 1986, s 122(1)(f).

[13] Insolvency Act 1986, s 123(1)(e). It seems that the courts may take into account debts that will fall due in the future when making this assessment, see *In re Cheyne Finance plc (No 2)* [2007] EWHC 2402 (Ch), [2008] Bus LR 1562 [53]–[57].

insolvency, meaning that the company's assets are worth less than its liabilities.[14] Moreover, a company will be deemed unable to pay its debts in the presence of certain facts indicating its inability to do so.[15] In *German law*, the grounds for opening insolvency proceedings differ according to whether the opening of the proceedings is requested by a creditor of the company or the company itself. The company's inability to pay debts that are due is always a sufficient ground.[16] When the company requests the opening of insolvency proceedings, it also suffices that it will likely be unable to pay debts that mature in the future.[17] Another ground is that the company's debts exceed its assets.[18] In *Norwegian law*, the court will – upon receiving a request from the company or a creditor – open proceedings if the company is insolvent.[19] A debtor is considered insolvent when two conditions are satisfied. First, the debtor must be permanently unable to pay its debts as they fall due. The assessment of whether this condition is satisfied involves considering whether the company is able to meet debts that have matured, as well as whether it will continue to do so in the future. Secondly, the value of the debtor's future income and assets must be insufficient for paying its liabilities.[20]

What all of the jurisdictions have in common is that they leave it to private parties to initiate insolvency proceedings. Creditors will have an incentive to do so when the benefits – ie removing the assets from the company – outweigh the costs of submitting a request for the court to open the proceedings. To induce the management of hopelessly insolvent companies to seek insolvency proceedings, all jurisdictions contain the possibility of legal sanctions for their failure to do so.[21]

Liquidation proceedings involve the appointment of a liquidator, an insolvency professional instructed to wind up the company. The liquidator assumes the power to sell assets on the company's behalf. Across all three jurisdictions, the commencement of the proceedings has certain immediate effects on the rights of *unsecured creditors* that are similar. Outside of insolvency proceedings, unsecured creditors can enforce unpaid claims through the courts or public authorities. Once liquidation proceedings have commenced, such enforcement is no longer possible: The commencement of English law winding-up proceedings affects the creditors' ability to enforce their rights against the company's assets. The precise effects differ somewhat between a creditors' voluntary winding up and a compulsory winding up.

[14] Insolvency Act 1986, s 123(2). On the interpretation of this clause, see *BNY Corporate Trustee Services Ltd v Eurosail-UK 2007-3BL plc and others* [2013] UKSC 28, [2013] 1 WLR 1408.

[15] Insolvency Act 1986, s 123(1)(a) and (b).

[16] InsO § 17. See also Gerner-Beuerle and Schillig (n 4) 914–15 for discussion on how German courts carry out this test.

[17] InsO § 18.

[18] InsO § 19. A company will not be considered to be overindebted if it is highly likely that the company is willing and able to continue its business.

[19] Konkursloven (kkl.) § 60.

[20] kkl. § 61. Certain circumstances give rise to a rebuttable presumption of insolvency, see kkl. §§ 62 and 63.

[21] Insolvency Act 1986, s 214 (English law); InsO § 15a (German law); allmennaksjeloven § 17-1 (Norwegian law).

The court's order for a compulsory winding up automatically results in the suspension of the enforcement rights of the unsecured creditors.[22] Conversely, a voluntary winding up does not automatically have this effect but the liquidator can apply to the court for an order that suspends the individual enforcement actions of unsecured creditors.[23] Unsecured claims also cease to be enforceable during a German law *Insolvenzverfahren*.[24] The same applies in a Norwegian law *konkurs*.[25]

In German and Norwegian law, the commencement of the proceedings results in a temporary suspension of rights to enforce security interests over certain assets.[26] Conversely, English law contains no such restrictions.[27]

The liquidator is tasked with disposing of the company's assets. The liquidator may to varying degrees continue the company's business with a view to facilitate its sale. A company becoming subject to insolvency does not necessarily lead to the cessation of its business: there is generally nothing that prevents a person from purchasing all or a substantial part of the company's assets with a view to continuing its operations. Whether the liquidator pursues such a sale or a piecemeal sale, will depend upon which avenue he expects to result in the highest sale proceeds.

The sale of the company's assets and the subsequent distribution of the proceeds give the unsecured creditors recourse to the assets that the company had when the proceedings commenced. Conversely, any assets that the company transferred prior to the commencement of the proceedings do not form part of the pool of assets available for distribution. Moreover, any rights in the assets, such as security interests, continue to subsist. There are exceptions to these principles, however. Notably, various transaction avoidance rules operate to either invalidate or empower the liquidator to 'reverse' otherwise valid and effective transactions made by the company prior to the commencement of the insolvency proceedings. Such rules potentially result in an increase of assets available for distribution among unsecured creditors.[28]

Some proceedings do not fit easily on either side of the liquidation/restructuring divide, such as English law administration. The commencement of an administration produces many of the same immediate effects as a winding up: An administrator assumes the powers of the company's bodies and creditor rights are suspended.[29] An administration may result in a similar outcome as a winding up: a sale of the company's assets and a distribution of the proceeds among its

[22] Insolvency Act 1986, s 130(2).

[23] K van Zwieten, *Goode on Principles of Corporate Insolvency Law*, 5th edn (London, Sweet & Maxwell, 2018) para 5-08.

[24] InsO § 89.

[25] VI Løvold, *Brækhus' Omsetning og Kreditt 1: Tvangsfullbyrdelse, gjeldsforhandling og konkurs* (Oslo, Universitetsforlaget, 2015) 262.

[26] InsO § 166 and kkl. § 117.

[27] H Beale et al, *The Law of Security and Title-Based Financing*, 3rd edn (Oxford, Oxford University Press, 2018) para 20.02.

[28] These rules are addressed at 4.2 insofar as they are of importance for the relative priority among creditors.

[29] Insolvency Act 1986, Sch B1 para 43(2).

creditors. However, this is not necessarily the case: The objectives of an administration depend on the economic circumstances surrounding the company's entry into administration. The administrator shall principally seek to rescue the company in administration.[30] Failing this, the administrator shall seek to produce a better outcome for the creditors than that which winding-up proceedings would yield.[31] If the achievement of this objective is not possible, the administrator shall realise the company's assets to make distributions to the company's secured or preferential creditors.[32] Accordingly, administration is not a liquidation procedure in the strictest sense.

3.1.4. Restructuring Proceedings

Liquidation proceedings mostly involve the end of the entity under liquidation. In recent years, attention has been drawn to the issue of restructuring distressed, but viable, companies. The restructuring of such companies need not conflict with the interests of the creditors. Indeed, it is possible in many cases for a company to restructure its debts through informal negotiations with its creditors and shareholders, especially if the company is of a certain size. Creditor involvement in such restructurings will typically be restricted to 'financial' creditors, that is, banks and investors in debt securities. As such informal restructurings are consensual and restricted to parts of the company's creditors, they stand in stark contrast to the mandatory and collective nature of liquidation proceedings.

It will, however, not always be possible for the negotiating parties to arrive at a solution that is palatable to everyone. An emerging consensus holds that the law should facilitate the rescue of viable businesses by establishing proceedings whereby a majority of creditors may force debt restructuring plans on a non-consenting minority. In 2019, the EU adopted the Preventive Restructuring Directive, which to some extent harmonises national restructuring proceedings by requiring that Member States have in place 'a preventive restructuring framework that enables them to restructure, with a view to preventing insolvency and ensuring their viability'.[33] The directive sets out minimum requirements for such frameworks. However, it does not prohibit Member States from retaining alternative national restructuring frameworks that come in addition to a framework in line with the directive's requirements. Moreover, there are several questions in

[30] Insolvency Act 1986, Sch B1 para 3(1)(a).
[31] Insolvency Act 1986, Sch B1 para 3(1)(b).
[32] Insolvency Act 1986, Sch B1 para 3(1)(c).
[33] Directive (EU) 2019/1023 of the European Parliament and the Council on preventive restructuring frameworks, on discharge of debt and disqualifications, and on measures to increase the efficiency of procedures concerning restructuring, insolvency and discharge of debt, and amending Directive (EU) 2017/1132 [2019] OJ L172/18.

respect of which the directive allows Member States to choose between different solutions.[34] Accordingly, the directive is unlikely to bring about uniform restructuring legislation within the EU. The adoption of the directive necessitated reform of the German restructuring framework. To this end, the German legislator adopted the *Unternehmensstabilisierungs- und -restrukturierungsgesetz* (StaRUG) in December 2020.

As a result of the UK leaving the EU, it was not necessary to implement the Preventive Restructuring Directive in English law. The directive has been designated by the EU as of relevance for the EEA Agreement, but the position of the EEA EFTA States is that it is not, and therefore should not be incorporated into the EEA Agreement. It is therefore uncertain whether the directive will ever become part of the EEA Agreement, and thus binding upon Norway. Insolvency law reform was nonetheless underway in both the UK and Norway at the start of 2020. Fears that COVID-19 would lead to mass liquidation of viable companies sped up the reform.

English, German and Norwegian law all contain restructuring frameworks. English law now contains three frameworks that allow for amendments to a company's liabilities even if not all affected creditors consent thereto. The first is the possibility for having a scheme of arrangement adopted pursuant to Part 26 of the Companies Act 2006. The adoption of a scheme of arrangement essentially involves three stages. First, the court receives an application to summon creditors and, possibly, shareholders to vote on a proposed scheme of arrangement, holds a hearing and decides whether to summon one or more meetings of the company's creditors and shareholders. Secondly, if meetings are summoned, these are held and the different classes of creditors and shareholders vote on the proposal. Thirdly, if a requisite majority within each class approves the proposal, the court holds a hearing and decides whether to sanction the scheme.

The Corporate Insolvency and Governance Act 2020 inserted a new Part 26A into the Companies Act 2006. That part now sets out a separate restructuring framework. The framework closely resembles that of Part 26. The most important difference for present purposes is that the protection of dissenting creditors is lower under Part 26A than under Part 26: While the sanctioning of a scheme of arrangement requires that all affected classes vote in its favour, this is not an absolute requirement for the sanctioning of a restructuring plan under Part 26A. The dissent of a class notwithstanding, the court may sanction the restructuring plan if: (i) the members of the dissenting class will not be worse off under the restructuring plan than under the scenario most likely to occur if the restructuring is not sanctioned, and (ii) at least one class that 'would receive a payment, or have a genuine economic interest in the company' in that scenario has voted in its favour.[35] However, the scope of companies to which restructuring under Part 26A is available is narrower, as a company must have encountered, or be likely

[34] G McCormack, *The European Restructuring Directive* (Cheltenham, Edward Elgar, 2021) 198.
[35] Companies Act 2006, s 901G(5).

to encounter, 'financial difficulties that are affecting, or will or may affect, its ability to carry on business as a going concern'.[36]

The third English restructuring framework is the company voluntary arrangement (CVA). The process of having a CVA approved is initiated by a company's directors or, if it is in administration or is being wound up, by the administrator or liquidator, respectively.[37] Following a proposed arrangement being drawn up, a qualified insolvency practitioner (a 'nominee') shall consider whether the proposal has a reasonable prospect of being approved and implemented and submit a report to the court.[38] If the nominee's verdict is positive, separate meetings of the company and its creditors shall then be summoned unless the court orders otherwise.[39]

A requisite majority of shareholders and creditors must approve the proposed CVA at the meetings of the company and the creditors, respectively. In contrast to a scheme of arrangement and a restructuring plan, a CVA may take effect without any decision by a court.[40] However, courts may become involved *ex post*, as creditors may apply to the court for a revocation of the CVA on the grounds that it unfairly prejudices their interests.[41]

German law contains two avenues for restructuring a company's liabilities. The first framework is the *Insolvenzplanverfahren*. This is a framework for adopting a restructuring – an *Insolvenzplan* – in respect of a company that is subject to insolvency proceedings pursuant to InsO. It thus follows that this option is only available for companies that meet the conditions for the opening of such proceedings. It is therefore necessary that the company is (imminently) unable to pay its debts or has liabilities that exceed its assets. It may be necessary to divide creditors and shareholders into classes for the purposes of voting over the proposed restructuring. The restructuring becoming effective requires the sanctioning of the court.

The recent adoption of StaRUG provides an alternative route for non-consensual restructuring of company debts.[42] This route is available for companies that are *imminently* unable to pay their debts.[43] The process towards having a restructuring sanctioned involves presenting a restructuring proposal to creditors and shareholders, and having them vote on the proposal, potentially as separate classes.[44] If the requirements set out in StaRUG are satisfied, the proposal may be sanctioned by a court.

In Norwegian law, the restructuring framework is currently set out in *rekonstruksjonsloven* (rkl). The framework consists of two tracks for adopting a

[36] Companies Act 2006, s 901A.
[37] Insolvency Act 1986, s 1.
[38] Insolvency Act 1986, s 2(2)(a).
[39] Insolvency Act 1986, s 3(1).
[40] Insolvency Act 1986, s 4A(2).
[41] Insolvency Act 1986, s 6.
[42] See T Pogoda and C Thole, 'The new German "Stabilisation and Restructuring Framework for Businesses"' (2021) *European Insolvency and Restructuring Journal*, www.eirjournal.com/content/EIRJ-2021-6.
[43] StaRUG § 63.
[44] StaRUG § 9.

restructuring. The first (*frivillig rekonstruksjon*) necessitates the actual or implied consent of all affected creditors. The second (*rekonstruksjon med tvangsakkord*), which is of interest in this context, allows for restructuring notwithstanding the dissent of some minority creditors. The process is initiated by the company or a creditor requesting that the court opens restructuring proceedings.[45] The creditors are consulted before a restructuring proposal is put forward. If a requisite majority votes in favour of the proposal eventually put forward, a court-appointed insolvency professional, who is tasked with assisting and supervising the company during the proceedings, sends the case to the court. The court then decides on whether the conditions for sanctioning the restructuring are satisfied, and if so, sanctions the restructuring.[46]

The design of restructuring frameworks raises several issues. The restructuring frameworks discussed above address these in different ways. In the following paragraphs, we identify four fundamental issues and briefly discuss how the abovementioned regimes approach these.

A first issue concerns whether the company is to enjoy protection from individual creditor enforcement attempts while the restructuring proposal is being negotiated. A company undergoing restructuring in a German *Insolvenzverfahren* or Norwegian *rekonstruksjonsforhandling* enjoys such protection.[47] Conversely, a company seeking to achieve a restructuring under the frameworks set out in StaRUG or the English restructuring frameworks does not automatically benefit from a stay on creditor enforcement. Under StaRUG, companies must apply to the courts for a stay.[48] In English law, companies may obtain a moratorium by filing documents with the court that, among other things, include a statement from a qualified insolvency professional proposed to monitor the moratorium that, in their view, 'it is likely that a moratorium for the company would result in the rescue of the company as a going concern'.[49]

A second issue concerns whether the company during the restructuring proceedings is to be supervised by the courts or a person appointed or approved by a court. This issue is closely related to that of whether a stay on creditor enforcement should be available for companies pursuing a restructuring, as there is a concern that hopelessly insolvent companies could misuse a stay to delay the unavoidable liquidation of the company. If no stay results from the restructuring efforts, this concern does not arise. In line with this idea, the restructuring frameworks examined only mandate the appointment of a supervisor insofar as the company benefits from a stay.

A third issue is whether in principle there should apply restrictions as to what claims may be subject to non-consensual restructuring. This is in other words a

[45] Rekonstruksjonsloven (rkl.) § 2.
[46] See rkl. §§ 47–51.
[47] InsO § 89; rkl. § 18.
[48] StaRUG § 49.
[49] Insolvency Act 1986, s A6(1)(e).

question of whether individual consent should always be a prerequisite for amending certain claims. Norwegian law contains restrictions in this regard: Neither the claims of creditors benefitting from a security interest or right of set-off, nor those of preferential creditors may be subject to a non-consensual restructuring under *rekonstruksjonsloven*.[50] This means that the restructuring of such claims is only possible with the consent of each individual creditor concerned. A similar restriction applies for an English law CVA.[51] StaRUG does not permit the restructuring of claims for wages, certain tort liabilities and claims that are sanctions for illicit behaviour.[52]

A fourth issue concerns the majority requirements for adopting a restructuring proposal. Some restructuring frameworks may potentially require that creditors are divided into separate classes, with each class voting separately over the proposal, while other frameworks do not. The adoption of an Insolvenzplan, a StaRUG-restructuring, a scheme of arrangement and a restructuring plan may require that creditors are divided into classes. The proposed restructuring will, as a main rule, require approval from all classes. A class will be considered to have approved a restructuring if a sufficient majority – the exact requirement differs between the frameworks – votes in its favour. Approval from all affected classes is not always a condition for the adoption of a restructuring proposal. Save for the scheme of arrangement framework, all the class-based frameworks discussed make it possible to have a restructuring approved even if one or more classes do not approve thereof, subject to additional conditions being satisfied. The conditions for the adoption of a restructuring giving such a result – which is often referred to as a 'cross-class cram down' – differ across regimes. The requirements for the adoption of a proposal in the presence of dissent from minority creditors are a matter of priority among creditors. Accordingly, these requirements will be subject to more comprehensive discussion in chapter four.

3.2. Why are General Insolvency Proceedings Deemed Unsuitable for Banks?

3.2.1. The Difference between the Objectives Pursued

Any justification for having a bank-specific insolvency regime must identify a bank-specific issue that general insolvency law does not address adequately. While the problem could be as fundamental as that bank insolvency proceedings should pursue other objectives than general insolvency law does, the problem could also be that the means for achieving general insolvency law objectives are inappropriate

[50] rkl. § 54.
[51] Insolvency Act 1986, ss 4(3) and 4(4).
[52] StaRUG § 4.

in this sector-specific context. This section addresses the extent to which society's goals for bank insolvency resolution could conflict with the objectives of general insolvency law.

An analysis of the perceived conflict between the objectives of general insolvency proceedings and bank resolution necessitates an understanding of the respective objectives. As discussed at 2.1.4, BRRD's resolution regime purports to pursue five objectives: (i) to ensure the continuity of critical functions, (ii) to avoid a significant adverse effect on the financial system, (iii) to protect public funds by minimising reliance on extraordinary public financial support, (iv) to protect depositors covered by the Deposit Guarantee Scheme Directive and investors covered by Directive 97/9/EC, and (v) to protect client funds and client assets.[53]

A goal frequently ascribed to general insolvency law is the maximisation of the amount of means available for distribution among the creditors.[54] Together with the distribution of those means in a normatively defensible manner, this objective constitutes one of the primary purposes of general insolvency law.[55] Wealth maximisation does not figure among BRRD's resolution objectives. However, the directive does not disregard the interests of the bank's creditors entirely. The resolution authority shall seek to 'avoid the destruction of value' when conducting its tasks.[56] Given that this goal contributes towards maximising the value of the company's assets, the directive thereby requires the resolution authority to consider the interests of the creditors as a whole when making decisions on the course of the resolution. This duty is not absolute, as it applies only insofar as it does not conflict with the resolution objectives. BRRD thus implies that there is conflict between the resolution objectives and the creditors' interests. The literature often highlights this supposed tension through statements about general insolvency law's lack of concern for broader public interest.[57]

Exactly how does this tension manifest itself? One possible conflict concerns the uncertainty that attaches to the likely course of events in the absence of resolution. Take, for instance, the case of a bank that is suffering from withdrawals from depositors and other short-term creditors. The resolution authority may view it as desirable to resolve the bank in the interest of putting an end to possible contagion

[53] BRRD art 31(2).

[54] English, German and Norwegian law all contain statutory provisions that reflect such a view. See the Insolvency Act 1986, Sch B1 para 3(2) (generally requiring an administrator to 'perform his functions in the interests of the company's creditors as a whole'), InsO § 1 and konkursloven §§ 85, 88 and 119, respectively.

[55] RJ Mokal, 'Liquidity, Systemic Risk, and the Bankruptcy Treatment of Financial Contracts' (2015) 10 *Brooklyn Journal of Corporate, Financial & Commercial Law* 15, 33.

[56] BRRD art 31(2).

[57] W-G Ringe, 'Bank Bail-in Between Liquidity and Solvency' (2018) 92 *American Bankruptcy Law Journal* 299, 301–303; SL Schwarcz, 'Beyond Bankruptcy: Resolution as a Macroprudential Regulatory Tool' (2018) 94 *Notre Dame Law Review* 709, 717; M Dewatripont and X Freixas, 'Bank Resolution: Lessons from the Crisis' in M Dewatripont and X Freixas (eds), *The Crisis Aftermath: New Regulatory Paradigms* (London, Centre for Economic Policy Research (CEPR), 2012) 117.

effects caused by the bank's response to the withdrawals, which could include fire sales that destabilise market prices, as discussed at 2.1.4. However, the bank could be in talks with potential investors over a share issuance. If the creditors deem the share issuance sufficiently likely, they will have an interest in that the resolution authority refrains from taking resolution actions that interfere with their claims. BRRD's solution to this conflict is found in the resolution conditions.[58] The resolution authority may only resolve a bank when it rules out that private-sector measures could prevent the bank's failure.[59] In the example above, the authority may only resolve a bank when it considers there to be 'no reasonable prospect' that a share issue will prevent failure 'within a reasonable timeframe'.

The above example of tension between resolution objectives and creditor interests presupposes that a disagreement exists about whether the bank is heading towards insolvency. A different question is whether tension is present when it is clear that a bank will fail in the absence of the resolution authority's intervention. Conceptually, there could be tension if the resolved bank's business is worth less than it would be if the bank entered liquidation and the official tasked with the liquidation sold off the assets piece by piece. But how likely is it that such tension will be present? The common view is that this is unlikely to be the case, as a bank that continues to operate will generally be worth more to its creditors than they can expect from a winding up, that is, the aggregate sum of its pieces minus the liquidation costs.[60]

This leaves us with the possibility for conflict between the interests of the creditors and the resolution objectives in terms of how a bank's business will be maintained. Such a conflict is conceivable. Take, for instance, a case of the bank's business being sold to a private purchaser. On the one hand, there is broad consensus that the swift completion of resolution is necessary to attain the resolution objectives.[61] However, a speedy sale will make it more difficult for a potential purchaser to assess the business offered for sale. Potential purchasers may therefore lower their bids to account for the uncertainty involved in having to assess the resolved bank's assets over a short time span.

Accordingly, we may conclude that while the interests of the creditors as a whole will often coincide with the implementation of the resolution objectives, the potential for conflict cannot be ruled out. We will now discuss whether the application of general insolvency law to banks could nonetheless be inappropriate even when the public interest and the creditors' interests coincide.

[58] See 3.4.2.

[59] BRRD art 32(1)(b).

[60] J Armour et al, *Principles of Financial Regulation* (Oxford, Oxford University Press, 2016) 341; S Gleeson and R Guynn, *Bank Resolution and Crisis Management: Law and Practice* (Oxford, Oxford University Press, 2016) para 1.05; Ringe (n 57) 302.

[61] Dewatripont and Freixas, 'Bank Resolution' (n 57); Karl-Philipp Wojcik, 'Bail-in in the Banking Union' (2016) 53 *CML Rev* 91, 92; Ringe (n 57) 302.

3.2.2. The Substantive Scope of the Official's Powers

This section discusses whether the protection of critical functions necessitates transfers of assets or debt restructuring that are not possible in general insolvency law. As discussed at 2.1.4, a bank's lending activities could constitute a critical function. To what extent would it be possible to continue the lending services of a bank that goes into liquidation under general insolvency law? A liquidation could involve the sale of an insolvent lender's operations to a purchaser. The operation of a bank often relies on the provision of ongoing services from external sources. For example, it is impossible to ensure the continuance of a bank's business if a provider of crucial IT services discontinues these services. Accordingly, the assumption and continuation of a bank's business by a purchaser would require either the transfer of the contracts or the purchaser entering into corresponding contracts with the service provider. It is often the case that general insolvency law does not permit the transfer of contracts without the counterparty's assent.[62] This means that a purchaser would have to negotiate new contracts with service providers – which, again, could hamper the seamless assumption of the business. BRRD solves this issue by empowering the resolution authority to transfer such contracts when exercising one of the transfer powers.

In taking deposits and providing access to payment services, banks also provide services that some would label critical functions. The liquidation of a bank could potentially affect its depositors as follows. First, depositors with outstanding balances would temporarily lose access to their deposits and could – depending on the applicable priority rules – possibly recover less than the balance. Coverage by a deposit guarantee scheme solves this issue for the covered deposits, as they stand to receive the guaranteed amount within seven working days at most.[63] However, the guarantee does not shield covered depositors entirely from any disadvantage. These depositors could be without access to their deposits for some days, which could leave them unable to purchase goods and pay bills. A second implication for depositors is that they would have to use another bank to deposit funds and access the payment system, though this should normally not give rise to any problems. The failure of a large bank could, however, result in an undersupply of deposit-taking capacity, as other banks active in the same market could be unwilling to expand their balance sheets to the extent necessary to absorb all the deposits previously held with the failed bank.

Ideally, a liquidation would involve the seamless transfer of account services to a purchaser along with the parts of the deposit balances that depositors will recover through the operation of the applicable priority hierarchy. Certain features of liquidation proceedings could prevent this, however. One issue is that the transfer of liabilities requires the consent of the creditors. While such consent would

[62] Eidenmüller (n 5) 1029.

[63] DGSD art 8(1). Pursuant to transitional rules, the repayment period may currently be up to 10 working days, see art 8(2).

often be forthcoming, the process of collecting consents could prove a logistical nightmare. A second, more fundamental issue is that a transfer of deposits could reduce the price a purchaser of the bank's business would be willing to pay. This, in turn, could leave other creditors worse off than would a mere asset sale. It is conceivable, then, that such a sale would be off the table under the general insolvency laws of some jurisdictions. Whether a combined transfer of assets and deposits leaves other creditors worse off than a transfer restricted to assets depends on whether the deposits in question enjoy priority over other creditors. BRRD solves this issue by combining the transfer power with granting priority to certain depositors ahead of the bank's general unsecured creditors.[64]

Restructuring proceedings offer alternative means for allowing the bank's operations to continue, as such proceedings allow the legal entity to live on. A restructuring does not, therefore, presuppose that a private purchaser is willing to assume the failed entity's business. Moreover, some forms of restructuring proceedings could serve to better facilitate uninterrupted access to deposits and payment services than could liquidation proceedings: Given that the bank's operations would subsist in the same legal entity, the abovementioned hurdles associated with transferring liabilities are not an issue. Under some regimes such as English law schemes of arrangement, it would be possible to allow depositors to continue to access outstanding deposit balances during the restructuring, as such proceedings do not result in a 'stay' on creditor rights. However, this would also entail the risk of a bank run during the restructuring process. To avoid this risk from materialising, the depositors would have to be certain that their deposits are unaffected by the restructuring. If the proposed restructuring only comprises the claims of bondholders and other long-term creditors, which is increasingly common in UK practice for restructuring larger companies by way of a scheme of arrangement,[65] and short-term bank creditors are confident that this practice will be followed, the lack of a stay is not necessarily prejudicial.[66]

3.2.3. The Procedural Aspects of the Official's Powers

A difference between general insolvency liquidation proceedings and resolution concerns the circumstances that allow the respective proceedings to commence. While liquidation proceedings necessitate the presence of some form of insolvency-related circumstances, the bank resolution authority may intervene at an earlier point in time. This is because BRRD deems a bank 'failing or like to fail' when it

[64] BRRD art 108.

[65] S Paterson, 'Rethinking Corporate Bankruptcy in the Twenty-First Century' (2016) 36 *OJLS* 697, 712.

[66] The lack of a stay does not necessarily rule out the restructuring of all types of debt. Recently, a UK bank, The Co-operative Bank plc, had sanctioned a scheme of arrangement that converted its subordinated debt to equity, see *Re The Co-Operative Bank Plc* [2017] EWHC 2269 (Ch).

is unable to satisfy certain regulatory obligations.[67] At first blush, it thus appears as if BRRD facilitates intervention at an earlier stage than general liquidation proceedings. Our discussion at 3.1.4 showed how national restructuring proceedings are more heterogeneous than liquidation proceedings in several respects. One difference concerns the conditions that must be present to open such proceedings. Completing an English law CVA or scheme of arrangement does not require that the company is distressed. Therefore, there are no legal barriers for restructuring a bank's debt at an early stage. Conversely, restructuring under the other frameworks discussed requires the presence of distress. It could seem that resolution also allows for intervention at an earlier stage than is the case for the latter category of restructuring proceedings.

Upon closer analysis, the differences between resolution and general insolvency law in this respect may be less pronounced than they appear at first sight. A bank's status as 'failing or likely to fail' is merely one of three conditions necessary for empowering the resolution authority to resolve the bank. Intervention is inter alia subject to the additional condition that no alternatives can remedy the failure. This requirement operates to narrow down the situations where the authority can resolve banks without establishing that they will likely be unable to pay their debts. Take the case of breaches of regulatory requirements that would justify the bank's supervisor withdrawing its authorisation, which under BRRD qualifies a bank as 'failing or likely to fail'.[68] If the source of the breach is of a financial nature – eg insufficient equity or liquidity – the bank could remedy the breach if it is able to issue shares at a price sufficient to restore compliance with the applicable requirement. In other words, a bank's breach of the capital requirements only justifies resolution if it is reasonably unlikely to be able to raise capital and thereby avoid losing its authorisation. There is reason to query whether allowing resolution under such circumstances involves a radical departure from the conditions of general insolvency law. Any company that: (i) finances itself with demandable debt to the same extent as banks, and (ii) stands to lose an authorisation necessary to conduct its business, will soon become unable to pay its debts.

A different issue concerns the procedural requirements applicable to the transfer of a bank's business or a restructuring of its debt. As discussed at 3.2.1, a common view in the literature is that the successful handling of bank distress necessitates quick and decisive action. More specifically, it should be possible to implement a transfer or debt restructuring during the period starting when the US markets close on Friday and ending with the opening of Asian markets on the following Monday. Would it be possible to transfer a bank's business or restructure its liabilities this swiftly within the confines of applicable procedural requirements? Unless a requirement to consult with the creditors applies, an insolvency professional could, in principle, complete a swift transfer during a liquidation.

[67] BRRD art 32(4)(a).
[68] BRRD art 32(4)(a).

A remaining issue, which we will discuss at 3.2.4, is whether the insolvency professional would be sufficiently prepared for such a task. As regards the use of general restructuring frameworks, suffice to say that it would be very difficult to complete a restructuring that involves creditor meetings during such a short time span. BRRD does away with all requirements to obtain the consent of the bank's creditors. The directive thus breaks with the creditor participation of general insolvency law to solve what many perceive as a potential problem.

3.2.4. The Decision-Makers

A potential issue with general insolvency proceedings is the combination of a public interest in the bank's continued operations and the allocation of decision-making powers to creditors and, in restructuring proceedings, also shareholders. The source of the problem is as follows. A restructuring necessitates some form of majoritarian approval among the creditors whose claims are subject to interference.[69] At the outset, obtaining creditor approval should not be a problem when the resolution objectives coincide with the interests of the creditors as a whole. However, as noted in the literature, the circumstances surrounding a bank failure could cause strategic behaviour on the part of the investors who must approve the restructuring.[70]

The problem of strategic behaviour is well known in general insolvency law theory.[71] In this context, the problem manifests when some creditors (or shareholders) refuse to consent to a debt restructuring, even though their economic rights are worth more in the event the restructuring is successful than if the company instead becomes subject to liquidation proceedings. Creditors could have an incentive to behave in this manner where other creditors stand to lose more (in absolute terms) if the restructuring does not receive sufficient investor approvals, as these other creditors would have an incentive to compensate the creditors threatening to withhold their consent. This problem explains the power of courts to sanction restructuring proposals that do not receive unanimous support.

When there is public interest in a bank's continued business, the strategic behaviour problem takes another form. Another stakeholder enters the picture,

[69] When the restructuring involves creditors receiving shares issued by the company in exchange for suffering a write-down, the approval of the company's shareholders will also be required.

[70] R de Weijs, 'Too Big to Fail as a Game of Chicken with the State: What Insolvency Law Theory Has to Say About TBTF and Vice Versa' (2013) 14 *European Business Organization Law Review* 201, 219. The same argument also applies insofar as shareholder approval is required, see V Babis, 'The impact of bank crisis prevention, recovery and resolution on shareholder rights' (2012) 6 *Law and Financial Markets Review* 387, 389; M Čihák and E Nier, 'The Need for Special Resolution Regimes for Financial Institutions – The Case of the European Union' (2012) 2 *Harvard Business Law Review* 395, 401; C Hadjiemmanuil, 'Special Resolution Regimes for Banking Institutions: Objectives and Limitations' (2013) LSE Law, Society and Economy Working Papers 21/2013, 22.

[71] See eg de Weijs (n 70) 210–15; M Schillig, 'Corporate Insolvency Law in the Twenty-First Century: State Imposed or Market Based?' (2014) 14 *Journal of Corporate Law Studies* 1, 8–9.

namely the state. If the creditors and shareholders believe that the state stands to lose more than they do in the event the bank fails, they have an incentive to 'hold out' to pressure the state to provide financial support on terms that result in a more favourable outcome for them than a restructuring. For example, creditors will have little reason to consent to a restructuring if they believe that the state, in the absence of a restructuring, will boost the bank's equity through solvency support measures. Were this to occur, the creditors would stand to receive full repayment of their claims. As put by de Weijs: 'Why would a creditor be satisfied with anything less than payment in full of its claim if it believes … that the state will not let the institution fail?'[72]

The bail-in power mitigates the problem of strategic behaviour on the part of the creditors and shareholders. The resolution authority's exercise of the bail-in power does not necessitate the consent of either creditors or shareholders. Accordingly, the investors do not have a means for pressuring the state into using public support to save the bank.

Even if the obligations and incentives of courts, insolvency professionals, creditors and any other decision-makers aligned perfectly with the resolution objectives, problems of implementation would remain. While it is not unprecedented to obligate private parties to assess threats to financial stability,[73] BRRD seems to reflect a view that the better solution is to leave the responsibility for decision-making with a resolution authority that employs expert personnel dedicated to the task of resolving banks. Proponents of a bank resolution framework hold the view that judges do not possess the necessary insight to properly assess issues of financial stability.[74] To the extent this argument bears merit, one could generalise it to apply to all other decision-makers normally involved in general insolvency proceedings.

As we shall discuss at 3.4.3, BRRD requires resolution authorities to draw up plans for how they will approach the failure of banks under their remit. This feature sets BRRD's resolution framework apart from general insolvency law. The directive's requirement for a specialised resolution authority could be seen as a measure for ensuring that decision-makers have sufficient expertise. Moreover, the requirements for the resolution authority to engage in planning exercises reflects an attempt at making sure that the authority procures the information necessary for handling a bank failure.

[72] de Weijs (n 70) 219.

[73] Under the Market Abuse Regulation art 17(5)(a), banks with listed financial instruments may postpone the publication of inside information if this is in the interest of preserving financial stability, see Regulation (EU) No 596/2014 of the European Parliament and of the Council of 16 April 2014 on market abuse (market abuse regulation) and repealing Directive 2003/6/EC of the European Parliament and of the Council and Commission Directives 2003/124/EC, 2003/125/EC and 2004/72/EC [2014] OJ L173/1.

[74] A Campbell and RM Lastra, 'Definition of Bank Insolvency and Types of Bank Insolvency Proceedings' in RM Lastra (ed), *Cross-Border Bank Insolvency* (Oxford, Oxford University Press, 2011) para 2.82. For a more mixed view in the US literature, see TH Jackson and DA Skeel, Jr, 'Dynamic Resolution of Large Financial Institutions' (2012) 2 *Harvard Business Law Review* 435, 449, 459.

3.3. Fragmentation: The Different Approaches to Bank Insolvency Prior to the Global Financial Crisis

While the bulk of the EU legislative acts that harmonise bank insolvency law stem from the period following the GFC, pre-crisis times also featured some harmonisation in this area. In 1999, the European Commission published the Financial Services Action Plan (FSAP), which established a plan for the integration of the EU securities markets.[75] Two of the plan's action points required Member States to ensure that certain contractual arrangements remained effective in any insolvency proceedings applicable to banks. The first was the implementation of the Settlement Finality Directive (SFD), which the EU had already adopted in 1998. This directive requires Member States, where necessary, to exempt the contractual provisions of payment and securities settlement systems from the ambit of certain general insolvency law provisions that could impede their effectiveness.

The second of FSAP's action points concerned the adoption of a directive to ensure the enforceability of cross-border collateral arrangements. The EU adopted such a directive in 2002 in the form of the Financial Collateral Directive (FCD). This directive seeks to accord sector-specific exemptions from general insolvency rules to 'financial collateral arrangements'. Financial collateral arrangements are, roughly speaking, contractual arrangements intended to secure claims with cash, financial instruments or loan receivables originated by banks. Both SFD and FCD remain in force today. We will discuss the details of their requirements for bank insolvency law in chapter five.

The execution of the FSAP coincided with the adoption of the Credit Institutions Winding Up Directive (CIWUD) in 2001.[76] This directive coordinates jurisdictional and private international law questions regarding the insolvency of a bank with links to more than one Member State. Importantly, the directive establishes a home state principle, which entails that a bank's home state – the Member State that has authorised the bank and supervises its affairs – shall have the exclusive power to adopt reorganisation measures or wind up the bank.[77] CIWUD does not harmonise the procedural and substantive features of national bank insolvency regimes. We will discuss the implications of this directive in chapters five and six.

Apart from the above requirements, Member States remained free from EU law requirements in forging insolvency proceedings for failing banks. This allowed for heterogeneous approaches to the issues posed by bank insolvency. An apt illustration is how English, German and Norwegian law dealt with the issue.

[75] Commission, 'Implementing the framework for financial markets: action plan' COM (1999) 232 final.

[76] Directive 2001/24/EC of the European Parliament and of the Council of 4 April 2001 on the reorganisation and winding up of credit institutions [2001] OJ L125/15.

[77] CIWUD arts 3(1) and 9, respectively.

English law contained no special bank insolvency framework prior to the GFC; only general insolvency law applied to banks. One bank-specific modification did exist, however: the bank supervisor had standing to petition the commencement of the compulsory winding up and administration proceedings addressed at 3.1.3.[78] However, the insolvency professional's duties were left unaltered: it appears that the insolvency professional would not be subject to an explicit duty to consider the public interest in financial stability in exercising its office. A compulsory liquidation would require the revocation of the bank's licence, which would rule out the continued existence of the bank.[79] While the making of an administration order would entitle the bank supervisor to revoke the licence, such an order would not require the bank supervisor to do so.[80] In principle, then, an administration could be used to restructure a bank, but such a restructuring would have to conform to the substantive and procedural requirements that would apply to the restructuring of any company in administration.

Although the insolvency procedure applicable to German banks in the pre-crisis period was the generally applicable insolvency procedure addressed at 3.1.3, some modifications did apply. Importantly, courts could only open such proceedings following a request from BaFin, the German supervisory authority. Both court and creditor control were to prevail once BaFin had submitted the request: the courts retained the power to open insolvency proceedings and to review whether the grounds for opening an insolvency proceeding were satisfied. This meant that insolvency proceedings could not be opened until the bank was (imminently) unable to pay its debts or was balance-sheet insolvent. Moreover, the court – rather than the government – was to appoint the insolvency professional.

As an alternative to requesting the opening of insolvency proceedings, German authorities had the power to suspend the repayment rights of an insolvent bank's creditors.[81] Exercising this power would also suspend the enforcement actions of individual unsecured creditors.[82] The underlying idea was that a suspension of payments would facilitate the bank's rehabilitation. As public authorities had no power to write down claims or otherwise permanently amend creditor rights, a successful restructuring would only occur where it was possible to recapitalise the bank through other means or through a creditor-approved Insolvenzplan.

In contrast to English and German law, Norwegian law contained a bank-specific insolvency procedure prior to the crisis termed *offentlig administrasjon*. This translates verbatim to public administration, which we will subsequently term

[78] M Phillips and L Tamlyn, 'Choice and Initiation of Insolvency Procedure' in F Oditah (ed), *Insolvency of Banks: Managing the Risks* (London, FT Law & Tax, 1996) 43, 51.

[79] Phillips and Tamlyn (n 78) 52.

[80] ibid 49.

[81] K Pannen, *Krise und Insolvenz bei Kreditinstituten*, 3rd edn (Cologne, Luchterhand, 2010) 36. This power was previously set out in the Kreditwesengesetz (KWG) § 46a as that provision read until 31 December 2010.

[82] KWG § 46a, subsection 1 sentence 5 as that provision read until 31 December 2010. See also J-H Binder et al, 'The choice between judicial and administrative sanctioned procedures to manage liquidation of banks: A transatlantic perspective' (2019) 14 *Capital Markets Law Journal* 178, 206.

this process. Public administration supplanted the ordinary insolvency proceedings discussed at 3.1, as banks were excluded from the scope of these proceedings.[83]

The Ministry of Finance had the exclusive power to place a bank in public administration.[84] In principle, it was not required that the Ministry receive a petition to do so in advance. However, Finanstilsynet, the Norwegian supervisory authority, was obligated to notify the Ministry should it consider that a bank was no longer capable of prudently continuing its business.[85] When giving such a notification, Finanstilsynet was to provide its assessment of whether the bank should be placed under public administration.[86] These obligations suggest that an underlying premise of the legal framework was that the Ministry would act following the initiative of Finanstilsynet.

Two scenarios would empower the Ministry of Finance to place a bank under public administration. First, the Ministry could exercise this power if the bank was unable to service its obligations as they fell due and no measures would enable the bank to continue its business in a prudent manner.[87] Secondly, the Ministry could intervene if a bank was unable to satisfy its capital requirements.[88]

The immediate effects of a decision to place a bank under public administration included elements from both liquidation proceedings and restructuring proceedings. The bank's corporate bodies would cede their powers to an administration board (*administrasjonsstyre*) appointed by Finanstilsynet. However, the bank could assume new business during the administration procedure, albeit subject to the prior consent of Finanstilsynet.

Banksikringsloven § 4-8 established the overall goals to be pursued by the administration board. Read in isolation, the instructions were quite open ended: The board was to facilitate the continuation of the bank's business, to transfer the bank's business to other banks or to wind down the bank. The legal framework arguably expressed a preference for the continuance of the bank's business, however, as the administration board was under a duty to propose that the Ministry of Finance should lift the administration if it was possible to continue the bank's business.[89] The Ministry's decision to lift the administration could be accompanied by a decision to write down claims against the bank.[90] Moreover, the framework expressed a preference for the transfer of business over a winding down, as the administration board was to wind down the bank only if it did not see a transfer of the bank's business as feasible.[91] A power to write down the bank's shares was employed on two occasions in connection with publicly funded recapitalisations of large Norwegian

[83] See banksikringsloven (bsl.) § 4-2.
[84] bsl. § 4-5.
[85] bsl. § 4-4.
[86] bsl. § 4-4.
[87] bsl. § 4-5(1).
[88] bsl. § 4-5(1).
[89] bsl. § 4-9(1).
[90] bsl. § 4-9(3).
[91] bsl. § 4-10.

banks at the height of the Norwegian banking crisis in 1991.[92] The recapitalisation did not involve any creditors taking losses, however.

3.4. Consensus: The Adoption of the Bank Recovery and Resolution Directive

3.4.1. The Origins of the Bank Recovery and Resolution Directive

The GFC prompted several countries to adopt bank-specific insolvency regimes. The UK Parliament adopted emergency legislation in 2008 to nationalise the failing bank Northern Rock.[93] The following year, the adoption of the Banking Act 2009 saw the permanent introduction of a crisis regime. The adoption of the Restrukturierungsgesetz in 2010 introduced a bank-specific restructuring proceeding[94] and a resolution framework in German law.[95] This period also saw the launch of international initiatives for harmonising national resolution regimes. In the EU, the Commission made a communication in 2009 that spelled out measures it viewed as necessary for effective crisis management and resolution of banks.[96] Steps were also taken in other international forums. The Group of 20 (G-20) – of which the EU, France, Germany, Italy and the UK are members – called upon the Financial Stability Board (FSB) to develop measures to resolve financial institutions.[97] The FSB, which is an international body established by the G-20, went on to publish its *Key Attributes of Effective Resolution Regimes for Financial Institutions* in 2011.[98] This document sets out principles for approaching the problems posed by the failure of banks of global systemic importance. The G-20 endorsed the FSB's recommendations at its summit in Cannes the same year.

In 2012, the Commission put forward a proposal for a directive to establish a framework for the recovery and resolution of banks and investment firms.[99]

[92] B Vale, 'The Norwegian banking crisis' in TG Moe, JA Solheim and B Vale (eds), *The Norwegian Banking Crisis* (2004) Norges Bank Occasional Papers No 33, 14.

[93] Banking Act (Special Provisions) 2008.

[94] See M Schillig, *Resolution and Insolvency of Banks and Financial Institutions* (Oxford, Oxford University Press, 2016) para 14.42ff.

[95] See generally R Chattopadhyay, *Bridge Banks in Deutschland: Abwicklung und Restrukturierung systemrelevanter Banken durch Vermögensübertragung* (Weisbaden, Springer, 2017).

[96] Commission, 'An EU Framework for Cross-Border Crisis Management in the Banking Sector' COM (2009) 561 final.

[97] G-20, 'The G-20 Toronto Summit Declaration' (26–27 June 2010) para 21.

[98] Financial Stability Board, 'Key Attributes of Effective Resolution Regimes for Financial Institutions' (October 2011). This document was subsequently updated in 2014.

[99] Commission, 'Proposal for a Directive of the European Parliament and of the Council establishing a framework for the recovery and resolution of credit institutions and investment firms and amending Council Directives 77/91/EEC and 82/891/EC, Directives 2001/24/EC, 2002/47/EC, 2004/25/EC, 2005/56/EC, 2007/36/EC and 2011/35/EC and Regulation (EU) No 1093/2010' COM (2012) 280 final.

This proposal sparked the legislative procedure that culminated in European Parliament's and the Council's adoption of BRRD in 2014. While BRRD's preamble primarily refers to FSB's *Key Attributes*, some see the UK Banking Act 2009 as an important source of inspiration for BRRD.[100]

3.4.2. Resolution and Early Intervention

The resolution regime established by BRRD represents an effort to create a procedure that ensures the continuity of important services provided by failing banks without resorting to the use of public funds to save the banks from insolvency. More precisely, BRRD seeks to further this ambition by requiring Member States to establish dedicated *resolution authorities* equipped with *resolution tools* – that is, powers to transfer and restructure the assets and liabilities of failing banks.

The resolution authority is a public authority charged with both resolving distressed institutions and planning for resolution. In the UK, the resolution authority is the Bank of England. In Norway, the functions are split between the Ministry of Finance and Finanstilsynet, the supervisory authority.[101] The German resolution authority is the Bundesanstalt für Finanzdienstleistungsaufsicht (BaFin), which is also the bank supervisor.[102]

The resolution authority may exercise the resolution powers if three conditions are met.[103] First, the bank in question must be 'failing or likely to fail'. As defined by the directive, four sets of circumstances make an institution failing or likely to fail. Some of these are familiar to general insolvency law: A bank is failing or likely to fail if it is, or 'there are objective elements to support a determination that [it] in the near future' will be, unable to honour its obligations.[104] The same is the case if it suffers from actual or impending balance-sheet insolvency.[105] Other circumstances that qualify a bank as failing or likely to fail are not insolvency-related per se. The directive deems a bank failing or likely to fail if it breaches or is likely to breach regulatory requirements in a manner that could justify the withdrawal of its authorisation to perform banking services.[106] Subject to some exemptions, the same is the case when a bank is to receive public financial support.[107]

[100] Gleeson and Guynn (n 60) para 12.01.
[101] Finansforetaksloven (ffl.) § 20-3.
[102] Gesetz zur Sanierung und Abwicklung von Instituten und Finanzgruppen § 3. However, as Germany participates in the Single Resolution Mechanism (SRM), which centralises decision-making over large banks and cross-border groups established in the participating Member States, BaFin will merely act on the instructions given at the EU level in resolution cases regarding banks covered by the SRM. We will briefly discuss the SRM at 3.4.4.
[103] BRRD art 32(4).
[104] BRRD art 32(4)(c).
[105] BRRD art 32(4)(b).
[106] BRRD art 32(4)(a).
[107] BRRD art 32(4)(d).

As a main rule, the resolution authority does not assess whether a bank is 'failing or likely to fail'. Rather, the bank supervisor shall determine this question.[108] By derogation, Member States can entrust the 'failing or likely to fail' assessment to the resolution authority if the resolution authority has the necessary capabilities to assess whether the circumstances meet the criterion.[109] Regardless of the choice made in this respect, the determination will be made by an agency. In contrast to what is usually the case in general insolvency law, there is no judicial control of the bank's financial state before the commencement of a bank resolution.[110]

The second condition for resolving a bank requires that there is no reasonable prospect of any alternative private sector measures or supervisory action that would prevent the institution's failure within a reasonable timeframe.[111]

As a third condition, any use of the resolution powers is conditional upon this being in the public interest.[112] This is the case where the exercise of the resolution power is a *necessary* and *proportionate* means for achieving one of the five *resolution objectives* set out in BRRD Article 31.[113] The objectives are:

(a) to ensure the continuity of critical functions;
(b) to avoid a significant adverse effect on the financial system, in particular by preventing contagion, including to market infrastructures, and by maintaining market discipline;
(c) to protect public funds by minimising reliance on extraordinary public financial support;
(d) to protect depositors covered by Directive 2014/49/EU [DGSD] and investors covered by Directive 97/9/EC; and
(e) to protect client funds and client assets.

BRRD states that the requirement of necessity rules out resolution actions unless a 'winding up of the institution under normal insolvency proceedings would not meet those resolution objectives to the same extent'.[114] Resolution is therefore the exception rather than the rule, at least in theory.

We now turn to the immediate effects of a decision to place a bank under resolution. The rationale of the resolution framework is to provide for a swift procedure to ensure the continued existence of a bank's business. The rehabilitation of the bank or the transfer of its business to another entity constitute means towards this end. A common view holds that the achievement of the resolution objectives necessitates that the resolution authority completes the main steps of the resolution within a 'weekend window' – that is, the space between the closing of US markets on Friday

[108] BRRD art 32(1)(a).
[109] BRRD art 32(2).
[110] However, Member States may introduce some *ex ante* judicial control, see BRRD art 85.
[111] BRRD art 32(1)(b).
[112] BRRD art 32(1)(c).
[113] BRRD art 32(5).
[114] BRRD art 32(5).

and the opening of Asian markets the subsequent Monday.[115] This explains why resolution differs from general insolvency proceedings with respect to immediate effects. For instance, the commencement of liquidation proceedings normally results in the automatic cessation of the functions of the company's management bodies. This is not necessarily the case in resolution. While the resolution authority has the power to remove the bank's board and senior management,[116] it is not required to use this power. Another special feature is the immediate effects on creditor rights. As discussed above, the commencement of liquidation proceedings often results in a 'stay' that involves suspending the rights of unsecured and, in some cases, secured creditors. Moreover, the commencement of restructuring proceedings either automatically leads to a stay or makes a stay available to companies insofar as this is necessary to facilitate a successful restructuring. The commencement of the 'normal insolvency proceedings' discussed at 3.5 often has a similar effect as the commencement of liquidation proceedings. Resolution differs in this respect, as no such automatic effects occur. Instead, the resolution authority has the power to suspend creditor rights for very short periods following publication of its intention to take resolution actions: The resolution authority may suspend the bank's obligations until midnight at the end of the business day following the date of publication.[117] Subject to certain exceptions, the resolution authority can also impose a stay on the enforcement of security interests for a period of similar length.[118]

The resolution tools are at the heart of BRRD's resolution regime. Roughly speaking, the resolution tools are the resolution authority's power to transfer the bank's assets and liabilities to other entities or to permanently amend the bank's obligations towards its creditors. Different resolution powers enable different forms of restructuring a failing bank's business. We can distinguish between powers that facilitate the continuation of the failing bank's business in another legal entity and powers that facilitate the bank's continued existence. Two powers, which we collectively will term the 'transfer tools', fall within the first category. These are *the sale of business tool* and *the bridge institution tool*.[119] Both enable the resolution authority to transfer either the shares issued by the bank or its assets and liabilities to another legal entity. These powers operate to preserve the business

[115] See eg SN Grünewald, *The Resolution of Cross-Border Banking Crises in the European Union* (Alphen aan den Rijn, Kluwer Law International, 2014) 15; Ringe (n 57) 328.

[116] BRRD art 63(1)(l).

[117] BRRD art 69. There are certain claims to which this power does not extend, see BRRD art 69(4). Following the amendments resulting from BRRD II, resolution authorities shall have the power to suspend some of a failing bank's obligations for a short period insofar as this is necessary to determine whether a resolution is in the public interest or to ensure the effectiveness of the application of the resolution tools, see BRRD art 33a.

[118] BRRD art 70.

[119] See BRRD arts 38 and 40, respectively. In addition, the directive conceptualises the 'asset separation tool' as a fourth resolution tool. This is a power to transfer assets and liabilities to an asset management entity. This is not an independent resolution power, however, as the resolution authority can only exercise it if the authority also exercises one of the three other powers.

of the bank under resolution rather than preserving the bank itself. The difference between the two powers lies in the identity of the transferee who assumes assets and liabilities from the failing bank. The sale of business tool involves the sale to a private-sector purchaser. The bridge institution tool involves a transfer to a government-controlled entity that shall temporarily carry on the resolved bank's business until it is possible to sell the business to a private-sector purchaser.[120] Whatever remains of the resolved entity shall be liquidated in accordance with the applicable 'normal insolvency proceedings' of its home state.

A resolution does not necessarily imply the end of the legal entity that has entered resolution. The *bail-in tool* facilitates its continued existence.[121] This is the resolution authority's power to write down parts of the claims against the bank.[122] Any creditors suffering a write-down may receive shares as compensation. A reduction in a bank's aggregate liabilities towards its creditors will improve its ability to repay the debt obligations that remain following the bail-in. The purpose of a bail-in is thus to restore the market's trust in the bank and enable it to continue its operations.

BRRD distinguishes resolution from crisis prevention measures. Crisis prevention measures are those that authorities may employ at an earlier stage in the course of a bank's financial deterioration.[123] Such measures can affect creditor rights: The resolution authority may write down capital instruments – that is, shares and debts issued on terms that qualify the debt as counting towards regulatory capital requirements.[124]

3.4.3. Financing Arrangements and Obligations to Prepare for Resolution

Our discussion thus far reveals some fundamental differences between general insolvency proceedings and resolution. However, the two share the same broad contours. For instance, the writing down of claims under a general insolvency law restructuring proceeding and the exercise of the bail-in power yield qualitatively similar results. The primary difference is that a debt restructuring under general insolvency law usually requires approval from some majority among the affected creditors, while the decision of the resolution authority suffices in the context of a resolution. BRRD does, however, establish certain ancillary arrangements that lack a counterpart in general insolvency law.

[120] As a main rule, the resolution authority shall terminate the operation of the bridge bank if privatisation has not occurred within two years of the transfer, see BRRD art 41(5).

[121] See BRRD art 43ff.

[122] BRRD art 2(1)(57). The resolution authority also has the power to bail-in liabilities following their transfer to another bank or a bridge institution under one of the transfer tools.

[123] BRRD art 2(1)(101).

[124] BRRD art 59. See also the discussion at 2.3.2 of capital requirements applicable to banks.

BRRD requires that Member States establish resolution financing arrangements that the banks themselves finance through contributions.[125] The purpose of these arrangements, which often take the form of a fund, is to provide solvency and liquidity support where the losses absorbed by bank shareholders and creditors are insufficient to ensure the bank's continued business. Member States shall ensure that the financing arrangements have financial means in an amount of at least one per cent of the covered deposits – ie the deposits which DGSD accords protection – of all banks authorised in their territory.[126] Limits apply to the resolution authority's use of the resolution financing arrangements.[127] Importantly, the resolution fund is largely prohibited from recapitalising the legal entity that is undergoing resolution.

Another feature of the resolution framework unparalleled in general insolvency law is that BRRD places explicit obligations on both individual banks and public authorities to plan for how the bank will be resolved should it fail.[128] In a sense, this development represents an extension of the prudential regulatory requirements that have long applied to banks.[129] These requirements seek to minimise the risk of bank failure by requiring banks to hold minimum levels of equity capital and liquidity to protect themselves from shocks. The planning requirements in BRRD now complement these requirements, as their objective is to minimise the damage caused if a bank should fail despite regulation and supervision. Essentially, the resolution authorities must draw up a plan of the actions they intend to take to preserve the resolution objectives if a bank fails. This can potentially involve the resolution authority requiring banks to remove impediments to the successful execution of the preferred course of action.

One important element of the preparatory framework is the minimum requirements for own funds and eligible liabilities (MREL).[130] MREL requires that a minimum part of a bank's financing must stem from equity or debt instruments with certain qualities. The underlying idea is to ensure that banks have sufficient liabilities remaining upon resolution so that the resolution authority then may use its powers effectively. Generally, the resolution authority determines MREL for banks and bank groups on a case-by-case basis. However, large banks classified as global systemically important institutions (G-SIIs) are subject to minimum requirements set out in the Capital Requirements Regulation (CRR).[131]

[125] BRRD art 100.
[126] BRRD art 102.
[127] BRRD art 101.
[128] See BRRD arts 5ff and 10ff, respectively.
[129] See ch 2.
[130] See ch 8.
[131] Regulation (EU) No 575/2013 of the European Parliament and of the Council of 26 June 2013 on prudential requirements for credit institutions and investment firms and amending Regulation (EU) No 648/2012 [2013] OJ L176/1 (CRR).

3.4.4. Cross-Border Resolution and the Single Resolution Mechanism

European banks frequently operate beyond the borders of their home states. This is in line with the political project to create a single market for financial services within the EU. Efforts to this end include the harmonisation of banking regulation and the introduction of the so-called passport system, where EU banks can operate throughout the internal market by obtaining authorisation from and submitting themselves to prudential supervision in one Member State.[132]

EU bank insolvency law builds on what one may term home state jurisdiction, where a bank's home state has the exclusive power to resolve or wind up that bank.[133] A Member State may therefore not take action regarding a bank authorised by another Member State, even if the bank has a branch in the first Member State. Because of the integration of markets for banking services, the effects of a bank's failure may extend beyond its home state. This, again, means that several Member States could take an interest in how a failing bank is resolved. Exclusive home state jurisdiction increases the risk that the chosen course of action does not account for the interests of other Member States.

EU law currently deals with the issue of coordinating national interests, albeit with a low degree of prescriptiveness. The generally applicable framework for cross-border resolution imposes certain high-level obligations on resolution authorities when they take resolution actions with cross-border implications.[134] A banking group operating on a cross-border basis could consist of entities authorised in different Member States, thereby placing the entities under the remit of different resolution authorities. BRRD contains provisions that require the various resolution authorities to cooperate when planning for the resolution of an entity that is part of a cross-border group.[135] Moreover, if one resolution authority intends to take resolution actions, it is required to notify the other resolution authorities of this intention with a view to agreeing on a joint resolution scheme.[136] BRRD establishes what can be described as a 'comply or explain' regime: A resolution authority is seemingly free to not follow an established course of action or otherwise enter into a joint resolution scheme, but it must state its reasons for not doing so.[137]

The adoption of BRRD coincided with the centralisation of resolution powers in parts of the EU through the establishment of the Single Resolution Mechanism (SRM). SRM operates to transfer the decision-making powers of the resolution authorities of the members of the Banking Union – ie eurozone Member States and Member States that join voluntarily – to the Single Resolution Board (SRB) with respect to banks subject to direct ECB supervision or otherwise part of a

[132] CRD IV art 33.
[133] CIWUD arts 3(1) and 9, respectively.
[134] BRRD title V.
[135] BRRD art 88.
[136] BRRD arts 91 and 92.
[137] BRRD arts 91(8) and 92(4).

cross-border group. The SRB is an EU agency created in connection with the SRM's conception.[138] The establishment of SRM also entailed centralisation of resolution financing arrangements, as members contribute to a Single Resolution Fund set up to support resolution action under the SRM.[139]

Within the SRM, the SRB does not act alone in placing an institution under resolution. Rather, SRB draws up a resolution scheme that is passed on to the Commission.[140] The Commission then decides whether to endorse the scheme or object on account of discretionary aspects other than the determination of whether resolution is in the public interest. Moreover, the Commission may propose that the Council shall object to the resolution scheme on account of it not being in the public interest or approve amendments proposed by the Commission with respect to use of the Single Resolution Fund. If neither the Commission nor the Council raises objections within 24 hours of the SRB sending the scheme to the Commission, the resolution scheme enters into force.[141] The national resolution authorities then implement the resolution by exercising their resolution powers under national legislation implementing BRRD.[142]

3.5. Winding-Up Proceedings for Smaller Banks

While the adoption of BRRD has drawn much attention to the resolution framework contained therein, it is important to recognise that BRRD does not foresee resolution as the sole insolvency procedure applicable to banks. BRRD presupposes that Member States shall have a two-tracked system where banks are either wound up under 'normal insolvency proceedings' or, where necessary in the public interest, resolved in line with BRRD's resolution framework. This section introduces BRRD's requirements to 'normal insolvency proceedings' and the main features of these proceedings in English, German and Norwegian law.

BRRD defines 'normal insolvency proceedings' as

> collective insolvency proceedings which entail the partial or total divestment of a debtor and the appointment of a liquidator or an administrator normally applicable to institutions under national law and either specific to those institutions or generally applicable to any natural or legal person.[143]

[138] SRMR art 42.

[139] Agreement on the Transfer and Mutualisation of Contributions to the Single Resolution Fund (21 May 2014); Regulation (EU) No 806/2014 of the European Parliament and of the Council of 15 July 2014 establishing uniform rules and a uniform procedure for the resolution of credit institutions and certain investment firms in the framework of a Single Resolution Mechanism and a Single Resolution Fund and amending Regulation (EU) No 1093/2010 [2014] OJ L225/1 (SRMR) art 76(1).

[140] SRMR art 18(6).

[141] SRMR art 18(7). For a more detailed discussion on the grounds on which the Commission and the Council may object to a resolution scheme, see eg D Busch, 'Governance of the European Banking Union's Single Resolution Mechanism' (2017) 28 *European Business Law Review* 447.

[142] SRMR art 18(9).

[143] BRRD art 2(1)(47).

BRRD builds on the premise that Member States have some form of procedure for winding up banks. As the directive defines the term, Member States can choose to liquidate banks under general liquidation proceedings or under a bank-specific procedure.

BRRD conceptualises normal insolvency law as the main approach to bank insolvency. The power to place an institution under resolution is inter alia conditional upon resolution being necessary in the public interest.[144] When determining the question of necessity, the resolution authority must compare the resolution's likely outcome to the likely outcome of 'normal insolvency proceedings'.[145] If normal insolvency proceedings sufficiently safeguard the public interest, the condition of necessity is not satisfied.

EU law harmonises national 'normal insolvency proceedings' to a limited extent. However, as discussed briefly at 3.3, EU law has since pre-crisis times contained directives that require Member States to protect security arrangements entered into to secure exposures under certain financial market contracts. These requirements continue to apply, and the normal insolvency proceedings must therefore respect such security arrangements. BRRD introduced some requirements to the priority of deposits in normal insolvency proceedings. As we shall discuss in more detail in chapter five, the directive requires that Member States accord priority over general unsecured creditors to deposits that are either protected under the Deposit Guarantee Scheme Directive (DGSD) or held by natural persons or micro-, small- or medium-sized enterprises.[146] Apart from these requirements, EU law currently allows Member States great discretion in shaping their national normal insolvency proceedings. For instance, Member States remain free to determine the objectives of the national winding-up proceedings that apply to banks. They can choose to require that decisions made during the proceedings should seek to maximise recoveries for the creditors as a whole. Alternatively, the national regime could require decisions that benefit one creditor group, such as retail depositors. The Member States also remain free to determine institutional features, such as whether the power to open proceedings and appoint a liquidator or administrator should rest with the courts or a public authority.

A quick glance at the 'normal insolvency proceedings' found in English, German and Norwegian law reveals that these states have chosen different solutions in the absence of EU law that would harmonise such proceedings. The different approaches also reflect those adopted by the jurisdictions concerned prior to the GFC.

The German law normal insolvency proceedings follow the general insolvency proceedings set out in InsO subject to bank-specific modifications. As seen at 3.3, this was also the German approach to bank insolvency law in pre-crisis times.

[144] BRRD art 32(1)(c).

[145] BRRD art 32(5).

[146] Directive 2014/49/EU of the European Parliament and of the Council on deposit guarantee schemes [2014] OJ L173/149.

The modifications largely remain the same. Once commenced, the insolvency proceedings will thus proceed in a similar manner as any other insolvency proceeding.

Norwegian law represents the opposite side of the spectrum. As discussed at 3.3, Norwegian law already excluded banks from the scope of general insolvency proceedings prior to the GFC. Instead, banks were subject to bank-specific and government-controlled public administration. As noted above, public administration was open-ended in terms of outcome – in principle, a bank taken under public administration could either end up liquidated or emerge intact following a restructuring. The legislative reform that implemented BRRD in Norwegian law brought about two important amendments. First, the reform reduced the public administration regime to a liquidation regime. Secondly, the administration board in charge of the liquidation shall pursue the objective of having another institution assume the deposits of depositors covered by the Norwegian deposit guarantee scheme.[147] Apart from these amendments, the recast public administration regime largely resembles its pre-crisis counterpart.

The English approach lies somewhere between the German and Norwegian approaches. While banks are not excluded per se from the scope of generally applicable insolvency proceedings, English law contains a bank-specific winding-up procedure termed bank insolvency that takes precedence over the general form.[148] The objectives of the bank insolvency procedure are to ensure that another bank assumes the deposits of the failed bank insured by the UK deposit guarantee scheme and to achieve the best result for the bank's creditors as a whole.[149] The former objective takes precedence over the latter.[150]

There have been calls for the EU to further harmonise the insolvency framework applicable to banks. We will briefly discuss these in chapter ten.

[147] Finansforetaksloven § 20-31(3).
[148] Banking Act 2009, s 119.
[149] Banking Act 2009, s 99.
[150] Banking Act 2009, s 99(4).

4

Creditor Priority in General Insolvency Proceedings

4.1. Introduction

This chapter turns to creditor priority in general insolvency law. The question of creditor priority arises whenever it becomes evident that a company's current assets and future income are insufficient to satisfy its obligations. In such a scenario, some creditors will not recover their claim against the company. In other words, questions of creditor priority are questions that concern the allocation of a scarce resource. In liquidation proceedings, priority manifests itself in the rules that govern which creditors get what out of the pool of assets that the company owns at the commencement of the proceedings. Restructuring proceedings also embody a system of creditor priority. A successful restructuring of a company's debts necessitates that some creditors forgo their claims against the company. The legal framework for restructuring proceedings often puts constraints on how a restructuring plan can allocate this burden among a given set of creditors – eg by ruling out the non-consensual restructuring of claims with a given priority in liquidation insofar as the claims of all subordinate creditors have not first been fully written down.

The default approach to creditor priority is *pari passu* distribution.[1] In a liquidation proceeding, the *pari passu* principle requires that creditors are paid in an amount pro rata to their claim against the debtor. If an insolvent company that enters liquidation proceedings owes its creditors in aggregate four million euro and the funds available for distribution are worth two million euro, a pro rata distribution involves each creditor receiving 50 per cent of their individual claims. A restructuring procedure that adheres fully to the *pari passu* principle would

[1] K van Zwieten, *Goode on Principles of Corporate Insolvency Law*, 5th edn (London, Sweet & Maxwell, 2018) para 3-07 ('the *pari passu* principle is one of the most fundamental principles of corporate insolvency law'); R Bork, *Einführung in das Insolvenzrecht*, 10th edn (Tübingen, Mohr Siebeck, 2021) paras 1–2; MH Andenæs, *Konkurs* (Oslo, MH Andenæs, 2009) 11. But see RJ Mokal, *Corporate Insolvency Law: Theory and Application* (Oxford, Oxford University Press, 2005) 127–28, who (against the background of English law) argues that *pari passu* distribution is no more than a fall-back rule whose existence is owed to the fact that funds rarely are available for distribution among general unsecured creditors; it is therefore pointless to differentiate between the creditors that currently fall within the category general unsecured creditors.

require the pro rata reduction of all claims that exist at the commencement of the restructuring proceedings.

As this chapter will make clear, none of the sample jurisdictions – English, German and Norwegian law – adheres strictly to the *pari passu* principle. One source of such deviations is the broad possibilities for a company to grant security interests to a specific creditor. A security interest most often gives the secured creditor recourse to the secured assets ahead of all other creditors. Moreover, some jurisdictions provide that whatever may remain of value after the secured creditors have been paid shall go towards paying certain preferential creditors in full before the general body of unsecured creditors receive any payments.

Against this background, this chapter seeks to analyse two questions. The first question is descriptive: to what extent do individual creditors enjoy priority above or below the general body of creditors in English, German and Norwegian general insolvency law? The second question is of an explanatory nature: Which reasons can explain the significant possibilities for deviations from the *pari passu* principle? In answering these questions, 4.2 discusses what constitutes the two most significant exceptions to the *pari passu* principle in liquidation proceedings. The first is a company's power to grant security interests to specific creditors, thereby giving such creditors priority over other creditors in liquidation proceedings. The second is the rules that govern the distribution of the values available for sharing among unsecured creditors.[2] Thereafter, 4.3 considers the extent to which creditors that enjoy a certain priority position in liquidation proceedings are entitled to maintain the same priority vis-à-vis other creditors in restructuring proceedings. This is a question of the extent to which it is a condition for interfering with the claim of a given creditor that no creditors which would rank subordinate in liquidation proceedings maintain any value, and that other creditors of the same rank bear an equal burden. Finally, 4.4 discusses different theories of creditor priority and how their policy implications fit the approaches of the sample jurisdictions.

4.2. Priority in Liquidation Proceedings: The Tension between Party Autonomy and Prescriptive Rules

4.2.1. The Possibilities for Taking Security and the Priority of Security Interests

The sample jurisdictions contain few limitations on a company's ability to grant security interests over assets that dominate bank balance sheets: loan receivables,

[2] This is not an exhaustive account of the exceptions to the *pari passu* principle. Other rights, such as non-consensual security interests and set-off rights, also form part of the bigger picture.

equity instruments and debt instruments.[3] One limitation is that such assets must be transferable but there are no general restrictions as to their transferability. There are certain formalities that must be observed for the security interest to arise or for it to remain effective if the company becomes subject to insolvency proceedings – eg registration and notification requirements – but these do not appear to so burdensome as to effectively rule out the granting of security interests.

Having established the options for creating security interests, we now turn to discuss the priority of security interests in insolvency proceedings. When the applicable proceeding is among the liquidation proceedings discussed at 3.1.3, this question is relatively straightforward: is a secured creditor's recourse to the value of the secured asset absolute following the commencement of the proceedings? Or will unsecured creditors receive parts of the value that the secured asset represents, even if the secured creditor has not received full satisfaction of the secured claim?

English law distinguishes between fixed and floating charges (a non-possessory security interest). This distinction is of great importance in the context of the priority that secured claims enjoy vis-à-vis unsecured creditors in liquidation proceedings. A creditor secured by a fixed charge has recourse to the secured asset with absolute priority over unsecured creditors.[4] The unsecured creditors will thus only have recourse to the value that the secured asset represents if the asset value exceeds the secured creditor's claim. Conversely, creditors secured by a floating charge do not enjoy absolute priority. A floating security interest only gives the secured creditor recourse to the value of the assets net the expenses of the proceedings, the claims of creditors of preferential debts[5] and a 'prescribed part' of the floating charge assets, a sum designated for sharing among the unsecured creditors.[6] The size of the prescribed part depends on the value of what remains following the satisfaction of the expenses and the preferred claims.[7] It can be up to £800,000.[8]

Whether a security interest is floating or fixed depends on whether the chargor – as long as no default or similar event has occurred – remains free to dispose of the secured asset free of the security interest.[9] In *Spectrum*, Lord Scott stated that 'the essential characteristic of a floating charge, the characteristic that distinguishes it

[3] This discussion builds upon the findings of SS Ellingsæter, 'Creditor Priority and Financial Stability: A study of the emergence and rationales of the creditor hierarchy in EU and EEA bank insolvency law' (PhD thesis, University of Oslo, 2020) ch 10.

[4] L Gullifer (ed), *Goode and Gullifer on Legal Problems of Credit and Security*, 6th edn (London, Sweet & Maxwell, 2017) para 4-09.

[5] Insolvency Act 1986, s 175(2)(b); Sch B1 para 65(2).

[6] Insolvency Act 1986, s 176A.

[7] See Insolvency Act 1986, s 176A(6) and Insolvency Act 1986 (Prescribed Part) Order 2003, SI 2003/2097, art 3(1).

[8] Insolvency Act 1986 (Prescribed Part) Order 2003, art 3(2).

[9] A floating charge becomes a fixed charge on 'crystallisation', following which the chargor is deprived of its right to dispose of the secured assets, see H Beale et al, *The Law of Security and Title-Based Financing*, 3rd edn (Oxford, Oxford University Press, 2018) para 6.78 ff. Whether or not a floating charge has crystallised prior to the commencement of insolvency proceedings is not of relevance for the issues touched upon in this chapter, see ibid, para 6.87.

from a fixed charge, is that the asset subject to the charge is not finally appropriated as a security for the payment of the debt until the occurrence of some future event. In the meantime the chargor is left free to use the charged asset and to remove it from the security'.[10] Conversely, '[u]nder a fixed charge the assets charged as security are permanently appropriated to the payment of the sum charged, in such a way as to give the chargee a proprietary interest in the assets. So long as the charge remains unredeemed, the assets can be released from the charge only with the active concurrence of the chargee'.[11] This means that a security interest created under a security agreement that permits the security grantor to continue to deal with the secured assets would qualify as a floating security interest. Conversely, whether the security agreement purports to create a security interest over assets that the chargor may acquire in the future is not of relevance for the classification of the charge.[12]

The main rule in German insolvency law is that the commencement of insolvency proceedings does not affect the enforcement powers of the security grantee. Exceptions do apply, however. InsO provides that in some instances the insolvency professional shall have the power to sell assets subject to a security interest clear of the security interest to a third party. This applies to claims transferred as security,[13] which is the most commonly used technique for granting claims as security. The proceeds of the sale are applied to cover the insolvency professional's fees for identifying and selling the secured assets. Remaining funds thereafter go towards satisfying the secured claim. The insolvency professional could also have a power of sale where the secured assets are immobilised shares deposited with the German central securities depository Clearstream AG insofar as the shares form a part of the company's economic unit.[14] The insolvency professional's power to sell secured assets entails suspending the security grantee's power to initiate a forced sale and other enforcement steps unless the insolvency professional decides that the asset should be sold by the security grantee.

Insofar as the insolvency professional has the power to dispose of assets that are subject to a security interest, parts of the proceeds accrue to the pool of assets available for distribution among the unsecured creditors as a form of remuneration for the work the insolvency professional undertakes in identifying and disposing of the secured assets.[15] The contribution does not necessarily reflect the actual

[10] *Re Spectrum Plus Ltd (in liquidation)* [2005] UKHL 41, [2005] 2 AC 680 [111]. See also *Agnew v Commissioner of Inland Revenue* [2001] UKPC 28, [2001] 2 AC 710 [13] (per Lord Millett); Gullifer (ed) (n 4) para 4-04; Beale et al (n 9) para 6.101.

[11] *Spectrum* (n 10) [138] (per Lord Walker).

[12] *Spectrum* (n 10) [103] (per Lord Scott). See also Gullifer (ed) (n 4) para 4-07; Beale et al (n 9) para 6.69; H Bennett, 'Late Floating Charges' in J Armour and H Bennett (eds), *Vulnerable Transactions in Corporate Insolvency* (Oxford, Hart Publishing, 2003) paras 5.14, 5.17.

[13] InsO § 166(2). When the secured asset is a monetary claim, the insolvency professional can choose to collect the underlying claim rather than selling it.

[14] This does not follow directly from InsO § 166, but derives from a recent judgment of the Bundesgerichtshof, the German Federal Court of Justice. See BGH IX ZR 272/13, NZI 2016, 21 para 33.

[15] InsO §§ 170 and 171.

costs of the work undertaken by the insolvency professional for this purpose. Such a rule therefore has the potential to distribute value embodied in the secured assets to the unsecured creditors where the contribution exceeds the costs to the insolvency estate. Ascertaining whether the rule operates to this effect would necessitate empirically informed studies that are beyond the scope of this chapter.

Secured creditors enjoy absolute priority over unsecured creditors in Norwegian law liquidation proceedings. The proceeds of secured assets are only available for distribution among unsecured creditors to the extent any proceeds remain after the proceeds are applied towards covering the secured claim. The insolvency estate has recourse to secured assets for covering the expenses of the liquidation.[16] However, this presupposes that the debtor's unencumbered funds are insufficient for covering the expenses.[17] This means that the insolvency estate can have recourse to secured assets only in cases where unsecured creditors receive no distributions. Accordingly, this rule does not operate to confer an advantage to unsecured creditors at the expense of secured creditors.

4.2.2. Transaction Avoidance of Security Interests

As seen at 4.2.1, there are broad possibilities for creating security interests over the assets typically owned by banks. Moreover, the commencement of liquidation proceedings generally does not affect the recourse of secured creditors to secured assets. Through its power to grant security interests, a company generally exercises significant influence over which creditors get what in the event that it becomes over-indebted and is unable to satisfy all of its obligations. This section analyses the limits that *transaction avoidance rules* impose on a company's influence over creditor priority through the granting of security interests.

It could be said that transaction avoidance rules 'provide for the setting aside of transactions that were, at the time they were made, generally valid and not vulnerable to challenge'.[18] It is common to group avoidance rules in two subcategories.[19] The first category comprises rules aimed at gifts and other transactions made at an undervalue. Such transactions involve the enrichment of a third party – eg a dominant shareholder – without the company receiving comparable value in return, thus harming the creditors. The second category of transaction avoidance rules render avoidable transactions that do not harm the creditors as a whole but that impact the distribution among them. One example is the payment of unsecured

[16] Panteloven § 6-4(1).

[17] Rt. 2014 14 para 39.

[18] G McCormack, A Keay and S Brown, *European Insolvency Law: Reform and Harmonization* (Cheltenham, Edward Elgar, 2017) 130.

[19] Some regimes empower the insolvency professional to avoid the company's assumption of liabilities, see eg Norwegian law (dekningsloven § 5-9).

debt immediately before the commencement of insolvency proceedings. At least when viewed in isolation, the payment does not leave the creditors as a whole worse off, but it gives one creditor full satisfaction of its claim to the detriment of the others. Depending on the circumstances, the granting of security interests can involve elements of both a transaction at an undervalue and a transaction that affects the distribution among the creditors. For instance, if the company grants a security interest for an existing debt, the secured creditor receives a benefit without providing comparable compensation. At the same time, the grant of the security interest does not harm the creditors as a whole. The creditors will recover in aggregate the same amount of funds, regardless of whether the company grants the security interest.

In the following, we will consider whether security interests granted in two scenarios are susceptible to avoidance in the sample jurisdictions.[20] We will consider applicable transaction avoidance rules as they generally operate. Therefore, we will not consider any special rules that apply where the security grantee is a connected party of the company – eg a dominant shareholder or director.

In the first scenario, the secured claim arises in connection with the granting of security. For instance, the company could grant a security interest in order for the security grantee to advance a loan. Insofar as the security interest covers assets that the company owns at the time, a security interest arises prior to or simultaneously with the security grantee advancing the loan. When the security interest purports to cover assets that the company may acquire in the future, the security interest arises automatically upon the company acquiring such assets.

Security interests granted in this scenario are generally not at risk of being avoided if the company subsequently enters liquidation proceedings. Exceptions apply in cases where the security interest concerns future assets. Under the German regime, such security interests may be avoided under InsO § 130 to the extent they attach to assets acquired by the security grantor at a date falling later than three months prior to the petition for insolvency proceedings being made. However, avoidance will require that the company at the time the assets accrued to it, and the security interest thus attached to them, was either unable to pay its debts or subject to a petition for the opening of insolvency proceedings, and that the security grantee was aware of the inability to pay or the petition. In a similar vein, a security interest for a new loan could be avoided under Norwegian law insofar as it concerns future assets that accrue to the company within a three-month suspect period preceding the liquidation.[21]

In the second scenario, the company grants security for an outstanding debt that the parties originally intended to leave unsecured. Such a scenario could, for instance, occur if an unsecured creditor threatens to demand early repayment of

[20] The specifics of the national transaction avoidance regimes are set out in more detail in Ellingsæter (n 3) ch 10.

[21] Dekningsloven § 5-7.

its claim or request that the court opens insolvency proceedings in respect of the company unless the company grants a security interest for that creditor's claim.

All sample jurisdictions contain transaction avoidance rules that bite on security interests granted in respect of debts that originally were unsecured. However, there are considerable differences as to the conditions that must be satisfied to avoid the security interest.

At one end of the spectrum are general provisions that make avoidance conditional upon it being established that the grant of security is tainted by some form of impropriety. This category includes the German InsO § 133: if, in providing a security interest, the company willfully disadvantages its unsecured creditors, and if the security grantee is aware of this will, the security interest is avoidable insofar as it was granted during the four years preceding the petition for the opening of insolvency proceedings or between the petition and commencement of the proceedings. Reference could also be made to section 239 of the UK Insolvency Act 1986, which sets out the general conditions for the avoidance of *preferences*, which includes the granting of security in respect of originally unsecured debt. The mere existence of a preference is not sufficient to warrant avoidance under this provision, however. Among other things, section 239 requires that the company in granting the security 'was influenced in deciding to give it by a desire to produce' the preference that it represents.

At the other end of the spectrum are 'blunt' provisions that make any security interest granted in respect of antecedent debts avoidable. Such provisions deem irrelevant both subjective factors, such as the motivation of the company for granting the security and the knowledge of the security grantee, and the company's financial state when the security was granted. This category comprises the first ground for avoidance set out in InsO § 131, which among other things renders avoidable security interests granted for antecedent debts within either the month preceding the request for insolvency proceedings or in the interval between the request and the commencement of the insolvency proceedings. In a similar vein, the Norwegian dekningsloven § 5-7 renders avoidable any security interest granted for antecedent debts following the date that fell three months prior to the request for insolvency proceedings being received by the court.

An intermediate category comprises transaction avoidance rules that make avoidance of security interests granted in respect of antecedent debts conditional upon the company being in financial distress. One such example is the second avoidance ground set out in InsO § 131, which empowers the insolvency professional to avoid such security interests when granted in the interval between the first and third months preceding the request to commence insolvency proceedings insofar as the company at that time was unable to pay its debts. Another example is section 245 of the Insolvency Act 1986 which – subject to certain other conditions – operates to invalidate floating charges granted in respect of antecedent debts by a company unable to pay its debts.

The above discussion shows that transaction avoidance provisions rarely operate to frustrate security interests granted in respect of new debts. Accordingly, such rules do not affect a company's ability to determine that creditors of certain debts shall have recourse to specific assets ahead of other creditors. Conversely, the possibilities for avoiding originally unsecured debts are wider. However, it may prove difficult and costly for insolvency professionals to challenge security interests under provisions that require improper motivation to have been established on the part of the company for granting security. While there are provisions that do not make avoidance contingent upon establishing such motivation, these are generally only applicable to security interests granted within the months preceding the opening of insolvency proceedings.

4.2.3. Priority Among Unsecured Creditors

Roughly speaking, the funds available for distribution among unsecured creditors following liquidation proceedings equal the value of the company's assets less secured claims and the expenses of the proceedings. In the following paragraphs, we will turn to the criteria in English, German and Norwegian insolvency law for the distribution of any such funds among unsecured creditors. General insolvency law places most unsecured creditors in the same class, which ranks behind any preferential claims but ahead of subordinated claims. In the following text, we shall draw our attention to cases where unsecured creditors are treated differently than such general unsecured creditors. More specifically, we shall explore the extent to which certain categories of unsecured claims are either elevated to the position of a *preferential debt* or demoted to the status of *subordinated debt* when the insolvency professional distributes funds in liquidation proceedings.

English law accords preferential status to certain claims. Preferential debts are divided into two categories: ordinary preferential debts and secondary preferential debts.[22] Ordinary preferential debts take priority over secondary preferential debts, and include unpaid wages of up to £800 for services rendered within the four months preceding the insolvency proceedings and certain other employment-related claims.[23] Ordinary preferential debts share *pari passu* in the event that the available funds only suffice to cover the aggregate amount of such debts in part.[24]

Following a recent amendment to the Insolvency Act 1986 secondary preferential debts now include certain debts owed to the Commissioners for Her Majesty's Revenue and Customs.[25] First, this includes value added tax. Secondly, this category also comprises certain deductions that a company is required to make from payments made to another person and subsequently pay to the Commissioners,

[22] Insolvency Act 1986, s 386.

[23] For a detailed account, see A Keay, A Boraine and D Burdette, 'Preferential Debts in Corporate Insolvency: a Comparative Study' (2001) 10 *International Insolvency Review* 167, 176–78. In addition, levies on the production of coal and steel made by the European Union and certain related claims also constitute preferential debts, see Insolvency Act 1986, Sch 6 para 15A.

[24] Insolvency Act 1986, s 175(1A).

[25] Insolvency Act 1986, s 386(1B); Sch 6 para 15D.

and the payment to the Commissioners is credited against any liabilities of the other person. Accordingly, there are several tax debts that are not secondary preferential debts and thus do not rank ahead of the general unsecured creditors.

German general insolvency law does not give preferential status to any unsecured claim.[26] This has been the case since InsO entered into force and abolished the preferential status of certain creditors under the previous insolvency law regime.

Norwegian insolvency law provides that the proceeds of the insolvency estate shall be distributed among certain preferential claims (*fortrinnsberettigede fordringer*) prior to other general claims against the company. A two-level hierarchy applies among the preferential claims: Funds are first distributed *pari passu* across first-class preferential claims (*fortrinnsberettigede fordringer av første klasse*), which comprises claims for unpaid wages and certain other employment-related claims.[27] Claims for unpaid wages only enjoy priority up to an amount equal to six months' wages.[28] The preferential status does not apply to wages due to persons with influence over the company's business, such as members of a company's management bodies. Remaining funds are thereafter distributed among second-class preferential claims (*fortrinnsberettigede fordringer av annen klasse*), which comprises certain claims for taxes and VAT.[29]

All three jurisdictions subordinate some claims to the company's general unsecured debts, which means that the creditors of such claims receive distributions only insofar as the funds available for distribution cover the general unsecured debt in full.

In English insolvency law, any such surplus funds first go towards satisfying statutory interest accruing on preferential and unsecured debt during the course of the insolvency proceedings. Insofar as funds remain, the insolvency professional shall apply the funds to statutorily deferred claims.[30] This category includes certain administrative sanctions, loans payable at a rate of interest that varies according to the company's profit and claims due to any member of the company in his capacity as a member of the company.[31] Moreover, the courts have the power to subordinate the claims of creditors that have engaged in fraudulent trading or wrongful trading.[32] If any funds remain, these go towards satisfying the claims of creditors of non-provable liabilities.[33] The Insolvency Rules 2016 provides that this category comprises inter alia certain criminal pecuniary sanctions.[34]

[26] CG Paulus and M Berberich, 'National Report for Germany' in D Faber et al (eds), *Ranking and Priority of Creditors* (Oxford, Oxford University Press, 2016) para 10.50.

[27] Dekningsloven § 9-3. See Andenæs (n 1) 416–20.

[28] Dekningsloven § 9-3.

[29] Dekningsloven § 9-4. See generally Andenæs (n 1) 421–22.

[30] H Anderson, C Cooke and L Gullifer, 'National Report for England' in Faber et al (eds) (n 26) para 8.69.

[31] Anderson, Cooke and Gullifer (n 30) paras 8.69–8.75.

[32] Insolvency Act 1986, s 215(4).

[33] Anderson, Cooke and Gullifer (n 30) para 8.76.

[34] Insolvency (England and Wales) Rules 2016, SI 2016/1024, r 14.2(2). See also Anderson, Cooke and Gullifer (n 30) paras 8.21–8.25 for a discussion on other claims that fall within this category.

In addition, it is possible for a creditor to subordinate its claim voluntarily to a company's general unsecured debt through an agreement with the company to this effect.[35]

Under German law, certain claims are only paid to the extent funds remain after covering the expenses of the proceedings, general unsecured debt, interest accruing on general unsecured debt and the costs incurred by general unsecured creditors through their participation in the insolvency proceedings. The claims in question fall into three categories, with claims falling within the first category ranking ahead of claims in the second category, and claims within the second category ranking ahead of the third category. The first category comprises pecuniary sanctions imposed on the company due to breaches of criminal law or the failure to observe court orders.[36] The second category comprises claims for the performance of obligations that the company has assumed without receiving any corresponding right of counter-performance.[37] The third category comprises certain loans made to the company by a shareholder (or persons connected to a shareholder) that either holds more than 10 per cent of the company's shares or manages the company.[38] An exemption applies for creditors that became shareholders in connection with the restructuring of a distressed company.

Moreover, it is possible for a creditor to subordinate its claim to those of unsecured creditors by agreement with the company. Both the company and the creditor are free to choose the relative ranking of the claim among the claims that rank subordinate to general unsecured claims.[39] If there is doubt about what the company and the creditor have agreed concerning a contractually subordinated claim's priority relative to the claims subordinated by statute, the claim ranks behind all other claims.[40]

Norwegian law also subordinates certain claims to general unsecured debt. These claims only receive distributions to the extent that funds remain after the payment of preferential and general unsecured debts and the interest accrued thereon. The first category of such subordinated claims comprises pecuniary sanctions resulting from the breaches of tax law, criminal law or court orders.[41] The second category comprises claims of a gratuitous nature.[42]

It is also possible for the company and a creditor to subordinate the latter's claim to other unsecured creditors by way of agreement. The parties are free to determine the claim's priority relative to other forms of subordinated debt.[43] If the

[35] *Re Maxwell Communications Corporation Plc.* [1993] 1 WLR 1402.
[36] InsO § 39(1)(3).
[37] InsO § 39(1)(4).
[38] InsO § 39(1)(5) *cf* InsO § 39(4) and (5). See Paulus and Berberich (n 26) paras 10.58–10.68.
[39] K Schmidt and A Herchen, '§ 39' in K Schmidt (ed), *Insolvenzordnung: InsO mit EuInsVO*, 19th edn (Munich, CH Beck, 2016) para 23.
[40] InsO § 39(2).
[41] Dekningsloven § 9-7(4).
[42] Dekningsloven § 9-7(5).
[43] See NOU 1972: 20, 'Gjeldsforhandling og konkurs' 358. Andenæs (n 1) 424.

parties fail to specify the priority vis-à-vis other subordinated claims, the claim will rank behind interest on preferential and general unsecured debt, but ahead of other claims.[44]

4.3. Creditor Priority in Modern Restructuring Proceedings

4.3.1. English Law

As discussed at 3.1.4, English law contains three frameworks that can be used to restructure company debts notwithstanding that not all affected creditors consent thereto: the scheme of arrangement, a restructuring plan adopted pursuant to the Companies Act 2006, Part 26A and the company voluntary arrangement (CVA).

Both a scheme of arrangement and a restructuring plan can interfere with the rights of both secured and unsecured creditors, at least where the scheme or plan is proposed by a company that has not entered administration.[45] The adoption of a scheme of arrangement involves the holding of two court hearings and intermediate creditor meetings where the creditors vote over the proposed scheme. At the first hearing, the court considers whether to order a meeting of the creditors or class of creditors. At the second hearing, the court considers whether to sanction the proposed scheme. In order to gauge the risk that the court will sanction a scheme that interferes with the priority a creditor would have in the liquidation of the company, it is necessary to look to two features of the procedure for receiving the court's sanction.

First, the sanctioning of a scheme requires that creditors are separated into classes insofar as this is appropriate and that a requisite majority within each class must approve the scheme. It is thus not possible to 'cram down' a dissenting class; that is, to have a scheme approved despite its failure to receive the support of a requisite approval within each class.[46] A creditor is therefore only at risk of having a debt restructuring forced upon it insofar as a requisite majority of creditors

[44] Dekningsloven § 9-7(2).

[45] The administrator of a company in administration may propose a scheme of arrangement. It has been argued that an administrator is prevented from proposing a scheme that would amend the rights of secured creditors without the consent of all secured creditors, see N Segal, 'The Effect of Reorganization Proceedings on Security Interests: The Position under English and U.S. Law' (2007) 32 *Brooklyn Journal of International Law* 927, 976.

[46] It has been argued that it is possible for a company and its secured creditors to cram down the claims of unsecured creditors by placing the company in administration and thereafter receiving court sanction of a scheme of arrangement that transfers the company's business and the secured claims to a new entity, see J Payne, 'The Role of the Court in Debt Restructuring' (2018) 77 *CLJ* 124, 130. We will not explore this question further here, given that we are concerned with the opposite problem – the potential for restructuring proceedings to interfere with secured creditors' priority over unsecured creditors.

within its class favours the proposed arrangement. Such a scenario could arise due to disagreement among the creditors on whether a proposed restructuring is likely to bring about the highest recovery of their claims. However, disagreement over a proposal could also result from the class comprising creditors that have different rights or that have different economic interests.[47]

What then, is the decisive criterion for dividing creditors into classes? Pursuant to court practice, a class shall comprise 'persons whose rights are not so dissimilar as to make it impossible for them to consult together with a view to their common interest'.[48] The courts will focus on the *rights* of the creditors when determining whether they should be divided into different classes.[49] This involves a comparison of both the rights prior to the proposed arrangement and the rights the creditors will have should it take effect. Conversely, the courts will not look to whether the creditors share the same *interests*.[50] In evaluating the similarity of the rights, it is relevant whether the company is insolvent – ie whether or not the alternative to the scheme is the winding up of the company.[51]

To what extent does this protect the priority of a creditor? Some protection is offered by the requirement that a single class should comprise only creditors with similar rights. This prevents the creation of classes with both secured and unsecured creditors, as well as classes comprising secured creditors with different security interests. However, it does not prevent the creation of groups dominated by a majority of secured creditors with personal interests that make them willing to forgo parts of the economic value of their secured claim to the advantage of unsecured creditors. Such a scenario could arise if some of the company's secured creditors are also unsecured creditors or shareholders.[52]

Dissenting creditors are not without protection against exploitation at the hand of a creditor majority within its class. The courts have discretion as to whether to sanction a scheme and practice this in a manner that protects the interests of dissenting creditors. When making their sanctioning decision, courts will often focus on: (i) whether the majority in each class fairly represents that class, and (ii) whether the scheme is one that an intelligent and honest person could have approved.[53]

There are two scenarios in which a court is particularly likely to question whether the majority fairly represents its class.[54] The first is one where few creditors

[47] This point is also made more generally by Jennifer Payne, see 'The Role' (n 46) 130.

[48] *Sovereign Life Assurance Co v Dodd* [1892] 2 QB 573 (CA), 583; J Payne, *Schemes of Arrangement*, 2nd edn (Cambridge, Cambridge University Press, 2021) 215.

[49] Payne (n 46) 135.

[50] Payne (n 48) 67, citing *Re UDL Holdings Ltd* [2002] 1 HKC 172 (Final Court of Appeal of Hong Kong), at 184–85.

[51] Payne (n 48) 64.

[52] Payne (n 48) 223–24.

[53] Payne (n 48) 86 with further references.

[54] Payne (n 48) 91.

attend the meeting and vote. The second is one in which the court has reason to suspect that some or all the majority's votes were cast to promote an interest not shared by the other creditors in that class. When considering whether an intelligent and honest person could have approved the arrangement, the courts assess just that, but do not go as far as considering whether the scheme is the best for the creditors concerned.[55]

The courts have not drawn up a general 'absolute priority rule' that only permits interference with the rights of dissenting creditors if the scheme involves the full write-down of claims that rank with lower priority in liquidation. In principle, then, creditors are susceptible to schemes of arrangement that deviate from the priority regime applicable in liquidation proceedings in terms of loss distribution among creditors.

Given that the sanctioning of a scheme requires qualified majoritarian approval within each class and the satisfaction of a fairness test, it would seem that court sanctioning of such a scheme would presuppose economic benefits for the secured creditors to counterbalance the wealth transfer to the unsecured creditors. Accordingly, an individual secured creditor's priority over unsecured creditors is primarily at risk when other secured creditors in its class have a different opinion of whether the scheme is sensible for the secured creditors.

It is possible to have sanctioned a scheme that interferes with the claims of certain creditors that would rank as general unsecured creditors in a liquidation while leaving the claims of other such claims untouched. For instance, the scheme could convert the claims of unsecured bondholders to shares, while not including any measures that vary the claims of trade creditors. However, the sanctioning of such a scheme requires that a sufficient majority among the class of creditors affected votes in favour. Moreover, the court must be satisfied that an intelligent and honest person could take the view that the benefits of such a debt restructuring are sufficient to outweigh the fact that the creditors affected bear an unproportionate part of the burden of restructuring the company proposing the scheme.

As discussed at 3.1.4, the newly introduced Part 26A of the Companies Act 2006 sets out a framework for the adoption of a restructuring plan that can be accessed by companies facing financial difficulties. To what extent are secured and unsecured creditors at risk of having their claims compromised under this framework? The adoption of a restructuring plan essentially follows the same procedure as the adoption of a scheme of arrangement and thus requires court sanction. For the purposes of voting over a restructuring plan, affected creditors and shareholders are to be divided into classes based on their rights.

There are differences in respect of the conditions for the sanctioning of the restructuring. While the court may sanction a restructuring plan if a requisite

[55] See eg *Re McCarthy & Stone plc* [2009] EWHC 1116 (Ch) [12].

majority within all classes approve the restructuring plan,[56] Part 26A also offers the possibility of court sanction where not all classes have approved the restructuring plan. For the court to have jurisdiction to sanction the restructuring plan under such circumstances, two conditions (termed conditions A and B) must be satisfied.[57]

Condition A is that if the plan is sanctioned 'none of the members of the dissenting class would be any worse off than they would be in the event of *the relevant alternative*' (emphasis added).[58] The relevant alternative is defined as 'whatever the court considers would be most likely to occur in relation to the company if the compromise or arrangement were not sanctioned'.[59] In some cases this will be liquidation or administration while the facts in some cases will lead the court to consider it most likely that the company will continue trading profitably.[60]

It seems reasonable to expect that a court that considers the value of the secured assets to be sufficient to cover the secured claim and costs associated with enforcement would conclude that a restructuring plan that writes down a secured claim will leave the secured creditors worse off than in the event of the relative alternative. This would, in turn, mean that condition A is not satisfied in such circumstances, and that the court does not have jurisdiction to sanction a restructuring plan that the class of secured creditors have rejected. Accordingly, condition A can be seen as operating to protect the priority that secured creditors have to the value represented by the secured assets.

For unsecured creditors condition A does not ensure that they will have absolute priority ahead of lower ranking creditors. It is entirely conceivable that an unsecured creditor could be better off under a restructuring plan that writes down claims in a manner that does not conform to the hierarchy applicable in liquidation proceedings if the relevant alternative to the plan is a liquidation where the creditor stands to receive less.[61]

Condition B is that the plan has been approved by at least one class of creditors or shareholders 'who would receive a payment, or have a genuine economic interest in the company, in the event of the relevant alternative'.[62] If the relevant alternative to the plan is the liquidation of the company and the only class that has approved it consists of shareholders who would not stand to receive distributions in that event, condition B will not be satisfied. Conversely, condition B is satisfied

[56] As is the case for a scheme of arrangement, the court has discretion as to whether to sanction a restructuring plan that all classes have approved. The courts have so far taken the same approach to this question as in respect of a scheme of arrangement, see *Re Virgin Atlantic Airways Ltd* [2020] EWHC 2376 (Ch), [2021] 1 BCLC 105 [46].

[57] Companies Act 2006, s 901G(2).

[58] Companies Act 2006, s 901G(3).

[59] Companies Act 2006, s 901G(4).

[60] As was Zacaroli J's conclusion in *Re Hurricane Energy Plc* [2021] EWHC 1759 (Ch), [2021] BCC 989.

[61] *Re Virgin Active Holdings Ltd and others* [2021] EWHC 1246 (Ch), [2022] 1 All ER (Comm) 1023.

[62] Companies Act 2006, s 901G(5).

if the plan is approved by a class consisting of secured creditors that would make a recovery out of the secured assets in the event of liquidation.[63]

If conditions A and B are satisfied the court *may* sanction the restructuring plan notwithstanding the dissent of a class. The court is conversely not obliged to do so. Indeed, recent cases indicate that the court will take several other factors into account when deciding whether to sanction a restructuring plan under such circumstances.[64]

This raises up the question of whether there may be circumstances under which the courts will refuse to sanction a restructuring plan on account of the plan leaving a dissenting class of creditors that would rank as general unsecured creditors in a liquidation worse off than other creditors that also would rank as such in liquidation. In *Virgin Active*, Snowden J said that

> the key principle … appears to be that … it is for the company and the creditors who are in the money to decide, as against a dissenting class that is out of the money, how the value of the business and assets of the company should be divided.[65]

A creditor being 'out of the money' here means that he would not receive any value in the relevant alternative to the plan. A restructuring plan can thus generally receive court sanction notwithstanding that it accords different treatment to different groups of such creditors even though they would rank *pari passu* as general unsecured creditors in liquidation or administration. However, this principle may not be absolute. Snowden J indicated that the courts in principle could refuse to sanction a plan 'that discriminated arbitrarily or capriciously between different classes of unsecured creditors who were all equally out of the money', although the facts of the case did not necessitate further analysis of this issue.[66]

A CVA may not affect the rights of secured creditors unless they consent thereto.[67] As a result, a CVA cannot encroach upon the priority of secured creditors vis-à-vis unsecured creditors.

It is, however, possible for a CVA to write down unsecured debt. In contrast to what applies for the adoption of a scheme of arrangement or restructuring plan, the process for adopting a CVA does not require the separation of creditors into different classes.[68] Accordingly, all unsecured creditors vote on the proposal.[69] The adoption of the CVA necessitates the approval of a majority of three-quarters (calculated by reference to the value of the claims) of the creditors voting.[70]

[63] *Re DeepOcean I UK Ltd* [2021] EWHC 138 (Ch), [2021] BCC 483 [40].
[64] *Re DeepOcean*; *Re Virgin Active* [223]–[225].
[65] ibid [259].
[66] *Re Virgin Active* (n 61) [265].
[67] Insolvency Act 1986, s 4(3). See also Payne (n 48) 265.
[68] V Finch and D Milman, *Corporate Insolvency Law: Perspectives and Principles*, 3rd edn (Cambridge, Cambridge University Press, 2017) 436.
[69] In addition, the company's shareholders must approve the CVA.
[70] Insolvency Rules 2016, r 15.34(3).

Preferential creditors enjoy protection against CVAs interfering with their priority. Section 4(4)(a) of the Insolvency Act 1986 rules out the possibility of a CVA providing that 'preferential debt of the company is to be paid otherwise than in priority to such of its debts as are not preferential debts'. Moreover, the CVA shall not give a preferential claim worse treatment than other preferential claims of the same class.[71] A CVA thus cannot impose on non-consenting preferential creditors a restructuring scheme that deviates from their priority in liquidation.

The framework is less ardent in its protection of the priority of other unsecured claims. For instance, the Insolvency Act 1986 does not rule out a CVA that imposes higher losses on one subset of general unsecured creditors than another subset. The protection of an individual creditor primarily lies in the creditor's ability to apply for a court order to revoke or suspend a CVA on the grounds that the arrangement unfairly prejudices its interests.[72] The respective frameworks for adopting a scheme of arrangement and a CVA both constitute instruments for varying a company's unsecured debt claims without the consent of all affected creditors. This raises the question of whether the tests applied by courts when considering whether to sanction schemes of arrangement are relevant when assessing whether a CVA unfairly prejudices the rights of a creditor. As discussed above, courts asked to sanction a scheme of arrangement will consider whether the scheme is something an intelligent and honest person could have approved. In *Sisu Capital Fund Ltd v Tucker*, Warren J described the respective tests of the two regimes as 'effectively the same'.[73] A finding that an intelligent and honest person might have reasonably approved the CVA is a 'powerful, and probably conclusive, factor' against concluding that the claimants have been unfairly prejudiced.[74]

There is no single, universal test for judging whether unfair prejudice exists.[75] Unfairness can be assessed from different angles. A *vertical comparison* involves comparing the position of the creditor against its position on a liquidation of the company. If the terms of the CVA result in some creditors being worse off than if the company was liquidated, this is very likely to result in the CVA being deemed to unfairly prejudice the interests of these creditors.[76] However, the vertical comparison is not always conclusive.[77] Another type of comparison is a *horizontal comparison*, which involves comparing the position of a creditor with those of other creditors.[78] This involves examining whether the CVA involves differential treatment of creditors. Finding that the creditor is better off through the CVA than in a hypothetical liquidation scenario is thus not sufficient for dismissing its

[71] Insolvency Act 1986, s 4(4).
[72] Insolvency Act 1986, s 6(1)(a) and (4)(a).
[73] [2005] EWHC 2170 (Ch), [2006] BCC 463 [133].
[74] *Prudential Assurance Co Ltd v PRG Powerhouse Ltd* [2007] EWHC 1002 (Ch), [2007] BCC 500 [96].
[75] *PRG Powerhouse* (n 74) [74].
[76] *Re T & N Ltd* [2004] EWHC 2361 (Ch) [82]; *PRG Powerhouse* (n 74) [81].
[77] *PRG Powerhouse* (n 74) [83].
[78] *PRG Powerhouse* (n 74) [75].

application if the benefits of avoiding liquidation are distributed disproportionately among the company's creditors.[79] While differential treatment is a relevant factor for determining whether a creditor has been unfairly prejudiced, it is not necessarily sufficient for establishing unfair prejudice.[80] Differential treatment will for instance not be deemed as unfairly prejudicing creditor interests if the differences can be justified by the need to ensure business continuity.[81]

As mentioned, the adoption of a CVA does not involve separating creditors into different classes for the purposes of voting on the arrangement. It is therefore in principle possible to adopt CVAs that are unlikely to obtain support from all classes under the schemes of arrangement framework. However, the fact that a creditor would have been able to block a proposal for a given scheme is relevant for the determination of whether a CVA on the same terms unfairly prejudices the interests of that creditor. While such a finding is 'relevant and potentially important', this does not necessarily mean that the minority creditors have been unfairly prejudiced for the purposes of the fairness test applicable to CVAs.[82]

4.3.2. German Law

The commencement of German insolvency proceedings does not necessarily involve winding up the company. An alternative is a debt restructuring by way of an Insolvenzplan. Given that the adoption of an Insolvenzplan does not require the unanimous consent of all creditors affected by the plan, a restructuring could interfere with the rights of dissenting creditors.[83] Following the recent adoption of a new restructuring act, the *Gesetz über den Stabilisierungs- und Restrukturierungsrahmen für Unternehmen* (StaRUG), German law now also offers an alternative for businesses with financial difficulties to have sanctioned a restructuring plan notwithstanding that not all creditors whose claims are to be varied under the plan have consented thereto.

As discussed at 3.1.4, the adoption of an Insolvenzplan could require separating creditors into different voting classes. It is always necessary to separate secured creditors from unsecured creditors.[84] As a main rule, a requisite majority within each class must approve the proposed plan. However, InsO § 245 empowers the court presiding over the proceedings to 'cram down' the dissenting creditor classes

[79] *Mourant & Co Trustees Ltd v Sixty UK Ltd (in admin.)* [2010] EWHC 1890 (Ch), [2010] BCC 882 [81]–[82] and [85].

[80] *PRG Powerhouse* (n 74) [88].

[81] *Discovery (Northampton) Ltd & Ors v Debenhams Retail Ltd* [2019] EWHC 2441 (Ch), [2020] BCC 9 [110].

[82] *PRG Powerhouse* (n 74) [95].

[83] H Mordhorst, 'Verwertung von Kreditsicherheiten im Insolvenzverfahren über das Vermögen des Sicherungsgebers' in H-J Lwowski, G Fischer and M Gehrlein (eds), *Das Recht der Kreditsicherung*, 10th edn (Berlin, Erich Schmidt Verlag, 2018) para 87.

[84] InsO § 222(1).

if certain conditions are satisfied. The cram down power means that there are two routes for writing down a claim, despite a creditor's rejection of the restructuring proposal. First, one could rely on this power to force a plan upon a class of dissenting creditors. Secondly, a creditor could have a plan forced upon it by a requisite majority of creditors within its class.

We will first consider whether the cram down provision could interfere with the priority that secured creditors enjoy in the default course of a German insolvency proceedings. Among other conditions, it is not possible to cram down a dissenting class unless that class stands to receive a reasonable share of the benefits brought about by the plan.[85] Whether this is the case turns on whether certain conditions are satisfied. One of these conditions is that the plan does not retain any value for classes with lower priority than the dissenting class.[86] This effectively rules out a plan that interferes with the relative priority secured creditors enjoy vis-à-vis unsecured creditors in a liquidation.

A second scenario involving interference with secured claims is that of a requisite majority of secured creditors in a class approving a plan despite the dissent of other class creditors. Disagreement among creditors with similar rights over whether to consent to a restructuring could result from several reasons. Dissenting creditors do, however, benefit from some protection against majoritarian decisions, even when all classes have consented to the restructuring. An individual creditor can prevent the court's sanction of the plan if he can show that he will be worse off with the plan than without it.[87] The comparator is the hypothetical outcome of a liquidation pursuant to the default operation of the German insolvency proceeding involving the sale of the company's assets.[88] This means that an insolvency plan cannot, at least in principle, reduce the economic value of the secured creditors' claim below the economic value that those creditors would have received were the company instead subject to liquidation.

We now turn to analysing whether a German insolvency plan can deviate from InsO's default rules for loss sharing among general unsecured creditors. A first mechanism at play is the main rule that a proposed restructuring plan shall divide creditors into classes whenever their legal rights differ.[89] If their economic interests differ, there may be further division of unsecured creditors into different classes.

It is not an absolute requirement that all classes consent to the restructuring plan. Three conditions must be met to mandate court sanctioning of the plan in the absence of the consent of all classes.[90] As discussed, one such requirement is that the plan cannot leave any dissenting class worse off than a liquidation. Moreover, a majority of the classes must consent and creditors belonging to dissenting classes

[85] InsO § 245(1)(2).
[86] InsO § 245(2)(2).
[87] InsO § 251(1)(2).
[88] Mordhorst (n 83) para 95.
[89] InsO § 222.
[90] InsO § 245.

must receive a reasonable share of the economic surplus brought about by the plan. InsO § 245(2) defines when a dissenting class of creditors receives a reasonable share. Two conditions relate to the priority of the dissenting creditors vis-à-vis other unsecured creditors. First, no subordinated creditors can retain any value.[91] This means that all creditor classes consisting of general unsecured creditors must consent to plans that interfere with their rights and that do not fully write down the claims that rank with subordinated status in a liquidation. Secondly, the plan cannot leave any other general unsecured creditors better off than the dissenting creditors.[92] A restructuring plan that, in economic terms, provides for unequal treatment among general unsecured creditors will thus require the approval of all affected classes.

InsO § 245 does not protect individual dissenting creditors against insolvency plans approved by its class. In this scenario, however, the dissenting creditor can, by virtue of InsO § 251(1)(2), block the adoption of the plan if they can demonstrate that the plan is likely to leave them worse off than a liquidation. Conversely, the individual creditor does not have a right to receive a 'reasonable share' of the restructuring surplus. This means that individual creditors enjoy neither a right to absolute priority over subordinated creditors nor a right to receive equal treatment as all other creditors with the same ranking in a liquidation.

StaRUG sets out a restructuring regime available for businesses with financial difficulties. In terms of creditor priority, the StaRUG-regime builds on InsO's framework for the adoption of an Insolvenzplan but relaxes the requirements in certain respects.

A restructuring plan may generally vary both secured and unsecured claims. However, there are certain claims that cannot be varied without the consent of the creditors concerned, including the claims of employees.[93] StaRUG § 8 provides that the plan does not need to vary all other claims; the company may restrict the plan to certain claims provided that the selection of creditors whose claims are proposed varied follows appropriate criteria.

A plan shall divide creditors in different classes insofar as their rights differ.[94] Secured creditors, general unsecured creditors and subordinated creditors are not to be placed in the same class. It is possible to further divide creditors with the same priority in liquidation into separate classes insofar as their economic interests differ. As a main rule, the adoption of a plan necessitates that a requisite majority within each class vote in favour.[95]

An individual creditor voting against the plan may block the court sanctioning of the plan if they establish that the plan is likely to leave them worse off than they

[91] InsO § 245(2)(2).
[92] InsO § 245(2)(3).
[93] StaRUG § 4.
[94] StaRUG § 9(1).
[95] StaRUG § 25.

would otherwise be.[96] This presumably entails that an individual creditor whose claim is secured by assets of a value sufficient to ensure that the creditor upon enforcement will recover the claim in full does not have to accept a plan even if a requisite majority of other secured creditors in the same class vote in favour thereof.

StaRUG § 26 provides for the possibility of a cram down of dissenting classes. The conditions are prima facie the same as for a cram down in respect of an Insolvenzplan: First, a majority of the classes must have consented to the plan. Secondly, the plan cannot leave any dissenting class worse off than they would be in a scenario where the plan is not adopted. Thirdly, creditors belonging to dissenting classes must receive a reasonable share of the economic surplus brought about by the plan.

Like InsO § 245(2), StaRUG § 27 sets out the conditions for when a dissenting group is deemed to receive a reasonable share of the restructuring surplus. A difference between the two regimes concerns the requirement that the dissenting group of creditors cannot be worse off than creditors that rank with the same priority in liquidation. First, if a plan put forward under StaRUG leaves out the claims of certain creditors, as StaRUG § 8 may permit, a cram down is permissible notwithstanding that the outcome for a dissenting group comprising creditors with the same priority in liquidation as creditors exempt from the plan is worse than that of the exempt creditors. Secondly, StaRUG § 28 provides for an exemption for cases where differential treatment among creditors affected by the plan is justified by the economic difficulties the company is facing and other circumstances. The provision makes clear that such an exception is not deemed as justified if the dissenting class comprises creditors that have more than half of the total voting rights accruing to creditors with the same rank in liquidation.

As is the case under InsO, StaRUG does not permit using the cram down provision to force upon a dissenting class of general unsecured creditors a plan that varies their claims while leaving subordinated creditors with value.

4.3.3. Norwegian Law

Rekonstruksjonsloven, which currently sets out the Norwegian restructuring framework, does not offer the possibility of varying the claims of secured creditors or preferential creditors without the consent of each creditor concerned.[97] What therefore remains susceptible to a non-consensual restructuring is the claims of general and subordinated creditors.

A restructuring plan must receive court sanction to enter into force unless all affected creditors consent to the restructuring. Up until the recent reform of the

[96] StaRUG § 64.
[97] Rekonstruksjonsloven § 54.

Norwegian restructuring framework, courts were under an obligation to reject the sanctioning of restructurings that provided for differential treatment of unsecured creditors unless consented to by the creditors receiving a worse treatment than others.[98] Such a requirement is not a part of the current framework. However, the court may refuse to sanction the proposed restructuring if it finds that it is not reasonable and fair towards the creditors.[99] The preparatory works of rekonstruksjonsloven indicate that proposals that accord different treatment to different subsets of general unsecured creditors could be deemed to contravene this standard insofar as the differential treatment is not fair and reasonable.[100] While it is unclear whether the claims of certain creditors, such as critical suppliers, can be left out of a restructuring altogether, it is permissible to apply a lower haircut to their claims than other general unsecured debt as long as such differential treatment can be justified. Accordingly, dissenting creditors that would rank as general unsecured creditors in a liquidation do not enjoy absolute protection against restructurings that give other general unsecured creditors a more favourable treatment.

Following an application from a creditor, the court may also refuse to sanction a restructuring that is not in the common interests of the creditors. Rekonstruksjonsloven § 49 states that this condition could be satisfied if the recovery of the creditors is disproportionately low considering the company's ability to pay. If a liquidation is the most realistic alternative to the restructuring, the court is to compare the outcome for the creditors under the proposal with the likely outcome of a liquidation.[101] While the provision does not explicitly require the court to refuse sanction in cases where a liquidation would be better for the creditors, Norwegian courts are thus clearly authorised to refuse the sanctioning under such circumstances.

4.3.4. Conclusions

Our discussion shows that the rights of secured creditors enjoy strong protection under the restructuring frameworks examined. The English CVA framework and the Norwegian frameworks offer the strongest protection, as a restructuring cannot interfere with the rights of a secured creditor without its consent. Conversely, the non-consensual variation of secured claims can occur under the other English frameworks and those found in German law, though the protection remains strong in terms of priority vis-à-vis unsecured creditors: the sanctioning of a scheme of arrangement under English law will require the consent of a requisite majority of each separate class that consists of secured creditors. Accordingly, a company and

[98] Konkursloven § 48.
[99] Rekonstruksjonsloven § 48.
[100] Justis- og beredskapsdepartementet, 'Midlertidig lov om rekonstruksjon for å avhjelpe økonomiske problemer som følge av utbrudd av covid-19 (rekonstruksjonsloven)' Prop. 75 L (2019–2020) 73.
[101] Prop. 75 L (2019–2020) 74.

its unsecured creditors cannot force a restructuring upon the company's secured creditors. A minority of a class of secured creditors also enjoys some protection against a requisite majority of the same class that votes in favour of a restructuring for reasons other than maximising their return *qua* secured creditors, as English courts will as part of their consideration of whether to sanction a scheme consider whether an honest and reasonable person could approve that scheme. While it is now possible to cram down dissenting creditor classes under Part 26A of the Companies Act 2006, this requires that the restructuring will not leave these creditors worse off than they would be in the event of the scenario most likely to occur if the restructuring is not sanctioned.[102] This, in turn, means that a class composed of creditors whose claims are secured by assets of a value sufficient to ensure that they recover in full in 'the relevant alternative', enjoy protection against a cram down. The adoption of a German insolvency plan pursuant to InsO or a restructuring plan pursuant to StaRUG also involves the separation of creditors into classes. As a main rule, the adoption of a plan necessitates the consent of a requisite majority of creditors within all classes. While this rule is not absolute, the adoption of a restructuring without the consent of the majority within each class of fully secured creditors can only occur if the plan involves the full write-down of all unsecured claims.

Turning to general unsecured creditors, the protection of their priority is somewhat weaker. None of the restructuring frameworks analysed contain an absolute requirement for the equal treatment of all creditors that would rank as general unsecured creditors in liquidation. However, insofar as the restructuring framework requires class-based voting over the proposal, a class of general unsecured creditors that are asked to bear a higher burden than other such creditors may, as a main rule, block the restructuring by voting against it. Some restructuring frameworks contain exceptions to this rule by providing for cram-down powers to override the dissent of individual classes. The extent to which the conditions for applying such powers operate to protect the priority of general unsecured creditors vis-à-vis other such creditors, varies. In the framework set out in InsO, there is a requirement that no creditors with the same priority in liquidation as those of the dissenting class are better off.[103] Conversely, the frameworks set out in StaRUG and Part 26A of the Companies Act 2006 do not make a cram down conditional upon such a requirement being met. However, dissenting classes are not without protection, as StaRUG requires that differential treatment must be appropriate, and English courts have indicated that they may in the future refuse to use their jurisdiction to sanction a restructuring plan against the dissent of a class insofar as the plan discriminates 'arbitrarily or capriciously between different classes of unsecured creditors'.[104] The frameworks that do not contain class-based voting systems – the English law CVA framework and the Norwegian regime – protect the priority

[102] Companies Act 2006, s 901G.
[103] InsO § 245.
[104] *Re Virgin Active* (n 61) [265].

of individual general unsecured creditors vis-à-vis other such creditors through enabling dissenting creditors to challenge CVAs that unfairly prejudice their interests and giving the court the power to refuse to sanction restructuring plans that are not fair and reasonable to the creditors, respectively.

The priority of unsecured creditors vis-à-vis creditors that rank below them in liquidation proceedings differs between regimes. Again, insofar as approval from all affected classes is an absolute requirement in a class-based framework, which is the case for the adoption of a scheme of arrangement, a class of creditors may use their votes to block a restructuring that allows junior creditors to retain value. Where this is not an absolute requirement, other mechanisms could protect creditors. Both German frameworks explicitly make a cram down of a creditor class conditional upon no creditors with a lower priority retaining any value.[105] The other regimes that do not contain a similar absolute requirement could nonetheless offer protection through more general standards of fairness or propriety applied by courts when considering whether to sanction the proposed restructuring.

4.4. Understanding the Creditor Priority Regime of General Insolvency Law

4.4.1. Introduction

This chapter's point of departure was the *pari passu* principle: creditors should share rateably when a company is unable to honour all its debts. However, as the above sections have demonstrated, the sample jurisdictions deviate significantly from this principle in several respects.

In the following section we will discuss different arguments for deviating from a rule of equal treatment of creditors and how the laws of the sample jurisdictions conform to their implications. First, 4.4.2 and 4.4.3 will consider two distinct arguments for whether it should be possible for a company to grant security interest over its assets, thereby giving certain creditors priority over others. Thereafter, 4.4.4 will discuss the arguments regarding whether deviations from the *pari passu* principle among unsecured creditors is permissible.

4.4.2. Property-Oriented Arguments for the Priority of Secured Credit

One line of argument is that security interests are property rights. Since legal systems permit the transfer of property, the presumption is that security interest

[105] InsO § 245; StaRUG § 27.

should also be permissible. In the words of Harris and Mooney Jr, 'those who question secured transactions must attack the generally applicable treatment of party autonomy in property and contract law or must explain why secured transactions differ from other transactions that the law respects'.[106] Likewise, Goode has argued that '[t]o deny recognition of the secured creditor's real rights upon the debtor's insolvency would be to use the very event against which the security interest was designed to give protection as the ground for its destruction'.[107] For him, the prioritised recourse of secured creditors to the secured assets does not constitute an exception to the *pari passu* principle because secured assets 'do not belong to the company and thus do not fall to be distributed among creditors on any basis' (footnote omitted).[108]

Property-oriented justifications for the power to grant security interests have attracted criticism. Mokal is unconvinced that companies' power to grant security interests can be justified merely by reference to property rights, 'given that the extent of these rights is a matter of what is allowed by the law, and whether and to what extent the law should allow security interests to be created is precisely what stands in need of justification'.[109] Others argue that security interests interfere with the rights of the unsecured creditors who, everything else being equal, receive less than they would have in the absence of the security interest. For instance, Bebchuk and Fried reject Harris and Mooney's argument on the basis that

> freedom of contract arguments have force only with respect to arrangements that do not create direct externalities. When a contract directly affects only the parties to the arrangement, in most cases it is believed that the parties should be allowed to choose for themselves whatever is best for them. But when the contract directly impinges on the rights of third parties, there is no prima facie presumption of freedom of contract.[110]

Bebchuk and Fried more or less turn Harris and Mooney Jr's argument upside down: While Harris and Mooney Jr view restrictions on the effectiveness of consensual security interests as a restriction on the security grantor's property rights, Bebchuk and Fried view the effectiveness of security arrangements as interfering with an unsecured creditor's payment rights.

The sample jurisdictions generally permit that companies grant security interests over receivables and financial instruments insofar as these are transferable. This fits with the prescriptions of the property-oriented theories of security interests. However, the company may not always be able to give the secured creditor a

[106] SL Harris and CW Mooney Jr, 'A Property-Based Theory of Security Interests: Taking Debtors' Choices Seriously' (1994) 80 *Virginia Law Review* 2021, 2052. See ibid at 2053 for a similar formulation of their position.

[107] van Zwieten (n 1) para 2-29.

[108] ibid para 8-17.

[109] Mokal (n 1) 138.

[110] LA Bebchuk and JM Fried, 'The Uneasy Case for the Priority of Secured Claims in Bankruptcy' (1996) 105 *Yale Law Journal* 857, 933. See also Mokal (n 1) 137; E Warren, 'Making Policy with Imperfect Information: The Article 9 Full Priority Debates' (1997) 82 *Cornell Law Review* 1373, 1375.

prioritised recourse to the secured assets that is absolute in all regards. Most notably, English law gives preferential debts priority over recoveries from assets subject to a floating charge ahead of creditors secured by such charges, and also reserves a sum of the recoveries – 'the prescribed part' – for distribution among the general unsecured creditors. Accordingly, the law does not perfectly align with the normative prescription of a property-oriented justification.

4.4.3. Efficiency-Oriented Theories of Secured Credit

Most of the literature on whether companies should have the power to create security interests centres on whether this is efficient. The literature does not always explicitly articulate the efficiency criterion employed, but it seems reasonable that what the relevant authors have in mind is the Kaldor-Hicks criterion. The introduction of a rule is Kaldor-Hicks efficient if the gains brought about are larger than the losses.[111] Accordingly, the question is whether the benefits brought about by permitting security interests outweigh the associated costs.

While the use of security interests is pervasive, scholars have yet to reach consensus on whether – and, if so, exactly how – a regime that allows for security interests is more efficient than other criteria for loss allocation among creditors. According to an early formulation of the problem by Schwartz, economic theory fails to explain what companies can gain by issuing security interests if we assume that all creditors are able to react to a company's granting of security.[112] Essentially, the argument proceeds as follows: while it is correct that offering a security interest to a creditor lowers the riskiness of that creditor's loan and, accordingly, the interest rate it demands for lending the company money, this benefit is not the only effect brought about by granting security. By giving the secured creditor a larger share of the pie in the event of insolvency, the company reduces the share available to the other creditors. These creditors will respond by raising their demanded interest rate. The increase in the interest that the company must pay in respect of unsecured debts would cancel out the decrease in interest demanded by the secured creditor. The company therefore stands to gain nothing from granting security interests. If the granting of the security interest involves transaction costs, the net result would in fact leave the company worse off by granting a security interest.

Following Schwartz's formulation of what he subsequently termed 'the puzzle of secured debt',[113] several scholars have presented arguments that purport to show

[111] RA Posner, *Economic Analysis of Law*, 9th edn (New York, Wolters Kluwer Law & Business, 2014) 14; R Cooter and T Ulen, *Law & Economics*, 6th edn (Boston, Pearson Addison-Wesley, 2012) 42.

[112] A Schwartz, 'Security Interests and Bankruptcy Priorities: A Review of Current Theories' (1981) 10 *Journal of Legal Studies* 1, 7–8. More specifically, the assumptions are that 'creditors (i) can learn of and react to the existence of security; (ii) can calculate risks of default reasonably precisely; (iii) are risk-neutral; and (iv) have homogenous expectations respecting default probabilities'.

[113] A Schwartz, 'The Continuing Puzzle of Secured Debt' (1984) 37 *Vanderbilt Law Review* 1051.

why the grant of security interests is efficient. One strand of works challenges a premise implicit in Schwartz's argument, namely that the size of the 'pie' to be shared in the event of insolvency, and the probability of insolvency, is not affected by whether applicable law provides that companies may grant security interests.

One such argument is that the granting of security interests reduces the costs of *monitoring* the company. To unpack this argument, it is necessary to present the key premises that underlie it. First, that the persons managing companies act in the interests of the shareholders. Secondly, that creditors and shareholders have different preferences as regards the riskiness of the activities the company chooses to take on. This assumption stems from the fact that the economic rights of creditors and shareholders differ. The upside for the creditors is limited, as they will at best be paid the agreed principal and interest. Conversely, shareholders are protected by limited liability and reap the benefit of earnings after debts have been paid. If the company's directors run the business activities in the interest of the shareholders, this may result in choices that are suboptimal for the creditors. For instance, the company may sell the assets it uses for its current operations and reinvest the proceeds in risky projects.

The company may overcome this issue if it is able to credibly commit itself to not make choices that disadvantage the creditors. One option is for the company to assume a contractual obligation to not sell material assets without the consent of the lender. It is common in corporate finance practice that loan agreements contain covenants that restrict the business activities of the borrowing company and the extent to which it may leverage its business through debt financing.[114] However, the lenders may need to monitor whether the company in fact observes these restrictions. If, for instance, the company has undertaken to not sell an asset that is key to business it carries out when the loan is taken out, the lenders must periodically check whether that asset remains the property of the company. It has been argued that the granting of a security interest is a superior device for controlling such restrictions. The argument centres on the notion that security interests are property rights that restrict the company's power to dispose of the secured assets even outside of insolvency proceedings. More specifically, the security grantor generally cannot dispose of the security free of the security interest.[115] This gives lenders assurance that the company will not sell off key assets and reinvest the proceeds in more risky ventures. Furthermore, consider the enforcement of restrictions on the extent to which the company may finance itself by issuing debt. The existence of a security interest could effectively prevent the company from obtaining further loans to finance excessively risky investments,[116] thereby preventing the company from acting in breach of contractual restrictions on leverage. This is because the

[114] L Gullifer and J Payne, *Corporate Finance Law*, 3rd edn (Oxford, Hart Publishing, 2020) 204ff.

[115] This is not always the case under English, German and Norwegian law.

[116] GG Triantis, 'Secured Debt Under Conditions of Imperfect Information' (1992) 21 *Journal of Legal Studies* 225, 248; BE Adler and G Triantis, 'Debt Priority and Options in Bankruptcy: A Policy Intervention' (2017) 91 *American Bankruptcy Law Journal* 563, 567.

existence of a security interest makes the prospects of repayment less certain for prospective lenders. They must more carefully scrutinise the company's prospects, and this would reduce the company's access to new loans.[117]

One criticism of this argument takes issue with the premise that the net benefits of the 'self-enforcement' exceed creditor enforcement of contractual prohibitions.[118] Another criticism is that even if one accepts this premise, it does not necessarily follow that one creditor must be given priority over both existing and prospective creditors.[119] Take, for instance, the risk that the company will incur further debt financing in order to take on increased risk. An alternative solution to this problem is to subordinate the claim of a prospective lender to all existing debt, not just that of the secured creditors.[120]

What, then, are the policy implications of the monitoring theories? From the perspective of reducing overall monitoring costs, it should be possible to enter into security agreements over all kinds of assets, and security interests should have absolute priority over unsecured claims. As the analysis at 4.2.1 demonstrates, this is largely the case. However, the emphasis on security interests as 'self-enforcing' restrictions on the company's ability to sell off key assets is difficult to reconcile with the fact that it in many cases is possible for the security grantor and grantee to agree that the grantor is authorised to sell secured assets free and clear of the security interest if no default has occurred.

We now turn to a different argument for why it is efficient that companies can issue security interests with absolute priority, which we will term the debt overhang argument. In brief, the argument proceeds as follows. There are circumstances in which all of a company's existing creditors stand to benefit if the company receives additional credit to finance continued trading or new investments. In given circumstances, the possibility for granting a security interest to a prospective lender could be indispensable for the company's prospects for raising new debt financing. Accordingly, the power to grant security interests would benefit all creditors, at least in some cases.

As with the monitoring theories, it is necessary to take a step back and consider a more general problem of corporate finance as we unpack this argument. The debt overhang problem occurs when a company's existing financial commitments render it unable to finance its ongoing business or new investments, even though the business is profitable.[121] The reason is that a new lender will have to share pro rata with existing lenders should the company become insolvent. In other words, the company's existing debt causes it to miss out on debt funding.

[117] J Armour, 'The Law and Economics Debate about Secured Lending: Lessons for European Lawmaking' (2008) 5 *European Company and Financial Law Review* 3, 8.
[118] Bebchuk and Fried (n 110) 878–79.
[119] Warren (n 110) 1382 ff.
[120] ibid 1383.
[121] GG Triantis, 'Financial Slack Policy and the Laws of Secured Transactions' (2000) 29 *The Journal of Legal Studies* 35, 38. For an early study of the problem that a firm's capital structure may lead to suboptimal investment decisions, see SC Myers, 'Determinants of Corporate Borrowing' (1977) 5 *Journal of Financial Economics* 147.

How can secured credit help to solve this problem? Essentially, the power to grant a security interest equips the company with a device that gives the new lender priority over existing creditors.[122] This increases lenders' willingness to extend loans to the company. If the company uses the fresh funds to finance a project with a value that exceeds the financing costs, the granting of the security interest also operates to the benefit of the existing creditors.[123] Under such circumstances, it is likely that the investment will increase the recovery of the unsecured creditors.

The debt overhang argument implies that companies should be able to grant security interests with full priority for new debt.[124] This is in line with the main rule in English, German and Norwegian insolvency law. Given that the debt overhang argument centres on how security interests facilitate a company's access to new funds, the argument generally does not offer a justification for the effectiveness of security interests that a company grants to secure existing debt, however. The possibilities for avoiding security interests granted in respect of antecedent debts are thus compatible with the debt overhang argument.

We have thus far discussed different attempts at justifying the power to grant security interests on account of contributing to efficiency. Bebchuk and Fried's article *The Uneasy Case for the Priority of Secured Claims in Bankruptcy* is a well-known and thorough efficiency-oriented *critique* of the priority of security interests.[125] The source of Bebchuk and Fried's beef with giving absolute priority to secured creditors is that a company will have 'non-adjusting' creditors, that is, creditors that for some reason do not increase their demanded interest rate in response to a company's decision to grant a security interest to one or more individual creditors.[126] This could comprise involuntary creditors, such as tort claimants or tax authorities. Moreover, suppliers that deliver goods or services on credit are non-adjusting creditors insofar as their sale prices do not incorporate the credit risk involved in extending credit to a particular customer. Finally, even sophisticated lenders could be non-adjusting if they extend an unsecured loan with an interest rate that remains the same regardless of whether the borrowing company subsequently grants a security interest to another creditor.

What Bebchuk and Fried essentially argue is that the presence of non-adjusting creditors will cause companies to grant security interests even when this is not optimal from the perspectives of their creditors as a whole. In other words, their argument is that

> a borrower and a secured creditor may adopt a security interest that gives the two parties a larger slice of the pie at the expense of non adjusting creditors even though the security interest at the same time reduces the size of the total pie.[127]

[122] Triantis, 'Secured Debt' (n 116) 248–49; SL Schwarcz, 'The Easy Case for the Priority of Secured Claims in Bankruptcy' (1997) 47 *Duke Law Journal* 425, 441–45.
[123] Mokal (n 1) 184–85; Schwarcz (n 122) 472–74.
[124] Mokal (n 1) 182–84; Schwarcz (n 122) 485.
[125] For a critique of Bebchuk and Fried, see Mokal (n 1) 164–73.
[126] Bebchuk and Fried (n 110) 882–91.
[127] Bebchuk and Fried (n 110) 896.

Their reasoning proceeds as follows. By offering a prospective lender a security interest for its claim, the company can borrow from that creditor at a lower interest rate than what it would have to pay to borrow on an unsecured basis. Insofar as other creditors are non-adjusting creditors, these creditors cannot offset any increase in the riskiness of their claim by increasing their demanded interest rate. Accordingly, the company will choose to borrow against a security interest under such circumstances.

If the new lender could not lend against a security interest with absolute priority, that lender would take precautions that would benefit the creditors as a whole.[128] Among other things, it would require the company to undertake contractual commitments to abstain from actions adverse to the interests of its creditors. The creditor would also monitor and enforce the company's compliance with such commitments. Moreover, removing the option to grant security interests with absolute priority would reduce the borrowing opportunities of a company that takes excessive risks. This would be beneficial, as a company that is aware that its risk-taking today would affect its ability to attract debt financing tomorrow would abstain from excessive risk-taking.

Bebchuk and Fried do not go so far as to propose that security interests should be ineffective in insolvency proceedings. Instead, they advocate a 'fixed-fraction priority rule'.[129] Under this rule, '75% of a secured claim would be given full priority over unsecured claims, and the remaining 25% would become an unsecured claim'.[130] This rule resembles the 'prescribed part' of assets subject to a floating charge that English insolvency law reserves for distribution among unsecured creditors. However, one difference is that the formula that determines the prescribed part is somewhat more intricate than a fixed-fraction formula, and the contribution can be £800,000 at most.[131] Another difference is that Bebchuk and Fried's proposed rule would apply to all security interests, while the English rule only applies to floating security interests.

As mentioned, German law contains a rule that makes the insolvency estate entitled to a lump sum contribution from certain secured assets. This rule conceivably operates to the effect of reserving part of the value of the secured assets for the unsecured creditors. As we have noted, it is difficult to ascertain whether the rule in practice operates to this effect. In any event, Bebchuk and Fried's proposal goes much further than the current German rule. It is interesting to note that Bebchuk and Fried seem to have drawn inspiration from a rule proposal put forth by a government-appointed committee at an early stage of the law reform that culminated in the Insolvenzordnung.[132] The committee's proposal – which was

[128] ibid 896–903.
[129] ibid 909–11.
[130] ibid 909.
[131] Insolvency Act 1986 (Prescribed Part) Order 2003, art 3.
[132] Bebchuk and Fried (n 110) 909.

subsequently discarded – would have reserved 25 per cent of the value of certain secured assets for distribution among unsecured creditors.[133]

Norwegian law does not contain any rules that reserve parts of the value of the secured assets for the unsecured creditors. In connection with its work on the reform of the Norwegian legal framework for the taking of security interests (which resulted in the adoption of panteloven in 1980), the Ministry of Justice considered whether to introduce a rule that would reserve parts of the value of the secured assets for liquidation expenses and distribution among unsecured creditors.[134] However, the Ministry of Justice concluded that the likely benefits that such a rule would bring about for unsecured creditors were insufficient to justify such a radical reform of the priority of secured creditors.

4.4.4. Priority Among Unsecured Creditors

In this section, we analyse how different normative ideals for priority among unsecured creditors resonate with the current general insolvency law of the sample jurisdictions. A common argument for granting priority to certain unsecured creditors is that unsecured creditors exhibit different needs for protection. While some unsecured creditors are sophisticated debt investors who seek to profit from assuming risk, other unsecured creditors cannot realistically abstain from extending credit or demand interest payments that reflect the credit risks they undertake.[135] The latter category includes inter alia tort creditors and most employees. The implication of this view is that creditors that are involuntary in some sense should enjoy priority over other unsecured creditors.

The funds available for distribution among unsecured creditors will often be scarce and may not always be sufficient to cover debts owed involuntary creditors, even if they were to enjoy priority ahead of other unsecured creditors. This raises the question of whether the creditor hierarchy should prioritise the interests of some vulnerable creditors at the expense of others. Finch and Milman argue that employees 'are seldom able to spread default risks and so will suffer considerable hardship' were they to rank *pari passu* with other unsecured creditors.[136] The implication of this view seems to be that creditors that are both involuntary (in a wider sense) and poorly diversified ought to enjoy priority ahead of creditors that are involuntary but better able to withstand a loss due to their other sources of income.

There are several arguments against giving preferential status to certain unsecured creditors. One such argument is that it is impossible to identify all creditors

[133] HG Ganter, 'Vorbemerkungen vor §§ 49 bis 52' in H-P Kirchhof, R Stürner and H Eidenmüller (eds), *Münchener Kommentar zur Insolvenzordnung*, 4th edn (Munich, CH Beck, 2019) para 8.

[134] Justis- og politidepartementet, 'Om pantelov' Ot.prp. nr. 39 (1977–1978) 19–20.

[135] See also Finch and Milman (n 68) 518–19.

[136] ibid 519. See also Mokal (n 1) 119.

worthy of priority over the general mass of creditors and to rank their relative need for priority. Many creditors cannot bargain for a security interest to secure their claim and are therefore, in some sense, involuntary creditors. The reason for their status as unsecured creditors could stem from circumstances other than a consensual decision to extend credit (tort creditors) or because they lack the negotiation power to demand that their claim is secured (employees, small trade creditors).

A second argument against giving certain unsecured creditors preferential status is that there are alternative means for protecting vulnerable creditors. It is possible to insure their claims by establishing public funds or requiring companies to take out insurance or procure third-party guarantees to secure such claims.[137] Moreover, it is possible to introduce an exemption to the rule that a company's shareholders enjoy limited liability towards company creditors.[138] In either case, the vulnerable creditor receives full payment from a third party without an exemption to the *pari passu* principle being necessary.

How, then, does the positive law fit with the above arguments? It is easiest to conclude with respect to German law where rules preferring certain unsecured creditors are absent. The preparatory works of InsO justify this by reference to the impossibility of protecting everyone in need of protection against credit risk.[139] Moreover, the existence of an insurance scheme served as a justification for removing the employee preference found in InsO's predecessor.[140] It could be said that English and Norwegian law partly reflect a perceived need to protect vulnerable creditors. Both jurisdictions provide preferential status to the claims of employees, who constitute a creditor group viewed as unable to bargain for a security interest or additional wages to reflect their risk of not receiving owed wages should the company become insolvent. The so-called Cork Report – which was a key source of inspiration for the Insolvency Act 1986 – also drew attention to the existence of the insurance of employment claims when proposing the abolition of the preference of wage claims in English law.[141] As employee preference still exists in English insolvency law, the Cork Report's recommendation apparently failed to sway the UK Parliament.

As discussed at 4.2.3, certain tax claims enjoy priority in Norwegian law. Two committees appointed to reform Norwegian insolvency law have recommended that the preferential status of such claims should be repealed.[142] However, these

[137] See K Lilleholt, 'Kor mykje skal bankane sitje att med?' in *Forhandlingerne ved det 37. nordiske Juristmøde i Reykjavík 18.–20. August 2005* (2005) 233 and Mokal (n 1) 151–52 for this argument in respect of the conflict between secured creditors and vulnerable unsecured creditors.

[138] For an analysis of the desirability of unlimited shareholder liability for tort claims, see H Hansmann and R Kraakman, 'Towards Unlimited Shareholder Liability for Corporate Torts' (1991) 100 *The Yale Law Journal* 1879.

[139] Bundesregierung, 'Entwurf einer Insolvenzordnung' BT Drucksache 12/2443 (1992) 90.

[140] ibid.

[141] Insolvency Law and Practice: Report of the Review Committee (Cmnd 8558) paras 1428–1433.

[142] Konkurs- og akkordutvalget, 'Innstilling til lov om fordringshavernes prioritet i konkurs m.v. (prioritetsloven)' (1961) 26 and NOU 1993: 16, 'Etterkontroll av konkurslovgivningen m.v.' 119–20.

proposals have failed to result in reform. English law abolished the preferential status of claims for the payment of VAT and similar taxes through the adoption of the Enterprise Act 2002, which amended the Insolvency Act 1986,[143] but subsequently reintroduced such preferential status in 2020.

Apart from this development, the general trend in the sample jurisdictions is that preferential creditor treatment is on the decline. Through the adoption of InsO in 1994, the German legislator put an end to preferential status as such.[144] Norwegian legislative reform in the 1960s rolled back the preferential status of several claims.[145]

While the trend regarding priority among unsecured creditors in liquidation is one towards equal treatment of all such creditors, the opposite is the case for restructuring frameworks. As noted at 4.3, most restructuring frameworks now make possible debt restructuring that provides for differential treatment among creditors that would have the same priority in liquidation proceedings.

The underlying logic is as follows. Fully paying certain creditors, such as key employees and suppliers of goods and services critical for the company's business, could be indispensable for maintaining relationships that will allow the business to thrive following the restructuring.[146] Increasing the company's profitability, in turn, benefits impaired creditors as this improves the company's ability to repay their residual claims.

Moreover, the impaired creditors may have received shares in the company as part of the restructuring, and increased profitability improves the company's ability to distribute dividends to its shareholders. Differential treatment could in fact be to the advantage of impaired creditors, provided that the payments and shares they stand to receive following the restructuring are of a greater value than what they would likely receive in its absence. If this is the case, they have no reason to complain.

[143] For an overview of the debts that enjoyed preferential status prior to the amendment, see Keay, Boraine and Burdette (n 23) 175.

[144] In the aftermath of the financial crisis, the reintroduction of the preferential status for tax claims was discussed, see Paulus and Berberich (n 26) para 10.51.

[145] See Lov om rekkjefylgja for krav i konkurs o.a. (prioritetslova).

[146] S Paterson, 'Rethinking Corporate Bankruptcy in the Twenty-First Century' (2016) 36 *OJLS* 697, 708.

5

Creditor Priority in the Winding-Up of Banks

5.1. Introduction

While the resolution regime set out in BRRD undoubtedly attracts the most attention in the post-crisis discussion on bank insolvency regimes, BRRD actually envisages resolution as the exception rather than the rule for handling bank failures. At least formally, the main approach to bank insolvency is what BRRD terms 'normal insolvency proceedings' – the winding-up procedure that applies to banks in a Member State.

Whereas bank resolution is now subject to detailed harmonisation at EU level following the adoption of BRRD, normal insolvency proceedings are subject to a low degree of harmonisation. In other words, EU law does not contain a holistic framework for winding up banks in circumstances that do not require application of the resolution powers. In principle, Member States are at liberty to design the rules for creditor priority and other aspects of normal insolvency proceedings as they see fit. Certain EU law constraints do apply, however. A fragmented body of EU legislation requires Member States to protect certain creditors and contractual arrangements in whatever insolvency proceedings a Member State uses to wind up insolvent banks.

This chapter analyses the extent to which EU law requires Member States to adopt rules that cause the loss distribution in a bank winding up to deviate from that of their general insolvency laws. We will first at 5.2 discuss the rules that potentially require Member States to improve the position of secured creditors compared to what applies in general insolvency law. Thereafter, 5.3 goes on to consider the extent to which EU law requires Member States to give certain unsecured claims priority superior or inferior to the bank's general unsecured creditors. Creditor priority in the winding up of banks that are part of groups or have engaged in cross-border activities is then considered at 5.4.

5.2. Secured Claims

5.2.1. Introduction

Chapter four showed that companies generally exercise great influence over priority among their creditors. This results from the wide powers to grant security interests and that security interests generally remain effective in insolvency proceedings. However, chapter four also showed that some limitations apply. Secured creditors do not always enjoy absolute priority over unsecured creditors. In some instances, avoidance provisions may reverse the effects of otherwise valid security interests. For reasons that we will explore in subsequent chapters, EU (and EEA) directives have sought to render certain transactions into which banks frequently enter immune from such limits. This section examines how the transposition of these legal acts caused Germany, Norway and the UK (when it was an EU member) to introduce exceptions from generally applicable insolvency law provisions.

5.2.2. The Settlement Finality Directive and the Financial Collateral Directive

The EU adopted two directives around the turn of the millennium that require Member States to protect certain contractual arrangements typically employed by banks. The level of protection could potentially require exceptions from rules that apply in general insolvency law. The first of the two is the Settlement Finality Directive (SFD) of 1998, which seeks to insulate payments and settlement systems from the effects of a participant's insolvency.[1] The second is the Financial Collateral Directive (FCD) of 2002, which, among other things, protects secured financial market transactions against the vagaries of general insolvency law.[2]

The adoptions of SFD and FCD coincide with two developments in the EU. First, 1999 saw the launch of the Commission's Financial Services Action Plan.[3] This initiative was an answer to the European Council's call for the development of a framework for actions to improve the single market in financial services.[4] The Commission's plan placed both directives under the headline 'Containing systemic risk in securities settlement'.[5] This objective, in turn, formed part of the wider objective of achieving a single EU wholesale market.[6] We will return below to the role of security in reducing settlement risk. A second development of importance was the introduction of the euro. A significant number of Member States adopting a common currency created the potential for a more integrated European market

[1] Directive 98/26/EC of the European Parliament and of the Council on settlement finality in payment and securities settlement systems [1998] OJ L166/45 (the Settlement Finality Directive or SFD).

[2] Directive 2002/47/EC of the European Parliament and of the Council on financial collateral arrangements [2002] OJ L168/43. The directive's personal scope causes it to apply to contractual relationships far beyond those usually considered 'financial market transactions', see L Gullifer, 'What Should We Do about Financial Collateral?' (2012) 65 *Current Legal Problems* 377, 401–03.

[3] Commission, 'Implementing the framework for financial markets: action plan' COM (1999) 232 final.

[4] COM (1999) 232 final 1.

[5] COM (1999) 232 final 18–19.

[6] COM (1999) 232 final 17. 'Wholesale' is jargon for the sophisticated segment of financial market actors.

in repurchase agreements and other securities transactions. Moreover, the market operations of central banks had developed towards the taking of collateral, and there was thus a rationale to introduce legislation that would ensure that collateral granted to central banks enjoys protection from transaction avoidance rules and the like if the provider of collateral becomes subject to insolvency proceedings.[7]

With this background in mind, we now consider exactly how SFD and FCD require Member States to relax the limits to secured transactions commonly found in general insolvency law. We will first consider the requirements of SFD. Before embarking on that analysis, it is helpful to discuss the background for these requirements, namely the credit exposures that arise within settlement systems.

SFD aims to protect the operations of payment systems and securities settlement systems. As discussed at 2.1.4, banks are considered to provide a critical service by giving their clients access to payment systems. These systems allow people and companies to transact with one another, despite having deposit accounts with different banks. The ultimate result of a payment transaction is that the payer's bank account is debited, while the payee's bank account is correspondingly credited. Securities settlement systems, meanwhile, facilitate the settlement of trades in securities – that is, the process whereby securities and money change hands.

When a payee's bank credits the payee's account, it receives a corresponding sum from the payer's bank. This interbank payment takes place through dedicated systems for settling payments. The crediting of the payee's bank account does not necessarily occur simultaneously with its bank's receipt of funds from the payer's bank. This interval creates a credit risk for the payee's bank: If it does not receive the funds, it will have assumed an obligation without receiving any corresponding benefit.

Whether such a credit risk arises depends on the settlement system in question. Some systems are so-called real-time gross settlement systems. In these systems, individual payments are settled one by one.[8] If the settlement of a payment takes place within such a system, the payee does not assume a credit risk. Other settlement systems are net settlement systems. In these systems, funds are not immediately transferred. Instead, the approach is to offset all recorded transfers in a given period against one another.[9] Insofar as banks wish to give their clients access to transferred funds before settlement occurs, this approach gives rise to credit risk. A bank that is a net creditor in the system runs the risk of not receiving the funds owed to it by other participants. Securities settlement systems create a similar credit risk if there is a gap between the delivery of financial instruments and payment.

[7] SFD recital 10.

[8] T Kokkola (ed), *The Payment System: Payments, Securities and Derivatives, and the Role of the Eurosystem* (Frankfurt am Main, European Central Bank, 2010) 116.

[9] General insolvency law provisions could render such contractual netting provisions ineffective. SFD art 3 requires that a system's netting arrangements shall remain enforceable in insolvency proceedings.

One way of mitigating credit risk in settlement systems is for the rules of the settlement system to require participants to grant security for their potential payment obligations.[10] SFD operates to protect this risk-mitigation technique, as the directive's Article 9(1) states that security received by a participant or a system operator in connection with the system 'shall not be affected' by the insolvency of the security grantor and that '[s]uch collateral security may be realised for the satisfaction of [the secured claim]'. The provision also requires that national central banks and ECB shall enjoy a similar privilege in respect of the security that they receive in their functions as central banks.[11]

The wording of SFD Article 9(1) seems to indicate that the directive does not require Member States to remove restrictions on the creation of security interests. Accordingly, the provision does not require Member States to permit the granting of security interests to a greater degree than what follows from its general laws.

A different question is whether so-called perfection requirements are permissible. Both English and Norwegian law distinguish between the question of whether a security interest exists and whether it is enforceable in insolvency proceedings. The Companies Act 2006 established a framework for the registration of charges and certain other non-possessory security interests created by companies.[12] The failure to register such a security interest renders the security interest ineffective in insolvency proceedings.[13] In Norwegian law, the perfection of a security interest usually requires some form of exterior act – eg registration or notification – which differs between asset classes. While it is not necessary to observe perfection requirements to create security interests, the failure to do so renders the security interest ineffective in insolvency proceedings.

The wording of SFD Article 9(1) indicates that perfection requirements are not permissible: as long as a security interest has arisen prior to insolvency proceedings, that security interest shall remain enforceable as it is outside of the insolvency proceedings.[14] The counterargument would be that this gives rise to an arbitrary distinction. Jurisdictions that require the performance of some form of act – eg registration or notification – for the security interest to come into existence as such will be able to retain these requirements, while those that make an act a precondition for protection in insolvency will not. For this reason, it is submitted that Article 9(1) should not be taken to prohibit perfection requirements.

What interpretation underpinned the implementation of SFD in English and Norwegian law? It appears that English law does not contain a rule that exempts all security interests within the scope of SFD Article 9(1) from the registration requirements necessary to make the security interest effective in insolvency proceedings,

[10] See Kokkola (ed) (n 8) 116–17 for other risk mitigation techniques.

[11] SFD art 9(1); art 1(c).

[12] Companies Act 2006, pt 25.

[13] Companies Act 2006, s 859H(3). Section 859A(6) sets out certain exemptions to the registration requirement, none of which are relevant in the present context.

[14] See also J-P Deguée, 'The Winding Up Directive Finally Establish Uniform Private International Law for Banking Insolvency Proceedings' (2004) 15 *European Business Law Review* 99, 114.

although the Banking Act 2009, section 252 provides an exemption for charges in favour of central banks. Norwegian law does not contain a provision that exempts such security interests from the applicable perfection requirements. In the process of drafting legislation to implement SFD in Norwegian law, it was not discussed whether such requirements would contravene the requirements of Article 9(1).[15]

Turning to the question of priority, the wording of Article 9(1) suggests that the secured creditor shall have absolute priority over the secured assets.[16] In particular, the requirement that 'collateral security may be realised for the satisfaction of [the secured claim]' would seem to prohibit insolvency law interfering with the secured creditor's recourse to the value of the secured assets. As discussed at 4.2.1, English insolvency law reserves part of the value of assets secured by a floating charge for unsecured creditors. First, preferential creditors have priority over the secured creditor. By virtue of an exemption in the UK Settlement Finality Regulations, this rule does not apply if the secured claim is owed to a participant in a settlement system, a system operator or a central bank.[17] Secondly, the Insolvency Act 1986, section 176A generally reserves a 'prescribed part' of floating charge assets for the company's general unsecured creditors. The Settlement Finality Regulations do not provide for an equally explicit exemption from this provision, however.[18] German law exempts creditors secured by system-related security interests from contributing to the insolvency estate as potentially required by the operation of general insolvency law.[19]

Finally, we turn to the question of avoidance. Again, the wording of SFD Article 9(1) suggests that avoidance rules shall not apply. This interpretation seems to underpin how the directive was implemented in English and Norwegian law. In response to the adoption of SFD, English law exempts system-related security interests from the 'zero-hour rule' of the Insolvency Act 1986, section 127.[20] When read together with section 129(2), this rule provides that transactions completed immediately prior to the commencement of a compulsory winding up are void unless the court orders otherwise.[21] Generally, this rule bites on transactions made between: (i) the presentation of a petition for the commencement of compulsory liquidation, and (ii) the court's decision to commence such proceedings. Moreover, it follows from the Settlement Finality Regulations 1999 that 'the provision of collateral security' is not subject to other avoidance provisions that may conceivably apply: sections 238 (transactions at an undervalue), 239 (preferences) and 245 (late floating charges) of the Insolvency Act 1986.[22] This effectively means

[15] The discussion was confined to the applicability of the avoidance rules, see Finans- og tolldepartementet, 'Om lov om betalingssystemer m.v.' Ot.prp. nr. 96 (1998–1999) 45–46.

[16] Bundesregierung, 'Entwurf eines Gesetzes zur Änderung insolvenzrechtlicher und kreditwesenrechtlicher Vorschriften' (1999) BT Drucksache 14/1539 11.

[17] Financial Markets and Insolvency (Settlement Finality) Regulations 1999, SI 1999/2979, reg 14(6).

[18] Settlement Finality Regulations 1999, reg 14(5) and (6).

[19] InsO § 166(3).

[20] Settlement Finality Regulations 1999, reg 16.

[21] A voluntary winding up results from a resolution made by the company's shareholders, while a compulsory winding up results from the decision of the court.

[22] Settlement Finality Regulations 1999, regs 16 and 17.

that such security interests are not liable to be avoided on grounds of securing antecedent debts.

Norwegian law exempts security interests from avoidance under dekningsloven § 5-7.[23] This provision states that security interests granted after the date falling three months prior to the petition for the commencement of insolvency proceedings may be avoided insofar as either the security interest was granted for antecedent debts or the parties failed to perfect the security without undue delay.

The implementation of SFD in German law included no amendment to the avoidance rules in the Insolvenzordnung. Nor did the government's explanatory proposal for the implementation of SFD in German law address the compatibility of applying avoidance rules to security interests that fall within the scope of SFD Article 9(1).

Having explored SFD's requirements for the treatment of security interests in insolvency, we now turn to the Financial Collateral Directive (FCD). Adopted by the EU in 2002, FCD essentially seeks to protect certain secured transactions that were already prevalent in some jurisdictions, thereby laying the foundations for an EU-wide market for such transactions. The directive has subsequently been subject to revisions. In 2009, an amendment expanded the directive's scope to protecting security arrangements involving the grant of security interests over loan receivables as collateral for central bank funding to banks hit by the effects of the financial crisis. BRRD thereafter amended FCD to roll back some of the protections that FCD originally offered so that the enforcement of security interests would not interfere with successful resolution.[24] FCD's protection of the priority of security interests over 'financial collateral' remains unchanged, however.

FCD aims at protecting certain financial market transactions, including sale and repurchase agreements – or, in market parlance, 'repos'.[25] Essentially, a repo involves two steps (or 'legs'). The first is that a seller sells a security (eg a government bond) to a buyer for cash. The parties agree that the original buyer shall resell the security to the original seller at a future date for a predetermined price. Accordingly, the seller receives liquidity during the term of the repo.

The second step involves the original seller repurchasing the sold security for the agreed price. The difference between the original sale sum and the resale sum represents a financing cost for the original seller, while the difference between the resale sum and the original sale sum is income for the original buyer. The predetermined resale price means that the buyer does not generally assume the risk of movements in the price of the asset; the seller's obligation to repurchase at the predetermined price remains in force even if the value of the security deteriorates during the term of the repo. If the seller defaults on its obligation to repurchase the security, the buyer is not obliged to re-transfer the security and can therefore

[23] Lov om betalingssystemer § 4-4.
[24] BRRD art 118.
[25] FCD recital 3.

apply the security's economic value to any loss caused by the seller's default. These features result in repos being seen as an alternative to secured lending.[26] The terms of the Global Master Repurchase Agreement (GMRA) – which is a model agreement developed and published by two financial industry associations – further amplify this resemblance. For instance, the GMRA stipulates that the original buyer shall transfer to the original seller any returns accruing on the security – eg interest payments where the sold security is a bond – during the term of the repo.[27] Should either party default, the non-defaulting party has the right to terminate the transaction.[28] The obligations of the parties are, in turn, valued and set off against each other.[29]

Margin security arrangements constitute another transaction technique that benefit from FCD's protection.[30] Essentially, such contractual arrangements empower a party to a transaction to demand that its counterparty provides security upon the occurrence of a pre-defined contingency, such as a decrease in the counterparty's creditworthiness or when the first party's unsecured exposure exceeds a certain threshold. There are different reasons why parties enter into margin security arrangements instead of granting the security upfront. One reason could be that the secured obligation is fluctuating. This is often the case when the secured claim arises under a derivatives contract. Another reason is a party wishing to have the option to demand security if its counterparty's creditworthiness deteriorates. The benefit for the counterparty of not immediately providing security is that it then avoids tying up assets as security, which, insofar as the assets are liquid, means that the assets may be employed for other uses. This is particularly beneficial if the security grantor must use cash to meet any margin demands, as is common.

The provision of security under margin security arrangements usually takes the form of a title transfer. As noted, repo transactions also involve title transfer rather than the granting of a security interest. What explains this practice? One possible explanation is that parties can circumvent the formalities and restrictions attached to the use of security interests in English law.[31] Despite the economic similarities, English law recognises a title transfer as something distinct from a security interest.[32] Presently, using this legal form rather than a security interest allows the parties to avoid the need to register company charges, as well as restrictions on both the security grantee's enforcement by way of appropriation and its use of secured assets during the term of the security agreement.[33]

[26] G Yeowart et al, *Yeowart and Parsons on the Law of Financial Collateral* (Cheltenham, Edward Elgar, 2016) paras 18.01–18.03; ER Morrison, MJ Roe and CS Sontchi, 'Rolling back the Repo Safe Harbors' (2014) 69 *The Business Lawyer* 1015, 1020.

[27] Global Master Repurchase Agreement (2011 version) (GMRA) para 5(a).

[28] GMRA para 10.

[29] GMRA para 10(d).

[30] FCD recital 5, which refers to the provision of margin security as 'top-up collateral'.

[31] Yeowart et al (n 26) para 17.62.

[32] H Beale et al, *The Law of Security and Title-Based Financing*, 3rd edn (Oxford, Oxford University Press, 2018) para 7.70; M Haentjens (ed), *Financial Collateral: Law and Practice* (Oxford, Oxford University Press, 2020) para 7.16ff.

[33] Yeowart et al (n 26) para 17.62.

Against this background, we will now discuss FCD's requirements. We will examine the scope of the directive before discussing its operative provisions. Importantly, the directive applies only to 'financial collateral arrangements',[34] which it defines as either a 'title transfer collateral arrangement' or a 'security financial collateral arrangement'.[35] A title transfer collateral arrangement is 'an arrangement … under which a collateral provider transfers full ownership of, or full entitlement to, financial collateral to a collateral taker for the purpose of securing or otherwise covering the performance of relevant financial obligations'.[36] A security financial collateral arrangement is 'an arrangement under which a collateral provider provides financial collateral by way of security to or in favour of a collateral taker, and where the full or qualified ownership of, or full entitlement to, the financial collateral remains with the collateral provider when the security right is established'.[37] To qualify as a financial collateral arrangement, the secured assets must thus constitute 'financial collateral' and the secured claim must be a 'relevant financial obligation'. We will consider these two concepts in the following paragraphs.

'Financial collateral' comprises three defined categories of assets: financial instruments, cash and credit claims.[38] The directive defines cash as money credited to an account and similar claims for the repayment of money.[39] Financial instruments comprise inter alia shares and debt instruments that are negotiable on capital markets.[40] Credit claims are credit institutions' loan receivables.[41]

A 'relevant financial obligation' is an obligation that gives 'a right to cash settlement and/or delivery of financial instruments'.[42] A 'right to cash settlement' comprises any claim for the payment of money.[43] This means that most bank liabilities constitute relevant financial obligations.

FCD's operational provisions kick in only when the financial collateral 'has been provided and if that provision can be evidenced in writing'. Article 2(2) states that

> [r]eferences … to financial collateral being 'provided', or to the 'provision' of financial collateral, are to the financial collateral being delivered, transferred, held, registered or otherwise designated so as to be in the possession or under the control of the collateral taker or of a person acting on the collateral taker's behalf.

[34] In addition, the directive contains a private international law rule for issues pertaining to 'book entry securities collateral', see FCD art 9.

[35] FCD art 2(1)(a).

[36] FCD art 2(1)(b).

[37] FCD art 2(1)(c).

[38] FCD art 1(4)(a).

[39] FCD art 2(1)(d).

[40] See FCD art 2(1)(e) for the full definition.

[41] FCD art 2(1)(o). Member States may choose to not give special protection to security arrangements under which the secured asset is a claim against a consumer or a micro- or small enterprise, see FCD art 1(4)(c). This discretion does not extend to security arrangements under which either the security grantor or security grantee is a central bank or among the supranational institutions listed in FCD art 1(2)(b).

[42] FCD art 2(1)(f).

[43] Case C-156/15 *Private Equity Insurance Group* ECLI:EU:C:2016:851, para 31.

Any right for the collateral provider to substitute the security or to withdraw excess security does not prejudice the security having been provided for the purposes of the Directive. The same applies to a right for the security grantor to continue to collect payments on credit claims until further notice from the security grantee.[44]

There is some uncertainty about exactly what the 'provision' of financial collateral involves. Some clarification was given by the ECJ's judgment in *Private Equity Insurance Group*. First, the Court stated that the criteria of 'possession' or 'control' are autonomous concepts of EU law.[45] Secondly, the judgment clarified that the security grantee acquires 'possession or control' of monies credited to a bank account if the collateral provider is prevented from disposing of these sums.[46] The merits leave unanswered the question of when a collateral provider is prevented from disposing of the balance on the account. It is clear that this will not be the case unless the security grantor undertakes not to dispose of the funds. It is unclear whether it is also necessary that the deposit-taking bank must be under an obligation to refuse to honour attempts by the security grantor to draw on the account.[47]

Among the three national jurisdictions that this book explores, the question of what entails 'possession or control' is most pressing in English law. This is because the statutory instrument that implemented FCD in English law only protects a 'security financial collateral arrangement' if the financial collateral is 'delivered, transferred, held, registered or otherwise designated *so as to be in the possession or under the control of the collateral-taker or a person acting on its behalf* (emphasis added).[48] Conversely, the definition of a financial collateral arrangement in German law does not make explicit reference to 'provision', as that term is defined by FCD.[49] Meanwhile, the applicability of the Norwegian implementing legislation is contingent upon the security interest having been perfected, ie having *rettsvern*. Rettsvern does not necessarily imply 'possession or control'. While it is not problematic to make rettsvern a sufficient ground for protection under the Directive,[50] it is more problematic to make the observance of this requirement a necessity for this protection. We will revisit this issue below.

We now turn to the personal scope of FCD. At the outset, the directive only protects financial collateral arrangements insofar as one of the parties is among the institutions listed in Article 1(2)(a)–(d) and the other person is not a natural person. In brief, the list includes public authorities, central banks, certain

[44] FCD art 2(2).

[45] Case C-156/15 *Private Equity Insurance Group* (n 43) para 39.

[46] ibid para 44.

[47] L Gullifer (ed), *Goode and Gullifer on Legal Problems of Credit and Security*, 6th edn (London, Sweet & Maxwell, 2017) para 6-44. Others seem to argue that such 'practical control' is necessary in addition to the 'legal control' that the security grantee has when the security grantor undertakes not to dispose over the account, see Beale et al (n 32) para 3.56.

[48] Financial Collateral Arrangements (No. 2) Regulations 2003, SI 2003/3226 (FCAR), reg 3(1).

[49] KWG § 1(17).

[50] *cf* K van Zwieten, *Goode on Principles of Corporate Insolvency Law*, 5th edn (London, Sweet & Maxwell, 2018) para 1-70.

supranational entities, financial institutions and central counterparties, settlement agents and clearing houses. Member States may further limit the scope of the protection offered by the directive to financial collateral arrangements to which both parties are among the institutions listed in Article 1(2)(a)–(d). Neither the UK nor Norway made use of this opt-out possibility. The German implementing legislation makes use of the possibility to some extent. If the security grantor does not fall within the scope of Article 1(2)(a)–(d), the arrangement only constitutes a financial collateral arrangement insofar as the secured claim is related to the purchase or sale of financial instruments, repos, securities lending or a loan for the acquisition of financial instruments.[51]

Having discussed the FCD's scope, we turn to the protection that the directive requires Member States to afford to financial collateral arrangements. Following the structure of the discussion at 4.2 on the priority of security interests in general insolvency law, we will discuss what the directive requires in terms of the national rules governing: (i) the available forms of consensual security interests, (ii) the priority of secured claims in insolvency proceedings, and (iii) the avoidance of security interests.

FCD requires that Member States shall recognise title transfer collateral arrangements. The directive does not spell out an equivalent requirement regarding security interests over financial collateral. Rather, it seems to build on the premise that it is possible under the laws of the Member States to grant security interests over such assets. One could argue that FCD Article 4, in providing that security financial collateral arrangements shall be enforceable in accordance with their terms, also implies that it must be possible to provide security interests that qualify as security financial collateral arrangements. This is a somewhat moot point, as English, German and Norwegian law all recognise security interests over the assets that constitute financial collateral under the Directive.[52]

As discussed, the parties to a security arrangement must ensure that collateral is 'provided' and that the provision is evidenced in writing to benefit from the protection that the Directive offers. Once the steps necessary to 'provide' collateral have been observed, no other actions shall be necessary to ensure the arrangement becoming effective.[53] Member States must do away with any rules that make the 'creation, validity, perfection, enforceability or admissibility in evidence of a financial collateral arrangement or the provision of financial collateral under a financial collateral arrangement … dependent on the performance of any formal act'.[54]

[51] KWG § 1(17).

[52] See SS Ellingsæter, 'Creditor Priority and Financial Stability: A study of the emergence and rationales of the creditor hierarchy in EU and EEA bank insolvency law' (PhD thesis, University of Oslo, 2020) ch 10.

[53] FCD art 3(1).

[54] FCD art 3(1).

Legal systems sometimes make the creation of security interests conditional upon the observance of certain steps. This raises the question of whether such requirements constitute the formalities that FCD Article 3(1) prohibits. FCD's recital provides that 'acts required … as conditions for transferring or creating a security interest on financial instruments, other than book entry securities … should not be considered as formal acts'.[55] Following an amendment in 2009, FCD Article 3(1) now also states that the provision of a credit claim as financial collateral cannot be conditional upon registration or notification of the debtor of the claim.

Under German law, the creation of a security interest is sometimes conditional upon the making of certain formal acts. This applies to a Pfandrecht over a claim.[56] German law does not provide an exemption for this requirement insofar as the underlying claim is a credit claim and the arrangement otherwise constitutes a financial collateral arrangement. This would seem to contravene Article 3(1).

To some extent, it is necessary in English and Norwegian law to observe certain requirements in order to create a security interest and/or to render a security arrangement effective in insolvency proceedings against the security grantor. In the following paragraphs, we will consider the extent to which such requirements are incompatible with FCD Article 3(1) and whether the jurisdictions have relaxed such requirements to comply with this provision.

As discussed above, it is necessary to register security interests granted by English companies to ensure their effectiveness should the security grantor become subject to insolvency proceedings. Such requirements are likely incompatible with FCD Article 3(1). By virtue of the FCAR reg 4(4), the registration requirement does not apply to security interests that form part of a financial collateral arrangement.

Lov om finansiell sikkerhetsstillelse (fsl.), which seeks to implement FCD in Norwegian law, makes the application of the special provisions contained therein conditional upon the parties observing the requirements necessary in order for the rettsvern of the security interest or title transfer (as applicable). Fsl. defines financial collateral as being 'provided' when the security interest achieves rettsvern.[57] Accordingly, the operative provisions of fsl. apply only insofar as the security interest achieves rettsvern. Achieving rettsvern for a security interest requires the observance of the applicable perfection act. The perfection act is notification to the debtor of the claim where the secured asset is a monetary claim,[58] and registration

[55] FCD recital 10. The cited text indicates that similar acts should not apply to the creation of financial collateral arrangements over 'book entry securities', that is, 'financial instruments, title to which is evidenced by entries in a register or account maintained by or on behalf of an intermediary' (FCD art 2(1)(g)).

[56] Conversely, this is not necessary where the security arrangement takes the form of a security transfer (*Sicherungsabtretung*).

[57] fsl. § 2(2).

[58] Panteloven § 4-5.

in the applicable central securities depository where the secured asset is a bond or a share issued by a public company.[59]

This requirement likely contravenes FCD Article 3(1). The failure to achieve rettsvern results in the security interest being ineffective in insolvency proceedings and limits the enforceability of the security interest in certain cases. This would seem to constitute a requirement that makes the 'perfection [and] enforceability … of … the provision of financial collateral under a financial collateral arrangement … dependent on the performance of any formal act', which Article 3(1) prohibits.

We now turn to FCD's implications for the priority of secured creditors vis-à-vis unsecured creditors. The directive requires that 'a financial collateral arrangement can take effect in accordance with its terms notwithstanding the commencement or continuation of winding-up proceedings or reorganisation measures in respect of the collateral provider or the collateral taker'.[60] A security agreement will often state that the security grantee shall have the right to sell the collateral and apply the sale proceeds towards the secured claim. A statutory provision that reserves parts of the proceeds of the secured assets for insolvency expenses or the claims of other creditors would prevent the operation of such a contractual enforcement clause. Accordingly, such statutory provisions would negate the collateral arrangement 'tak[ing] effect in accordance with its terms' and thus breach the requirement of FCD Article 3(1).

The legislative instruments that implemented FCD in English, German and Norwegian law all reflect this interpretation. In English law, the relevant provision is FCAR Regulation 10, which provides that the Insolvency Act 1986, sections 175, 176ZA and 176A do not apply to financial collateral arrangements. Sections 175 and 176A provide that floating charge creditors have priority behind preferential debts and the 'prescribed part' that the latter provision reserves for the unsecured creditors. Section 176ZA, meanwhile, subordinates floating charge claims to the expenses of liquidations and administrations. In German law, InsO § 166(3)(3) provides that financial collateral arrangements enjoy an exemption from the regime discussed at 4.2.1, where the insolvency estate potentially receives a contribution from creditors secured by a security transfer of monetary claims.

As discussed at 4.2.1, secured creditors enjoy absolute priority over unsecured creditors in Norwegian insolvency proceedings. However, the exemption of financial collateral arrangements from panteloven § 6-4, which in certain circumstances gives the insolvency estate recourse to secured assets with priority ahead of the secured creditor(s) in order to cover expenses, indicates that the Norwegian legislature has also taken the view that FCD Article 4 requires absolute priority for claims secured under a financial collateral arrangement.

[59] Panteloven § 4-1.
[60] FCD art 4(5).

In summary, FCD prompted German, Norwegian and UK lawmakers to remove any impediments to a secured creditor under a financial collateral arrangement achieving priority ahead of all other claims.

We now turn to FCD's implications for transaction avoidance. FCD Article 8 sets out certain limits for transaction avoidance rules. First, 8(1)(b) prohibits so-called 'zero-hour rules': Member States shall ensure that financial collateral arrangements are not susceptible to avoidance solely by virtue of the security being provided in a prescribed period prior to the insolvency proceedings. It appears that among the jurisdictions analysed in chapter four only English law contains a general insolvency law rule that qualifies as the kind of 'zero-hour rule' that FCD prohibits. Section 127 of the Insolvency Act 1986 renders void transactions made immediately prior to the court ordering a company's compulsory winding up.[61] By virtue of FCAR, this provision does not apply to financial collateral arrangements.[62]

FCD Article 8(3) establishes limits for the avoidance of security provided in accordance with the margin security arrangements discussed above. Among other things, the provision states that '[w]here a financial collateral arrangement contains … an obligation to provide financial collateral or additional financial collateral in order to take account of changes in the value of the financial collateral or the amount of the relevant financial obligations', the security grantor's performance of its obligation to provide security shall not be subject to avoidance 'on the sole basis' that the security grantor incurred the secured claim prior to the provision of the financial collateral.

This provision protects some, but not all, margin security arrangements. The protection extends only to cases where the obligation to provide security arises due to 'changes in the value of the financial collateral or the relevant financial obligations'. Conversely, the provision does not protect security that the security grantor became obligated to provide because of a reduction in its creditworthiness (eg its credit rating being downgraded).[63] Moreover, margin security arrangements only enjoy protection from avoidance provisions that make the provision of security avoidable on the basis of there being an interval between: (i) the creation of the secured claim, and (ii) the provision of the security interest.

Among the transaction avoidance provisions of English law, section 245 of the Insolvency Act 1986 is the only provision that could contravene FCD Article 8(3). Section 245 renders void in liquidation proceedings a floating charge insofar as it is granted without the security grantor receiving contemporaneous consideration in the form of new money, goods or services. FCAR Regulation 10(5) provides that section 245 shall not apply to 'any charge created or otherwise arising under a security financial collateral arrangement'.

[61] Insolvency Act 1986, s 127 read together with s 129(2). This rule is not absolute, as the court may order otherwise.

[62] FCAR reg 10(1).

[63] K Rosén, *Lov om finansiell sikkerhetsstillelse* (Oslo, Gyldendal, 2011) 61.

No other English law avoidance provisions empower the insolvency professional to avoid security interests solely on the basis that the secured claim arose prior to the security interest. The avoidance of security interests under section 239 requires that the security grantor granted the security interest with a desire to prefer the security grantee. Moreover, section 238, if at all applicable, requires an element of undervalue. Avoidance under these provisions will therefore not occur 'on the sole basis' that the security grantor incurred the secured claim prior to the provision of the financial collateral As a result, FCD did not require the UK to amend either section 238 or 239.[64]

The German implementation of FCD Article 8(3) takes the form of an exemption from InsO § 130, which generally renders avoidable the provision of security that a company unable to pay its debts grants within a three-month suspect period insofar as the security grantee is aware of the company's inability to pay. The exemption provides that this rule shall not apply insofar as the company satisfies an obligation to grant financial collateral and the obligation results from fluctuations in either the value of existing financial collateral or the secured claim.[65] Accordingly, the amendment of InsO § 130 is limited to what FCD Article 8(3) requires.

Among other things, InsO § 131 empowers the insolvency professional to avoid any incongruent provision of a security interest made either within a month prior to the request for the opening of insolvency proceedings being made or after this. It is not a condition that the company is insolvent when the security interest is granted. It seems that the provision of security under a margin security arrangement does not constitute such incongruent performance that the provision aims at as long as the security grantor does not have any discretion as to how it is to satisfy its contractual obligation to provide security.[66] Accordingly, if the agreement gives rise to an obligation to provide a specific quantity of a specific issue of German government bonds, the security grantor's performance of this obligation would seemingly qualify as congruent.

However, it is not uncommon to encounter margin security arrangements containing a list of assets that the security grantor may use to satisfy a demand for margin security. For instance, the arrangement could give the security grantor the choice between different currencies or government bonds for satisfying its obligation to provide security. In other words, the security grantor could enjoy some discretion in deciding how to satisfy its obligation. It is clear that too much discretion on the part of the security grantor could render the provision of security incongruent.[67] It therefore appears possible that security granted under some margin security arrangements could constitute incongruent performance. This, in turn, would be sufficient to render the security susceptible to avoidance

[64] Yeowart et al (n 26) para 5.28.

[65] InsO § 130(1).

[66] H Schoppmeyer, 'Anfechtung von Kreditsicherheiten' in HJ Lwowski, G Fischer and M Gehrlein (eds), *Das Recht der Kreditsicherung*, 10th edn (Berlin, Erich Schmidt Verlag, 2018) para 15.

[67] ibid.

if granted within one month prior to the request for the opening of insolvency proceedings.

The German implementation of FCD did not include exemptions to InsO § 131. How does the absence of an exception conform to FCD Article 8(3)? The preparatory works to the implementing legislation did not address this question in very much detail. A possible defence of the German position is that avoidance of margin security under InsO § 131 is not caused only by the fact that the security secures an existing debt obligation. Rather, what may render the grant of security avoidable is that the security grantor's obligation to provide security is too open-ended. In other words, the argument would be that InsO § 131 does not make the provision of margin security susceptible to avoidance 'on the sole basis' that the security grantor incurred the secured claim prior to the date of the provision of the financial collateral, and hence does not contravene FCD Article 8(3).

The avoidance rules set out in dekningsloven § 5-7 could render margin security avoidable. Fsl. § 5 represents the Norwegian law implementation of FCD Article 8(3) and states that financial collateral cannot be avoided solely on the basis that the security was *provided* for an existing financial obligation. As discussed above, fsl. considers security as 'provided' when the security interest obtains *rettsvern*. Accordingly, the provision operates to negate any avoidance provision that otherwise would render a security interest avoidable due to the security having achieved rettsvern after the secured claim arose.

Security granted in a three-month suspect period is avoidable under dekningsloven § 5-7(1)(b) if the security interest did not achieve rettsvern without undue delay following the incurrence of the secured claim. Fsl. § 5 thus operates to make this provision inapplicable to financial collateral arrangements.

Dekningsloven § 5-7(1)(a) empowers the insolvency professional to avoid a security interest that: (i) the company granted within three months before the request for the opening of insolvency provisions, and (ii) secures debt that the security grantor incurred prior to the time when the parties agreed upon the security interest. Some uncertainty attaches to when the provision deems the parties to have 'agreed upon the security interest'. The most convincing interpretation is that the provision refers to the point in time when the parties entered into the security agreement.[68] Under this interpretation, the parties first 'agree upon the security interest' when the security grantor satisfies its obligation to provide security under the margin security arrangement. This often occurs after the security grantor incurred the secured claim. However, the provision is not crystal-clear. The working group appointed to draft legislation to implement FCD in Norwegian law interpreted the provision so that it refers to the potentially earlier point in time when the security grantor assumed a contractual obligation to grant security upon the occurrence of some future event.[69] The consequence of this interpretation is that

[68] MH Andenæs, *Konkurs* (Oslo, MH Andenæs, 2009) 340; K Lilleholt, 'Finansiell trygdgjeving' in K Høivik et al (eds) *Håkonarmål 2006* (Bergen, 2006) 30.

[69] Finansdepartementet, 'Om lov om finansiell sikkerhetsstillelse' Ot.prp. nr. 22 (2003–2004) 57.

margin security is not susceptible to avoidance under dekningsloven § 5-7(1)(a) as long as the margin security arrangement was in place prior to the security grantor incurring the subsequently secured liabilities. This, in turn, would mean that § 5-7(1)(a) could not conflict with FCD Article 8(3). Based on this understanding, the proposal for what eventually became fsl. § 5 did not exempt financial collateral arrangements from § 5-7(1)(a).

If the correct interpretation is that the parties 'agree upon the security interest' when the security grantor satisfies its obligation to provide security under the margin security arrangement, what makes a security interest avoidable under dekningsloven § 5-7(1)(a) is that the secured claim arose prior to the security interest. Conversely, a security interest's susceptibility to avoidance does not turn on when it achieves rettsvern and thereby is 'provided' for the purposes of fsl. The application of § 5-7(1)(a) would therefore not conflict with fsl. § 5. The avoidance of margin security under § 5-7(1)(a) would, in turn, involve a breach of the requirement in FCD Article 8(3) not to render margin security arrangements susceptible to avoidance 'on the sole basis' that the security grantor incurred the secured claim prior to the provision of the financial collateral.

In this section, we have analysed the requirements under SFD and FCD and the implementation of these directives in the laws of England, Germany and Norway. The adoption of SFD represented a first step at the EU level towards insulating transactions between banks and other financial market participants from the effects of generally applicable insolvency rules, as it protects security granted in accordance with the rules of payment and settlement systems. FCD extended this approach further to protect financial collateral arrangements more generally. It is not always entirely clear what the directives require of national bank insolvency law. The differences in the changes made to national laws in response to the directives serve to indicate that the Member States may interpret them differently.

5.2.3. Covered Bonds

The EU recently adopted the Covered Bonds Directive (CBD), which harmonises national regimes for the issuance by credit institutions of covered bonds.[70] As was the case for SFD and FCD, the Directive forms part of a wider programme for the integration of EU financial markets as it is one of several measures composing the Commission's efforts to create a Capital Markets Union.[71] The main imperative of the Capital Markets Union initiative is to strengthen equity and debt capital markets to make European businesses less reliant on bank funding. It is somewhat ironic that the initiative includes an effort to harmonise covered

[70] Directive (EU) 2019/2162 of the European Parliament and of the Council of 27 November 2019 on the issue of covered bonds and covered bond public supervision and amending Directives 2009/65/EC and 2014/59/EU [2019] OJ L328/29.

[71] COM (2015) 468 final.

bonds, as an important rationale underpinning covered bonds frameworks is to stimulate bank lending. However, given the Commission's view that a harmonised regime will lower the financing costs of banks,[72] a plausible underlying rationale is that harmonisation is conducive to the initiative's overarching objective of strengthening Europe's economy and stimulating investment to create jobs.[73]

The issuance of covered bonds is reserved for credit institutions.[74] Pursuant to the definition of a 'covered bond' in CBD Article 3(1), a defining feature of such bonds is that the issuer's payment obligation 'is secured by cover assets to which covered bond investors have direct recourse as preferred creditors'. 'Cover assets' are assets that are included in a 'cover pool', which, in turn, is 'a clearly defined set of assets securing the payment obligations attached to covered bonds that are segregated from other assets held by the credit institution issuing the covered bonds'. Accordingly, covered bonds shall have priority ahead of other creditors to the assets that are designated as part of the cover pool.

A second defining feature of covered bonds under CBD is that they are issued in accordance with national frameworks that implement the directive's requirements. This includes obligations on issuing institutions to ensure that the cover assets are always sufficient to cover the payment obligations under the bonds.[75] Moreover, the cover assets must satisfy qualitative criteria that restrict eligibility in the cover pool to low-risk assets.[76]

CBD requires that Member States shall ensure that claims under the covered bonds have priority over the assets of the cover pool if the issuer becomes subject to insolvency proceedings or is resolved.[77] This means that the credit institution's insolvency estate shall not have recourse to the cover pool unless the bonds have been paid in full.[78]

The above discussion shows that the issuance of covered bonds essentially involves reserving a pool of assets for satisfying the bonds. The assets that compose the pool are not necessarily the same during the term of the outstanding bonds. As mortgage loans and other cover assets are repaid, the proceeds are often being reinvested in new cover assets.

While the harmonisation of covered bonds issuance at EU level is a novel development, many jurisdictions, including the sample jurisdictions, already had in place legislative frameworks that facilitate the issuance of such bonds. In the following, we will discuss the extent to which these frameworks enable banks to offer bond investors better priority than what is possible in the absence of special legislation.

[72] COM (2015) 468 final 22.
[73] COM (2015) 468 final 3.
[74] CBD art 2.
[75] CBD art 15(1).
[76] CBD art 6.
[77] CBD art 4(1)(b).
[78] CBD art 12(1)(c).

The Regulated Covered Bonds Regulations (RCBR) lay out the English law framework for regulated covered bonds. As the deadline for the implementation of CBD fell after the UK's exit from the EU, these regulations have not been amended to satisfy the requirements of this Directive. The legal structure of UK covered bonds is as follows.[79] First, a bank issues the bonds and on-lends the proceeds to a special purpose vehicle. Secondly, the special purpose vehicle (SPV) uses the loan to purchase an 'asset pool' from the issuing bank. Thirdly, the SPV guarantees the issuing bank's payment of the sums due under the bond and grants a security interest over the asset pool that secures the claim against the issuer. By virtue of the RCBR, the covered bondholders have absolute priority ahead of the SPV's other creditors, as the regulation provides for an exemption from sections 175 and 176A of the Insolvency Act 1986 in liquidation proceedings against an SPV set up for the purpose of issuing covered bonds.[80]

The fundamental structure of the UK covered bonds arrangements predates the adoption of RCBR.[81] One likely benefit of the arrangement is that the bondholders' security interest over the asset pool has priority ahead of the bank's unsecured creditors, regardless of whether the security interest is floating, as sections 175 and 176A of the Insolvency Act 1986 only apply to security interests over the insolvent company's assets, not those of its subsidiaries. This outcome, however, is dictated by the operation of generally applicable insolvency rules and not bank-specific legislation.

What RCBR achieves that is not possible under general insolvency law is to give the bondholders absolute priority ahead of all of the SPV's unsecured creditors. RCBR provides that sections 175 and 176A of the Insolvency Act 1986 do not apply in the insolvency of an SPV involved in a covered bonds transaction. Were it not for this provision, the covered bondholders would, insofar as their claims are secured by a floating security interest, have recourse to the secured assets after preferential creditors and the 'prescribed part' reserved for general unsecured creditors. Given that the SPV conducts no operations and hence will not have many unsecured creditors, it is debatable whether RCBR's exemption adds significant protection in practice.

In German law, the issuance of covered bonds does not involve the use of a subsidiary. Instead, special legislation enables banks to issue covered bonds that have prioritised recourse against a cover pool that the bank designates as being reserved for the bondholders.[82] The legal framework seeks to shield covered bond

[79] G Benteux et al, 'Regulated covered bonds: a comparative review' (2009) 4 *Capital Markets Law Journal* 341, 377–78.

[80] Regulated Covered Bonds Regulations, SI 2008/346 (RCBR), Sch, para 2(4). The provision does not appear to modify s 176ZA of the Insolvency Act 1986, which provides that liquidation expenses have priority over assets subject to a floating charge ahead of the claims of creditors secured by a floating charge.

[81] HM Treasury, 'Proposals for a UK Regulated Covered Bonds legislative framework: summary of responses and final Impact Assessment' (February 2008) para 1.10.

[82] Pfandbriefgesetz § 30(1).

investors from adverse effects should the issuer become subject to insolvency proceedings.[83]

To what extent does the special framework enable German banks to offer covered bondholders better priority than what is possible under general insolvency law? Given that the German covered bond framework relies on the use of just one legal entity, the obvious comparator is that the bank itself would grant a security interest.

Insofar as the secured asset is a monetary claim, the security grantor can either grant a Pfandrecht or transfer the claim by way of security.[84] If a Pfandrecht is granted, the secured creditors will have unfettered priority – but it will be necessary to give notice to the debtor of the claim to be granted as security in order to give rise to the security interest. A security transfer does not necessitate such a notification, but the insolvency professional's power to sell the assets thereby secured could result in the secured creditor having to hand over a percentage of the value of the assets to the insolvency estate as a lump sum compensation for the insolvency professional's costs of identifying the secured assets and, potentially, her sale of these assets.[85] The covered bonds legislation enables the parties to circumvent this administrative burden, as it is sufficient that that the bank records that a loan receivable is part of the relevant cover pool.[86]

Another general limitation in German general insolvency law for giving secured creditors priority is that the creation of a security interest in respect of antecedent debts could be susceptible to avoidance. The source of this risk is that a company's satisfaction of an obligation to ensure that the aggregate value of the security at all times exceeds the secured claims could constitute incongruent performance. Accordingly, any security granted in the last month before the request to open insolvency proceedings against the bank could thus be avoidable pursuant to InsO § 131. The special legislation does not contain any provision that explicitly states that the bank's designation of new assets as reserved for the covered bondholders is not susceptible to avoidance. It appears that the question has not received much scholarly attention. Some scholars have argued that *payments* on covered bonds made by a bank with assets that do not form part of the cover pool could be subject to avoidance, but they do not discuss in detail the application of the various avoidance grounds in German insolvency law.[87] It therefore appears as unclear whether the bank's inclusion of additional assets in the cover pool could be subject to avoidance.

[83] Upon the issuer becoming subject to insolvency proceedings, the different asset pools are carved out of the bank, see Pfandbriefgesetz § 30. The insolvency estate will only receive whatever remains when the covered bonds have been repaid in full.

[84] See Ellingsæter (n 52) ch 10 and the references contained therein.

[85] See 4.2.1.

[86] Pfandbriefgesetz § 5.

[87] W Henckel, '§ 130' in W Henckel and W Gerhardt (eds), *Insolvenzordnung*, vol 4 (Berlin, De Gruyter Recht, 2008) para 30; G Kayser and N Freudenberg, '§ 130' in H-P Kirchhof, R Stürner and H Eidenmüller (eds), *Münchener Kommentar zur Insolvenzordnung*, 4th edn (Munich, CH Beck, 2019) para 18.

The Norwegian covered bonds legislation reserves the issuance of covered bonds for credit institutions whose purpose is: (i) to grant or acquire loans secured by real estate or other assets capable of registration in a public asset register or loans to public institutions, and (ii) to finance its lending primarily by issuing covered bonds.[88] Accordingly, it is not possible for a deposit-taking bank to issue covered bonds.[89] In the event the issuer is wound up, the holders of covered bonds have recourse to the asset pool designated for those bonds ahead of all of the issuer's unsecured creditors.[90] The Norwegian government has recently put forward a proposal for legislative amendments intended to ensure that the covered bonds legislation satisfies CBD's requirements.[91] However, the proposed amendments would not alter the fundamental features of the framework.

It is debatable whether the special regime gives the bondholders better recourse to the assets composing the cover pool than what is generally achievable. The appropriate comparator is a scenario in which a bank establishes a subsidiary credit institution which issues bonds to finance the purchase of loan receivables from the parent bank and grants the bondholders a security interest over the loan receivables. This would not be problematic. As discussed at 4.2.1, such a financing structure would give the secured creditors absolute priority ahead of the SPV's unsecured creditors (if any) to the loan receivables. To the extent the loan receivables would mature during the term of the bonds, the SPV could place the proceeds in a bank account over which the bondholders have been granted a security interest. The SPV could use the proceeds to purchase new loan receivables over which the bondholders would receive security interests.

Were the SPV to acquire new loans to replace repaid loans, there is a risk that the security interests over such newly acquired loan receivables could be susceptible to challenge under dekningsloven § 5-7 as a security interest granted for antecedent debts insofar as the SPV granted the security within the applicable three-month suspect period. However, insofar as the SPV acquires the receivables in question with funds credited to a bank account over which the bondholders enjoy a security interest, it is likely that the grant of security would steer clear of avoidance: it is generally accepted that a security interest that arises in the context of the substitution of secured assets does not constitute a security interest for existing debt for the purposes of § 5-7.[92]

[88] Finansforetaksloven (ffl.) § 11-7(1).

[89] However, banks may control credit institutions authorised to issue covered bonds. In practice, most Norwegian covered bonds issuers are controlled by one or more banks.

[90] ffl. § 11-15.

[91] Finansdepartementet, 'Endringer i finansforetaksloven og verdipapirfondloven (obligasjoner med fortrinnsrett) og samtykke til deltakelse i en beslutning i EØS-komiteen om innlemmelse av forordning (EU) 2019/2160 og direktiv (EU) 2019/2162 i EØS-avtalen' Prop. 42 LS (2021–2022).

[92] Andenæs (n 68) 342; K Huser, *Gjeldsforhandling og Konkurs: Omstøtelse*, vol 3 (Bergen, Juristinformasjon, 1992) 399ff; R Myhre, 'Må boet lide et tap for å kunne omstøte etter de objektive omstøtelsesregler?' (1992) 105 *Tidsskrift for Rettsvitenskap* 84, 126–127 and the references therein.

5.3. Unsecured Claims

5.3.1. Depositor Preference

BRRD requires that two categories of deposits enjoy priority ahead of general unsecured creditors in normal insolvency proceedings. The first category is covered deposits. 'Covered deposits' is a term defined by the Deposit Guarantee Scheme Directive (DGSD). In essence, covered deposits are deposits that must be subject to coverage under the national deposit insurance schemes that DGSD requires Member States to establish.[93] EU law does not use a specific term to denote the second category of deposits with special priority. We will therefore refer to these deposits as 'other prioritised deposits' in the following paragraphs.

A defining characteristic of a covered deposit is that the deposit constitutes an 'eligible deposit'.[94] An eligible deposit is any deposit that does not fall within the 11 categories set out in DGSD Article 5(1). These categories cover deposits held by public authorities, other banks and other financial firms. Conversely, deposits held by natural persons and non-financial companies generally constitute eligible deposits.

As a main rule, DGSs guarantee eligible deposits up to 100,000 euro. Where a deposit exceeds this level, the guarantee only applies to the first 100,000 euro of the deposits and the excess is not a covered deposit. There are some exemptions from this coverage level. For instance, deposits resulting from the sale of private residential properties may for a limited period of time be covered in full.[95]

BRRD sets out the following requirements for the priority of covered deposits in normal insolvency proceedings.[96] Covered deposits shall have priority ahead of the other prioritised deposits.[97] Since the other prioritised deposits shall have priority ahead of general unsecured debt,[98] this means that covered deposits shall also have priority ahead of general unsecured debt.

In order to implement BRRD, English law now accords the same priority to covered deposits as the ordinary preferential debts discussed at 4.2.3.[99] In Norwegian law, covered deposits conversely rank below the debts that enjoy preferential status in general insolvency law, but ahead of other prioritised deposits and general unsecured debt.[100] The question of the priority of covered deposits vis-à-vis other preferential creditors does not arise in German law, as no claims enjoy priority in liquidation proceedings beyond what BRRD requires. Kreditwesengesetz § 46f(4) now provides that covered deposits rank ahead of other prioritised deposits, which in turn rank ahead of general unsecured debt.

[93] DGSD arts 6(1) and 8(1).
[94] DGSD art 2(1)(5).
[95] DGSD art 6(2)(a).
[96] BRRD art 108.
[97] BRRD art 108(1)(b).
[98] BRRD art 108(1)(a).
[99] Insolvency Act 1986, s 386(1A); Sch 6 para 15B.
[100] ffl. § 20-32.

Where the deposit guarantee scheme makes a payment to a covered depositor, the scheme subrogates into the claim of the depositor. BRRD requires that this claim shall have the same priority as a covered deposit.[101]

We now turn to the second category of deposits that pursuant to BRRD shall have priority ahead of general unsecured debt, namely the other prioritised deposits. This category comprises deposits that would have qualified for coverage under the deposit guarantee scheme but for exceeding the 100,000 euro threshold and that are held by natural persons or micro-, small- and medium-sized enterprises.[102] Micro-, small- and medium-sized enterprises are entities that employ fewer than 250 persons and that have an annual turnover not exceeding 50 million euro and/or assets with a value of less than 43 million euro.[103] As already touched upon, deposits that fall within the said category shall have priority ahead of general unsecured debt, but behind covered deposits. BRRD also protects depositors in third states where EU banks have a presence, as deposits made through one of the bank's non-EU branches have the same priority as other prioritised deposits.[104]

5.3.2. Bondholder Subordination

An amendment to BRRD was introduced in 2017 to facilitate the issuing of debt that ranks below ordinary debt, but above debt instruments that qualify as own funds.[105] As we shall discuss in more detail in subsequent chapters, the background is that resolution authorities have the power to require that a minimum of a bank's financing stems from own funds instruments or certain other loans that are subordinated to its general unsecured debt.

BRRD Article 108(2) now provides that

> ordinary unsecured claims [shall] have, in … normal insolvency proceedings, a higher priority ranking than that of unsecured claims resulting from debt instruments that meet the following conditions:
>
> (a) the original contractual maturity of the debt instruments is of at least one year;
> (b) the debt instruments contain no embedded derivatives and are not derivatives themselves;
> (c) the relevant contractual documentation and, where applicable, the prospectus related to the issuance explicitly refer to the lower ranking under this paragraph.

[101] BRRD art 108(b)(ii).

[102] BRRD art 108(1)(a)(i).

[103] See BRRD art 2(1)(107), which adopts the definition in Commission Recommendation 2003/361/EC of 6 May 2003 concerning the definition of micro, small and medium-sized enterprises [2003] OJ L124/36 annex, art 2(1).

[104] BRRD art 108(1)(a)(ii).

[105] Directive (EU) 2017/2399 of the European Parliament and of the Council of 12 December 2017 amending Directive 2014/59/EU as regards the ranking of unsecured debt instruments in insolvency hierarchy [2017] OJ L345/96.

Taken at face value, the effect of the provision is limited to requiring that Member States enable banks to issue debt that by virtue of contract is subordinated to claims that rank as 'ordinary unsecured claims' in the applicable insolvency proceedings. Given that EU law does not contain any requirements that positively define 'ordinary unsecured claims', and that the term therefore cannot plausibly refer to anything else than the ranking under the proceedings pursuant to which insolvent banks are wound up under national law, it would seem that BRRD Article 108(2) seemingly does not prevent Member States from subordinating certain debt claims by statute. Germany briefly had legislation that, subject to some exceptions, subordinated debt instruments that are tradable on capital markets to general unsecured debts.[106]

However, the legislative history of BRRD Article 108(2) suggests that the provision was introduced to limit statutory subordination. The recital of the amending Directive that inserted Article 108(2) into BRRD refers to divergent approaches to subordination that had arisen following the adoption of BRRD.[107] Moreover, the recital states that '[i]nstitutions should remain free to issue debt in both the senior and the non-preferred senior classes'.[108] This is not possible if all long-term debt is subordinated by virtue of statute. Statements to the same effect are also found in the explanatory memorandum of the Commission's proposal to adopt such a provision.[109]

As Germany has repealed the statutory subordination of debt instruments issued by banks, this controversy is of little importance in the present context. What is clear is that BRRD Article 108(2) does not represent a departure from the general insolvency law principles of English, German and Norwegian law: All jurisdictions recognise contractual subordination.[110] Nonetheless, all jurisdiction adopted statutory provisions that explicitly implement the requirements of BRRD Article 108(2).[111]

5.4. Creditor Priority in Group and Cross-Border Settings

EU law contains a fragmented set of rules of relevance for creditor priority in the winding up of a bank. There are thus several aspects Member State remain free to govern as they see fit. One of these is the extent to which there should apply special

[106] See KWG § 46f as it read between 1 January 2017 and 20 July 2018.
[107] Directive (EU) 2017/2399 recital 7.
[108] Directive (EU) 2017/2399 recital 10.
[109] Commission, 'Proposal for a Directive of the European Parliament and of the Council on amending Directive 2014/59/EU of the European Parliament and of the Council as regards the ranking of unsecured debt instruments in insolvency hierarchy' COM (2016) 853 final 6.
[110] See 4.2.3.
[111] See Insolvency Act 1986, s 176AZA; KWG § 46f(6); Finansforetaksloven § 20-32.

priority rules where the bank being wound up is part of a group of financial institutions, and thus may owe other group members debts under intragroup financing arrangements. It appears that none of the sample jurisdictions have adopted bank-specific priority rules aimed at this scenario.

The Credit Institutions Winding Up Directive (CIWUD) coordinates jurisdictional issues and questions of private international law arising in connection with insolvency proceedings initiated against a bank with links to more than one Member State.[112] The directive establishes a home state principle, which entails that a bank's home state – the Member State that has authorised the bank and supervises its affairs – shall have the exclusive power to adopt reorganisation measures or commence winding up proceedings with respect to the bank.[113] This eg means that Germany shall always have exclusive jurisdiction to wind up a bank authorised and supervised by German authorities even if it has significant branches in other Member States.

CIWUD Article 10 provides that the home state's laws (*lex domus*) as a main rule govern all aspects of the winding-up proceedings.[114] This includes 'the rules governing the distribution of the proceeds of the realisation of assets [and] the ranking of claims'.[115] Moreover, it is, subject to an exemption in Article 30, the home state's transaction avoidance rules that are applicable.[116]

The home state is not permitted to discriminate against creditors from other Member States. CIWUD Article 16(2) provides that:

> The claims of all creditors whose domiciles, normal places of residence or head offices are in Member States other than the home Member State shall be treated in the same way and accorded the same ranking as claims of an equivalent nature which may be lodged by creditors having their domiciles, normal places of residence, or head offices in the home Member State.

It would therefore not be permissible for a Member State's insolvency laws to eg provide that other banks shall have priority ahead of general unsecured creditors in the winding up of a bank but only insofar as such other banks are authorised by that Member State.

Member States retain more room for manoeuvre to discriminate against creditors outside of the EU (and the EEA). However, as discussed above, BRRD Article 108(1)(a)(ii) requires that 'deposits that would be eligible deposits from natural persons and micro, small and medium-sized enterprises were they not made through branches located outside the Union of institutions established within the Union' shall have priority behind covered deposits but ahead of general

[112] Directive 2001/24/EC of the European Parliament and of the Council of 4 April 2001 on the reorganisation and winding up of credit institutions [2001] OJ L125/15.

[113] CIWUD arts 3(1) and 9(1), respectively.

[114] B Wessels, 'Commentary on Directive 2001/24/EC on the Reorganisation and Winding Up of Credit Institutions' in G Moss, B Wessels and M Haentjens (eds), *EU Banking and Insurance Insolvency*, 2nd edn (Oxford, Oxford University Press, 2017) para 3.62.

[115] CIWUD art 10(2)(h).

[116] CIWUD art 10(2)(l).

unsecured creditors. Among other things, this means, roughly speaking, that deposits taken by an EU bank through a UK branch shall have priority ahead of the bank's general unsecured creditors if the depositor is a natural person or a micro, small and medium-sized enterprise.

There are exceptions to the principle of *lex domus*. Importantly, it follows from CIWUD Article 21(1) that winding up-proceedings

> shall not affect the rights in re of creditors or third parties in respect of tangible or intangible, movable or immovable assets – both specific assets and collections of indefinite assets as a whole which change from time to time – belonging to the credit institution which are situated within the territory of another Member State at the time of the adoption of such measures or the opening of such proceedings.

CIWUD Article 21(2)(a) goes on to state that 'rights in re' includes 'the right to dispose of assets or have them disposed of and to obtain satisfaction from the proceeds of or income from those assets, in particular by virtue of a lien or a mortgage'. When Article 21 applies, secured creditors are thus to be entitled to enforce security interests and apply the proceeds to the secured claim to the extent they are entitled to do so outside of insolvency proceedings. The effect is to prohibit the application of any provisions of *lex domus* reserving parts of the value of the secured assets for sharing among unsecured creditors, such as the Insolvency Act 1986, section 176A.[117]

CIWUD Article 21 applies insofar as the secured assets – whether tangible or intangible – are situated in another Member State when the winding-up proceedings commence. This raises the question of how one determines the location of intangible assets, such as loan receivables, deposits and financial instruments. The directive does not provide any guidance in this respect. Guidance could perhaps be sought in the Insolvency Regulation, which coordinates issues of jurisdiction and private international law with respect to general insolvency proceedings.[118] This Regulation contains a provision (Article 8) that is nearly identical to CIWUD Article 21. By contrast to CIWUD, however, the Insolvency Regulation governs in which Member State assets shall be considered as situated.

The Insolvency Regulation deems cash held in bank accounts as situated in the Member State indicated in the account's International Bank Account Number (IBAN), or, if the account does not have an IBAN, the Member State where the bank 'has its central administration or, where the account is held with a branch, agency or other establishment, the Member State in which the branch, agency or other establishment is located'.[119] Other claims against third parties are deemed situated in the Member State where the debtor has its 'centre of its main interests'.[120]

[117] See 4.2.1.

[118] Regulation (EU) 2015/848 of the European Parliament and of the Council of 20 May 2015 on insolvency proceedings (recast) [2015] OJ L141/19.

[119] Insolvency Regulation art 2(9)(iii).

[120] Insolvency Regulation art 2(9)(viii). The 'centre of its main interests' is determined in accordance with art 3(1) of the Regulation.

It is not necessarily the case that the determination of where assets are situated for the purposes of CIWUD Article 21(1) must follow the criteria of the Insolvency Regulation. The two are separate legal acts. Nonetheless, it is submitted that it seems sensible to adopt this approach in the absence of any guidance in CIWUD.

For security interests over financial instruments, CIWUD Article 24 solves the question regarding the effects of winding-up proceedings by providing a private international law rule. This Article states that the enforcement of security interests

> the existence … of which presupposes their recording in a register, an account or a centralised deposit system held or located in a Member State shall be governed by the law of the Member State where the register, account, or centralised deposit system in which those rights are recorded is held or located

CIWUD Article 30 makes an exemption to the rule in Article 10(2)(l) that avoidance actions are governed by *lex domus*.[121] The exemption requires that two conditions are satisfied. First, the potentially voidable act – eg the granting of security for antecedent debts – must be subject to the laws of a Member State other than *lex domus*. Secondly, the laws of that other Member State must not allow any means of challenging the act in question.

[121] On the scope of acts to which CIWUD art 30 applies, see the EFTA Court's judgment in Case E-28/13 *LBI hf. v Merrill Lynch Int Ltd.* [2014] EFTA Ct. Rep. 970.

6

Creditor Priority in Bank Resolution

6.1. Introduction

This chapter discusses creditor priority under the bank resolution framework of BRRD. First, we will at 6.2 discuss how creditor priority manifests itself under the different resolution powers. We will then address the priority of secured credit at 6.3 before discussing priority among unsecured creditors at 6.4. This is followed by a discussion at 6.5 of creditor priority in the resolution of banks that are part of groups or have engaged in cross-border activities At 6.6 we will examine BRRD's framework for compensating creditors who suffer a disadvantage when the bank is subject to resolution rather than liquidation under normal insolvency proceedings.

6.2. Priority Under the Different Resolution Powers

While the various resolution powers involve different legal effects, all are essentially means for preserving bank activity that society deems to merit protection. On the one hand, the bail-in power allows the resolution authority to write down claims against the bank under resolution. This strengthens the bank's solvency and is supposed to facilitate the bank's continued existence. On the other hand, the transfer tools give the resolution authority the power to transfer the bank's assets and liabilities to another entity. While the bank's *business* may live on in the transferee entity, the transfer signals the 'death' of the legal entity that is under resolution: Following the transfer, the transferor entity shall be wound up.[1]

As discussed at 3.1.2, some view the concept of general insolvency proceedings as comprising two subsets of proceedings: liquidation and restructuring proceedings. Under a much-simplified view, liquidation proceedings aim at selling the assets of the company, while restructuring proceedings seek to preserve its continued existence through a debt reduction. Resolution proceedings do not fall neatly on either side of such a dichotomy. The intended use of the bail-in tool is to ensure the continued existence of the entity under resolution. Meanwhile, the rationale for giving the resolution authority the sale of business tool and the bridge institution tool is to enable the business of the resolved entity to live on in a transferee entity through a transfer of assets and liabilities to another bank or a state-owned bridge bank.

[1] BRRD art 37(6).

Does the difference in legal effects mean that the loss distribution among bank creditors must differ between the various resolution powers? Not necessarily.[2] To illustrate this point, it is helpful to think of a bank's balance sheet as consisting of a pool of assets and two sets of liabilities: Liabilities A and Liabilities B. Liabilities A represent claims that must receive protection to achieve the resolution objectives, while Liabilities B represent all other claims.

Consider the case of using a simplified version of the bail-in tool. **Table 1** illustrates the effects of the bail-in tool. As the table shows, the resolved entity has equity of −5 upon entering resolution. Suppose that the resolution authority considers that the entity needs equity equal to 10 per cent of its assets to continue operating. As its assets equal 100, the desired equity level is 10. In order to increase the equity to this level, the aggregate amount of liabilities must be reduced to 90. This, in turn, means that the writing down of liabilities in an aggregate amount of 15 is required.

This brings us to the first stage of loss distribution, which involves identifying the liabilities that are susceptible to bail-in and those that are not. Consider a failing bank with two subsets of liabilities: Liabilities A and Liabilities B. Suppose that the resolution authority can lawfully choose to write down Liabilities B without also writing down Liabilities A, and that the resolution authority considers that the bail-in should be restricted to Liabilities B to prevent any negative effects on the functioning of the financial system. Therefore, the resolution authority chooses to write down liabilities that fall into this category in an aggregate amount of 15, reducing the outstanding Liabilities B from 35 to 20. Liabilities A are meanwhile safe, as the resolution does not affect their claims.

The second stage of loss distribution under the bail-in power involves identifying how the burden of the write-down shall be borne by the creditors that are susceptible to write-down, in our example the creditors of claims falling into the category Liabilities B. This is a question of priority. If, for the sake of simplicity, we assume that these creditors are to share losses *pari passu*, the result of the resolution is that these creditors retain approximately 57 per cent of their claim (as well as any shares received in exchange for the partial writing down of their claims).

Table 1

A. The state before bail-in

Assets		*Liabilities and Equity*	
Assets	100	Liabilities A	70
		Liabilities B	35
		Equity	−5
	100		100

(continued)

[2] See also TH Tröger, 'Too Complex to Work: A Critical Assessment of the Bail-in Tool under the European Bank Recovery and Resolution Regime' (2018) 4 *Journal of Financial Regulation* 35, 37.

Table 1 ***(Continued)***

B. The state after bail-in

Assets		*Liabilities and Equity*	
Assets	100	Liabilities A	70
		Liabilities B	20
		Equity	10
	100		100

We now turn to the use of the bridge institution tool. **Table 2** shows how it is possible to recapitalise *the business* of the institution through this power. Again, the recapitalisation potentially involves two stages of loss distribution. The first stage is to select the liabilities, if any, that the bridge entity shall assume along with the resolved bank's assets. As every liability assumed by the bridge entity is likely to be paid in full, the transfer of a liability is akin to exempting the claim from being written down under the bail-in power. In our example, the resolution authority will wish to have the transferee assume Liabilities A along with the resolved bank's assets. Leaving a claim behind in the transferor entity is akin to making a claim susceptible to write-down. In our example, rather than writing down Liabilities B in an amount of 15, the transfer leaves this amount of Liabilities B in the resolved entity while moving all other assets and liabilities to the bridge institution. The first stage of the loss distribution therefore leads to identical results as under the bail-in power.

The above assumes that the criteria for loss distribution are the same for the bail-in tool and the transfer tools. This assumption does not hold, however. As we shall

Table 2

A. The state before the transfer

Resolved entity				**Bridge institution**			
Assets		*Liabilities and Equity*		*Assets*		*Liabilities and Equity*	
Assets	100	Liabilities A	70		0		0
		Liabilities B	35				
		Equity	−5				
	100		100		0		0

B. The state after the transfer

Resolved entity				**Bridge institution**			
Assets		*Liabilities and Equity*		*Assets*		*Liabilities and Equity*	
Assets	0	Liabilities A	0	Assets	100	Liabilities A	70
		Liabilities B	15			Liabilities B	20
		Equity	−15			Equity	10
	0		0		100		100

see in the following sections, there are even differences between the bail-in and the transfer tools in terms of priority. The bail-in tool is largely prescriptive in terms of claims that are potentially subject to bail-in and claims that are not. Moreover, the exercise of the bail-in power is subject to strict rules that govern the priority among creditors that are susceptible to bail-in. Conversely, at the outset, the transfer tools are only subject to general principles insofar as questions of priority are concerned.

6.3. Secured Claims

6.3.1. The Bail-in Tool

BRRD Article 44(2)(b) states that the bail-in power shall not extend to

> secured liabilities including covered bonds and liabilities in the form of financial instruments used for hedging purposes which form an integral part of the cover pool and which according to national law are secured in a way similar to covered bonds.

Accordingly, the resolution authority is neither required nor empowered to write down claims that fall within this category. In other words, the claims in question are 'immune' from bail-in; there are no circumstances under which the claims are susceptible to the resolution authority's write-down power.

BRRD defines a secured liability as 'a liability where the right of the creditor to payment or other form of performance is secured by a charge, pledge or lien, or collateral arrangements including liabilities arising from repurchase transactions and other title transfer collateral arrangements'.[3] In line with FCD's approach of eliminating the distinction between security interests and title transfer security arrangements, it is not only secured claims in a strict sense that are exempt from the scope of the bail-in power, but also the payment or delivery rights of counterparties to title transfer collateral arrangements.

As defined by BRRD, a covered bond comprises two categories of instruments.[4] First, instruments falling within the Covered Bonds Directive's definition of covered bonds.[5] Secondly, instruments that: (i) were issued prior to 8 July 2022 (the deadline for applying national measures implementing the Covered Bonds Directive), and (ii) satisfied the conditions set out in Article 52(4) of the UCITS Directive as that provision read on the date of its issue.

The third subparagraph of BRRD 44(2) states that resolution authorities – 'where appropriate' – shall have the power to bail in secured liabilities to the extent they exceed the value of the secured assets. As discussed on earlier occasions, a

[3] BRRD art 2(1)(67).
[4] BRRD art 2(1)(96).
[5] See 5.2.3.

premise underlying the resolution framework is that the process shall only last a few days. Ascertaining whether secured claims exceed the value of the security over such a short period will likely only be feasible if the secured assets have an easily observable market price. Even then, this could involve a heavy administrative burden. This could lead resolution authorities to argue that a bail-in of parts of the secured claim is not 'appropriate' and that some claims are fully exempt from bail-in despite the secured claim exceeding the value of the secured asset.

6.3.2. The Transfer Tools

The transfer tools generally contain few explicit constraints on what liabilities the resolution authority should select to transfer to the transferee entity. However, security interests and the like enjoy special protection. BRRD Article 76(2) establishes the principle that such arrangements shall enjoy 'appropriate protection' in a resolution that involves the use of one of the transfer tools. Other provisions operationalise the application of this principle to different security arrangements.

One category is security arrangements where 'a person has by way of security an actual or contingent interest in the assets or rights that are subject to transfer, irrespective of whether that interest is secured by specific assets or rights or by way of a floating charge or similar arrangement'.[6] Pursuant to BRRD Article 78, such arrangements enjoy protection through four constraints on the resolution authority's power. First, the resolution authority cannot transfer secured assets without also transferring the '[secured] liability and the benefit of the security'.[7] Secondly, the same is the case 'unless the benefit of the security are also transferred'.[8] Thirdly, the resolution authority is barred from effecting a 'transfer of the benefit of the security unless the secured liability is also transferred'.[9] Fourthly, the resolution authority shall not have the power to modify or terminate a security arrangement to the effect that the secured liability ceases to be secured.[10]

The essence of BRRD Article 78(1) seems to be that secured creditors shall have the same recourse to the secured assets after the transfer as they had upon the commencement of the proceedings, regardless of whether the secured assets are transferred. The protection is not limited to security interests that secure certain specified subsets of liabilities. This stands in contrast to the scope of the protection offered under the FCD, which is conditional upon the liability being a 'relevant financial obligation'. Nor is the protection limited to security arrangements concluded between specific categories of persons. The scope of protection is thus also wider in this respect than that offered by SFD and FCD.

[6] BRRD art 76(2)(a).
[7] BRRD art 78(1)(a).
[8] BRRD art 78(1)(b).
[9] BRRD art 78(1)(c).
[10] BRRD art 78(1)(d).

Another category of security arrangements that enjoy protection comprises title transfer financial collateral arrangements where

> collateral to secure or cover the performance of specified obligations is provided by a transfer of full ownership of assets from the collateral provider to the collateral taker, on terms providing for the collateral taker to transfer assets if those specified obligations are performed.[11]

Generally, the resolution authority cannot choose to transfer only some of the rights and liabilities that form part of the collateral arrangement.[12] The resolution authority must thus choose between transferring all of these rights and liabilities or leave them all behind in the residual entity.

BRRD defines 'title transfer financial collateral arrangement' as FCD defines that term. As FCD has a limited personal scope,[13] the question arises as to whether BRRD's protection of title transfer arrangements is also limited in this respect. To put the question in more specific terms: given that FCD does not require Member States to apply the directive's requirements to transactions between physical persons and banks, will a person that has effectively extended a secured loan to the bank by selling it government bonds under a repo trade enjoy protection from bail-in? Seeing that BRRD only refers to FCD's definition of a title transfer collateral arrangement and that this definition does not refer to the parties to the transaction,[14] the answer appears to be yes.

Finally, the holders of covered bonds enjoy protection from the resolution authority exercising the transfer tools in a manner that prejudices their recourse to the underlying cover pool. The resolution authority cannot transfer only some of the assets and liabilities that comprise the 'structured finance arrangement' of which the covered bonds form a part.[15] Presumably, this means that the resolution authority shall have a binary option between either leaving the cover pool and the claims under the covered bonds in the residual entity or transferring all these assets and claims to the transferee.

6.4. Unsecured Claims

6.4.1. The Bail-in Power: Scope

As discussed, BRRD Article 44 lays out the scope of the bail-in power. Unless exempted by that provision, all liabilities are in principle susceptible to bail-in.

[11] BRRD art 76(2)(b).
[12] BRRD art 77(1).
[13] See 5.2.2.
[14] FCD art 1(2) lays out the limits on the directive's personal scope. An arrangement can thus fall under the definition of a 'title transfer financial collateral arrangement' and nonetheless fall outside the scope of FCD due to the identities of the parties to the arrangement.
[15] BRRD art 79(1).

BRRD Article 44 contains two avenues for exempting liabilities from the scope of the bail-in tool. First, the directive exempts certain liabilities by reference to one or more of their attributes, such as the identity of the creditor or the legal relationship that gave rise to the claim.[16] Secondly, resolution authorities have the power to exempt specific liabilities on a case-by-case basis if one of four conditions is satisfied.[17] In the following, the two sets of exemptions are termed *mandatory exemptions* and *discretionary exemptions*, respectively. We will first examine the scope of the mandatory exemptions.

Three of the mandatory exemptions relate to certain forms of short-term debt. First, BRRD exempts covered deposits from the scope of the bail-in power.[18] As discussed at 5.3.1, the term 'covered deposits' refers to the deposits that, pursuant to DGSD, shall be guaranteed by a deposit guarantee scheme. Roughly speaking, this category consists of deposits that are held by depositors that are neither financial institutions nor public authorities and that do not exceed 100,000 euro. As such, covered deposits are not necessarily short-term liabilities, as term deposits may constitute covered deposits. However, the majority are demand deposits and are thus repayable upon demand by the depositor.

Secondly, liabilities owed to another 'institution' are exempt from bail-in insofar as the liability has an original maturity of seven days or less and the institution is not part of the same group as the bank under resolution.[19] An institution is a credit institution or an investment firm.[20]

Thirdly, the bail-in power does not extend to liabilities with a remaining maturity of less than seven days towards payment and securities settlement systems, their operators and participants as a result of the bank's participation in such a system, or a central counterparty (CCP) either authorised under EMIR or recognised as a third-country CCP.[21]

These three exemptions do not cover all potential short-term bank creditors. First, large companies whose liquidity management involves placing money in deposit accounts will easily have balances that exceed the coverage afforded by DGSD. The excess part of the balance does not enjoy immunity from bail-in. Moreover, the claims of financial market actors that are neither credit institutions nor investment firms – eg insurance companies – do not benefit from any of the three exemptions.

BRRD's bail-in provisions differ from what the Commission originally proposed when launching the legislative procedure that led to their adoption. The scope of the provisions that render short-term debt immune to the bail-in power is the aspect where the differences are the most pronounced. The Commission proposed excluding from bail-in all unsecured debt with an original maturity of

[16] BRRD art 44(2).
[17] BRRD art 44(3).
[18] BRRD art 44(2)(a).
[19] BRRD art 44(2)(e).
[20] BRRD art 2(1)(23).
[21] BRRD art 44(2)(f).

less than one month.[22] Under such a provision, all providers of short-term capital would benefit from protection from the bail-in power.

BRRD contains other exemptions from the bail-in power that appear to be motivated by a wish to protect certain liabilities to the same extent as they enjoy protection in 'normal insolvency proceedings' – ie the applicable proceeding for winding up banks in the Member State concerned. Exempt from bail-in is 'any liability that arises by virtue of the holding by the [bank] … of client assets or client money … provided that such a client is protected under the applicable insolvency law'.[23] Moreover, the bail-in power does neither extend to 'any liability that arises by virtue of a fiduciary relationship between the [bank] … (as fiduciary) and another person (as beneficiary) provided that such a beneficiary is protected under the applicable insolvency or civil law'.[24] Finally, liabilities to tax and social security authorities are exempt, 'provided that those liabilities are preferred under the applicable law'.[25] As the above discussion shows, the protection from bail-in under these exemptions is contingent upon such claims enjoying special protection under normal insolvency proceedings. If not, the claims are susceptible to bail-in.

Other exemptions from the bail-in power are harder to categorise. Claims of employees for salary, pension benefits and other fixed remuneration are generally exempt from the bail-in power regardless of whether such claims enjoy special status in normal insolvency proceedings.[26] The same is the case for claims owed for the provision of goods or services that are critical to the bank's operation.[27] Moreover, an exemption applies for contributions owed to deposit guarantee schemes.[28] Liabilities for contributions arise when such schemes are financed by levies imposed on deposit-taking banks. Finally, the most recent revision of BRRD introduced an exception for non-subordinated claims of certain group entities.[29] The exemption does not apply insofar as the creditor is a resolution entity – that is, an entity that the resolution authority envisages to resolve if it were to fail.[30]

The exemptions we have addressed so far are 'mandatory' in the sense that the resolution authority lacks the power to bail in the claims concerned. Even if the resolution authority deems it safe or even desirable to bail in such claims, the claims are nonetheless safe from bail-in. As mentioned at the outset of this section,

[22] See Commission, 'Proposal for a Directive of the European Parliament and of the Council establishing a framework for the recovery and resolution of credit institutions and investment firms and amending Council Directives 77/91/EEC and 82/891/EC, Directives 2001/24/EC, 2002/47/EC, 2004/25/EC, 2005/56/EC, 2007/36/EC and 2011/35/EC and Regulation (EU) No 1093/2010' COM (2012) 280 final, 86 (proposed art 38(2)(d)).

[23] BRRD art 44(2)(c).

[24] BRRD art 44(2)(d).

[25] BRRD art 44(2)(g)(iii).

[26] BRRD art 44(2)(g)(i).

[27] BRRD art 44(2)(g)(ii).

[28] BRRD art 44(2)(g)(iv).

[29] BRRD art 44(2)(h).

[30] BRRD art 2(1)(83a).

these exemptions are not the only route for the exemption of a claim from bail-in. The resolution authority has the power to exempt claims on a case-by-case basis in the presence of one of four sets of circumstances described in BRRD Article 44(3). Pursuant to its power under BRRD Article 44(11), the Commission has adopted a Delegated Regulation (the 'Bail-in Exclusion Regulation', or 'BER') that seeks to specify further the circumstances under which the resolution authority has the power to exclude claims from bail-in.[31]

Generally, the resolution authority makes the decision on whether to exempt a claim. However, if the exclusion of a claim necessitates funding from the resolution financing arrangements (ie the applicable resolution fund),[32] the Commission can block the decision.[33] Such a situation could arise if the resolution authority is either unable or unwilling to offset the exemption of certain claims by increasing the part of the write-down that falls on the non-exempted creditors. Subject to the constraints set out in BRRD Article 44,[34] the resolution authority may then make up for the deficit by using the resolution fund to recapitalise the bank under resolution.

We now turn to examine the four grounds that empower the resolution authority to exempt claims from bail-in. BRRD Article 44(3)(a) permits resolution authorities to exclude a liability from the scope of bail-in if it is 'not possible to bail-in that liability within a reasonable time notwithstanding the good faith efforts of the resolution authority'.[35] Relevant scenarios could consist of difficulties in valuing the claim or, if the claim is governed by the laws of a third state, the non-recognition of the resolution authority's powers.

Pursuant to BRRD Article 44(3)(b), the resolution authority shall have the power to exclude a liability from bail-in when doing so is 'necessary to achieve the continuity of *critical functions* and *core business lines* in a manner that maintains the ability of the institution under resolution to continue key operations, services and transactions' (emphasis added).[36] The provision gives rise to two sets of questions. The first question concerns the criteria to be employed when identifying services that are critical functions and core business lines, respectively. The second question concerns when the bail-in of a liability could prejudice the continuance of a service. In the following, we will first consider what BRRD and an associated Commission delegated regulation have to say about the concept of a critical

[31] Commission Delegated Regulation (EU) 2016/860 of 4 February 2016 specifying further the circumstances where exclusion from the application of write-down or conversion powers is necessary under Article 44(3) of Directive 2014/59/EU of the European Parliament and of the Council establishing a framework for the recovery and resolution of credit institutions and investment firms [2016] OJ L144/11.

[32] See 3.4.3.

[33] BRRD art 44(12). In other cases, the directive merely requires that the resolution authority shall notify the Commission.

[34] See BRRD art 44(5) and (8).

[35] BRRD art 44(3)(a).

[36] BRRD art 44(3)(b).

function and when the exclusion of a liability is necessary to protect the resolved bank's critical functions before we move on to consider the corresponding questions regarding core business lines.

BRRD Article 2(1)(35) defines 'critical functions' as

> activities, services or operations the discontinuance of which is likely in one or more Member States, to lead to the disruption of services that are essential to the real economy or to disrupt financial stability due to the size, market share, external and internal interconnectedness, complexity or cross-border activities of an institution or group, with particular regard to the substitutability of those activities, services or operations.

Pursuant to BRRD's definition, a critical function is either essential to the real economy of one or more Member States or is a function whose discontinuance would disrupt financial stability in one or more Member States.

Pursuant to Commission Delegated Regulation 2016/778 Article 6(1), a function must satisfy two conditions to constitute a critical function. First, the function must be provided to third parties that are not affiliates of the bank.[37] Secondly, the resolution authority must establish that 'the sudden disruption of that function would likely have a material negative impact on the third parties, give rise to contagion or undermine the general confidence of market participants due to the systemic relevance of the function for the third parties and the systemic relevance of the institution or group in providing the function'. When making this assessment, the resolution authority shall consider the 'size, market share, external and internal interconnectedness, complexity and crossborder activities of the institution or group'.

As BRRD's definition of critical functions makes clear, the substitutability of the function is of particular importance for assessing whether a function is critical. The underlying rationale appears straightforward: An individual bank's provision of a service is only indispensable for the wider economy if other banks are not able to fill the void that would result from that bank's exit from the market. Determining exactly when this is the case, is a task fraught with difficulties. An essential function shall be considered substitutable 'where it can be replaced in an acceptable manner and within a reasonable time frame thereby avoiding systemic problems for the real economy and the financial markets'.[38] It is debatable whether this provision clarifies the question, given that the provision is couched in the vague and value-laden standards 'acceptable' and 'reasonable'.

Under what circumstances is it necessary to exclude a liability from bail-in to safeguard a critical function? BER Article 7(1)(a) provides that an exclusion

[37] Commission Delegated Regulation (EU) 2016/778 of 2 February 2016 supplementing Directive 2014/59/EU of the European Parliament and of the Council with regard to the circumstances and conditions under which the payment of extraordinary ex post contributions may be partially or entirely deferred, and on the criteria for the determination of the activities, services and operations with regard to critical functions, and for the determination of the business lines and associated services with regard to core business lines [2016] OJ L131/41.

[38] Commission Delegated Regulation (EU) 2016/778 art 6(3).

is necessary when the resolution authority considers that either of two sets of circumstances is present. The first is that the bail-in of the claim in question 'would undermine the function due to the availability of funding or to a dependence on counterparties … which may be prevented from or unwilling to continue transactions with the institution following a bail-in'.[39] The underlying reasoning is that there could be cases where the bail-in of a creditor would affect the bank's ability to attract funding or other services from the same creditor in the future and that bank cannot source the same from another market actor.

BER Article 7(1)(b) provides a second ground for excluding a liability from bail-in on account of protecting critical functions, namely that 'the critical function in question is a service provided by the institution to third parties which depends on the uninterrupted performance of the liability'. This ground could be met if a bail-in of deposits that are not covered by the deposit guarantee would cause many depositors to be without liquid funds, which again could disrupt their ability to make payments for goods and non-financial services.[40]

We now turn to the power to exempt liabilities where necessary to protect core business lines. The term 'core business lines' denotes 'business lines and associated services which represent material sources of revenue, profit or franchise value for an institution or for a group of which an institution forms part'.[41] BER does not shed additional light on the circumstances under which it is necessary to exclude a liability in order to maintain business lines and ultimately facilitate the continuance of the bank's 'key operations, services and transactions'.[42]

BRRD Article 44(3)(c) empowers resolution authorities to exempt liabilities from bail-in where doing so is 'strictly necessary and proportionate to avoid giving rise to widespread contagion … which would severely disrupt the functioning of financial markets … in a manner that could cause a serious disturbance to the economy of a Member State or of the Union'. Following the wording of the provision, an exemption requires the resolution authority to establish that bailing in the liability entails a risk of seriously disturbing the economy of a Member State or the Union.

BER Article 8 requires the resolution authority to consider the risk of both *direct contagion* and *indirect contagion*.[43] The definition of direct contagion is 'a situation where the direct losses of counterparties of the institution, resulting from the write-down of the liabilities of the institution, lead to the default or likely default for those counterparties in the imminent'.[44] Indirect contagion denotes 'a situation where the write-down or conversion of institution's liabilities causes

[39] BER art 7(1)(a).
[40] Financial Stability Board, 'Recovery and Resolution Planning for Systemically Important Financial Institutions: Guidance on Identification of Critical Functions and Critical Shared Services' (16 July 2013) 15.
[41] BRRD art 2(1)(36).
[42] BER art 7(5).
[43] BER art 8.
[44] BER art 3(1).

a negative reaction by market participants that leads to a severe disruption of the financial system with potential to harm the real economy'.[45]

In line with the wording of BRRD Article 44(3)(c), the assessment of *direct* contagion under BER Article 8 requires not only an assessment of whether counterparties stand to fail because of a bail-in, but also whether such counterparties are of systemic importance.[46]

BER lists 12 indicators that could be of relevance for resolution authorities when assessing the risk of *indirect* contagion. Several of the indicators concern the risk that the bail-in causes depositors and other providers of short-term funding to lose confidence in other banks, thereby causing a bank run.[47] Other indicators appear to relate to the risk that a bail-in of certain counterparties could otherwise impair the counterparties' ability to provide critical functions.[48]

Finally, BRRD Article 44(3)(d) empowers resolution authorities to exclude liabilities from bail-in insofar as a bail-in of those liabilities 'would cause a destruction in value such that the losses borne by other creditors would be higher than if those liabilities were excluded from bail-in'.[49] An exemption on this ground could perhaps be justified if bailing in a given liability would lead to the termination of an executory contract and the termination would cause a loss larger than the bailed-in liability.

An issue is how one should approach situations where retail investors own a substantial amount of the bonds issued by the bank to be resolved. The bondholders could have come to purchase the bonds from the bank itself under circumstances that represent a breach of the duties applicable when banks market financial products. Would it be possible for the resolution authority to exempt retail bondholders from bail-in? The above discussion shows that none of the discretionary exemptions would clearly allow for an exemption from bail-in. Resolution authorities would likely be hard-pressed to argue that the bail-in of long-term bonds would cause a risk of depositor runs on other banks and that Article 44(3)(c) thus would provide a ground for exempting the bonds.

As discussed, the mandatory exemptions for short-term debt are narrower than what the Commission originally proposed. In contrast, the discretionary exemptions are wider than the proposal envisaged. The Commission originally proposed that the resolution authority should have the discretionary power to exclude claims under derivatives contracts from the scope of the bail-in when it is necessary to protect the continuity of critical functions or prevent contagion.[50] As the above analysis shows, the scope of the resolution authority's discretionary powers is considerably wider than under the Commission's proposal.

[45] BER art 3(2).
[46] BER art 8(1).
[47] BER art 8(2)(a), (b), (e), (f), (g), (j), (k) and (l).
[48] BER art 8(2)(c), (d) and (h).
[49] BRRD art 44(3)(d).
[50] COM (2012) 280 final, 86 (proposed art 38(3)).

6.4.2. The Bail-in Power: Priority

Having discussed the claims that are exempt from the scope of the bail-in tool, we now turn to discuss priority among the remaining claims that are liable to the resolution authority's write-down power.

BRRD provides that claims liable to bail-in shall be written down in an order inverse to that in which available funds are distributed among unsecured creditors in 'normal insolvency proceedings'.[51] The resolution authority therefore begins by writing down the instruments that have the most junior ranking in normal insolvency proceedings and then moves up the priority ladder to the extent necessary. The resolution authority cannot write down claims that fall within a priority class unless it also writes down all junior liabilities.[52] If only parts of the aggregate amount of claims belonging to a class are required to be written down, the claims are generally reduced pro rata to their notional value.[53]

BRRD's requirements mean that debt with priority senior to general unsecured debt can only be written down after the general unsecured debt has been fully written down. The priority in 'normal insolvency proceedings' will be the priority found in general insolvency proceedings (see chapter four) subject to the modifications that we discussed in chapter five and any additional modifications made at the national level. Moreover, general unsecured debt cannot be written down unless all subordinated debt has been written down in full. This is an important point, as it frames our subsequent discussions in chapter eight on regulatory requirements for how banks compose their debt financing.

As discussed at 5.3.1, BRRD requires that covered deposits as well as most deposits of natural persons and micro-, small- and medium-sized businesses shall have priority ahead of general unsecured creditors in normal insolvency proceedings. How the bail-in power operates in terms of priority is of little interest for the holders of covered deposits, as such depositors are immune from bail-in by virtue of the mandatory exemption addressed at 6.4.1. Conversely, the priority under the bail-in power is of importance for natural persons and micro-, small- and medium-sized businesses with deposits in excess of the 100,000-euro threshold. Such deposits cannot be written down unless the resolution authority first writes down all general unsecured debt that remains susceptible to bail-in following the application of the mandatory and discretionary exemptions.

Member States may further tailor the loss distribution among creditors by amending the creditor hierarchy applicable in normal insolvency proceedings beyond BRRD's requirements. In Member States that choose not to make any such amendments, BRRD's priority principles mean that long-term 'financial' liabilities – ie debts owing under bonds – cannot be written down without also writing down some 'operational' liabilities such as large corporate deposits and unsecured claims

[51] BRRD art 48.
[52] BRRD art 48.
[53] BRRD art 48(2).

under derivative trades, save to the extent long-term creditors have agreed to priority below the general unsecured debts of the bank. This is indeed the current situation in English, German and Norwegian law.

6.4.3. The Transfer Tools

The bridge institution tool and the sale of business tool give the resolution authority the power to transfer 'all or any assets, rights or liabilities of one or more institutions under resolution' to a bridge institution or another purchaser, respectively.[54]

In contrast to the bail-in tool, the transfer powers are not formulated in a manner that requires the protection of any unsecured claims against losses. Such protection would require that a transfer cannot be executed unless the transferee also assumes the liabilities sought protected. As BRRD does not contain such a requirement, there is no functional equivalent to the exclusion of certain unsecured claims from the scope of the resolution authority's bail-in power.

Another difference between the transfer tools and the bail-in tool is that BRRD does not explicitly require that the resolution authority exercise the transfer tools in a manner that respects the priority between claims in normal insolvency proceedings. Where the bail-in tool is applied, BRRD requires that claims that are not exempted from bail-in either per se or following the ad hoc decision of the resolution authority are written down pro rata in accordance with the priority hierarchy applicable under normal insolvency proceedings. However, when the transfer tools are applied, there is nothing that explicitly prevents the resolution authority from transferring an unsecured claim to the transferee while leaving behind in the residual entity other unsecured claims that enjoy priority to the transferred claim in normal insolvency proceedings. Liabilities qualifying as own funds cannot be assumed by the transferee, however, as such liabilities must be written down if it is determined that the conditions for resolutions are met.[55]

On closer inspection, the resolution authority may not enjoy such broad discretion when selecting the unsecured liabilities to be assumed by the transferee. BRRD Article 34 requires that the resolution authority takes 'all appropriate measures' to ensure compliance with certain general principles applicable to the exercise of the resolution powers. The principles thus apply to the exercise of the transfer powers. Several of the principles concern creditor treatment.[56]

Two of the principles overlap somewhat. First, 'creditors [shall] bear losses … in accordance with the order of priority of their claims under normal insolvency proceedings, save as expressly provided otherwise in [the] Directive'.[57] Secondly, creditors of the same class are treated in an equitable manner 'except where

[54] BRRD arts 40(1)(b) and 38(1)(b).
[55] BRRD art 59(3)(a).
[56] BRRD art 34(1)(b) and (f)–(i).
[57] BRRD art 34(1)(b).

otherwise provided in [the] Directive'.[58] The second principle purports to require *equitable* treatment, not equivalent treatment.[59] Nonetheless, the text could be read as referring to equivalent treatment. First, other language versions of the directive employ words that translate to 'equivalent'.[60] Secondly, it is implausible that the legislators meant to express what follows from a verbatim reading of the English version. As creditors of the same class are entitled to be treated in an equitable manner *except where otherwise provided in the Directive*, such an interpretation would involve an implicit admission on the part of the Council and the European Parliament that the creditor treatment under the directive is inequitable to some extent!

In any event, the effect of these principles is not entirely clear. It is common to view principles as being different to rules. A rule is prescriptive: When BRRD Article 44(2)(a) states that covered deposits fall outside the scope of rights subject to the bail-in tool, it unequivocally states that a bail-in decision cannot encroach upon such deposits. Conversely, principles represent objectives that potentially must yield if the achievement of other legitimate objectives is deemed more important. However, the above-cited provisions read more like rules than principles. By stating that the resolution authority shall observe the priority scheme of normal insolvency proceedings unless the Directive explicitly provides otherwise, BRRD Article 34(1)(b) seemingly indicates that the resolution authority lacks the discretion to deviate from the said priority rules as the extent of permissible deviation is already explicitly provided elsewhere in the Directive. Otherwise, the provision would effectively read as follows: 'creditors … bear losses … in accordance with the order of priority of their claims under normal insolvency proceedings, save as expressly provided otherwise in this Directive, *unless a different allocation of losses is necessary to achieve one or more of the resolution objectives*'.

A different question is what the two 'principles' require. On one reading, they could be taken to indicate that the resolution authority must exercise the transfer tools in a manner that fully corresponds to the priority hierarchy applicable in normal insolvency proceedings. As the provisions governing the transfer tools do not explicitly state that the resolution authority can exercise these powers in a manner that leads to results deviating from the ordinarily applicable priority rules, no deviations would be permissible. The counterargument is that in omitting to include any restrictions on the transfer powers in the directive, the Council and the European Parliament have determined that the resolution authority shall have the power to deviate from the priority scheme. However, as the resolution authority's exercise of the bail-in power, in contrast to the exercise of the transfer powers, is subject to explicit rules, this interpretation would make BRRD Article 34(1)(b) and (f) devoid of content.

[58] BRRD art 34(1)(f).

[59] MA Schillig, 'The (Il-)Legitimacy of the EU Post-Crisis Bailout System' (2020) 28 *American Bankruptcy Institute Law Review* 135, 180; V Santoro and I Mecatti, 'Write-down and Conversion of Capital Instruments' in MP Chiti and V Santoro (eds), *The Palgrave Handbook of European Banking Union Law* (Cham, Palgrave Macmillan, 2019) 358. See also BRRD recital 13.

[60] See the Danish (*ens*), German (*gleich*) and Swedish (*likvärdigt*) versions of the directive.

To conclude, the most plausible interpretation of the 'principles' set out in Article 34(1)(b) and (f) is that they require the resolution authority to observe the priority scheme set out in the applicable normal insolvency proceedings when the authority uses the transfer powers. The resolution authority cannot rely on the resolution objectives to justify deviations from the applicable priority scheme.

Article 34 lays out additional principles. The resolution authority shall observe the principle that 'covered deposits are fully protected'.[61] This principle appears somewhat ambiguous. In one sense, covered deposits are protected, as such claims are guaranteed by the relevant deposit guarantee scheme. Interpreting this principle as requiring only this would render it entirely redundant, however, as BRRD does not alter the protection required under DGSD. On the other hand, the protection offered by the deposit guarantee scheme does not render depositors entirely unaffected by the failure of the deposit-taking bank. DGSD does not require that they have immediate access to their deposits following the failure of the bank. It is therefore possible to interpret this principle as requiring that any transfer must include the transferor's assumption of the covered deposits of the institution under resolution. In contrast to the 'principles' discussed above, the wording of the principle of protection of covered deposits is compatible with this being a principle and thus not a goal that must be achieved in all cases.

Another principle set out in BRRD is that 'no creditor shall incur greater losses than if the [entity] … had been wound up under normal insolvency proceedings in accordance with the safeguards in Articles 73 to 75'.[62] This principle merely replicates what already follows from BRRD Articles 73 to 75, namely that creditors have a right to compensation for any disadvantage caused by the institution being resolved rather than wound up.[63] We will discuss these provisions at 6.6.

The final principle that we will mention is that 'resolution action is taken in accordance with the safeguards in [the] Directive'.[64] It is difficult to see that this principle results in any additional limitations on the decision-making of the resolution authority, as the safeguards are prescriptive.

6.4.4. The Discretion of the Resolution Authority

The preceding sections show that the loss allocation among the creditors of a bank in resolution to some extent depends on decisions made by the resolution authority. Such discretion is present where the resolution authority exempts liabilities from bail-in under BRRD Article 44(3) or chooses the extent to which liabilities shall be transferred to a purchaser or a bridge bank. This feature sets resolution apart from general insolvency proceedings.

[61] BRRD art 34(1)(h).
[62] BRRD art 34(1)(g).
[63] See 6.6.
[64] BRRD art 34(1)(i).

The resolution authority's powers are formulated in vague language. It is thus difficult to discern the limits to its powers. The above analysis shows that the rules that govern the distribution of losses among creditors in resolution employ conditions that reference the likely effects of imposing losses on certain creditors. This requires projections of the future developments in alternative scenarios. The structure of BRRD Article 44(3)(c) illustrates this general point. In essence, the provision permits the resolution authority to exempt a claim from bail-in where

> the exclusion is strictly necessary and proportionate to avoid giving rise to widespread contagion which would severely disrupt the functioning of financial markets … in a manner that could cause a serious disturbance to the economy of a Member State or of the Union.

The provision contains several vague terms. The decision-maker will have to make up their mind about when financial markets are 'severely disrupt[ed]' and what constitutes 'a serious disturbance to the economy of a Member State or the Union'. While the Commission's Delegated Regulations seek to provide guidance on when such circumstances are present, it remains the case that the applicable rules are vague.

Article 44(3)(c) is not a unique case. Several provisions of the directive contain vague standards and/or employ conditions that necessitate very difficult projections. A fundamental question is whether one should view these provisions as substantive limits to the resolution authority's power. This question has been discussed in the literature with respect to the public interest test in BRRD Article 32. As discussed at 3.4.2, Article 32 sets out three conditions for resolution. The third of these conditions is that a resolution is in the public interest, which is the case if resolution is necessary for the achievement of one or more of the resolution objectives set out in Article 31. Taken at face value, the provision requires 'a fully fledged cost-benefit analysis'.[65] Some have argued that this provision should not be viewed in this manner. Rather, what is required is no more than 'an informed guess *ex ante*'.[66] This would come close to conceiving BRRD's provisions as requirements of a procedural nature, merely involving a duty on the part of the resolution authority to demonstrate that it acted in good faith in considering resolution actions necessary. It is, however, difficult to square this interpretation with the wording of both Articles 32 and 44(3), which clearly suggests that the limits to the resolution authority's power are of a substantive nature.

Nonetheless, there are reasons to suspect that court review of the resolution authority's exercise of its resolution powers will not be particularly intrusive. In principle, there exists some point where the risk of contagion is too small to justify exempting a claim that is normally susceptible to bail-in. Having identified this threshold, the court would thereafter be able to consider whether the evidence

[65] J-H Binder, 'Resolution: Concepts, Requirements, and Tools' in J-H Binder and D Singh (eds), *Bank Resolution: The European Regime* (Oxford, Oxford University Press, 2016) para 2.45.
[66] ibid para 2.46.

shows the risk of contagion was sufficiently serious to justify an exception. This, of course, is an idealised account of the practice of adjudication. It is not possible to derive from the text of Article 44(3)(c) that a measure is necessary and proportionate to avoid a serious disturbance to the economy of a Member State when, for example, the failure to exclude a liability with probability *p* will reduce annual gross domestic product growth in an amount of at least *X*. This, in turn, could lead the court to treat the question as one of fact and apply administrative law standards of court deference to the resolution authority's conclusion that the measure was necessary. As discussed at 2.1.4, the ECJ's approach in cases concerning financial stability follows this pattern. The Court has limited its judgments to state that the protection of financial stability is a legitimate aim. The merits spell out little about the circumstances under which interference is necessary to achieve this aim.

This brings us to the question of what BRRD has to say about court review of the resolution authority's decisions. BRRD requires Member States to give all persons affected by a crisis management measure a right to appeal against the decision.[67] In terms of the standard of judicial review, the sole explicit requirement is that the national courts shall 'use the complex economic assessments of the facts carried out by the resolution authority as a basis for their own assessment'.[68] This wording suggests that the resolution authority's assessment has authority as such, but that the authority is not absolute.

BRRD's recital 89 explains the background as follows:

> Crisis management measures taken by national resolution authorities may require complex economic assessments and a large margin of discretion. The national resolution authorities are specifically equipped with the expertise needed for making those assessments and for determining the appropriate use of the margin of discretion. Therefore, it is important to ensure that the complex economic assessments made by national resolution authorities in that context are used as a basis by national courts when reviewing the crisis management measures concerned.

However, the recital goes on to state that:

> … the complex nature of those assessments should not prevent national courts from examining whether the evidence relied on by the resolution authority is factually accurate, reliable and consistent, whether that evidence contains all relevant information which should be taken into account in order to assess a complex situation and whether it is capable of substantiating the conclusions drawn therefrom.

In light of this, a court using the resolution authority's economic assessments 'as a basis for [its] own assessment' seems to involve the review of whether the assessment relies on an accurate and complete set of facts. Moreover, the courts shall assess whether the resolution authority is 'capable of substantiating the conclusions drawn' from the factual material. It is clear that this does not involve the

67 BRRD art 85(2).
68 BRRD art 85(3).

court substituting its judgement for that of the resolution authority. The wording seemingly refers to a form of plausibility test where the court may find a decision *ultra vires* if the resolution authority presents an implausible argument.

The wording of the standard of review appears to be inspired by the CJEU's jurisprudence on annulment actions against Commission's enforcement of EU competition law. The CJEU has stated several times that it will only set aside the Commission's 'complex economic assessments' in cases of 'manifest error of assessment'.[69] In *Tetra Laval*, the ECJ stated that while the Commission 'has a margin of discretion with regard to economic matters', there is a role for the CJEU to review the Commission's assessments.[70]

The Court went on to describe the scope of the review as follows:

> [n]ot only must the Community Courts, inter alia, establish whether the evidence relied on its factually accurate, reliable and consistent but also whether that evidence contains all the information which must be taken into account in order to assess a complex situation and whether it is capable of substantiating the conclusions drawn from it.

Note the similarity in the Court's statement and the above-cited language contained in BRRD's recital. It is therefore reasonable to expect that the CJEU will apply a similar standard when dealing with disputes over the legality of resolution actions.[71] It is also reasonable to interpret BRRD Article 85(3) as requiring national courts to adopt the same standard when reviewing the decisions of resolution authorities. This would, at least on paper, indicate that the courts shall generally not substitute their view for that of the resolution authority insofar as economic assessments are concerned.[72]

Statements made by the General Court in its recent judgment in *Dr. K. Chrysotomides & Co* support the hypothesis that the courts will apply a deferential standard when reviewing the legality of the resolution authority's decisions. When considering whether the Commission's and the ECB's involvement in the Cypriot ad hoc bail-in measures in 2013 breached the bailed-in creditors' right to property, the Court stated that:

> [w]here, as in the present case, the institutions of the EU are required, in a complex and changing environment to make technical choices and undertake forecasts and complex assessments, those institutions must, nevertheless, be granted a wide margin of discretion with respect to the nature and the extent of the measures supported by them or with respect to which they require maintenance or continuous implementation.

[69] See generally A Kalintiri, 'What's in a name? The marginal standard of review of "complex economic assessments" in EU competition enforcement' (2016) 53 *CML Rev* 1283.

[70] Case C-12/03 P *Commission v Tetra Laval* ECLI:EU:C:2005:87, para 39. Numerous subsequent judgments confirm this approach, see eg Case C-525/04 P *Spain v Commission* ECLI:EU:C:2007:698, para 57 and Case C-290/07 P *Commission v Scott* ECLI:EU:C:2010:480, para 65.

[71] M Schillig, *Resolution and Insolvency of Banks and Financial Institutions* (Oxford, Oxford University Press, 2016) para 5.15.

[72] Whether this will be the case in practice remains to be seen. Some argue that the CJEU's review is more intense than the above-cited statements would suggest, see eg Kalintiri (n 69).

> In such a situation, the condition relating to the unlawfulness of the conduct complained of requires it to be established that the institution concerned manifestly and gravely disregarded the limits of its discretion (citations omitted).[73]

The statement is phrased in general terms. It is seemingly the case that a similar standard of review would apply should the CJEU review in the future any resolution decisions made by the Single Resolution Board (SRB), the Commission or the Council within the Single Resolution Mechanism's decision-making procedure. This means that it would be difficult to challenge the legality of a resolution scheme invoking the power to exempt claims from bail-in under the discretionary exemptions set out in SRMR Article 27(5), which corresponds to BRRD Article 44(3).

The General Court's recent judgment in *Algebris* is in line with the above predictions.[74] The judgment concerned an action for the annulment of the Commission's decision to endorse the resolution scheme drawn up by SRB for the Spanish bank Banco Popular. The Court started its assessment by elaborating upon the principles applicable to the CJEU's review of decisions made by the SRB. The Court described SRB's decisions as being based on 'highly complex economic and technical assessments'. This, in turn, meant that the CJEU, in line with established case law, could not substitute its assessment of scientific and technical facts, or economic questions for that of the SRB.[75] However, the CJEU would nonetheless be called upon to

> not only establish whether the evidence relied on is factually accurate, reliable and consistent but also ascertain whether that evidence contains all the information which must be taken into account in order to assess a complex situation and whether it is capable of supporting the conclusions drawn from it.[76]

In dealing with the applicants' action, the Court was, among other things, required to consider whether the Commission committed a manifest error in its assessment that a valuation of the resolved bank's assets and liabilities carried out by a consultancy was 'fair, prudent and realistic' and thus satisfied the requirement set out in SRMR Article 20(1) for the commissioning of such valuation. The Court deduced from the general principles governing its review that in order for it to find manifest error of assessment, the applicants would be required to adduce sufficient evidence to render the valuation 'implausible'.[77] What was already an uphill struggle for the

[73] Case T-680/13 *Dr. K. Chrysostomides & Co. LLC and Others v Council of the European Union and Others* ECLI:EU:T:2018:486, para 291. The ECJ subsequently set aside parts of the judgment on appeal, but this decision was not related to the view expressed in the cited text. See Joined Cases C-597/18 P, C-598/18 P, C-603/18 P and C-604/18 P, *Dr. K. Chrysostomides & Co and others* ECLI:EU:C:2020:1028.

[74] Case T-570/17 *Algebris (UK) Ltd and Anchorage Capital Group LLC v European Commission* ECLI:EU:T:2022:314.

[75] Case T-570/17 *Algebris (UK) Ltd and Anchorage Capital Group LLC v European Commission*, para 107.

[76] Case T-570/17 *Algebris (UK) Ltd and Anchorage Capital Group LLC v European Commission*, para 108.

[77] Case T-570/17 *Algebris (UK) Ltd and Anchorage Capital Group LLC v European Commission*, para 229.

applicants became even more daunting as the Court noted that 'some uncertainties and approximations' were inherent in the valuation to be carried out under SRMR Article 20(1), as such valuations have to be produced within a tight time frame and subject to limited information.[78] The applicants' critique of the valuation report failed to sway the Court, which concluded that the Commission had not committed a manifest error.

The judgment in *Algebris* suggests that the CJEU would adopt a deferential approach should it be called upon to review the legality of a resolution scheme making use of the exemptions set out in SRMR Article 27(5), which, as mentioned, correspond to BRRD Article 44(3). First, this follows from the General Court confirming that decisions made in the context of a resolution is among the complex economic and technical assessments that warrant deferential review. Secondly, the Court acknowledged that resolution decisions – which include whether to exclude creditors from bail-in on an ad hoc basis – inherently involve decision-making under temporal and informational constraints. This presumably further raises the threshold for how unimpressed the reasons for a decision must leave the Court for it to find the decision vitiated by a manifest error of assessment.

The legality of the exercise of resolution powers could be challenged before both national courts and the CJEU. There remains room for national differences beyond what BRRD and general EU law principles require in terms of the intensity of judicial review of the resolution authority's decisions. There could therefore be differences in the standard of review that different courts adopt.[79] We will for present purposes not explore the different standards that the various national courts are likely to employ when adjudicating disputes over the legality of resolution measures.[80]

6.5. Creditor Priority in Group and Cross-Border Settings

While members of a corporate group are deemed individual entities from a legal perspective, they may collectively compose a unit for economic purposes. The traditional approach in general insolvency law has nonetheless been to treat group members as separate entities and conduct individual proceedings for each entity.[81]

[78] Case T-570/17 *Algebris (UK) Ltd and Anchorage Capital Group LLC v European Commission*, para 242.

[79] See also J-H Binder, 'Resolving a bank – Judicial review with regard to the exercise of resolution powers' in C Zilioli and K-P Wojcik (eds), *Judicial Review in the European Banking Union* (Cheltenham, Edward Elgar, 2021) para 22.32.

[80] For discussion of the legal framework for review of resolution actions in Germany and the UK, see Schillig (n 71) paras 5.17–5.21.

[81] I Kokorin, 'The Rise of "Group Solution" in Insolvency Law and Bank Resolution' (2021) 22 *European Business Organization Law Review* 781, 782.

Recent years have seen efforts aimed at coordinating insolvency proceedings simultaneously initiated against several group members.[82]

Several of BRRD's provisions reflect the view that disregard for the economic linkages between group members may cause suboptimal outcomes. The directive requires that members of cross-border groups shall be permitted to enter into intra-group arrangements providing for financial support to distressed group members beyond what may generally be legal under relevant company law.[83] Moreover, resolution authorities may designate one entity within a group of banks and other financial institutions as the entity to be resolved (the 'resolution entity'),[84] and require that the group's external long-term financing is obtained through that entity and on-lent to other group members. This makes it possible to recapitalise the group by resolving the resolution entity and writing down its external liabilities while avoiding disruption to the operations and business relationships of the other group members. It could also be mentioned that BRRD contains provisions requiring the resolution authorities responsible for the members of cross-border groups to draw up common plans for resolving the group – although individual resolution authorities remain free to not follow such plans.[85]

Nonetheless, group members are generally treated as distinct entities for the purposes of resolution. If two group members are simultaneously resolved, the two will be subject to separate resolution actions. With respect to priority among a bank's creditors, the approach is generally to treat debts owed by a resolved entity to other group members in the same manner as corresponding debts owed to external parties. One group-specific rule does apply, however. As mentioned at 6.4.1, liabilities owed to entities that are part of the same resolution group as the resolved bank shall generally not be bailed-in insofar as such entities are not themselves resolution entities.[86] An exception applies for liabilities that at the time of the transposition of the Directive ranked with priority below general unsecured debt in applicable normal insolvency proceedings; such debts may thus be bailed-in.

Turning to creditor priority in cross-border resolution, it is useful to note that CIWUD not only coordinates jurisdiction and private international law with respect to winding-up proceedings but also 'reorganisation measures'. CIWUD Article 2 defines this term to include the application of the resolution tools and the exercise of resolution powers set out in BRRD. Accordingly, CIWUD Article 3(1) gives the resolution authority of a bank's home state exclusive power to take resolution actions in respect of the bank.

BRRD Article 66(1) requires that other Member States give effect to the home state resolution authority's transfer of assets and liabilities located in their territory or subject to their laws, respectively. The resolution authority's power to transfer

[82] ibid.

[83] BRRD art 19ff.

[84] BRRD art 2(1)(83a).

[85] BRRD arts 91 and 92. Within the SRM, the SRB adopts decisions that are binding on the resolution authorities of Member States participating in the Banking Union.

[86] BRRD art 44(2)(h).

assets pursuant to BRRD's transfer tools is accordingly to extend to all assets located in EU (and EEA) Member States. A third party with proprietary rights over the bank's assets is thus not to have the possibility of challenging the transfer on account of the assets concerned being situated in another Member State. The location of the secured assets is therefore not of relevance for whether a secured creditor will be affected by a resolution involving the transfer of assets.

If the home state resolution authority decides to use the bail-in tool to write down liabilities governed by the laws of another Member State, that other Member State shall give effect to the decision.[87] Subject to the modifications discussed in this chapter, it follows from BRRD Article 48 that the order in which creditors are bailed-in follows the priority rules of the home state's normal insolvency proceedings. As discussed at 5.4, it is not permissible for the priority rules applicable in winding up proceedings to discriminate against creditors of other Member States. This has the indirect implication that BRRD Article 48 operates to ensure that all creditors within the EU (and the EEA) are all subject to bail-in on equal terms.

6.6. The 'No Creditor Worse Off' Principle

When BRRD exempts a creditor from the scope of the bail-in tool, other creditors could be required to bear a larger burden to reach the targeted debt reduction. Likewise, a purchaser could be willing to pay less for assets transferred from the resolved entity if the transfer also includes the assumption of liabilities. As a result, the ratio of assets available for distribution in the liquidation of the resolved entity following a transfer of assets and liabilities is lower than it would have been if only assets were transferred. It is therefore possible that resolution makes the creditors that do not benefit from special treatment worse off than they would have been had the banks instead been wound up under normal insolvency proceedings.

BRRD sets out a scheme for compensating disadvantaged creditors. For this purpose, an independent person is appointed to make two valuations.[88] The first valuation shall estimate the treatment creditors would have received if the resolved entity had entered normal insolvency proceedings at the time the resolution authority decided to take a resolution action.[89] This estimate shall disregard any

[87] BRRD art 66(4).

[88] Commission Delegated Regulation (EU) 2016/1075 of 23 March 2016 supplementing Directive 2014/59/EU of the European Parliament and of the Council with regard to regulatory technical standards specifying the content of recovery plans, resolution plans and group resolution plans, the minimum criteria that the competent authority is to assess as regards recovery plans and group recovery plans, the conditions for group financial support, the requirements for independent valuers, the contractual recognition of write-down and conversion powers, the procedures and contents of notification requirements and of notice of suspension and the operational functioning of the resolution colleges [2016] OJ L184/1, ch IV.

[89] BRRD art 74(2)(a).

provision of public financial support to the resolved bank.[90] This means that the estimate does not necessarily reflect the market value of claims against the bank immediately prior to its resolution, as such prices could reflect the possibility of state aid.

Thereafter, the value retained by the creditor following the resolution actions is subtracted from the hypothetical outcome of normal insolvency proceedings.[91] If the difference is positive, meaning that the creditor is deemed disadvantaged by the resolution, the creditor is entitled to compensation from the resolution fund.[92]

The relevant comparator is thus the hypothetical outcome of the bank being wound up. In contrast to the criteria discussed at 6.4.4, the decisive criterion for whether a creditor has the right to compensation is conceptually clear. However, this is not to say that the decision is straightforward. As highlighted by several commentators, uncertainty attaches to any estimate made by the valuer.[93] For instance, if the bank is large enough, a liquidation could have produced effects on the prices of its assets different from those caused by the resolution. Moreover, an estimate of the outcome of a liquidation requires a projection of all relevant decisions taken by liquidators and courts under the proceedings.[94] This can be particularly challenging when the resolved entity holds assets in several jurisdictions, as different assets will then be subject to different substantive laws.[95]

The valuation exercise could nonetheless result in the conclusion that general unsecured creditors stood to receive substantial distributions had the bank been wound up rather than resolved. It is important to bear in mind that the valuation shall assume that the bank was wound up on the day the decision to place the bank under resolution came into effect. Given that the resolution authority has the power to resolve entities before they become insolvent, the outcome of a hypothetical winding up could – at least in theory – be a payment of 100 per cent of the principal amount owed to general unsecured creditors.

[90] BRRD art 74(3)(c).
[91] BRRD art 74(2)(b) and (c).
[92] BRRD art 75.
[93] J-H Binder, 'The position of creditors under the BRRD' in Bank of Greece's Center for Culture, Research and Documentation (ed), *Commemorative Volume in memory of Professor Dr. Leonidas Georgakopoulos* (2016) 43–48, at www.ssrn.com/abstract=2698086; MF Hellwig, 'Valuation reports in the context of banking resolution: What are the challenges?' (Brussels, European Parliament: The Economic Governance Support Unit, 2018) 6.
[94] Tröger (n 2) 63.
[95] Binder (n 93) 48.

7

The Rationales of Bank-Specific Creditor Priority Rules

7.1. Introduction

The preceding chapters have mapped the creditor priority hierarchy applicable in both the winding up and the resolution of a bank. In this chapter, we will try to identify rationales that may explain the existence of these sector-specific priority rules. To this end, we will identify different arguments for bank-specific priority rules and analyse the extent to which the priority rules correspond to the implications of these arguments.

It is necessary to make one caveat regarding the scope of the analysis. Most bank-specific priority rules derive from EU law. Naturally, a rationale for the adoption of directives and other legal acts is to promote the functioning of the internal market for financial services by harmonising the laws of the Member States. The adoption of uniform rules and the removal of legal impediments to cross-border activity are conducive to this end. However, the objective of market integration does not necessarily say anything about what the rules should look like. As we are concerned with the policy rationales that inform the design of the rules, we will therefore not discuss the objective of market integration further.

7.2. A Matter of Adapting General Principles to Special Circumstances?

One possible explanation for the existence of special priority rules in bank insolvency law is that sector-specific circumstances render such rules necessary for achieving the objectives pursued by the priority rules of general insolvency law. Under such a view, differences in terms of creditor priority are not due to differences in the *ends* sought achieved. Rather, the peculiarities of banks call for employing different *instruments* than under the normal approach. We will in the following consider whether this is a plausible explanation for the bank-specific priority rules examined in preceding chapters.

Banks benefit from sector-specific legislation that enables them to create security interests to a greater extent than what is generally possible for companies.

In 4.4, we outlined two normative theories on this question: (i) that companies should be able to grant security interests to the same extent they may alienate their property (the property right justification), and (ii) that security interests contribute to lowering overall financing costs (the funding costs justification). We then analysed whether English, German and Norwegian law fit with the implications of these theories. We found that both theories fit well, but that there are some aspects of current regimes that seem irreconcilable with both theories.

How compatible is the sector-specific protection of secured credit in the Settlement Finality Directive (SFD), the Financial Collateral Directive (FCD) and the Covered Bonds Directive (CBD) with these justifications? We can first quickly discard the property right justification, as banks generally do not have wider powers to dispose of their assets than other companies do. Accordingly, the property rights justification does not imply that banks should have broader powers to grant security interests than other companies.

What remains as a possible justification is the wish to give banks access to cheaper financing. This argument figures in the recitals of FCD and the CBD.[1] While we will not revisit the arguments for and against whether secured credit generally serves this objective, it should be noted that the financial structure of banks would likely compound any misgivings over how secured credit offers borrowers a device for taking on risk at the expense of non-adjusting creditors. Due to both their low sophistication and the existence of deposit insurance, covered depositors appear as fitting squarely into Bebchuk and Fried's category of 'non-adjusting creditors' that do not respond to changes of their priority vis-à-vis the debtor's other creditors.[2] Lenders of last resort, such as central banks and governments, are arguably also non-adjusting (contingent) creditors, as they cannot necessarily exercise any influence over a bank's financial structure before they are called upon to extend emergency financing amidst a crisis.

As our analysis has shown, currently applicable law contradicts the policy implications of such a pessimistic view. Several directives require Member States to ensure that banks may enter into certain secured transactions without being subject to the vagaries of generally applicable law. In the following, we will seek to rationalise this approach. Accordingly, we will examine whether there are arguments that suggest that banks possess special features that justify an expansion of the possibilities to create security interests beyond what is generally justifiable.

This question has attracted strikingly little attention. One exception found in US scholarship is Steven L Schwarcz's analysis of the benefits of covered bonds.[3] As touched on at 4.4.3, Schwarcz was one of the proponents of a general justification for security interests based on the need to overcome a form of debt overhang – that is, a situation where a company's existing debt load makes it unable to attract debt

[1] FCD recital 3; CBD recital 5.
[2] See 4.4.3.
[3] SL Schwarcz, 'The Conundrum of Covered Bonds' (2011) 66 *The Business Lawyer* 561, 582–85.

financing, despite having profitable business opportunities. His argument is that security interests constitute a device for companies to obtain liquidity in circumstances where they are unable to obtain funding otherwise. Does this argument hold when the company is a bank and the security interest takes the form of a covered bond? Given that banks do issue covered bonds even when they are able to attract unsecured debt, the factual premise is problematic in the present context. This does not change Schwarcz's conclusion, however. Based on the assertion that lenders will not lend to a company even on a secured basis if the bank has 'a realistic chance' of becoming subject to insolvency proceedings, it will not be possible for an insolvent bank to borrow on a secured basis with a view to 'gamble for resurrection' or otherwise finance behaviour that reduces the recovery prospects of its non-adjusting creditors.[4]

Some also view the option for issuing covered bonds as an important means for banks to overcome debt overhang in times of distress. For instance, Norges Bank's work with liquidity stress testing shows that this option has a material impact on the survival rate of Norwegian banks in adverse liquidity scenarios.[5] It has also been reported that the issuance of covered bonds provided a means for banks to attract liquidity when banks in certain Member States could no longer place ordinary long-term bonds with investors during the Eurozone crisis.[6]

Regardless of the general merits of the debt overhang argument, it does not explain why SFD, FCD and CBD are sector specific. Intuitively, one would expect that if expanding the scope for security arrangements in the financial sector reduces the funding costs of banks, the same benefits would result from expanding the scope more generally. In summary, the funding cost argument does not provide a full explanation of bank-specific priority rules.

The demand for 'safe assets' is another possible rationale for the adoption of FCD. Insured deposits are perceived as sufficiently safe to serve as a store of value. The limitations on deposit insurance do, however, complicate things for clients that wish to store money with banks, as a winding up or resolution could see them lose their deposits. The removal of restrictions on the possibilities for creating security interests with absolute priority to other creditors, which FCD mandates with respect to banks, contributes to solving this issue by facilitating the transformation of uninsured bank liabilities into 'safe assets'.[7] This, again enables clients with deposits above the threshold of the applicable deposit guarantee scheme to store excess liquidity safely.

[4] Schwarcz (n 3) 583. Schwarcz does note that the requirement of continuous 'overcollateralisation' of covered bonds could prejudice the interests of non-adjusting unsecured creditors, however.

[5] Norges Bank, 'Financial Stability Report: Vulnerabilities and Risks' (2018) 47–48.

[6] See High-level Expert Group on reforming the structure of the EU banking sector, 'Final Report' (2 October 2012) 9.

[7] See eg G Gorton and A Metrick, 'Securitized banking and the run on repo' (2012) 104 *Journal of Financial Economics* 425, 426–27; GB Gorton, *Slapped by the Invisible Hand: The Panic of 2007* (Oxford, Oxford University, Press 2010) 6–7.

This 'transformation' consists of banks and clients entering into 'repos', repurchase agreements where the bank (the 'seller') sells a safe security (eg a AAA-rated government bond) to a creditor (the 'buyer') and undertakes to repurchase the bond at a date in the immediate future. Pursuant to the terms of the agreement, the buyer is not under an obligation to transfer the security back to the seller at the end of the repo if the seller in the meantime has become subject to insolvency proceedings. Rather, the buyer may retain the security and set-off its value against the 'repurchase price' to be paid by the seller. Insofar as the value of the security suffices to cover the repurchase price, the buyer does not suffer a loss if the seller becomes subject to winding up or resolution during the term of the repo.

The more the value of the security exceeds the sale price at the time of the initial sale, the more assured the buyer is that the value of the sold security will not fall below the repurchase price during the term of the repo. The amount of such 'overcollateralisation' demanded by buyers depends on the volatility of the security's market value. If the parties continuously renew the contract with short intervals at a time (eg one day or one week), the buyer will have similar access to the funds on demand as a depositor (they can merely refuse to renew the contract) while avoiding the exposure to the bank's default that an uninsured depositor normally has.

Everything else being equal, a bank obtaining financing through repos instead of unsecured deposits will increase the credit risk of other unsecured creditors. As one would expect that the unsecured creditors respond to repo activity by increasing the interest rate they demand, this raises the question of whether the increased costs in borrowing from such creditors would offset the decrease in the interest costs paid to repo counterparties. In theory, there are two reasons why the response of the unsecured creditors will not fully offset the isolated benefit of lending through repos. First, some repo counterparties will attach an independent value to the safeness and liquidity of a repo, which in turn reduces the amount of interest the bank pays for the credit that the buyer effectively extends during the term of the repo. In such a case, the reduction of funding costs could exceed the increase that the remaining unsecured creditors will demand to make up for the increased risk they face as repo counterparties receive priority ahead of them. Secondly, not all unsecured creditors will view the bank's borrowing funds through repos as prejudicial to their interest. This is because covered deposits often form a substantial part of a bank's liabilities. As discussed at 2.4.4, deposit insurance dampens the incentive of these depositors to exert market discipline.

To what extent could EU law be viewed as facilitating the transformation of uninsured deposits into safe assets? We have already answered this question to some extent by noting that such transformation necessitates certain legal preconditions. FCD requires Member States to establish these preconditions. First, absolute priority enables lower overcollateralisation requirements. As our discussion at 5.2.2 showed, FCD requires that the secured party under a financial collateral arrangement have absolute priority to the secured assets. Another precondition is that banks can 'replenish' collateral shortfalls. In the case of a repo, this is achieved by transferring margin security. In some jurisdictions, avoidance rules could render the margin security ineffective should the security grantor subsequently fail. FCD removes the risk of this occurring, as the directive requires Member States to shield the provision of 'top-up' collateral from otherwise applicable avoidance provisions.

It may be possible to see the covered bonds framework as facilitating the issuance of safe assets. One of the explanations for the Covered Bonds Directive is that it creates a safe investment.[8] Indeed, covered bonds give the holders absolute priority to the cover pool assets ahead of the bank's other creditors. Unlike FCD, this directive does not contain explicit protection from avoidance rules, however. In any event, our discussion at 5.2.3 concluded that the risk of avoidance of replenishments of the asset pool backing the bonds is not particularly grave in the sample jurisdictions.

So far, we have discussed the funding cost argument in relation to SFD, FCD and CBD. To some extent, the implications of this argument are consistent with such bank-specific rules. More difficulties attach to reconciling the funding cost argument with BRRD's priority rules. BRRD's rules differ fundamentally from those of the abovementioned directives. These directives expand the powers of banks to grant security interests. Accordingly, they facilitate rather than prescribe that different bank creditors shall rank with different priority. An implicit rationale is that it is best to leave it to banks to determine whether to use this power. Conversely, BRRD's priority rules are prescriptive and thus do not follow the logic of the funding cost argument.

7.3. Falling Like Dominoes: Creditor Priority and Direct Contagion

The prevention of contagion is one of the most prominent justifications for society's special concern with bank insolvencies. Broadly speaking, contagion refers to the process through which the problems of one bank spread to other banks. Given the direct and indirect linkages between banks, a bank's failure inevitably involves some degree of contagion. However, contagion first becomes an issue of concern where the losses give rise to sufficiently grave effects. A case in point is BRRD Article 44(3)(c). This provision empowers the resolution authority to exempt claims from bail-in where contagion 'could ultimately cause a serious disturbance to the economy of a Member State or the Union'. In other words, the potential costs of contagion must be sufficiently high. In the following, we will use the term 'contagion' as shorthand for a form of contagion that exceeds this threshold.

As discussed at 2.1.4, there are conceptually different forms of contagion. In the following, we will analyse the argument that priority rules can contribute to mitigate *direct contagion* and discuss the extent to which the bank-specific priority

[8] CBD recital 5.

rules conform with its implications. Direct contagion refers to the process through which a bank's failure causes problems for another financial market actor because the latter has financial exposures to the bank.[9]

It is possible to view SFD and FCD as responses to the need to protect banks against direct contagion: an obvious measure whereby parties can reduce credit risk is to enter into a security arrangement. A policy implication of the need to reduce credit risk is to make it as easy as possible for parties to do so.[10] Moreover, the operation of the security arrangement should enjoy protection against otherwise applicable avoidance provisions.[11] Both SFD and FCD require that the provision of margin security shall remain immune to avoidance challenges in insolvency proceedings. Judging by their recitals, the prevention of direct contagion appears to have been an important goal of the two directives. SFD's recital speaks of the protection of collateral arrangements as necessary for reducing systemic risk.[12] This rationale could also explain FCD's protection of the provision of margin security, as the directive's recital speaks of margin security arrangements as constituting a 'sound market practice favoured by regulators'.[13]

Prescriptive priority rules constitute another approach to reducing the risk of direct contagion. BRRD includes such rules in that short-term interbank debt is to be immune from bail-in per se.[14] The resolution authority's aforementioned power to mitigate contagion by exempting claims on a case-by-case basis is also a form of prescriptive creditor protection. As already noted, this prescriptive approach differs from that of FCD, which seeks to enable banks to give secured creditors absolute priority over financial assets. However, FCD's approach is one of facilitating choice rather than prescription. Nothing in the directive prohibits banks and their creditors from choosing to maintain unsecured exposures towards one another. This element of optionality is not present in the case of the claims exempt from the bail-in power, as the parties are unable to contract out of the exemption.[15]

The above discussion shows that several bank-specific priority rules are reconcilable with a policy of preventing direct contagion. This approach is oriented towards the effects that priority rules have *if* a bank fails. This is understandable, as the concept of direct contagion presupposes the occurrence of a bank defaulting on its debt obligations. Conversely, the approach does not involve analysis of

[9] See eg the definition of direct contagion in Commission Delegated Regulation (EU) 2016/860 of 4 February 2016 specifying further the circumstances where exclusion from the application of write-down or conversion powers is necessary under Article 44(3) of Directive 2014/59/EU of the European Parliament and of the Council establishing a framework for the recovery and resolution of credit institutions and investment firms [2016] OJ L144/11 (BER) art 3(1).

[10] RH Weber and S Grünewald, 'Settlement Finality and Financial Collateral Directives: ignored but crucial in financial turmoil' (2009) 24 *Butterworths Journal of International Banking and Financial Law* 70, 73.

[11] P Paech, 'The Value of Financial Market Insolvency Safe Harbours' (2016) 36 *OJLS* 855, 872–73.

[12] SFD recital 9.

[13] FCD recital 16.

[14] BRRD art 44(2)(e).

[15] They could, of course, agree upon a maturity that is sufficiently long to disqualify the claim from the exception in BRRD art 44(2)(e).

how priority rights might affect the behaviour of banks, their creditors and other market actors *prior to* a bank's failure. By contrast, this is reflected in arguments oriented towards indirect contagion, to which we now turn.

7.4. Creditor Priority and Indirect Contagion: Fire Sales and Informational Contagion

A bank's failure may cause indirect forms of contagion. As discussed at 6.4.1, BER defines indirect contagion as 'a situation where [a bail-in] causes a negative reaction by market participants that leads to a severe disruption of the financial system with potential to harm the real economy'.[16] By drawing attention to the effects of a resolution, this definition also embodies the *ex post* approach inherent in arguments relating to direct contagion. However, as our discussion at 2.1.4 showed, the debate on contagion also includes analysis of the *ex ante* effects of the resolution regime. More specifically, this perspective includes predictions on how the possibility that a struggling bank might be resolved and the priority rules that will then apply may affect the behaviour of the struggling bank, its creditors and other financial market participants in the period leading up to the resolution. In other words, we can also speak of contagion to the extent that the prospects of a resolution causes shifts in the behaviour of financial market participants that in turn impair the provision of financial services.

A source of indirect contagion risk is the asset-side channel. As discussed at 2.1.4, the sale of the assets of a distressed or failed bank could cause the market price of such assets to fall. Such 'fire sales' have a negative effect on the aggregate asset values of other banks that hold similar assets. This, in turn, could impair the ability of these other banks to maintain all their short-term financing and force them to cut back on lending or sell illiquid assets at prices that further push down asset prices. In other words, actions that in isolation are individually rational could prove detrimental to the stability of the banking system.

Could the bank-specific priority rules plausibly be construed as a policy response to the issue of indirect contagion? Fire sales stem from a need for liquidity. Wide possibilities for granting security interests could increase the possibilities of banks to attract liquidity in times of stress.[17] Everything else being equal, the option for distressed banks to grant security interests in times of trouble could prevent fire sales, thus benefiting the stability of the financial system. This argument resembles the debt overhang argument made in the discussion on whether companies generally should be able to grant security interests.[18] The difference is

[16] BER art 3(2).

[17] European Central Bank, 'Main features of the repo market in the euro area' (October 2002) ECB Monthly Bulletin 64.

[18] See 4.4.3.

that while the beneficiaries in that context are the company's existing creditors, an additional benefit in the present context is the maintenance of financial stability.

Some scholars view this argument with scepticism. Rather than reducing the risk of liquidity squeezes and fire sales, rules akin to those set out in FCD may *increase* this risk. Their argument is that such special rules cause financial institutions to assume more risks in the form of unstable funding sources. As fragile funding structures increase systemic risk, the effect of insolvency privileges – eg priority ahead of other creditors – ends up being the opposite of the stated goal of such rules. One criticism of special treatment of repos is that it causes banks to finance themselves with 'more easily runnable debt'.[19] The underlying premise seems to be that banks would finance themselves to a larger degree with long-term debt were it not for the special insolvency protection of repos.[20] This, in turn, would reduce the risk of bank runs. A similar criticism is that the priority of secured creditors increases the expected losses of unsecured creditors and therefore gives the unsecured creditors a stronger incentive to run, compared to the result if losses were shared equally among the creditors.[21]

The above shows that the question of whether special protection of financial collateral arrangements mitigates fire sale risk is controversial. We now turn to discuss how EU law reflects the different views on the issue. The first view is that fire sales stem from a debt overhang problem. Accordingly, insofar as the special protection offered by FCD contributes to solving debt overhang issues, the directive will also help reduce systemic risk. As we have noted in earlier encounters with the debt overhang argument, the argument seems to imply that distressed banks should have wider powers for issuing secured instruments when they suffer from distress than they do otherwise. It is clear, however, that FCD itself does not fully conform to this standard, as the directive's protection of financial collateral arrangements does not merely function as a means for securing distressed banks access to funding. This conclusion derives from the directive's lack of provisions that limit the use of financial collateral arrangements to liquidity crises. In other words, the directive accords special protection to repos and similar transactions, regardless of whether the borrowing bank is able to attract unsecured funding. However, recent regulatory developments represent a move towards such a rule. As discussed at 2.3.6, EU law now contains a liquidity coverage requirement. Banks are henceforth under an obligation to maintain a liquidity buffer upon which they

[19] MJ Roe, 'The Derivatives Market's Payment Priorities as Financial Crisis Accelerator' (2011) 63 *Stanford Law Review* 539, 563; ER Morrison, MJ Roe and CS Sontchi, 'Rolling back the Repo Safe Harbors' (2014) 69 *The Business Lawyer* 1015, 1028.

[20] Morrison, Roe and Sontchi (n 19) 1028–30, 1036. It is not entirely apparent why banks would not instead respond by financing themselves with ordinary short-term secured loans in lieu of repos, however.

[21] See H Nabilou and A Prüm, 'Shadow Banking in Europe: Idiosyncrasies and their Implications for Financial Regulation' (2017) working paper, 29–30, at www.ssrn.com/abstract=3035831.

can draw in times of stress.[22] Assets must be unencumbered if they are to count towards the liquidity requirement.[23] In other words, banks must maintain a higher amount of unencumbered assets in good times than in bad times. This, in turn, means that parts of a bank's assets can only be subject to repos in times when the bank is likely suffering from a debt overhang problem.

Still, nothing prevents a bank and its secured creditors from exploiting the special protection of FCD, even if the bank is able to borrow on an unsecured basis. Accordingly, the function of the directive's special protection is not restricted to being a means for allowing banks to overcome debt overhang, thereby reducing the risk of disruptive fire sales.

As discussed above, some view the protection of financial collateral arrangements as adverse to financial stability. The policy implication of this view is to repeal FCD. It is easy to conclude that this view has failed to gain traction among EU policymakers, as FCD remains in force.

Turning to the priority of unsecured credit, BRRD's creditor hierarchy could be interpreted as attempts to make banks less susceptible to runs, which again would reduce the risk of fire sales. As our discussion at 6.4 showed, BRRD contains two kinds of rules that protect unsecured creditors. First, some of the rules are prescriptive and require that certain claims are immune from bail-in or enjoy priority to unsecured debt in all circumstances. Secondly, the resolution authority has the power to exempt claims on a case-by-case basis in the presence of certain circumstances. As the two types of rules raise distinct issues, we will discuss the mandatory rules before moving on to discuss those that give the resolution authority discretion.

As the discussion at 6.4.1 and 6.4.2 showed, certain types of short-term debt enjoy protection by being exempted from the bail-in power or by having priority over general unsecured creditors. A possible rationale for these rules runs along the following lines. Creditors will only run insofar as they possess two attributes. First, the creditor must have the right to demand immediate repayment from the bank. Short-term creditors clearly possess this attribute. A demand deposit entitles the depositor to receive repayment upon demand. A creditor holding a claim with a short and fixed term does not have to demand repayment; he will receive repayment upon maturity unless he and the bank actively agree to roll over the loan. Secondly, the creditor must have an incentive to run. Short-term creditors will not run insofar as they have assurance that someone else will bear the cost of failure. A priority rule can provide this assurance insofar as it guarantees that the relevant creditor will not bear losses should the bank become subject to resolution.

This argument could be susceptible to different forms of criticism. The benefit of making short-term creditors less prone to run would obviously be lost if the

[22] Commission Delegated Regulation (EU) 2015/61 to supplement Regulation (EU) No 575/2013 of the European Parliament and the Council with regard to liquidity coverage requirement for Credit Institutions [2015] OJ L11/1 art 4.

[23] LCRR art 7(2).

protection of short-term creditors increases the incentive of long-term creditors to seek early repayment of their claims. If the long-term creditors were also able to demand repayment by accelerating their loans, this would defeat the attempt at reducing the risk of bank runs. A crucial assumption, therefore, is that such creditors do not have a right to demand early repayment because of doubts arising over the issuer's financial health. While it cannot be ruled out that the long-term financial arrangements of some banks are subject to such terms, it appears that such terms rarely feature in the bonds and other long-term instruments that banks issue. Another argument against giving short-term creditors priority is that priority rules favouring short-term debt could cause banks to shift their funding towards this kind of debt. As we will show in chapter eight below, this concern is mitigated by banks being under an obligation to maintain a minimum amount of debt with a remaining maturity of at least one year.

A different argument against giving short-term creditors priority ahead of other creditors is that the objective of containing run risk must be balanced against the need to maintain market discipline, as short-term debt contributes to this end.[24] The purported benefits on market discipline of banks issuing unsecured short-term debt derive from two factors. The first factor is that the debt is unsecured and the creditors of such debt stand to lose if the bank becomes subject to insolvency proceedings before they have received repayment. The second factor is that the debt has a short maturity. This allows the creditors to respond to an increase in a bank's risk-taking by demanding a higher rate of interest or repayment. As they are aware of this, the bank's management will avoid excessive risks.

The market discipline argument does not necessarily mean that all unsecured short-term debt must be susceptible to losses. The related debate on the effects of deposit insurance on market discipline provides an interesting parallel. Some participants in this debate argue that deposit insurance may not be detrimental to the extent that the bank maintains other short-term unsecured debt, such as uninsured deposits and interbank claims.[25] Applied to the case of the bail-in power, the logic underlying this argument implies that at least some short-term claims should remain susceptible to being bailed-in when a bank is resolved.

Some advocates of adjusting priority rules to reduce run risk recognise the market discipline argument but do not view it as detrimental to a policy of prioritising short-term bank debt. From one view, the market discipline that long-term creditors exert is sufficient to prevent banks from taking on a suboptimal high level of risk.[26] A different argument against placing too much emphasis on the policy

[24] TH Jackson and DA Skeel, Jr., 'Dynamic Resolution of Large Financial Institutions' (2012) 2 *Harvard Business Law Review* 435, 448; T Philippon and A Salord, *Bail-ins and Bank Resolution in Europe: A Progress Report* (Geneva Reports on the World Economy, ICMB/CEPR 2017) 50.

[25] DW Diamond and RG Rajan, 'Liquidity Risk, Liquidity Creation, and Financial Fragility: A Theory of Banking' (2001) 109 *Journal of Political Economy* 287, 319.

[26] P Davies, 'The Fall and Rise of Debt: Bank Capital Regulation After the Crisis' (2015) 16 *European Business Organization Law Review* 491, 503.

prescriptions of advocates of market discipline is more fundamental. It consists of questioning the basic premise of the market discipline argument, namely that placing certain bank creditors at risk of being bailed in will make such creditors, by way of monitoring, pressure banks to assume less risk.[27] Their reason for questioning this premise is that banks are 'complex and opaque', and that it is therefore difficult for creditors to monitor their operations.

We now turn to discuss how BRRD balances the above argument in its protection of run-prone creditors. It seems plausible that the wish to reduce run risk motivates the protection of short-term debt. It is not clear whether BRRD's scope of protection is the most rational means to this end. As noted at 6.4.1, not all short-term unsecured debt enjoys protection from bail-in.[28] One possible rationale for this is that it simply is not possible to provide all short-term creditors with protection without risking that the remaining (long-term) debt is insufficient for recapitalising the bank. However, it is arguable that BRRD's solution differs from what would be optimal from the perspective of preventing runs. Under such a policy, the short-term creditors that are most likely to run should enjoy the highest priority. Four categories of short-term creditors currently enjoy special protection under BRRD. The first category is covered depositors. The second category is depositors that are natural persons, micro-, small- or medium-sized enterprises with deposit balances that exceed the coverage threshold under the applicable deposit guarantee scheme. The third category comprises other credit institutions whose claims have an original maturity of seven days or less. The fourth is claims that arise through participation in settlement systems with a remaining maturity of seven days or less. Not all short-term creditors benefit from an exemption, however. While such short-term creditors could have been run-prone even under a creditor hierarchy based on *pari passu* distribution, BRRD's protection of other short-term claims could accentuate their incentives to run on struggling banks, as they are now more vulnerable if the bank subsequently fails. This residual category of short-term creditors includes professional asset managers and larger companies with dedicated treasury personnel. It is reasonable to assume that these creditors will be among the first to react should they sense trouble.[29] This is also reflected in EU liquidity regulation, which deems such creditors as more likely to run than, for example, retail depositors.[30] Given the premise that not all short-term debt can be

[27] M Andenas and IH-Y Chiu, *The Foundations and Future of Financial Regulation* (London, Routledge, 2014) 325–26.

[28] See also J Armour et al, *Principles of Financial Regulation* (Oxford, Oxford University Press, 2016) 360; JN Gordon and W-G Ringe, 'Resolution in the European Banking Union: The Unfinished Agenda of Structural Reform' in D Busch and G Ferrarini (eds), *European Banking Union* (Oxford, Oxford University Press, 2015) para 15.18; Davies (n 26) 508.

[29] Financial Stability Board, 'Recovery and Resolution Planning for Systemically Important Financial Institutions: Guidance on Identification of Critical Functions and Critical Shared Services' (16 July 2013) 15; Norges Bank (n 5) 34–35.

[30] For instance, a comparison of LCRR arts 25 and 28 shows that the regulation implicitly deems an uninsured retail depositor as less likely to withdraw money from a distressed bank than other unsecured short-term creditors.

protected, some would therefore be inclined to conclude that BRRD's protection of small depositors is perhaps not the best if the goal is to contain run risk.

However, BRRD's approach of not insulating all short-term creditors is consistent to some extent with a market discipline rationale. The asset managers and large companies that remain exposed to bail-in risk are among the creditors perceived as the most apt at observing and reacting to a bank's excessive risk-taking. However, it appears somewhat inconsistent with the market discipline rationale to exclude short-term interbank liabilities from the scope of the bail-in power, presuming that other banks are at least as well placed to react to increased credit risk as asset managers and corporate treasury departments.

To summarise, the scope of the protection for short-term creditors embodied in BRRD's exclusions from the bail-in power as well as the priority of non-insured deposits held by natural persons and SMEs conform to a rationale of reducing the risk of fire sale-inducing bank runs. It is, however, arguable that the exact configuration of this protection is not entirely coherent with a single rationale. In a similar vein, the implications of a policy aiming at fostering market discipline by exposing sophisticated short-term creditors to bail-in risk is partially consistent with the scope of the bail-in power and the priority among creditors susceptible to bail-in.

As mentioned, BRRD Article 44(3)(c) raises distinct issues. The provision gives the resolution authority the power to exclude a liability from bail-in where necessary to avoid contagion. As a matter of law, creditors are not assured protection until the resolution authority has made the decision to exercise its power to exempt claims from bail-in. This approach has attracted criticism, as some view this as prejudicial for the purposes of mitigating the incentive of short-term creditors to run on the bank in the period preceding the resolution.[31] As put by Armour et al, why would short-term creditors 'wait around to discover whether, exceptionally, it was to be exempted in this particular case?'[32] In a similar vein, Paul Davies argues that resolution authorities facing a systemic crisis should announce the intention to exclude all short-term debt from bail-in.[33]

Others view Article 44(3) as one of several instances of BRRD leaving outcomes to vague standards and the discretion of the resolution authority and the other authorities involved.[34] In turn, this uncertainty makes it harder for creditors to gauge how a bank failure will affect their claims against the bank, which ultimately makes it more difficult for the creditors to exert market discipline.[35] Given the tendency of the debate on bank creditor priority to frame the design of the loss distribution criteria as a trade-off between stable funding structures and the

[31] Armour et al (n 28) 360–61.

[32] ibid 361.

[33] Davies (n 26) 508. As the power to exclude liabilities pursuant to BRRD art 44(3) is intended to be used on a case-by-case basis, such an announcement may be incompatible with the directive, however.

[34] TH Tröger, 'Too Complex to Work: A Critical Assessment of the Bail-in Tool under the European Bank Recovery and Resolution Regime' (2018) 4 *Journal of Financial Regulation* 35, 59.

[35] ibid 37.

maintenance of market discipline, it is interesting to note that BRRD Article 44(3) is susceptible to criticism of accomplishing neither of the two objectives.

Our discussion has so far been concerned with the asset-side contagion that occurs through fire sales of assets commonly held by banks. Another form of indirect contagion is informational contagion. As addressed at 2.1.4, informational contagion occurs when the news of the failure of one bank ('Bank A') causes the creditors of one or more other banks ('Bank B') to begin questioning the financial soundness of Bank B. In certain circumstances, the failure of Bank A could trigger a systemwide run. As noted, it is reasonable to assume that informational contagion not only requires that the creditors of Bank B start to question that bank's soundness, but that the creditors must also fear they will suffer losses if the bank should fail. Rearranging creditor priority to protect the creditors most susceptible to run could therefore be beneficial for preventing runs. However, many of the same counterarguments addressed above would also apply in this context.

In summary, the fire sale argument and the informational contagion argument partially offer plausible rationales for the bank-specific priority rules found in EU law. First, FCD's expansion of banks' powers to create 'insolvency-proof' security interests could be viewed as a means for facilitating the access of distressed banks to liquidity, which – again – would prevent fire sales and bank failures that cause informational contagion. Given that the banks use these powers in normal times and could therefore have few unencumbered assets available in a crisis, this argument offers a partial explanation at best.

Turning to the scope of BRRD's bail-in power and its rules on priority among unsecured bank creditors, the protection of some short-term unsecured creditors is compatible with a policy of mitigating fire sales and informational contagion. However, assuming that not all short-term creditors can enjoy protection and that protection should be given to the most run-prone creditors, it might be argued that the protection of sophisticated short-term creditors is the policy that would best prevent fire sales and informational contagion. The current rules only do so in part. This result is nonetheless understandable considering the political outcry that would likely ensue from a proposal to protect financial creditors at the expense of retail depositors. The lack of rules protecting all short-term creditors could, however, also be explained by a policy oriented towards maintaining market discipline. Under such a policy, exposing sophisticated short-term creditors to losses could cause them to exercise market discipline, thus stymieing excessive risk-taking on the part of banks with such creditors.

7.5. The Reorientation of Bank-Specific Creditor Priority Rules: From Party Autonomy to Prescriptive Rules

The above discussion justifies the conclusion that bank-specific priority rules do not merely involve the adaption of general insolvency law principles to fit the peculiar features of banks. Although it proved futile to draw up a single and coherent rationale that explains all the rules, the best-fitting rationale is the prevention of different forms of contagion.

While preventing contagion serves as a rationale for priority rules dating both prior to and following the GFC, there appears to have been a shift in the types of contagion with which the rules are concerned. The special protection offered by directives of a pre-crisis vintage, such as SFD and FCD, seems to build on the logic of protecting the secured creditors of banks. Given that the secured creditors of banks often could be other banks, these directives embody an approach to contagion that is oriented towards the immediate effects of a bank failure once the failure has occurred. In other words, the underlying idea seems to be that if banks transact with each other on a secured basis, the financial system should be safe. This echoes the logic many ascribe to the pre-crisis banking regulation. As discussed at 2.3.4, it is common to refer to this approach to banking regulation as microprudential. The microprudential approach has attracted criticism for failing to reflect how actions that are rational for individual institutions in sum may produce adverse outcomes for the financial system as a whole.

Conversely, the post-crisis priority rules exhibit an orientation towards the *ex ante* effects that priority rules may have on the behaviour of banks and their creditors, which in turn affects other parts of the financial system. This approach views the prevention of bank runs as imperative because a run could harm banks that have no dealings with the bank in question and could ultimately reduce the capacity of the banking sector to provide financial services. The emergence of this approach to bank creditor priority coincides with the adoption of a host of initiatives aimed at shifting banking regulation in a more macroprudential direction. As discussed at 2.3.4, a macroprudential approach involves an orientation centred directly on safeguarding the financial system rather than pursuing this end indirectly by safeguarding its constituent parts.

Another shift in the approach to bank creditor priority concerns the structure of the rules. The pre-crisis Directives were oriented towards removing barriers for banks granting each other security interests with absolute priority, but they did not prescribe that banks should actually use this autonomy. Conversely, the approach of BRRD's priority rules is one of prescriptive rules that partly dictate how losses are to fall on different constituencies among a bank's creditors. These developments mirror more broad regulatory trends. As discussed at 2.2.2, the calculation of pre-crisis capital requirements increasingly relied on the internal risk models of banks, particularly in the case of large banks. The recent inclusion in CRR of the leverage ratio requirement – ie the unweighted capital requirement discussed at 2.3.5 – involves a more prescriptive approach to capital regulation and thereby reflects a distrust of the developments in pre-crisis banking regulation.

It is also noteworthy that BRRD employs two approaches for determining creditor priority. The first approach consists of the provisions that exclude certain claims from the scope of the bail-in power and requires that certain claims shall have priority above or below general unsecured creditors in winding-up proceedings and resolution. These rules leave no discretion: if a claim falls within one of the categories listed in BRRD Article 44(2), the resolution power lacks the power to bail-in that claim.

However, BRRD also employs a second approach: giving the resolution authority direct influence over how a bank's creditors share losses in resolution. As discussed at 6.4.1, the authority may exclude claims from bail-in on a case-by-case basis insofar as one of the grounds set out in Article 44(3) is met. The provision employs vague conditions – eg 'not possible … within a reasonable time'; 'strictly necessary and … proportionate to achieve the continuity of critical functions'; and 'strictly necessary and proportionate to avoid giving rise to widespread contagion'. Moreover, these conditions require projections of the outcome of a given claim being bailed-in or not. The making of such projections requires technical expertise. Considering whether bailing-in the claims of eg non-insured deposits will cause runs on other banks requires a model of the effects of such claims being bailed-in.

Rather than opting for 'blunt' and clear rules pursuant to which certain creditors are *always* exempt from bail-in, while other creditors are *never* excluded as such, the EU legislature adopted an approach where the resolution authority may intervene on a case-by-case basis with a view to optimising the outcome of the resolution. This approach falls in line with the broader trend towards technocratic fine-tuning in banking regulation to which we shall return in chapter nine.

While bank insolvency law has evolved towards a more prescriptive approach to issues of creditor priority, it is important to note that priority rules still leave banks with ample room to influence the loss distribution among their creditors. Banks may place certain creditors in a position that is better than that of general unsecured creditors by granting security interests. Likewise, a bank and a creditor may agree that the creditor shall rank behind general unsecured creditors, thus leaving that creditor worse off in a winding up or resolution. An interesting trend is the emergence of public law requirements that dictate how banks are to use this influence over loss sharing among their creditors. The requirements in question thus complement the priority rules in forging the loss distribution among bank creditors. The next chapter will analyse these requirements.

8

Administrative Law and Creditor Priority: The Case of MREL* (Minimum Requirements for Own Funds and Eligible Liabilities)

8.1. How Administrative Law and Decisions Increasingly Influence Private Contracting Over Priority

Chapter two discussed the various capital requirements that apply to banks, namely the minimum own funds requirements, pillar 2 requirements adopted by bank supervisors and the capital buffer requirements. All of these requirements concern the liabilities side of bank balance sheets. While the capital requirements essentially establish a minimum requirement for their equity-to-debt ratio, our discussion at 2.3.2 showed how banks may in part satisfy some of these requirements with instruments that may count as liabilities for accounting purposes – AT1 and Tier 2 instruments.

The adoption of BRRD in 2014 saw the introduction of further requirements with implications for how banks finance themselves. Banks must now observe MREL, a 'minimum requirement for own funds *and eligible liabilities*' (emphasis added). Eligible liabilities are long-term liabilities that meet certain conditions.[1] The MREL framework is of interest from a creditor priority perspective, as one such condition may be that the liability must rank with priority below general unsecured debt in a winding up under normal insolvency proceedings or resolution. In other words, banks may be under a regulatory obligation to ensure that a certain portion of their financing is subordinated to general unsecured creditors. As satisfying this requirement could require banks entering into agreements with some of their creditors to subordinate their claims to those of other creditors, MREL is an example of a regulatory requirement for how banks should exercise the discretion that bank insolvency law leaves for them to contract with creditors over priority in a winding up or resolution. The MREL framework is not the

[1] BRRD art 2(1)(71a).

sole example of such requirements. As discussed at 2.3.7, the European Market Infrastructure Regulation (EMIR) in some cases requires banks trading in derivatives to enter into security arrangements with their counterparties, thus obliging banks to use their power to enter into such arrangements as guaranteed by the Financial Collateral Directive.[2] An analysis of creditor priority in bank insolvency law is incomplete without a discussion of MREL, as such requirements are of great importance for loss distribution among bank creditors.

In 2019, the MREL framework underwent numerous amendments as part of a wider reform of EU banking law. It is now composed of provisions scattered across CRR and BRRD. CRR contains fixed, directly applicable minimum requirements that apply to global systemically important institutions (G-SIIs).[3] BRRD, meanwhile, sets out a regulatory regime where resolution authorities on a case-by-case basis shall determine the MREL of the banks under their remit.

A key driver for the recent amendments of the MREL framework was the publication of the Financial Stability Board's principles for total loss-absorbing capacity (TLAC) in 2015.[4] In contrast to BRRD's original MREL regime, which in principle applied to all banks, the TLAC standard only applies to G-SIIs. The recent amendments to CRR implemented the TLAC standard in EU law.[5] However, the EU chose to go beyond what was necessary for EU law to conform to the standard and revised the general MREL framework to align technical aspects with CRR's new regime for G-SIIs. In addition, the reform introduced limits on the resolution authority's powers in terms of both quantitative and qualitative aspects of their MREL decisions.

This chapter examines the MREL regime. We will shed some light on the background and rationale of the MREL regime (8.2), before discussing its evolution from BRRD's first iteration (8.3), via the subsequent adoption of the TLAC principles (8.4) to the adoption of the current framework (8.5). This discussion will analyse the extent to which debt has been, or is, required to be subordinated to general unsecured debt to count towards satisfying a bank's MREL obligations. To complete the picture of how the MREL regime operates to distribute losses among bank creditors, we discuss the regulation of the sale of and investment in MREL-eligible instruments at 8.6.

The current MREL framework distinguishes between entities designated as 'resolution entities' and other entities. This distinction is of relevance when a group

[2] See the discussion at 5.2.2.

[3] On the designation of banks as G-SIIs, see 2.3.4.

[4] Financial Stability Board, 'Principles on Loss-absorbing and Recapitalisation Capacity of G-SIBs in Resolution: Total Loss-absorbing Capacity (TLAC) Term Sheet' (9 November 2015).

[5] Regulation (EU) 2019/876 of the European Parliament and of the Council of 20 May 2019 amending Regulation (EU) No 575/2013 as regards the leverage ratio, the net stable funding ratio, requirements for own funds and eligible liabilities, counterparty credit risk, market risk, exposures to central counterparties, exposures to collective investment undertakings, large exposures, reporting and disclosure requirements, and Regulation (EU) No 648/2012 [2019] OJ L150/1.

comprises several entities potentially subject to resolution.[6] Resolution entities are the entities that the resolution authority envisages to resolve to recapitalise the group. The MREL framework treats the two categories somewhat differently, but the principles are the same. For convenience, we will in this chapter primarily draw our attention to the framework that applies to resolution entities.

In some cases, the resolution entity will be a bank's holding company. The group will then satisfy MREL requirements by the holding company issuing debt to external bond investors and thereafter, to the extent necessary, lending on the loan proceeds in the form of subordinated loans within the group. Upon the resolution entity being resolved, its external liabilities are bailed-in and its claims under the intragroup loans are written down, thereby recapitalising the other group members.[7] For an external bond investor, there is not much difference between investing in a bond issued by a holding company or a subordinated bond issued by an operational entity within the group. In both cases, the investor will have recourse to the operational entity's assets after the (other) creditors of the operational entity.[8] For convenience, we will therefore refer to the issuer of MREL-eligible debt as a bank in the following sections, notwithstanding that the issuer may be a holding company.

8.2. Background

The MREL framework consists of highly technical rules. To facilitate the ensuing discussion, we will first provide a brief account of the rationale for the MREL framework and its relationship with the capital requirements discussed at 2.3.

To this end, we must return briefly to the components that comprise the capital requirements regime and their functions.[9] The higher of the own funds requirement and the leverage ratio requirement, each possibly supplemented by a pillar 2 requirement, represents the minimum amount of capital that banks must maintain. In principle, it is not permissible for a bank to operate with capital below this threshold. Breaches of the minimum capital requirements could result in the bank's supervisor withdrawing its authorisation or the resolution authority resolving the bank.

Following the GFC, the EU added capital buffers to its capital requirements framework. The buffer requirements differ from the traditional capital requirements

[6] The entities subject to the resolution powers are credit institutions, investment firms, certain holding companies and financial institutions controlled by credit institutions or investment firms, see BRRD art 1(1).

[7] BRRD art 59(1).

[8] For a different view, see JN Gordon and W-G Ringe, 'Resolution in the European Banking Union: The Unfinished Agenda of Structural Reform' in D Busch and G Ferrarini (eds), *European Banking Union* (Oxford, Oxford University Press, 2015) para 15.18.

[9] See the discussion at 2.3.

in that banks may continue to operate despite breaching these requirements. Rather than triggering the withdrawal of the bank's authorisation or resolution, the sanction for breaching the buffer requirements is that the bank in question must restrict distributions to shareholders, and awarding and paying out bonuses until it has shored up its capital ratio by raising new equity, retaining earnings or selling assets to pay off debt.

In a sense, minimum requirements and buffer requirements represent different philosophies. The underlying idea of a minimum requirement is to ensure that a loss-making bank is shut down and wound up before it has become deeply insolvent. It is therefore now common to view the minimum requirements as oriented towards a microprudential objective of preventing banks from taking on excessive risk at the expense of insured depositors or, perhaps more realistically, their home state as the ultimate deposit insurer.[10] Conversely, the buffer requirements build on the idea that it is necessary to ensure that banks can incur certain losses and still be able to maintain their operations. This reflects the increased focus of post-crisis banking regulation on maintaining the continuity of financial services in times of stress.

MREL follows the approach of the capital buffer requirements and further increases the amount of losses that a bank should be able to withstand and still be able to continue its operations, even if this necessitates recapitalising the bank through resolution. It is important to note that MREL is a requirement for *own funds and* eligible liabilities. The acronym MREL is thus somewhat misleading – MROFEL would be more accurate. What this means is that a bank that falls short of its MREL requirement has the choice between issuing additional own funds or eligible liabilities to comply.

The parallel between the underlying logics of the MREL framework and the capital buffer requirements, respectively, is most apparent in the case of a bank that solely uses CET1 capital – ie roughly speaking, equity – to satisfy MREL. The bank's aggregate amount of equity would then be equal to the sum of: (i) the amount it needs to satisfy the own funds requirement, and (ii) the amount of losses it should be able to bear, as represented by the additional equity it holds to meet the capital buffer requirement and MREL. The bank could then burn through component (ii) without meeting the conditions for resolution, as component (i) would still be sufficient to satisfy the own funds requirement. It is then neither necessary nor legal for the resolution authority to place the bank under resolution and write down its liabilities.

Suppose instead that component (ii) consists of debt. It would still be possible to reach the result where the bank complies with the minimum own funds requirement notwithstanding the losses, but this would necessitate the intermediate step of a resolution where the debts composing component (ii) are written down, thereby increasing the bank's equity.

[10] See the discussion at 2.3.4.

If only CET1 capital counted towards meeting the MREL requirement, one would do away with the burden of having to execute a resolution. Why, then, does the current framework permit banks to meet MREL with debt? A key consideration is likely the view that increasing equity requirements increases banks' financing costs.[11] All else being equal, an increase in a bank's financing costs will, in turn, make lending to marginal borrowers unprofitable, and the bank will thus no longer lend to such borrowers. Accordingly, increases in capital requirements lead to less lending to the real economy. If one accepts this argument, the calibration of capital requirements involves a trade-off between the soundness of the banking sector and the sector's ability to provide finance.

It seems highly plausible that the financing cost argument is a key reason for why the MREL framework was introduced instead of increases in capital requirements beyond those of the minimum requirement and the buffer requirements. As discussed, resolution makes it possible to recapitalise banks by writing down their liabilities. A well-timed resolution can achieve the same results as an increased capital requirement. If resolution actions are indeed timely, it will thus be possible to meet the objective of increasing the loss-bearing capacity of banks at a lower cost than under increased capital requirements, seeing that debt carries lower financing costs.

Our account so far does not provide a rationale for why debt liabilities should count towards meeting MREL only insofar as they are long-term and subordinated to general unsecured debt. There are two different rationales that favour such policy. The first rationale is that the composition of a bank's debts is of importance for whether it will be feasible to recapitalise the bank through resolution. Importantly, as discussed in earlier chapters, some liabilities are excluded from the resolution authority's bail-in power. Examples include insured deposits and short-term interbank debt. All else being equal, these exceptions will likely affect the behaviour of banks and bank creditors. First, banks will have an incentive to finance themselves through debt that is excluded from the scope of the bail-in power. Secondly, bank creditors that are subject to the bail-in power will have incentives to exercise any repayment rights they may have upon the first sight of trouble at the bank. The design of the bail-in power thereby creates, or at least exacerbates, the risk that the debts that the resolution authority is empowered to bail-in will not be of an amount sufficient to recapitalise the bank.

Insofar as a sufficiently large portion of a bank's debts is long-term and subordinated, the above problems do not necessarily arise. While banks may in part finance themselves with debt excluded from bail-in, this is not problematic if the

[11] For a recent review of the literature on this issue, see Basel Committee on Banking Supervision, 'The costs and benefits of bank capital – a review of the literature' (June 2019). For a critique of the argument that increasing equity requirements result in increased social costs, see AR Admati et al, 'Fallacies, Irrelevant Facts, and Myths in the Discussion of Capital Regulation: Why Bank Equity is Not Socially Expensive' (2013) Rock Center for Corporate Governance at Stanford University Working Paper No 161.

amount of non-excluded debts is sufficient to recapitalise the bank. Moreover, if a subset of creditors – those who have agreed to a priority subordinate to that of general unsecured debt – will bear the burden of recapitalising the bank in the event of resolution, other creditors do not have an incentive to run if the bank appears to suffer from financial problems. Understood against this background, the underlying idea of MREL is to ensure that it is possible to recapitalise banks through bail-in. More specifically, this is achieved by requiring that a sufficient portion of bank liabilities are long term and therefore will remain outstanding come resolution. Moreover, requiring that liabilities must be subordinated to count towards MREL reduces the risks of bank runs. As put by Ringe, such a policy could be 'understood as avoiding destructive runs, fire sales, and contagion – in short, any transmission of shock to the real economy'.[12]

A second rationale for requiring that debt must be subordinated to count towards MREL is to reduce the risk of resolution triggering compensation claims against the resolution fund. As chapter six showed, resolution and normal insolvency proceedings do not necessarily lead to the same loss distribution among creditors. Importantly, some creditors are excluded from the scope of the bail-in tool. Other creditors could therefore end up retaining less value following resolution than they would if the bank had instead been wound up. However, this risk is not ultimately borne by any one creditor. As discussed at 6.6, the no-creditors-worse-off (NCWO) safeguard set out in BRRD Article 73ff provides that creditors shall have a claim for compensation against the resolution fund if resolution leaves them worse off than they would be if the bank had instead been wound up. This compensation scheme involves transferring the losses initially suffered by disadvantaged creditors to those that finance the resolution fund, namely the other banks required to make contributions. The potential liability of the resolution fund is viewed as problematic. Statements in both the Financial Stability Board's TLAC standard and the recital to BRRD II express a desire to eliminate the risk of such liabilities materialising.[13]

The risk of creditors being left worse off in resolution decreases with banks funding themselves with debt ranking below general unsecured debt in normal insolvency proceedings and resolution. Through the operation of BRRD Article 48, a resolution authority exercising the bail-in power must first fully write down subordinated debt before writing down general unsecured debt. Assuming that some general unsecured debt must be bailed-in to recapitalise the bank, the existence of a layer of subordinated debt will reduce the extent to which general unsecured debt must be written down for the bank to reach the desired level of capital post-resolution.

[12] W-G Ringe, 'Bank Bail-in Between Liquidity and Solvency' (2018) 92 *American Bankruptcy Law Journal* 299, 316.

[13] Financial Stability Board, 'Principles on Loss-absorbing and Recapitalisation Capacity of G-SIBs in Resolution: Total Loss-absorbing Capacity (TLAC) Term Sheet' (9 November 2015) 16; BRRD II recital 9.

8.3. The First Iteration of the MREL Regime

In its original iteration, BRRD Article 45 set out the resolution authority's power to impose individual MREL requirements on banks and other institutions. Resolution authorities were to consider six criteria when determining a bank's MREL requirement.[14] These were centred around the first rationale described at 8.2, that is, whether considerations of financial stability are likely to require that the relevant bank is resolved rather than wound up and, if so, the need to ensure that the bank will have a sufficient amount of debt available for bail in.

The original iteration of Article 45 did not itself establish any prescriptions as to the size of the MREL requirement. However, a Commission Delegated Regulation set out certain limits on the resolution authority's discretion.[15] Under the regulation, resolution authorities were to determine a 'loss absorption amount' and a 'recapitalisation amount'. A bank's MREL requirement was to be at least equal to the sum of those amounts. The loss absorption amount was, as a default rule, to equal the bank's capital requirements.[16] However, the regulation allowed for both upwards and downwards adjustments in certain cases.

The size of the recapitalisation amount depended on several variables. The recapitalisation amount would, as a main rule, be set to zero if the resolution authority considered it to be feasible and credible to let the bank be wound up under normal insolvency proceedings in the event of failure. In such cases, the bank's MREL would equal its minimum capital requirements. Accordingly, compliance with MREL would not involve any burden beyond obligations to which the bank in any event would be subject. The regulation's approach was thus that only banks that the resolution authority expected to resolve – ie banks of a certain size and systemic importance – were to have a recapitalisation amount exceeding zero. For such banks, the recapitalisation amount was to equal at least 'the amount necessary to satisfy applicable capital requirements necessary to comply with the conditions for authorisation after the implementation of the preferred resolution strategy'.[17] This meant that if the preferred resolution strategy for a bank was recapitalisation through a bail-in of its creditors, the recapitalisation amount had to at least equal the sum of the own funds requirement and the bank's individual pillar 2 requirement, if applicable. However, the resolution authority had the power to increase the recapitalisation amount insofar as this was deemed 'necessary to maintain sufficient market confidence after resolution'.[18] This allowed the

[14] BRRD art 45(6) as it read prior to the adoption of BRRD II.

[15] Commission Delegated Regulation (EU) 2016/1450 of 23 May 2016 supplementing Directive 2014/59/EU of the European Parliament and of the Council with regard to regulatory technical standards specifying the criteria relating to the methodology for setting the minimum requirement for own funds and eligible liabilities [2016] OJ L237/1.

[16] Commission Delegated Regulation (EU) 2016/1450 art 1(5).

[17] Commission Delegated Regulation (EU) 2016/1450 art 2(5).

[18] Commission Delegated Regulation (EU) 2016/1450 art 2(7).

resolution authority to also include the bank's combined buffer requirement in the recapitalisation amount.

As discussed, MREL is a requirement for own funds and eligible liabilities. BRRD Article 45(4) originally set out the requirements that a liability had to meet to count as an eligible liability. Importantly, one such requirement was that the liability had a remaining maturity of at least one year.[19] The resolution authority was to be empowered to require that a bank met MREL with instruments ranking below general unsecured debt in resolution and normal insolvency proceedings.[20] However, the authority was not under an obligation to use this power. The general policy of many resolution authorities was to require that institutions met MREL with subordinated liabilities insofar as the resolution plan contemplated a bail-in strategy.[21]

8.4. The Emergence of a Global Consensus: Total Loss-Absorbing Capacity (TLAC)

In 2015, the Financial Stability Board (FSB) published a document setting out a standard for the loss-absorbing and recapitalisation capacity of global systemically important banks (the TLAC standard).[22] FSB is an international body composed of senior officials of the central banks and financial supervisory authorities of the G20 countries and certain other states, as well as representatives from the Commission and ECB. Among other things, FSB develops regulatory standards. These standards, including the TLAC standard, are not formally binding on any state. As we shall see, the EU nonetheless chose to reform the MREL framework to bring it in line with the standard.

The TLAC standard differs from the original MREL framework in several respects. First, its scope is restricted to global systemically important banks. Conversely, the MREL framework applied to all banks. Secondly, unlike the original MREL framework, the TLAC standard contains a common quantitative minimum requirement: Banks shall have TLAC that exceeds the higher of 18 per cent of risk-weighted assets and 6.75 per cent of the Basel III leverage ratio denominator. Thirdly, the TLAC standard provides that equity capital employed towards meeting the capital buffer requirements cannot simultaneously be used to satisfy a TLAC requirement, whereas BRRD was originally silent on this issue.

[19] BRRD art 45(4) as it read prior to the adoption of BRRD II.

[20] BRRD art 45(14) as it read prior to the adoption of BRRD II.

[21] See Single Resolution Board, 'Minimum Requirement for Own Funds and Eligible Liabilities (MREL): 2018 SRB Policy for the second wave of resolution plans' (16 January 2019) 13–14; Bank of England, 'The Bank of England's approach to setting a minimum requirement for own funds and eligible liabilities (MREL)' (June 2018) 6.

[22] Financial Stability Board, 'Principles on Loss-absorbing and Recapitalisation Capacity of G-SIBs in Resolution: Total Loss-absorbing Capacity (TLAC) Term Sheet' (9 November 2015).

Fourthly, the TLAC standard contains more requirements that debts must satisfy to count towards the minimum requirement than BRRD's MREL framework originally did. Importantly for present purposes, the main rule is that debt instruments only count towards the TLAC minimum insofar as they rank with priority below debt that the standard deems as 'liabilities excluded from TLAC' – eg short-term deposits, debts ranking with priority ahead of general unsecured debt and liabilities arising under derivatives. As we will return to in the below discussion of the reformed MREL framework, this requirement effectively means that a debt obligation only counts toward meeting the TLAC minimum insofar as it is subordinated to general unsecured debt.

8.5. The Revision of the MREL Regime

8.5.1. Quantitative Requirements

Following the 2019 revision of the MREL framework, different frameworks apply for global systemically important institutions (G-SIIs) and other banks. G-SIIs are subject to numerical minimum requirements set out in CRR, with the resolution authority having the power to impose higher requirements on a case-by-case basis in line with a framework laid out in BRRD. Conversely, other banks are subject only to the resolution authority's administrative decision-making, which is also governed by BRRD.

In line with the TLAC standard, CRR Article 92a(1) now prescribes that all G-SIIs shall maintain own funds and eligible liabilities that exceed both 18 per cent of their risk-weighted *total risk exposure amount* (RWA) and 6.75 per cent of the *total exposure measure* (the unweighted denominator used for determining a bank's leverage ratio). Banks cannot simultaneously apply CET1 capital towards risk-weighted MREL and the capital buffer requirements.[23] If a bank is subject to an aggregate capital requirement of 16.5 per cent of RWA and the capital buffer requirement makes up 6.5 percentage points of the requirement, only the capital composing the first 10 percentage points will count towards satisfying CRR's minimum requirement. Accordingly, the bank must in this case maintain an additional amount of own funds or eligible liabilities equal to eight per cent of RWA to meet CRR's minimum requirement. In total, the bank must maintain own funds and eligible liabilities in an amount of at least 24.5 per cent of RWA to satisfy both the capital buffer requirements and CRR's risk-weighted MREL.

The basic idea of BRRD's MREL framework is that banks should maintain MREL-instruments in an amount sufficient to absorb the bank's losses and contribute to restoring its capital to a level sufficient for compliance with its risk-weighted

[23] BRRD art 16a.

and unweighted capital requirements. In line with this idea, BRRD instructs the resolution authority to determine both risk-weighted and unweighted MREL, the higher of the two requirements being binding.[24] BRRD conceptualises both requirements as being composed of two elements: a loss absorption amount and a recapitalisation amount.[25] This allows resolution authorities to set a bank's MREL according to the bank's importance, as well as whether the applicable resolution plan envisages that the entirety or only parts of the bank shall live on following resolution. In the following, we will examine a scenario where the resolution authority determines MREL for a large bank.

The default approach to determining unweighted MREL is straightforward. The requirement's loss absorption component equals the leverage ratio requirement.[26] By default, the recapitalisation component has the same value, meaning that the aggregate requirement generally is twice the leverage ratio requirement or, in other words, six per cent of the total exposure measure. If the value of a bank's assets exceeds 100 billion euro or the bank is considered a systemic risk, the MREL shall never be below five per cent of the total exposure measure.

The loss absorption component of risk-weighted MREL equals the own funds requirement and the pillar 2 requirement, where applicable.[27] The default rule is that also the recapitalisation amount is to equal this amount. The resolution authority may – insofar as this is deemed necessary to regain market confidence in the bank post-resolution – set a higher recapitalisation amount so that it also comprises an amount that reflects the capital buffer requirements to which the bank then will be subject. By default, this amount shall equal the sum of the combined buffer requirements less the countercyclical capital buffer requirement. However, after having consulted the bank's supervisor, the resolution authority may adjust the market confidence buffer both upwards and downwards. Banks whose assets are worth more than 100 billion euro or who otherwise pose a systemic risk in the event of failure must maintain MREL exceeding the higher of 13.5 per cent of RWA and five per cent of unweighted assets.[28]

As in the case of CRR's MREL requirement for G-SIIs, banks must meet capital buffer requirements and risk-weighted MREL separately, with noncompliance potentially being sanctioned by restrictions on distributions and bonuses.[29] A brief example illustrates the effect of this rule. Suppose that a bank is subject to a risk-weighted capital requirement equal to 16 per cent of the total risk exposure amount, of which eight percentage points reflect the own funds requirement, two percentage points reflect the pillar 2 requirement and six percentage points

[24] BRRD art 45c(3).
[25] BRRD art 45c(2).
[26] BRRD art 45c(3)(b).
[27] BRRD art 45c(3)(a).
[28] BRRD art 45c(5) and (6).
[29] BRRD art 16a; CRD IV art 128. See also European Systemic Risk Board, 'Report of the Analytical Task Force on the overlap between capital buffers and minimum requirements' (December 2021).

reflect buffer requirements. Assume furthermore that the bank's risk-weighted MREL equals two times the sum of the own funds requirement and the pillar 2 requirement, ie 20 per cent of RWA. In such a scenario, the bank must maintain instruments that constitute own funds or eligible liabilities in an amount of 20 per cent of RWA to meet risk-weighted MREL and an additional amount of CET1 capital equal to six per cent of RWA to meet the capital buffer requirements.

Article 45d sets out the resolution authority's power to impose a MREL requirement on G-SIIs that exceeds CRR's minimum requirement. The resolution authority may impose such additional requirements if CRR's minimum requirement is insufficient to meet the requirement that would follow from the resolution authority's approach for determining the MREL of individual banks. Accordingly, an additional requirement may be imposed if the resolution authority deems CRR's minimum requirement too low to ensure that the institution following resolution will be able to comply with the own funds requirement and any pillar 2 requirement, and regain the confidence of the market. The SRB's policy is to make use of this possibility, thus requiring G-SIIs to maintain MREL in excess of the TLAC minimum.[30]

8.5.2. Subordination and Other Qualitative Requirements

A liability must meet several requirements to count as an eligible liability under the present MREL framework. Importantly, the remaining tenor of the liability must exceed one year.[31] Moreover, the liability cannot be among those that CRR lists as 'excluded liabilities'.[32] This list includes, among other things, all liabilities that by virtue of BRRD Article 44(2) are excluded from the resolution authority's bail-in power and liabilities in respect of deposits that pursuant to BRRD Article 108 shall rank ahead of general unsecured debt.[33] What then remains of conventional bank liabilities that do not constitute excluded liabilities is likely to be little else than bond instruments with a remaining maturity of a year or more, as well as corporate time deposits of the same tenor.

The general rule under CRR's G-SII MREL framework is that a liability only counts towards MREL if it is subordinated to the liabilities that CRR lists as 'excluded liabilities'.[34] This list includes, among other things, all liabilities that by virtue of BRRD Article 44(2) are excluded from the resolution authority's bail-in power and liabilities in respect of deposits that pursuant to BRRD Article 108 shall rank ahead of general unsecured debt.[35] Insofar as some excluded liabilities, such

[30] Single Resolution Board, 'Minimum Requirement for Own Funds and Eligible Liabilities (MREL): SRB Policy under the Banking Package' (May 2021) 15.

[31] BRRD art 45b(1)(c); CRR art 72c(1).

[32] BRRD art 45b(1)(a); CRR art 72a(1).

[33] CRR art 72a(2).

[34] CRR art 72b(2)(d).

[35] CRR art 72a(2).

as short-term interbank debt, rank as general unsecured debt in normal insolvency proceedings, CRR's requirement effectively means that liabilities must rank below general unsecured debt in order to count towards MREL.

There are three ways to achieve the requisite subordination.[36] First, the liability could be contractually subordinated to the excluded liabilities. The bank would then rely on the possibilities for contractual subordination as guaranteed by Directive (EU) 2017/2399 as discussed at 5.3.2. Secondly, the liability could be subordinated by statute. Thirdly, liabilities issued by an entity with no excluded liabilities satisfy the subordination requirement. This third option is primarily of use to resolution entities that are holding companies and thus do not themselves incur any operational liabilities such as deposits.

The resolution authority may permit G-SIIs to meet CRR's minimum requirement in an amount of up to 3.5 per cent of the total risk exposure amount with liabilities that are not subordinated to the excluded liabilities.[37] Alternatively, the resolution authority may permit the bank to apply general unsecured debt towards satisfying MREL if the excluded liabilities ranking *pari passu* to or below such debt do not exceed five per cent of the bank's MREL.[38] In either case, the resolution authority must find that permitting the use of non-subordinated debt to satisfy the minimum requirement would not give rise to a material risk of successful legal challenge or compensation claims following a resolution.

The nominal main rule under BRRD's current regime is – unlike under CRR's MREL regime – that a claim may qualify as an eligible liability and thus count towards a bank's individual MREL even if it ranks as general unsecured debt.[39]

Exemptions apply for certain banks. Banks whose assets are worth more than 100 billion euro or whose failure constitutes a systemic risk are to be required to meet MREL with subordinated debt.[40] As mentioned above, such banks are subject to a minimum MREL requirement equal to the higher of 13.5 per cent of RWA and five per cent of non-weighted assets.[41] Non-subordinated liabilities do not count towards satisfying this minimum requirement.

Moreover, these banks must generally maintain own funds or subordinated eligible liabilities in an amount equal to eight per cent of the entity's 'total liabilities, including own funds' (hereinafter the '8%-requirement').[42] The choice of this amount is not accidental.[43] The use of government funds and/or the resolution fund to prop up a bank in resolution is prohibited unless shareholders and creditors through bail-in contribute an amount that at least equals this threshold.[44]

[36] CRR art 72b(2)(d).
[37] CRR art 72b(3).
[38] CRR art 72b(4).
[39] BRRD art 45b(1)(b).
[40] BRRD art 45c(5) and (6).
[41] BRRD art 45c(5) and (6).
[42] BRRD art 45b(4).
[43] BRRD II recital 10.
[44] See 2.4.3.

Accordingly, the underlying idea is to ensure that it is possible to recapitalise banks by sharing the burden between investors in subordinated instruments and public resources, thereby avoiding a bail-in of operational liabilities such as non-preferred deposits and derivatives.

As mentioned, banks may be subject to the 8%-requirement either by virtue of having assets that exceed 100 billion euro or their failure constituting a systemic risk. Insofar as a bank is subject to the 8%-requirement solely by virtue of the value of its assets, the subordination requirement shall never exceed 27 per cent of RWA (hereinafter the 27%-limit), provided that the applicable resolution plan does not contemplate use of the resolution fund.[45] Conversely, if the resolution authority finds that the bank's failure would pose a systemic risk, the 27%-limit will not apply.[46]

As discussed at 8.5.1, banks may not simultaneously use CET1 capital to meet both the combined capital buffer requirement and risk-weighted MREL. It seems intuitive to assume that the same applies in the case of a subordination requirement, meaning that an assessment of whether a bank meets the 8%-requirement will not take into account CET1 capital necessary to meet the capital buffer requirements. However, BRRD Article 45b(6) states that '[t]he own funds of a resolution entity that are used to comply with the combined buffer requirement shall be eligible to comply with the requirements referred to in paragraphs 4, 5 and 7'. As the 8%-requirement is set out in paragraph 4 of Article 45b, this suggests that capital employed to meet the capital buffer requirements may be employed towards satisfying the 8%-requirement.

The Commission has published a notice on its views on various interpretative questions concerning provisions introduced by the 'Banking Package', which included BRRD II. One question addressed concerns whether BRRD Article 45b(6) relates to both the subordination requirement expressed as percentages of the total risk-exposure amount (ie risk-weighted) and the total exposure amount (ie unweighted). In its answer, the Commission stated that 'CET1 capital used to comply with the [capital buffer requirements] cannot be used to meet any MREL requirement, whether subordinated or not, expressed [as percentages of the total risk-exposure amount]'.[47] It is, respectfully, not entirely clear what arguments the Commission relies on for arriving at this conclusion, which appears to contradict the plain meaning of Article 45b(6). One possible interpretation is that Article 45b(6) is intended to clarify that capital employed for meeting capital buffer requirements may be used to meet unweighted MREL. However, Article 45b(6) does not distinguish between risk-weighted and unweighted MREL.

[45] BRRD art 45b(4).

[46] BRRD II recital 12.

[47] Commission Notice relating to the interpretation of certain legal provisions of the revised bank resolution framework in reply to questions raised by Member States' authorities [2020] OJ C321/1 para 33.

It appears that the Single Resolution Board interprets SRMR Article 12c(6), which corresponds to BRRD Article 45b(6), in accordance with its plain meaning. In a recent policy communication, SRB writes that '[w]hen setting the subordinated component of the MREL ensuring the 8% TLOF target, the resolution authority should count CET1 eligible for capital buffers towards the 8% target'.[48] This seems to be in line with the most plausible interpretation of BRRD Article 45b(6): that CET1 capital employed to meet the capital buffer requirements may simultaneously be employed towards satisfying the 8%-requirement.

BRRD Article 45b(8) lays out three grounds that may justify a subordination requirement that exceeds the 8%-requirement. The first is that there are substantive impediments to the resolvability of the entity, and the resolution entity has omitted to take remedial action or the powers of the resolution authority are insufficient to remedy the impediment. The second ground is that the resolution authority considers the feasibility and credibility of the resolution strategy to be limited. The third ground is that the resolution entity is among the 20 per cent riskiest institutions under the resolution authority's remit. In addition, there is a cap on the number of banks to which the resolution authority may apply the increased subordination requirement. In principle, the increased requirement should apply to no more than 30 per cent of banks that are G-SIIs, that have assets in excess of 100 billion euro or that otherwise constitute a systemic risk.[49] However, Member States may set the percentage higher than 30 per cent. In determining whether to raise this cap, the Member States shall take 'into account the specificities of their national banking sector'.

Assuming that the conditions for a subordination requirement exceeding the 8%-requirement is met, how high may this requirement be? Pursuant to BRRD Article 45b(7), the requirement may be adjusted upwards insofar as the required amount of own funds and subordinated eligible liabilities does not exceed the so-called prudential formula – ie the sum of: (i) two times the own funds requirement, (ii) two times the pillar 2 requirement, and (iii) the combined buffer requirement.

As discussed at 8.5.1, the resolution authority may demand that G-SIIs maintain MREL in excess of CRR's minimum requirement. Subject to restrictions that are essentially the same as those just discussed, the resolution authority may require that instruments must be subordinated in order to count towards the parts of the aggregate requirement that exceed CRR's minimum requirement.

Finally, the resolution authority shall have the power to decide that liabilities shall only count towards meeting a bank's MREL insofar as they are subordinated even if the bank is not a G-SII, does not have assets in excess of 100 billion euro and does not otherwise pose a systemic risk.[50] This power is conditional upon the

[48] Single Resolution Board (n 30) 7. 'TLOF' is short for Total Liabilities and Own Funds.
[49] BRRD art 45b(8).
[50] BRRD art 45b(5).

presence of three conditions. First, non-subordinated MREL must have the same priority in normal insolvency proceedings as liabilities that are excluded from bail-in. Secondly, there must be a risk that some creditors will suffer greater losses in resolution than if the bank is instead wound up under normal insolvency proceedings. Thirdly, the subordination requirement shall not exceed what is necessary to ensure that no creditor is worse off from resolution. The subordination requirement cannot exceed the highest of: (i) the 8%-requirement, and (ii) the sum yielded by the formula set out in BRRD Article 45b(7).

The above discussion shows how the framework has grown in complexity. This raises the question of whether the amendments affect the ability of resolution authorities to pursue MREL policies forged against the backdrop of BRRD's original framework. As discussed at 8.3, this approach often consisted of requiring that banks were to satisfy MREL with subordinated liabilities. Although their discretion is now subject to numerous restrictions, the resolution authorities may often make exceptions. The conditions for such exceptions are often formulated in language which could effectively leave much to the authority's opinion. It might therefore be the case that the revised rules on subordination requirements will not do much to alter the approaches of the resolution authorities. This ultimately depends upon the extent to which courts are willing to substitute their assessments on matters of law and facts for that of the resolution authority. We will discuss this issue in the next section.

8.5.3. Judicial Review of MREL Decisions

The current MREL framework distinguishes between the following four categories of banks: First, G-SIIs. Secondly, non-G-SIIs that either own assets worth more than of 100 billion euro or whose failure poses a systemic threat. Thirdly, banks that do not fall into either the first or second category, but that the resolution authority nonetheless contemplates to resolve rather than wind up should they fail. Fourthly, banks that the resolution authority will allow to be wound up under normal insolvency proceedings.

The categorisation of a bank determines the extent to which it is, or the resolution authority may require it to, satisfy MREL exclusively with own funds or subordinated debt. The determination of the category to which a given bank belongs is thus ultimately of importance for whether the bank may only use subordinated instruments to meet MREL. Except for the criterion of having assets worth more than 100 billion euro, the criteria for these determinations are vague. One example is the criteria for placing a bank in the second category notwithstanding that the value of its assets is below the said threshold, which is that the resolution authority has determined that the bank is 'reasonably likely to pose a systemic risk in the event of its failure'.

The extent to which a bank is only allowed to satisfy MREL with subordinated instruments does not automatically follow from its categorisation. This is because the final calibration of the requirement in all cases involves decision-making on the part of the resolution authority, albeit to different degrees. CRR's G-SII regime is the most prescriptive in this regard, as the main rule is that debts only count towards the minimum requirement set out in Article 92a(1) if they are subordinated. However, the resolution authority is to some extent empowered to permit the use of non-subordinated debts. Moreover, insofar as the resolution authority uses its power to impose upon a G-SII an MREL requirement that exceeds CRR's minimum requirement, the resolution authority may – subject to the upper bound discussed at 8.5.2 – determine that the part of the requirement that exceeds CRR's minimum must be met with own funds or subordinated debt. Non-G-SII banks that either own assets worth more than 100 billion euro or whose failure represents a systemic threat are required to ensure that their own funds and subordinated debt exceed eight per cent of the sum of their own funds and liabilities. However, as discussed, the resolution authority may, subject to certain vaguely defined conditions being met, adjust this threshold both upwards and downwards. To summarise, it is not the case that the categorisation of a bank is entirely determinative of the extent to which it may use non-subordinated debt to meet MREL; the resolution authority has, within certain limits, the power to make the final determination on this issue.

The circumstance that an MREL decision may have implications for a bank's financing costs, and that the resolution authority's decision-making is subject to vague conditions, raises the question of how courts will deal with judicial challenges against such decisions. In some instances, the wording of the applicable provisions suggests that the resolution authority enjoys wide discretion. Take for instance the resolution authority's determination that a bank's failure poses a systemic risk, which, as discussed, will result in the bank being placed in the second of the above-listed categories. First, the bank must be one '*which the resolution authority has assessed as reasonably likely* to pose a systemic risk in the event of its failure' (emphasis added).[51] This wording indicates that it is for the resolution authority to decide whether the bank is reasonably likely to pose a systemic risk in the event of its failure. Secondly, the determination involves a complex economic assessment. This may constitute an independent reason for courts dealing with challenges against MREL decisions to defer to the resolution authority's view.

EU law does not generally harmonise the intensity with which national courts are to review administrative decisions that purport to be authorised by EU regulations or national provisions transposing directives.[52] Some courts could opt for a more intense standard of review than others. In the following paragraphs we will discuss how the CJEU may approach judicial review of an MREL decision adopted by the Single Resolution Board. This will not necessarily be representative of how

[51] BRRD art 45c(3b).

[52] See, by analogy, Case C-120/97 *Upjohn Ltd* ECLI:EU:C:1999:14, paras 32–33. See also Case C-71/14, *East Sussex County Council* ECLI:EU:C:2015:656, para 58.

all courts would approach judicial review of MREL decisions but will nonetheless illustrate the issues and dilemmas that both the CJEU and national courts will face.

The CJEU is often reluctant to substitute its views for that of an EU institution or agency insofar as that body's decision is based on complex economic assessments.[53] In accordance with this, the prevailing view in the literature is that the CJEU both should, and is likely to, subject MREL decisions and other resolution planning measures to marginal judicial control.[54] But what exactly does such marginal review entail? The CJEU is yet to deal with a challenge against an MREL decision made by the Single Resolution Board.[55] However, it is of interest to discuss how the General Court in *Crédit Mutuel Arkéa v European Central Bank* dealt with the challenge brought against a pillar 2 requirement determined by ECB.[56] As discussed at 2.3.3, a pillar 2 requirement is an entity-specific capital requirement determined by the bank's supervisor that comes in addition to CRR's minimum requirements. Such requirements are meant to capture risks not accounted for in the minimum requirements. A feature common to pillar 2 and MREL decisions is thus that both have financial stability as their ultimate goal and involve forecasting future events. It therefore seems reasonable to treat the General Court's approach to the challenge against the pillar 2 requirement in *Arkéa* as indicative of how the CJEU will approach challenges against MREL decisions.

The background for the contested pillar 2 decision was that the Crédit Mutuel Arkéa (hereinafter Arkéa), the applicant credit institution, was affiliated with the Confédération nationale du Crédit Mutuel, a central body in a network of local cooperative companies. The ECB considered that a conflict between Arkéa and a group of cooperative companies within the Crédit Mutuel network could result in Arkéa's exit. This outcome could have negative effects on its business and liquidity. Moreover, it would result in Arkéa having to calculate its capital requirements in accordance with the standardised approach rather than IRB approach,[57] which in turn would increase the amount of capital needed to satisfy its capital requirements.[58]

Against this background, the ECB found that the Single Supervisory Mechanism Regulation (SSMR) Article 16(1)(c) warranted supervisory measures.[59] This provision states that the ECB may adopt such measures when following supervisory

[53] M van der Woude, 'Judicial Control in Complex Economic Matters' (2019) 10 *Journal of European Competition Law & Practice* 415, 417.

[54] See S Grünewald, 'Judicial Control of Resolution Planning Measures' in C Zilioli and K-P Wojcik (eds), *Judicial Review in the European Banking Union* (Cheltenham, Edward Elgar, 2021) para 23.43 and the references contained therein.

[55] At the time of writing, an action for the annulment of an MREL decision is pending before the General Court, see Case T-71/22 *BNP Paribas v SRB*.

[56] Case T-712/15 *Crédit Mutuel Arkéa v European Central Bank* ECLI:EU:T:2017:900.

[57] On the difference between the standardised approach and the IRB approach, see 2.2.2.

[58] Case T-712/15 *Crédit Mutuel Arkéa v European Central Bank*, para 171.

[59] Council Regulation (EU) No 1024/2013 of 15 October 2013 conferring specific tasks on the European Central Bank concerning policies relating to the prudential supervision of credit institutions [2013] OJ L287/63.

review it determines 'that the arrangements, strategies, processes and mechanisms implemented by the credit institution and the own funds and liquidity held by it do not ensure a sound management and coverage of its risks'. SSMR Article 16(2)(a), on which the ECB relied, provides that one available measure is 'to require institutions to hold own funds in excess of the [own funds requirement and the capital buffer requirements] related to elements of risks and risks not covered by the relevant Union acts'.

One of Arkéa's pleas was that the possibility of the bank being excluded from the Crédit Mutuel network was so implausible that taking it into account vitiated the contested decision by an error of law. The General Court rejected the plea.[60] In doing so, the Court noted that CRD IV Article 97(1)(a) states that supervisory review of banks shall consider the risks to which they 'are or *might be* exposed' (emphasis added).[61] Accordingly, the ECB is entitled to take into account 'future events capable of altering their risk profile'. This in turn led the Court to recharacterise Arkéa's argument; what the bank 'really claim[ed]' was not that the ECB had committed an error in law, but rather that taking into account the possibility of Arkéa's departure from the group constituted an error of assessment.

The approach of the CJEU to challenges against administrative decisions is to conduct a full judicial review insofar as the applicant alleges that the decisions is vitiated by an error of law. Conversely, full review is not always the norm for alleged errors of assessment. Indeed, in *Arkéa* the General Court stated that the ECB enjoys broad discretion 'given the complexity presented by the assessment of the level of a credit institution's CET 1 capital requirements in the light of its risk profile and events likely to have an effect on that profile'.[62] Against this background, the Court's review of the ECB's decision was to be confined 'to verifying whether the rules on procedure and on the statement of reasons have been complied with, whether the facts have been accurately stated and whether there has been any manifest error of assessment or misuse of powers'.[63] The Court's description of the intensity of its review is in line with the CJEU's review of administrative acts made by EU bodies.[64]

The ECB's pillar 2 decision was based on the risk of Arkéa being excluded from the Crédit Mutuel network. Arkéa argued that the decision was thus motivated by a risk the realisation of which was 'so implausible' that it could not justify the

[60] The judgment was subsequently appealed to the ECJ, but the appeal did not turn on the pillar 2 requirement, see Joined Cases C-152/18 P and C-153/18 P *Crédit Mutuel Arkéa v European Central Bank* ECLI:EU:C:2019:810.

[61] Case T-712/15 *Crédit Mutuel Arkéa v European Central Bank*, para 176–177.

[62] Case T-712/15 *Crédit Mutuel Arkéa v European Central Bank*, para 181.

[63] Case T-712/15 *Crédit Mutuel Arkéa v European Central Bank*, para 178.

[64] M Ioannidis, 'The Judicial Review of Discretion in the Banking Union: From 'Soft' to 'Hard(er)' Look?' in C Zilioli and K-P Wojcik (eds), *Judicial Review in the European Banking Union* (Cheltenham, Edward Elgar, 2021) para 9.15. On the justification of such 'deference', see P Craig, 'Judicial review and judicial deference' in M Scholten and A Brenninkmeijer (eds), *Controlling EU Agencies: The Rule of Law in a Multi-jurisdictional Legal Order* (Cheltenham, Edward Elgar, 2020) 105–06.

decision. After having framed this claim as an alleged error of assessment, the General Court rejected the argument and concluded that the risk materialising did 'not seem so improbable that taking it into account [amounted] to a manifest error of assessment by the ECB'.[65] The merits do not address *how* likely the exclusion of Arkéa appeared. Accordingly, it is not possible to draw precise inferences about what, if any, level of probability the Court ascribed to this event occurring. What the wording of the conclusion does seem to indicate, however, is that the Court deemed the probability as not being insignificant. Or in the words of Ioannidis, '[m]anifest error meant, thus, going beyond the improbable'.[66]

As mentioned, Arkéa's claim that the ECB had committed an error of law was reframed as a claim of error of assessment. In dismissing this claim, the General Court did not need to interpret SSMR Article 16. It is unknown to me what arguments Arkéa's counsel put forward in support of the claim of error of law. But a conceivable argument is that SSMR Article 16(1)(c) must be interpreted to the effect that only risks whose probability of materialising exceed a certain threshold warrant the conclusion that the bank's arrangements are insufficient to ensure 'sound management and coverage of its risks', which in turn empowers the ECB to impose pillar 2 requirements on the bank. If, in a hypothetical scenario, the General Court had considered this argument, accepted it, and found that the ECB based its decision on an interpretation that does not require risks to pass such a probability threshold, this would likely have led to the conclusion that the ECB had committed an error of law. This is a question distinct from the question of whether the ECB – although its legal interpretation is correct – has incorrectly assessed the probability of the risk materialising, and that the error is of a degree that justifies the annulment of the decision for error of assessment. The difference between the two forms of assessments is that the first is normative – when are risks sufficiently grave to warrant imposing additional requirements on banks? – while the second is 'technical' – how high was the probability of the specific risk materialising?

What the General Court seems to do in *Crédit Mutuel Arkéa* is to confound these two steps. Implicit in its conclusion that the possibility of exclusion did 'not seem so improbable that taking it into account [amounted] to a manifest error of assessment by the ECB', the Court implicitly recognises that there is some, albeit vaguely defined, threshold for how probable the materialisation of a risk must be for it to justify a pillar 2 requirement. But by restricting its analysis to one on error of assessment, the Court treats both the normative and technical issue as technical issues.

The same issues that confronted the General Court in *Arkéa* will be at play if MREL decisions are challenged before the CJEU or national courts. Take for instance BRRD Article 45c(6),[67] which, as discussed, provides that if 'the resolution

[65] Case T-712/15 *Crédit Mutuel Arkéa v European Central Bank*, para 188.
[66] Ioannidis (n 64) para 9.16.
[67] The corresponding provision in SRMR is Article 12d(5).

authority has assessed [a bank] as reasonably likely to pose a systemic risk in the event of its failure', that bank may be subject to the same subordination requirements as banks belonging to a resolution group whose assets exceed 100 billion euro. If courts approach this issue in a manner akin to that of the General Court in *Arkéa*, the review will be confined to considering whether the resolution authority's forecasts are sufficiently plausible. This is a complex assessment, which under the CJEU's approach justifies restricting the review to whether the rules on procedure and on the statement of reasons have been complied with, whether the facts have been accurately stated, and whether there has been any manifest error of assessment or misuse of powers.

Unless the CJEU and national courts establish abstract criteria for when a bank 'pose[s] a systemic risk in the event of its failure' and assess whether the resolution authority's decision conforms to the court's interpretation, the ensuing result will be that judicial review is confined to assessing whether the forecasts are not so implausible that the courts find that the decision should be annulled. BRRD's constraints on MREL decisions may therefore prove less binding than they prima facie appear.[68]

8.6. Who Will Invest in MREL Instruments?

Subordination requirements will give rise to a new creditor class that is to assume the financial burden of recapitalising failing banks through resolution. Creditors that invest in such debt will represent a wedge in the priority hierarchy between own funds investors and general unsecured bank creditors. This raises the question of whether the identity of the investors purchasing such debt instruments is relevant for safeguarding financial stability and other public interests. EU law now answers this question in the affirmative following the introduction of regulation on both the sale and holding of subordinated debt instruments that count towards MREL. We will in the following section discuss the legal regime for the issuing bank's sale of such securities as well as the legal restrictions on banks investing in the same.

We will first discuss the sale of subordinated bank debt to the bank's retail clients, which has been a controversial issue in recent years. The sale of subordinated debt to such investors is subject to both generally applicable regulation as well as regulation that specifically governs the sale of subordinated bank debt. The Prospectus Regulation is a natural starting point for this discussion.[69]

[68] For a similar point as regards the interplay between the CJEU's standards of review and the criterion 'significant impediment to effective competition' in EU merger control, see PI Colomo, 'EU Merger Control Between Law and Discretion: When Is An Impediment to Effective Competition Significant?' (2021) 44 *World Competition* 347.

[69] Regulation (EU) 2017/1129 of the European Parliament and of the Council of 14 June 2017 on the prospectus to be published when securities are offered to the public or admitted to trading on a regulated market, and repealing Directive 2003/31/EC [2017] OJ L168/12.

The Regulation generally requires that a prospectus must accompany public offerings of debt. While this requirement is subject to certain important exemptions, the exemptions do not extend to sales to smaller retail investors. The Prospectus Regulation explicitly requires the prospectus to highlight risk pertaining to the subordination of the offered security.[70] If the issuer is a bank, the prospectus must address the potential impact of a resolution.[71] Moreover, a bank that 'self-places' own funds or other instruments counting towards MREL must inform clients of the differences between such instruments and bank deposits.[72]

Prospectus requirements form part of the 'disclosure paradigm' that has long permeated financial market regulation, where regulation reflects the belief that capital markets are well functioning if sufficient information is available.[73] Some would likely be inclined to argue that more information does not remedy the issue at hand, as the problem lies in retail investors not understanding how priority in resolution works.[74] The pre-crisis framework actually reflects how retail investors are often unsophisticated investors, as disclosure requirements were coupled with the more paternalistic approach of imposing duties on investment firms when providing investment services to retail clients.[75] The adoption of MiFID II constitutes a post-crisis reinforcement of this approach.[76]

Some cases of banks marketing their subordinated debt to retail investors could easily constitute investment advice for the purpose of MiFID II, in which case the bank must assess the suitability of the investment for the investor. MiFID II Article 4(1)(4) defines 'investment advice' as 'the provision of personal recommendations to a client, either upon its request or at the initiative of the investment firm, in respect of one or more transactions relating to financial instruments'. As the definition's emphasis on *personal* recommendations makes clear, not all recommendations constitute investment advice.[77] However, it seems reasonable to expect that the interactions surrounding a bank's marketing of its own bonds to existing depositors and other clients often will give rise to the provision of investment advice. Banks are unlikely to contact clients at random. It seems more plausible

[70] Prospectus Regulation arts 7(7)(a)(iv) and 16(2)

[71] Prospectus Regulation arts 7(7)(a)(iv) and 16(2).

[72] Commission Delegated Regulation (EU) 2017/565 of 25 April 2016 supplementing Directive 2014/65/EU of the European Parliament and of the Council as regards organisational requirements and operating conditions for investment firms and defined terms for the purposes of that Directive [2017] OJ L87/1 art 41(4).

[73] See eg E Avgouleas, 'The Global Financial Crisis and the Disclosure Paradigm in European Financial Regulation: The Case of Reform' (2009) 6 *European Company and Financial Law Review* 440, 442–43; N Moloney, *EU Securities and Financial Markets Regulation*, 3rd edn (Oxford, Oxford University Press, 2014) 54.

[74] The futility of providing information to investors without the capacity to understand said information has been addressed by several commentators, see Moloney (n 73) 59 and the references contained therein.

[75] Moloney (n 73) 771, 805.

[76] Directive 2014/65/EU of the European Parliament and of the Council of 15 May 2014 on markets in financial instruments and amending Directive 2002/92/EC and Directive 2011/61/EU [2014] OJ L173/349.

[77] L Enriques and M Gargantini, 'The Expanding Boundaries of MiFID's Duty to Act in the Client's Best Interest: The Italian Case' (2017) 3 *Italian Law Journal* 485, 494.

that a client receives an offer to purchase such instruments when a bank is aware that the client holds means available for investment. It is, in turn, reasonable to expect that the bank's sales representatives will highlight the fact that the client has means available for investment and that he could earn a higher interest rate by investing those means in subordinated bonds. A suggestion that a potential investor should rebalance its portfolio of financial assets is likely to constitute a personal recommendation that qualifies as investment advice under MiFID II. Such considerations may underpin the European Securities and Markets Authority's view that 'it is extremely likely' that a bank that seeks to place its own bonds with its clients will give investment advice.[78]

As mentioned, banks that provide investment advice are required to conduct a 'suitability test' and refrain from recommending investments that are unsuitable for the potential investor in light of factors such as the investor's experience, his ability to bear losses and his risk tolerance.[79] While it is necessary to assess compliance with the suitability test on a case-by-case basis, a breach generally occurs when a bank's sales representative solicits a retail investor of ordinary means and convinces him to place all or a substantial amount of his wealth in subordinated debt instruments issued by one bank.[80]

Pursuant to recent amendments to BRRD, banks and others that sell subordinated bank debt to retail clients shall be subject to obligations beyond those set out in the Prospectus Regulation and MiFID II. Member States may choose between two measures. The first consists of the following: The seller of the bonds must: (i) perform a suitability test, (ii) conclude that the bonds are suitable for the retail client, and (iii) document the test.[81] In addition, if the client's financial instrument portfolio is less than 500,000 euro, the seller must ensure that the client does not invest an aggregate amount exceeding 10 per cent of the portfolio in subordinated bank bonds and that the initial investment is at least 10,000 euro.[82] For present purposes, the financial instrument portfolio includes cash deposits and unencumbered financial instruments.[83] The first of these requirements resembles the suitability test under MiFID II. The difference lies in that BRRD appears to require that banks carry out such a test whenever they sell bonds to retail investors. Unlike under MiFID II, such an obligation is thus not restricted to cases where the issuing bank provides investment advice (or portfolio management) to the retail investor.

Instead of introducing the above measure, Member States may require that subordinated bank bonds have a minimum denomination of 50,000 euro.[84] Banks authorised by a Member State opting for this approach would, however,

[78] European Securities and Markets Authority, 'Statement: MiFID practices for firms selling financial instruments subject to the BRRD resolution regime' (2016) ESMA/2016/902 8.

[79] MiFID II art 25(2).

[80] P-H Conac, 'Subordinated Debt and Self-placement: Mis-selling of Financial Products' (Brussels, European Parliament: Policy Department A, 2018) 28.

[81] BRRD art 44a(1).

[82] BRRD art 44a(2).

[83] BRRD art 44a(4).

[84] BRRD art 44a(5).

not be free from the general MiFID II obligation to conduct a suitability test when providing investment advice. As noted above, unsolicited approaches by banks to their clients may easily constitute investment advice and thus require the bank to conduct a suitability test.

Finally, an exemption applies when the total assets of the resolution entities established in a Member State are less than 50 billion euro. Such Member States can choose not to apply either of the abovementioned measures and instead only subject sellers to the obligation that the initial investment of retail investors is at least 10,000 euro.[85] Again, such a choice would not free the Member State from requiring their banks to conduct suitability tests insofar as this is required under MiFID II.

The regulatory requirements of MiFID II should – at least on paper – prohibit the most perverse instances of banks inducing unsophisticated investors to invest substantial portions of their wealth in subordinated bank debt. Breaches of the requirements could occur, of course. Some argue that historic instances of the sale of subordinated debt to retail investors have resulted from weak enforcement rather than a lack of regulation.[86]

Having discussed the regulatory framework for the sale of subordinated bank debt to retail investors, we may now turn to discuss the legal framework that applies to the investments of banks in subordinated instruments issued by other banks. The extent to which it should be permissible for banks to make such investments is a pertinent issue. The objective of maintaining financial stability could be undermined if systemically important banks hold the subordinated MREL-instruments. The reason is that losses suffered by such other banks could cause them to rein in lending and other services.[87] A resolution would then at best relocate problems to other banks. Moreover, the risk of such contagion may move the resolution authority to invoke its power pursuant to BRRD Article 44(3)(c) to exclude the claims of such other banks from bail-in.[88]

The only piece of legislation that explicitly deals with this concern is Article 72e of CRR, which states that a G-SII's holding of subordinated MREL-instruments issued by another G-SII shall be deducted when determining whether the first G-SII complies with its MREL.[89] Accordingly, a G-SII's holding of such instruments issued by other G-SIIs is penalised in a sense; it must raise an additional unit of MREL-instruments for every unit it holds of subordinated MREL-instruments issued by other G-SIIs. Conversely, the legal framework does nothing specific to dissuade: (i) G-SIIs from purchasing subordinated bonds issued by non-G-SIIs, or (ii) non-G-SIIs from purchasing subordinated bonds issued by other banks.

[85] BRRD art 44a(6).

[86] Conac (n 80) 32.

[87] J Crawford, 'Credible Losers: A Regulatory Design for Prudential Market Discipline' (2017) 54 *American Business Law Journal* 107, 141–42.

[88] ED Martino, 'Towards an optimal composition of bail-inable debtholders?' (2021) 21 *Journal of Corporate Law Studies* 321, 348.

[89] G-SIIs are not always required to fully deduct such holdings, see CRR art 72e ff.

9

From Meta-Regulation to Technocratic Fine-Tuning: The Phases of Creditor Priority in Bank Insolvency Proceedings

9.1. The Phases of Creditor Priority in Bank Insolvency Proceedings

The preceding chapters have shown how the creditor priority framework in bank insolvency law is a result of several legal acts adopted over time, many of which follow rationales distinct from each other. Bank-specific creditor priority rules are one of several measures for safeguarding financial stability. As chapter two demonstrated, several other fields of law forge the legal framework for the prevention of bank failures that could lead to a sector-wide impairment of the provision of financial services. To complete the picture, this section ties together the findings on the development of the bank-specific creditor priority framework and places the different stages of this development within the shifting approaches to banking regulation in recent decades.

It is possible to distinguish between three phases of bank insolvency priority, each following distinct rationales. The first phase is the period that leads up to the adoption of the Settlement Finality Directive and the Financial Collateral Directive around the turn of the millennium. The second phase is the period from the adoption of these directives to the GFC. In the third and ongoing phase, the adoption of BRRD has further contributed to forging a sector-specific priority regime distinct from that of general insolvency law. We will also attempt to place the different phases in the context of broader trends in banking regulation.

The first phase saw no EU harmonisation of priority rules applicable to bank insolvencies. Save for certain provisions that protect the security interests of clearinghouses and central banks,[1] Member States generally did not adopt any special priority rules. This was in line with the broader approach to bank insolvency in English and German law, as banks remained subject to general insolvency law

[1] See Companies Act 1989 Part VII and Bundesbankgesetz § 19 (as it originally read following its restatement in 1992), respectively.

proceedings rather than sector-specific insolvency frameworks. While Norwegian law had already empowered the government to place banks under public administration and to restructure or wind-down banks, any losses were to be shared among creditors in accordance with the same priority rules that applied in general insolvency law. Accordingly, the applicable priority regime coincided with the priority rules applicable in general insolvency law, which were discussed in detail in chapter four.

While general insolvency proceedings nominally follow a principle of *pari passu* distribution, the deviations from this principle are substantial. First, companies may grant security interests to specific creditors. Limits do apply, however, with details differing between jurisdictions. Examples of such limits include the prescribed sharing of the proceeds of secured assets with other creditors and avoidance rules that allow for the reversal of certain transactions concluded prior to the opening of insolvency proceedings. A second deviation from the *pari passu* principle is that some, but not all, jurisdictions have rules that give certain preferential creditors a right to receive distributions out of the assets available for sharing among the unsecured creditors before other unsecured creditors.

Our discussion at 4.4 showed the difficulties attached to establishing a normative theory that perfectly accounts for the approach to creditor priority in general insolvency law. It was shown that a property-oriented view and an efficiency-oriented view are the two normative justifications whose policy implications correspond best with the companies' power to give individual creditors superior priority through the granting of security interests. The property-oriented view holds that a company should be able to grant security interests that remain effective in insolvency proceedings to the same extent as it is possible for the company to alienate its property. The efficiency-oriented view posits that the possibility of granting security interests leads to efficient outcomes, as companies may more easily access debt capital to finance profit-generating business activity. This, in turn, justifies broad possibilities for granting security interests. Conversely, the rules that govern priority among unsecured creditors appear to follow a different logic, as the justification that best – although not perfectly – explains their existence is a wish to protect creditors that have difficulties in avoiding (eg tax authorities) or responding to (eg employees) a credit risk exposure towards the company.

In the absence of bank-specific adjustments to the general insolvency law priority framework, the approach to creditor priority in this first phase restricted its attention to the competing interests of creditors *qua* creditors. How does this fit with the more general trends of banking regulation at this time? This phase coincides with the first efforts to harmonise the national regulatory regimes applicable to banks by implementing the Basel I accord in EU law. As discussed at 2.3.4, the pre-crisis capital regulation has since been characterised as *microprudential*, meaning that the aim is to prevent the failure of individual banks, which in turn serves to protect depositors and states as their ultimate guarantors. While it might be natural to supplement such a policy with priority rules that give depositors preferred status, no such rule was introduced in EU law or in English, German or Norwegian law. This is not to say that there was no concern whatsoever with the protection of certain creditors. Rather, different means were employed. Various forms of deposit insurance schemes had emerged in European countries during the later decades of the twentieth century. This trend led to the adoption of the first Deposit Guarantee Scheme Directive in 1994,[2] which obligated Member States to ensure that smaller bank deposits enjoyed a minimum level of protection.

The second phase of bank insolvency law in the EU was brought about as part of the execution of the Commission's Financial Services Action Plan, which more generally expanded the domain of EU financial market law. This period saw the adoption of SFD and FCD. In addition, CIWUD established rules on jurisdiction and choice of law in insolvency proceedings concerning banks. While EU law remained agnostic as to whether Member States should enact bank-specific insolvency procedures to supplant those of general insolvency law, SFD and FCD ensured that EU law would require that certain security arrangements received a minimum level of protection in any insolvency proceeding applicable to banks.

Within their respective scopes of application, SFD and FCD require that banks shall have the ability to grant other banks and financial market participants security interests that enjoy absolute priority over unsecured creditors. Moreover, parties may continuously adjust the amount of security to account for fluctuations in the secured exposure or value of the secured assets. Our analysis in chapter seven suggests that a rationale that fits well with these rules is a concern for direct contagion. Direct contagion occurs when the failure of a bank causes problems for other banks, as the failing bank fails to make good obligations assumed through their mutual dealings. The other banks thereby incur losses due to the failure, thus reducing their capital and, in the extreme, triggering a sequence of individual bank failures reminiscent of a chain of dominos falling down. The special protection offered by SFD and FCD is consistent with the view that this problem may be avoided by removing any barriers for banks to create security arrangements among themselves that remain effective in any insolvency procedure.

The adoption of FCD coincides with a period in which European repo and derivatives markets grew rapidly.[3] As a result, exposures between banks became more common. This second phase also coincides with the introduction of the meta-regulatory elements in capital requirements regulation discussed at 2.2. When the capital requirements framework was expanded to cover market risk – the risk banks face when holding securities for trading purposes – banks became able to influence their capital requirements by providing their own input.[4] The adoption

[2] Directive 94/19/EC of the European Parliament and of the Council on deposit-guarantee schemes [1994] OJ L135/5.

[3] See International Capital Market Association, 'European Repo Market Survey' (October 2018) 9 for the growth from June 2001 to June 2018. See Bank of International Settlements, 'Implications of repo markets for central banks' (9 March 1999) 34 for measures of repo markets in certain European states in 1995 and 1997, respectively.

[4] EU law was amended to allow for the use of internal models for calculating market risk following the adoption of Directive 98/31/EC of the European Parliament and of the Council amending

of the Basel II framework in 2004 and its implementation in 2006 through CRD I expanded this approach to the domain of lending,[5] as supervisors could consent to a bank's capital requirements for credit risk being calculated by reference to its internal models.

In a sense, SFD and FCD embody the same spirit as the shift in the capital requirements framework. The introduction of risk-weighted capital requirements based on internal bank data and models rather than the standardised risk weights of Basel I reflects a trust in the ability of banks to tailor a portfolio of assets that carries a risk below the threshold acceptable to society. In the same vein, SFD and FCD limit themselves to enabling banks to offer individual creditors security arrangements with absolute priority over other creditors. In other words, these directives remove restrictions on the power of banks to grant security with absolute priority rather than prescribing that certain counterparties should have priority over other creditors. The implicit logic is that the banks will exercise such powers in a manner that is conducive to the public interest in preventing the problems of one bank from spreading through the financial system, and that this is preferable to rigid priority rules and capital requirements determined by statute.

The third and current phase of bank-specific creditor priority rules marks the period from the global financial crisis up to the time of writing. The reform of the priority rules has primarily occurred in connection with the adoption of BRRD, a directive that for many Member States represented a clean break with their pre-crisis approaches of treating bank insolvency as any other corporate insolvency. Member States are now required to implement BRRD's bank resolution framework and appoint a resolution authority.

BRRD brought about further harmonisation of creditor priority. The approach is novel in several respects. First, in contrast to the earlier approach of enabling banks to give certain creditors absolute priority over other creditors – but ultimately leaving the decision with the bank – BRRD's rules are prescriptive. For instance, certain claims are exempted from the resolution authority's bail-in power regardless of which creditors the bank would prefer to protect. Another example is that certain depositors shall have priority over general unsecured debt in the winding up of banks.

It is not a novel idea as such for an insolvency framework to contain prescriptive priority rules. Suffice it to say that many general insolvency frameworks provide or, in the case of the German framework, have provided, that certain unsecured creditors shall receive distributions ahead of the general body of unsecured creditors. The development towards more prescriptive priority rules in bank insolvency law is nonetheless noteworthy, as the trend in general insolvency law has long consisted of abolishing rules that give certain unsecured creditors priority over other unsecured creditors. Moreover, a difference between the approach

Council Directive 93/6/EEC on the capital adequacy of investment firms and credit institutions [1998] OJ L204/13.

[5] Directive 2006/48/EC of the European Parliament and of the Council relating to the taking up and pursuit of the business of credit institutions (recast) [2006] OJ L177/1.

of the prescriptive priority rules of general insolvency law and those of BRRD lies in the identity of the beneficiaries of priority. When applied in the context of general insolvency law, statutory priority rules tend to favour creditors that are poorly equipped to look out for their own interests. Conversely, the list of debts exempted from the bail-in power includes short-term interbank debt. This exemption is clearly not motivated by concerns over the ability of banks to assess the creditworthiness of their counterparties.

A second change brought about by BRRD is the empowerment of resolution authorities to intervene in the loss distribution among creditors through decisions made at the same time as or after the decision to resolve a bank. As discussed at 6.4.1, the resolution authority has the power to exempt certain claims from bail-in on a case-by-case basis. Such a rule is foreign to the approach to priority in general insolvency law, where the loss distribution relies on a combination of the operation of statutory provisions and the existence of any security interests that the debtor has granted before the commencement of insolvency proceedings. Neither insolvency professionals nor the court supervising the proceedings has discretion to decide the order in which different creditors are to receive the funds available for distribution in a liquidation or restructuring proceeding.

A third and final change to note is the interplay between insolvency law and regulatory powers of public authorities. The earlier phases of creditor priority in bank insolvency law employed two techniques for governing creditor priority. The first technique consists of allowing companies and their creditors to contract for priority. The most famous example of this is the general recognition of the effectiveness of security interests in insolvency proceedings, which in turn empowers companies to decide upon the priority among their creditors. Moreover, it is also possible for banks and other companies to agree with specific creditors that those creditors shall rank behind general unsecured creditors in insolvency. The second technique is to fix by statute the order in which unsecured creditors are to share in the value of the company's unencumbered assets. Post-crisis EU law does, however, employ an additional, third technique: regulating how banks employ their power to contract with creditors over priority. The most prominent example is the MREL framework, which in practice empowers the resolution authority to demand that banks utilise the possibility of agreeing with specific creditors that those creditors shall rank subordinate to general unsecured creditors should the bank be resolved or wound up.

The power to demand that banks fund themselves with subordinated debt also marks a shift from the second phase's approach to creditor priority. While the earlier approach solely drew attention to identifying the creditors that should be protected from the risk of bank failure, the underlying logic of the resolution authority's power approaches the issue from the other end. Essentially, the approach consists of identifying 'credible losers', the creditors that shall bear the risk of failure.[6] While this approach effectively protects creditors that the resolution

[6] J Crawford, 'Credible Losers: A Regulatory Design for Prudential Market Discipline' (2017) 54 *American Business Law Journal* 107.

authority identifies as worthy of special protection, the layer of subordinated debt also protects other creditors.

As we argued at 7.4, a possible rationale for the changes brought about by BRRD with respect to creditor priority is an increased concern for *indirect contagion*. Indirect contagion denotes the risk of one bank's problems spreading to others through channels distinct from interbank lending and other mutual dealings. While priority rules concerned with direct contagion seek to prevent the risk of problems spreading once a bank has failed, an orientation towards indirect contagion also encompasses predictions on how the applicable priority rules affect the behaviour of a struggling bank's creditors – and those of other banks – even before the struggling bank has become subject to resolution or winding up.

However, directing attention to indirect contagion has not supplanted concerns regarding direct contagion. As SFD and FCD remain in force, we are rather witnessing an expansion of the concerns that underpin the bank-specific priority framework. Viewed as a whole, the current framework now seemingly seeks to mitigate several types of contagion risks and not only the risk of a single bank failure causing a cascade of failures due to direct links between banks. In broadening the risks sought mitigated by bank-specific priority rules, BRRD's priority rules follow a more general trend in post-crisis regulation. As briefly touched upon at 2.3, the capital requirements framework now contains capital buffer requirements that supplement the general own funds requirement. One of the purposes of the capital buffer requirements is to avoid distressed banks selling off assets or reining in lending to the potential detriment of the system. By giving certain short-term creditors special protection in resolution or liquidation, and indirectly protecting other short-term creditors by requiring banks to issue subordinated debt to satisfy MREL-requirements, the current framework seemingly contributes to this objective. Such measures reduce the incentive of short-term creditors to run at the first sign of distress, thus mitigating liquidity squeezes and ensuing fire sales. By ensuring that banks maintain a minimum of liquidity, the new liquidity coverage requirement and the net stable funding requirement, both discussed at 2.3.6, provide a second line of defence in case a run nonetheless occurs.

9.2. Technocratic Fine-Tuning and Creditor Priority

9.2.1. Technocratic Fine-Tuning

Chapter one presented the thesis that post-GFC reform of the creditor priority framework in bank insolvency law embodies an approach of technocratic fine-tuning (TFT), and that this is in keeping with broader developments in EU banking regulation during the same period. This section discusses this thesis and its implications against the discussions of the preceding chapters. We will first elaborate upon the concept of TFT regulation and discuss how it fits recent developments within banking regulation (9.2.1). Thereafter, we discuss some of the tensions and trade-offs involved (9.2.2), following which we at 9.2.3 argue that the creditor priority framework now contains elements that reflect a TFT approach.

As defined at 1.2.3, TFT regulation has the following attributes: first, the regulatory output – ie the obligations ultimately imposed on private parties – is complex. Complexity here refers to degree to which the output differs between individual targets of regulation and is intended to vary over time. Secondly, as the desired level of complexity exceeds what legislators have the capacity to decide upon, the current regulatory framework increasingly leaves it to supervisors and other administrative agencies to determine the content of the regulatory obligations. Thirdly, the powers of these executive bodies are often qualified by numerous, but vaguely formulated, legal conditions.

Under TFT regulation, requirements place concrete obligations on the targets, who must do as the regulator commands. This means that TFT regulation is what regulatory theory denotes as command-and-control regulation.[7] One implication is that so-called meta-regulation, which imposes upon regulatory targets an obligation to regulate themselves, is not TFT regulation.

Several pieces of the regulatory framework produce complex regulatory output. For instance, the pillar 2 requirements discussed at 2.3.3 are complex because they are individual requirements tailored to specific circumstances of individual banks. The counter-cyclical capital buffer requirement discussed at 2.3.4 is complex because it is intended to vary over time: the rate shall be high when the economy is booming, and low during slumps.

Not all command-and-control regulation is TFT regulation. General provisions that impose the same requirement across regulatory targets and time are not TFT regulation, as such provisions lack the complexity attribute. Accordingly, the leverage ratio requirement discussed at 2.3.5 is an example of command-and-control regulation that is not TFT regulation. Somewhat simplified, this requirement involves that all banks must ensure that their equity exceeds three per cent of the accounting value of their assets. The requirement applies to all banks and is intended to remain the same over time.

The second attribute of TFT regulation concerns the bodies who determine the regulatory requirements: regulatory output results from the decision-making of an agency. In other words, TFT regulation will in many political systems result from the exercise of authority delegated from legislatures. This means that complex and prescriptive rules are not necessarily instances of TFT regulation. Tax legislation is in many cases both prescriptive – the provisions establish an obligation to pay money to tax authorities – and complex – there may be several taxes and/or exemptions. Nonetheless, the relevant provisions are not TFT insofar as they are set out in legislation. The implication is also that CRR's provisions on computing the minimum capital requirements for credit risk under the standardised approach are not TFT regulation, as CRR emanates directly from the EU's legislative bodies.

[7] See 1.2.2.

Pillar 2 requirements, being determined through individual decisions adopted by bank supervisors, have this second attribute of TFT regulation. The supervisor will in such cases act in accordance with powers delegated pursuant to primary legislation. Likewise, CRD IV requires that the power to determine time-varying capital buffer requirements shall be delegated to a 'designated authority'.

The third attribute of TFT regulation concerns the legal base – ie the legislation delegating power to adopt regulatory requirements – on which the relevant authority relies to adopt rules or individual decisions. The legal base must subject the authority's decision-making powers to several constraints. This attribute sets TFT regulation apart from requirements adopted following broad delegation of legislative powers. One example of a power that for this reason would not be TFT is the original iteration of the Financial Services and Markets Act 2000, section 138. This provision empowered the Financial Services Authority – then the authority in charge of financial supervision in the UK – to make rules applying to, among others, banks insofar as such rules appeared 'to be necessary or expedient for the purpose of protecting the interests of consumers'. This condition is too vague for rules adopted under it to constitute TFT regulation.

A pillar 2 requirement has the third attribute of TFT regulation. CRD IV Article 104a(1) sets out six grounds that empower the bank supervisor to impose such requirements on banks. In addition, the power shall only be exercised 'to cover the risks incurred by individual institutions due to their activities', which means that the power cannot be used to impose additional requirements to cover risks that all banks face; such risks are to be addressed through other parts of the capital requirements framework. Furthermore, one ground for imposing additional requirements is that the bank 'is exposed to risks or elements of risk that are not covered or not sufficiently covered' by CRR's minimum capital requirements. This means, at least at the outset, that the decision-making is subject to constraints.

Countercyclical capital buffer requirements also have the third attribute of TFT regulation. Pursuant to CRD IV Article 136, the authority in charge of setting the buffer rate is to calculate a 'buffer guide'. This measure shall be based on the deviation of the ratio of credit-to-GDP from its long-term trend in the jurisdiction concerned. Based on the guide, guidance from ESRB and other variables considered relevant, the designated authority shall each quarter 'assess the intensity of cyclical systemic risk' and consider whether the then-applicable buffer rate is appropriate. Insofar as it is not, the authority shall adjust the rate upwards or downwards. This means that the authority's task is fairly concrete: to set a buffer rate that appropriately reflects cyclical systemic risk in the Member State concerned.

9.2.2. The Tensions and Trade-Offs Involved

As discussed, TFT regulation is characterised by complexity, understood as regulatory obligations varying across regulatory targets and/or over time. As a category, banks comprise a wide range of institutions, from small savings banks that lend to individuals and businesses in their local community to large and global banks combining lending with investment banking. Complex regulation may thus result from the view that regulatory requirements that are necessary for larger banks, are unnecessary for others. In the extreme, applying all requirements to all banks could force smaller banks to exit the market. The result may thus be to change the market structure by favouring larger institutions over smaller ones. Recent EU reform of CRD IV provides an example of such thinking. When the Commission put forward the relevant proposals in 2016, it was argued that they would decrease 'the administrative and compliance burden' for smaller banks.[8] A similar sentiment is reflected in the UK Prudential Regulation Authority's recent publication of a discussion paper that, among other things, sets out a vision of a 'strong and simple' regulatory framework for UK banks that are not systemically important.[9]

Another argument favouring complexity is that regulatory restrictions involve costs. Designing a regulatory regime therefore involves balancing the benefits of regulation against associated costs. If one subscribes to the view that higher capital requirements for banks decrease the supply of loans and other financial services,[10] determining whether to increase capital requirements beyond current levels involves a trade-off between, on the one hand, financial stability and, on the other, the interests of the marginal borrowers who are at risk of not receiving loans if requirements are raised. Complexity in banking regulation may therefore be interpreted as an attempt at achieving regulation that involves an optimal trade-off between benefits and costs.

While the aims of complex regulation are unproblematic, their operationalisation may clash with other values. A first tension could arise between complexity and rule of law ideals. Under some conceptions of the rule of law, norms must be general.[11] Accordingly, governance through ad hoc decisions is incompatible with this ideal. Generality does not require that all regulatory targets are subject to the same obligations, however. Accordingly, regulation that eg imposes more onerous obligations on banks with assets whose value exceeds a quantitative threshold, is not necessarily at odds with the generality requirement. Respect of the rule of law is thus not an argument against statutory provisions requiring any bank with assets above X billion euro to maintain capital beyond the minimum requirements common to all banks.

The imposition of regulatory obligations is only at odds with the generality requirement when such obligations derive from decisions specifically aimed at the regulatory target rather than generally worded legislation. In such cases, regulatory

[8] Commission, 'Proposal for a Directive of the European Parliament and of the Council amending Directive 2013/36/EU as regards exempted entities, financial holding companies, mixed financial holding companies, remuneration, supervisory measures and powers and capital conservation measures' COM (2016) 854 final, 7.

[9] Prudential Regulation Authority, 'A strong and simple prudential framework for non-systemic banks and building societies' (2021).

[10] See 8.2.

[11] See eg J Waldron, 'The Concept and the Rule of Law' (2008) 43 *Georgia Law Review* 1, 24.

obligations are imposed upon the regulatory target ('Bank A') by virtue of the regulator's view of what obligations Bank A should be subject to. This is different from the case where Bank A becomes subject to obligations because Bank A has certain attributes that, pursuant to the operation of a statutory provision, result in regulatory obligations, as in the above example.

Governance through administrative decisions, which is inherent in TFT regulation, is potentially in conflict with the generality requirement. The question as to whether there is such a tension, is one of degree. The tension is higher if the decisions are unconstrained than if numerous constraints apply. As we will return to below, this concern could be mitigated by imposing constraints on administrative discretion.

A second issue with complex regulation concerns its effectiveness. As discussed, complex regulation is an attempt at achieving an optimal level of regulation. In the context of banking regulation, the idea is to go no longer than necessary to achieve the desired level of financial stability. It is in line with this idea for regulation to differentiate between banks based on the threat they pose to financial stability. This rationale assumes that regulators can indeed identify the optimal level of regulation for each bank. If it turns out that some risk was higher than anticipated, the regulation is not in fact optimal. Insofar as the expected costs to society of underestimating risks are higher than overestimating them, a case can be made for 'simpler' regulation that sometimes goes further than may be strictly necessary.[12]

A third issue with complex regulation is that it may increase the risk of banks 'capturing' their regulators. The term 'regulatory capture' is used to refer to different concepts. In a broad sense, the term describes 'the process through which special interests affect state intervention in any of its forms'.[13] It is thus clear that any level of the state, including legislators, may be 'captured'.

One could reasonably take the view that capture is particularly problematic when occurring outside of the public sphere. In such cases, the public has no way of knowing what is going on. This in turn means that it will not be able to hold officials accountable insofar as their prioritising of special interests is considered unacceptable. If a regulatory framework is complex, it is prima facie less easy to detect capture. How is the public to unearth instances of capture when only experts can comprehend the regulatory framework?[14] The benefits of complex regulation must therefore be balanced against the risk of covert capture of regulators.

To sum up the discussion thus far, we have discussed arguments for and against complex regulation. The arguments favouring complexity are to avoid requirements that are only necessary for a certain subset of banks, being applied to all banks, and, more generally, to achieve an optimal trade-off between protecting financial stability and minimising costs. The arguments against are that the pursuit

[12] See D Aikman et al, 'Taking uncertainty seriously: simplicity versus complexity in financial regulation' (2021) 30 *Industrial and Corporate Change* 317.

[13] E Dal Bó, 'Regulatory capture: A review' (2006) 22 *Oxford Review of Economic Policy* 203, 203.

[14] P Gai et al, 'Regulatory complexity and the quest for robust regulation' (2019) European Systemic Risk Board Reports of the Advisory Scientific Committee No 8, 10.

of such goals could come at the cost of rule of law ideals, that the estimation of the regulatory optimum could be incorrect, and that complexity increases the risk of regulatory capture.

As discussed, the second attribute of TFT regulation is that agencies determine regulatory output. Delegation of regulatory powers raises the question of what types of bodies should be entrusted with fine-tuning the regulatory requirements. Should it be a governmental department or agency subject to governmental control, or, conversely, a body insulated from the control and instruction of the government? As we shall return to below, the answer to this question involves a trade-off between democratic legitimacy and preventing undue interference with administrative decision-making.

The idea of delegating decision-making to independent agencies is not new. It has been prevalent at the federal level in the US since the New Deal-era. As the 'regulatory state' emerged in Europe in the 1980s and 1990s,[15] legislators delegated rulemaking and enforcement powers to independent agencies in several economic sectors. Moreover, there has emerged an international consensus that central banks should have operational independence in matters of monetary policy, and this is a requirement under EU law.[16]

Nor is operational independence for bank supervisors a post-GFC invention. The current version of the BCBS's publication *Core Principles for Effective Banking Supervision* provides that the supervisor should have 'full discretion to take any supervisory actions or decisions on banks and banking groups under its supervision',[17] and has done so since its inception in 1997.[18] IMF has also for a long time taken the position that bank supervisors should not be subject to instructions from the government.[19]

CRD IV Article 4(4) requires that bank supervisors shall have, among other things, the 'independence necessary to carry out the functions relating to prudential supervision, investigations and penalties'. At present, the directive does not go on to specify what this requirement entails regarding the relationship between national governments and bank supervisors. However, it seems plausible that it at least prohibits governments from instructing supervisors in individual cases. Insofar as more detailed legislation concerning this issue has been adopted or proposed, the approach has been to insulate supervisors from elected officials: when the European Central Bank and bank supervisors of Member States that partake in the Banking Union act within the Single Supervisory Mechanism, they 'shall act independently', and institutions at EU and national level shall respect that independence.[20] This may soon become a general EU law requirement. The

[15] G Majone, 'The rise of the regulatory state in Europe' (1994) 17 *West European Politics* 77.

[16] TFEU art 130.

[17] Basel Committee on Banking Supervision, 'Core Principles for Effective Banking Supervision' (September 2012) 22–23.

[18] Basel Committee on Banking Supervision, 'Core Principles for Effective Banking Supervision' (September 1997) 13.

[19] See eg IMF, 'Norway: Financial System Stability Assessment' (July 2020) 29.

[20] SSMR art 19(1).

Commission has proposed the insertion of the following provision into CRD IV: 'Member State shall provide all the necessary arrangements to ensure that … competent authorities … can act independently and objectively, without seeking or taking instructions, or being subject to influence … from any government of a Member State …'.[21]

It is a wide-spread view that elected officials generally should have the final say on the balancing of competing interests. Their legitimacy derives from the voters having elected them in accordance with constitutional norms and the ability of voters to hold them to account in subsequent elections.[22] Why, then, are discretionary powers sometimes delegated to independent agencies? The heads of such agencies are not subject to the same accountability mechanisms as elected officials, and thus require some other basis for their legitimacy insofar as they are to make decisions that balance competing interests.

A first possible justification is that elected officials sometimes cannot credibly commit to pursuing a public interest objective.[23] The reason lies in their accountability: voters may through subsequent elections sanction unpopular decisions by replacing the responsible officials. Under this view, politicians are short-sighted and may therefore avoid adopting policies that are beneficial in the long run but involve immediate costs.

To give an example of how this problem supposedly unfolds, consider the case of banking regulation. Suppose the following: First, the person in charge of banking regulation may choose between several policies on a continuum from lax to strict, and there exists a policy that is optimal from a long-term perspective. Secondly, the benefits of the optimal policy accrue after the next election (eg lower risk of a financial crisis occurring), while the costs accrue prior to this election (eg a lower supply of loans to the public). Thirdly, politicians make decisions to maximise their utility. The utility of politicians is a function of the probability of re-election. Politicians therefore choose policies that maximise their chance of being re-elected.

Against this background, a politician in charge of banking regulation may choose a suboptimal policy to avoid imposing costs on the electorate. This is in the politician's self-interest, as choosing the optimal policy and thereby imposing an immediate cost on the electorate, may make the politician unpopular and cause him to lose the next election. The delegation of banking regulation and supervision to an agency that is independent of elected politicians mitigates this specific

[21] Commission, 'Proposal for a Directive of the European Parliament and of the Council amending Directive 2013/36/EU as regards supervisory powers, sanctions, third-country branches, and environmental, social and governance risks, and amending Directive 2014/59/EU' COM (2021) 663 final, proposed art 1(2).

[22] R Bellamy, 'Democracy without democracy? Can the EU's democratic "outputs" be separated from the democratic "inputs" provided by competitive parties and majority rule?' (2010) 17 *Journal of European Public Policy* 2.

[23] P Tucker, *Unelected Power: The Quest for Legitimacy in Central Banking and the Regulatory State* (Princeton, Princeton University Press, 2018) 98.

problem: the head of the agency does not stand for re-election and therefore does not have a personal interest in avoiding short-term costs.[24]

A second justification for delegating decision-making to independent agencies is that such agencies possess expertise that politicians do not have. In contrast to what we assumed above when we described the commitment problem that may arise when decisions are made by politicians, this view posits that politicians are not capable of identifying optimal policy. Accordingly, the choice of policy should be left to the experts that possess skills within the field concerned. This justification is susceptible to the criticism that leaving the final say with politicians in no way rules out them receiving advice from a bureaucracy appointed to provide the government with expert advice.[25]

The trade-off between democratic legitimacy and achieving public interest goals leads some to conclude that delegating decision-making powers to independent agencies is legitimate only insofar as such agencies receive a sufficiently precise mandate. Their actions must thus be limited to *implementing* rather than *making* policy.[26] If decisions involve distributional choices, the delegation of decision-making powers to an independent agency is at odds with democratic legitimacy.[27] In practice, the question of whether the agency makes policy is one of degree. Legislatures cannot adopt laws that specify how rights and obligations are to be distributed in all possible contingencies and it is therefore unavoidable that agencies must make some decisions in modern states.

This brings us to the third attribute of TFT regulation: that administrative decision-making is subject to numerous constraints. The degree of power transferred to an agency depends on how the delegating act is formulated. If the delegated powers are wide-ranging and unconstrained, the agency will either explicitly or implicitly balance competing interests when making decisions on their use. Conversely, if a legislature enacts a statute that carefully specifies when and to what ends an agency may act, there is less room for balancing competing interests. The agency's role then becomes one of implementing policy choices made at by the legislature: the legislative body determines the goal to be achieved but leaves it to an agency to determine how the goal sought is reached.

A paradigmatic instance of a narrowly defined task being delegated to an independent agency is the delegation of the operational implementation of monetary policy to a central bank and insulating it from influence from the government. Under such a model, the government retains control over the goal(s) of monetary

[24] This assumption is common, see eg A Alesina and G Tabellini, 'Bureaucrats or Politicians? Part I: A Single Policy Task' (2007) 97 *American Economic Review* 169, 170. See also Tucker (n 23) 99–102 for discussion of Alesina and Tabellini's model.

[25] Bellamy (n 22) 10; Tucker (n 23) 95.

[26] Tucker (n 23) 104–05.

[27] This point has also been made in the context of supervisory guidance on the compatibility of banks' lending with climate change objectives, see A Smoleńska and J van 't Klooster, 'A Risky Bet: Climate Change and the EU's Microprudential Framework for Banks' (2022) 8 *Journal of Financial Regulation* 51, 64.

policy but leaves it to the central bank to make the decisions to achieve that goal. Suppose that a central bank is under a statutory obligation to ensure that yearly inflation is two per cent. The central bank thereafter decides how to best achieve the desired level of inflation. As the mandate is restricted to achieving inflation of two per cent, the central bank will not have regard to negative effects that the pursuit of this goal could have on other interests. For example, if high interest rates are necessary to curb inflation, the central banks will aim to raise rates even if this will cause the unemployment rate to rise. Some may argue that the central bank of this example does not *make* policy choices but rather *implements* a choice made by the legislature.

This argument is susceptible to several types of criticism. First, it could be argued that even if there is certainty as to the policy goal, the independent agency could have several means for achieving the goal. The choice between different available means could have distributional implications. If this is the case, the premise that central bank operations are merely the implementation of policy choices made by elected officials no longer holds.[28]

Secondly, it is rarely easy to define policy goals as precisely as a quantitative inflation target.[29] Indeed, actual central banks mandates are often more nuanced or vague. If there are several possible interpretations of a mandate, this could enable the agency to define its task which unavoidably implies that the agency will determine matters of policy.

Consider for instance the conception of financial stability as a quality of a given financial system. As mentioned, the ECB until recently defined financial stability as 'a state where the build-up of *systemic risk* is prevented' (emphasis added).[30] Systemic risk was in turn described as 'the risk that the provision of necessary financial products and services by the financial system will be impaired to a point where economic growth and welfare may be materially affected'.[31] Pursuant to these definitions, answering the question of whether a society currently has financial stability requires the identification of the scenarios in which systemic risk materialises – ie the scenarios in which the impairment of financial products and services causes economic growth and welfare to be 'materially affected'. This is a vague criterion. Moreover, assuming that it is possible to pin down the relevant scenarios, the next step would be to determine what preventing the 'build-up' of such outcomes involves. Does this involve aiming for no systemic risk? Or are certain low levels of probability of systemic risk materialising acceptable? If so, what is the threshold for when systemic risk is unacceptably high? ECB's definition does not provide us with precise answers.

[28] See N de Boer and J van 't Klooster, 'The ECB, the courts and the issue of democratic legitimacy after Weiss' 57 *CML Rev* (2020) 1689, 1702.

[29] *cf* Bellamy (n 22) 9.

[30] European Central Bank, 'Financial Stability Review' (May 2017) 3.

[31] ibid.

The vagueness of financial stability as a concept exemplifies that although a policy objective is fixed, the precise policy implications may not be given.[32] This does not mean that it is possible or, for that matter, desirable that bank supervisors and other agencies should operate in a mechanical fashion. Rather, the point is that modern banking regulation often will require supervisors and resolution authorities to make decisions that could involve distributional choices.

The influence of agencies under TFT regulation depends on the possibilities of successful court challenge being brought against their decisions. If courts adopt an intrusive standard of review, delegation does not necessarily give the agencies much leeway. Conversely, if courts defer to the agency on matters of law and fact, what at the outset appears as constraints may have little effect in practice.

It seems reasonable to expect that a court's approach to judicial review of a given administrative decision will be a function of the nature of the conditions that must be satisfied for the agency to have the power to make the challenged decision. If the conditions are of a quantitative nature, courts may be more inclined to engage in scrutiny of whether the conditions are met in the case at hand.

Courts may be more reluctant to second guess agency interpretations of conditions that are not easily determined interpreted by reference to traditional sources of law within its jurisdictions. Consider a provision that gives a bank supervisor authority to impose regulatory requirements on individual banks when 'necessary to safeguard financial stability'. This will first require an interpretation of the terms 'necessary' and 'financial stability' and thereafter, the court considering whether the facts at hand justify the supervisor's conclusion that the contested decision was necessary to safeguard financial stability.

We will first consider what the court will do at the interpretative stage. The word 'necessary' is usually taken to require that the goal sought cannot be attained with less intrusive means.[33] At a conceptual level, it is clear what this means. The supervisor must choose the least intrusive measure available for achieving the goal.

Conversely, as argued above, the concept of financial stability is vague. Attempts at specifying its meaning involve some form of value judgement. In the absence of evidence that the legislature had a particularly precise conception of financial stability in mind when the provision was adopted, the court has two options: it can make up its mind as to what it thinks financial stability should mean or it can defer to the understanding that the agency adopted for the purposes of the contested decision.

How will courts review the supervisor's interpretation of what financial stability entails? Consider first a court whose attitude is that there is a correct answer to all questions of interpretation and that therefore seeks to establish the 'best interpretation' of what financial stability entails. For this court, the agency's interpretation

[32] *cf* M Andenas and IH-Y Chiu's point that different Member States may have different 'preferences in risk tolerance in financial activities', see 'Financial stability and legal integration in financial regulation' (2013) 38 *EL Rev* 335, 355–56.

[33] See eg Case C-493/17 *Weiss and Others* ECLI:EU:C:2018:1000, para 72.

carries no more weight than its argumentative force. Such an approach will narrow the space of the agency's ability to create policy through decision-making to interpretations that conform to the court's understanding of financial stability.

Consider next a court that to some extent defers to the interpretation of the agency. The court may have several reasons for doing so. It could be the case that the court finds it difficult to make up its mind regarding what financial stability entails, and thus adopts the agency's interpretation as a pragmatic measure. Another possible motivation is that the court recognises that specifying the meaning of a vague term unavoidably involves policy making and considers the agency as better situated to make such decisions. Under this approach, the court is thus willing to accept the agency's interpretation if it indeed *specifies* rather than *changes* the meaning of the provision. In other words, the court defers to the understanding of the agency if it appears to be plausible.[34]

Once the court has interpreted the terms 'necessary to safeguard financial stability', it will have to consider whether it is possible to protect financial stability (as that concept is understood by the court) through less restrictive means. Any vagueness surrounding the concept of financial stability will spill over into this assessment: it is not possible to consider the necessity of a measure unless it is clear what its goal is. Accordingly, difficulties in grasping what a provision refers to by references to 'financial stability' will cause difficulties for a court trying to determine whether a given measure is necessary to achieve this goal.

Conversely, the application of the necessity test to a regulatory measure is conceptually clear if the measure's goal is precisely defined. However, courts may be reluctant to substitute their view on the likely effects of the measure for that of an agency whose staff has technical expertise on the matter. Such considerations could rationalise CJEU's approach to reviewing administrative acts of EU institutions which require the institution 'to make choices of a technical nature and to undertake complex forecasts and assessments': CJEU case law provides that the institution 'must be allowed, in that context, a broad discretion'.[35]

The above example shows how the wording of the constraints on decision-making on the part of independent agencies conceivably could be of importance for whether courts will engage in a review of their decisions.

9.2.3. Creditor Priority in Bank Insolvency Law and Technocratic Fine-Tuning

BRRD provides that the resolution authority shall have decision-making powers that influence how losses are shared among bank creditors. More specifically, the authority's powers to determine MREL requirements and exclude liabilities

[34] *cf* the ECJ's reasoning in Case C-493/17 *Weiss and others* on the ESCB's specification of the objective of price stability.

[35] Case C-493/17 *Weiss and others*, para 73. See also the discussion at 6.4.4 and 8.5.3.

from bail-in means that loss sharing among bank creditors could be fine-tuned according to the individual circumstances of banks. These elements of the bank-specific creditor priority framework lack a counterpart in general insolvency law. This section argues that they are in line with the TFT approach encountered in post-crisis banking regulation and considers the extent to which the authority's discretion to exercise the said powers is subject to constrains.

Resolution authorities exercise influence over the ultimate distribution of losses in a resolution involving the bail-in power. BRRD Article 44(3) provides that the resolution authority may, subject to one of four conditions being satisfied, exempt certain creditors from bail-in. This adds to the possibilities for differential treatment among creditors, and hence the complexity of the output of the resolution framework. What sets decisions under Article 44(3) apart from the other elements of BRRD that contribute to this complexity, is that preferential treatment derives from the administrative decision-making of the resolution authority.

Since any differentiation among creditors pursuant to BRRD Article 44(3) will result from an administrative decision, this provision has the second attribute of TFT regulation.

How are the conditions from exempting creditors from bail-in worded? Our discussion at 6.4.1 showed that BRRD Article 44(3) seeks to constrain the resolution authority's discretion. We will discuss the degree of constraint with reference to Article 44(3)(b), which, among other things, empowers the resolution authority to exempt claims from bail-in when 'strictly necessary and … proportionate to achieve the continuity of *critical functions*' (emphasis added). This example is chosen because the definition of a critical function, which is further specified in Commission Delegated Regulation 2016/778 Article 6(1),[36] illustrates that some conditions are vague, thereby potentially leaving some value judgement to the resolution authority, while others may be clearer.

Pursuant to Article 6(1), an attribute of a critical function is that 'the sudden disruption of that function would likely have a material negative impact on the third parties, give rise to contagion or undermine the general confidence of market participants'. Accordingly, for a service to be a critical function, disruption of the service must be likely to result in at least one of the three effects listed in the definition. The first of these – 'a material negative impact on third parties' – is vaguely formulated and will require the resolution authority to form a view on when effects are sufficiently grave to cross the materiality threshold. This assessment implicitly involves the determination of whether the interests of such third parties are sufficient to justify other creditors potentially having to bear greater losses to cover

[36] Commission Delegated Regulation (EU) 2016/778 of 2 February 2016 supplementing Directive 2014/59/EU of the European Parliament and of the Council with regard to the circumstances and conditions under which the payment of extraordinary ex post contributions may be partially or entirely deferred, and on the criteria for the determination of the activities, services and operations with regard to critical functions, and for the determination of the business lines and associated services with regard to core business lines [2016] OJ L131/41.

the shortfall left by excluding creditors. By contrast, the second effect listed in the definition – disruption being likely to give rise to contagion – is more conceptually clear: is the disruption of the service likely to cause problems for other market participants?

Even if a condition is conceptually clear, disagreement may arise as to whether it is met in a case at hand. As discussed at 6.4.4, it is reasonable to expect that courts will exercise constraint when reviewing the resolution authority's projections of the effects of excluding or not excluding a claim from bail-in. The standard to be applied is one of 'manifest error of assessment'.

As discussed in chapter eight, resolution authorities determine MREL. The resolution authority can to some extent determine that a bank's debt obligations shall only count towards this requirement if the debt ranks below the bank's general unsecured debt. As banks will often prefer to meet such requirements by issuing debt rather than issuing new shares, the resolution authority's determination that debt shall only count towards MREL insofar as it is subordinated effectively is a requirement as to how banks structure the priority among their creditors.

Does the MREL framework constitute TFT regulation? It should first be noted that the framework is intended to produce different requirements for different banks. This is the case both with respect to the total requirement imposed on banks and the extent to which liabilities must be subordinated to count towards satisfying the requirement. There is a minimum MREL requirement that only applies to banks that have been designated as G-SIIs. Other banks are subject to decision-making on the part of the resolution authority. Accordingly, the framework produces complex regulatory outputs as we defined that term at 9.2.1.

Except for the minimum MREL for G-SIIs, which derives from CRR, MREL requirements are products of administrative decision-making on the part of the resolution authority. Accordingly, the MREL framework also has the second attribute of TFT regulation.

The question then is what constraints apply to the decision-making of the resolution authority? We gave an account at 8.5.2 of the conditions that apply for the resolution authority's power to determine that liabilities must be subordinated to count towards MREL. We will not repeat them here. What that section showed, is that there are several constraints, and the MREL framework therefore has the third attribute of TFT regulation. The conditions differ in terms of precision. On the one hand, there are conditions that either reference quantitative measures, such as the assets of a bank, or other easily verifiable information, eg whether the bank has been classified as a G-SII by the authority tasked with identifying such institutions.[37] On the other hand, a bank may be required to meet MREL with subordinated liabilities insofar as it 'pose[s] a systemic risk in the event of its failure'. As discussed at 9.2.2, the determination of whether conditions of this type are satisfied necessarily involves some form of value judgements with respect to what

[37] See CRD IV art 131.

risks society is willing to assume. To sum up, the MREL framework fits neatly into the TFT approach.

It is true that priority rules contained in legal acts such as SFD, FCD and CBD still embody an approach where the priority framework is merely facilitative: banks are empowered to give certain creditors priority over others but are not obliged to make use of this possibility. It is thus not the case that a TFT approach to creditor priority has completely replaced the pre-GFC approach. This is the same for banking regulation. While we have argued that key pieces of post-GFC reform embody a TFT approach, it remains the case that other parts of the framework follow other approaches, such as more traditional command-and-control regulation and meta-regulation. For instance, it remains a possibility for banks to receive permission to calculate capital requirements under the internal ratings-based approach (IRB), thus employing the bank's internal models to this end.[38]

The shift from meta-regulation to a TFT approach means that banking regulation and the creditor priority framework both remain complex. The difference is that agencies now have a more active role in forging the complexity as compared to under the frameworks of pre-crisis times. An implicit premise of post-GFC reform thus seems to be that the problem with earlier approaches was not complexity but too little technocratic involvement. It remains to be seen whether the new approach will fare better.

[38] See 2.3.2.

10

What is the Future of Bank-Specific Creditor Priority Rules?

10.1. The End of Creditor Priority?

What does the future hold for the bank-specific creditor priority regime? Will the trend towards more differentiation, and hence complexity, endure, or has the law reached a state that will remain stable in the future?

The most recent wave of priority rules is still fresh. Importantly, banks will need to issue large volumes of subordinated debt in the coming years to comply with MREL requirements. This could lead policymakers to give banks some breathing room in the immediate future.

However, there have been calls to amend BRRD so that all deposits will enjoy priority ahead of general unsecured creditors in liquidation and resolution.[1] The chair of the SRB has voiced the opinion that not only resolution, but also the national procedures for bank liquidation – 'normal insolvency proceedings', in BRRD's terminology – should be subject to harmonisation.[2] Such reform could very well involve further differentiation with respect to priority among the unsecured bank creditors.

This chapter considers how certain future scenarios could cause reform with implications for creditor priority. First, we discuss the link between the MREL framework's requirement for issuing subordinated liabilities and financial stability, and events that may discredit it (10.2). Thereafter, we discuss whether further reform within the Banking Union – the establishment of a European Deposit Insurance Scheme (EDIS) and/or expanding the scope of banks under the SRB's remit – could lead to further EU law harmonisation of the creditor priority framework (10.3).

[1] European Central Bank, 'Opinion of the European Central Bank of 8 March 2017 on a proposal for a directive of the European Parliament and of the Council on amending Directive 2014/59/EU as regards the ranking of unsecured debt instruments in insolvency hierarchy' (Opinion 2017) OJ C132/1 para 2.3.

[2] E König, 'Why we need an EU liquidation regime for banks' (2018), available at srb.europa.eu/en/node/622.

10.2. MREL and Financial Stability

The MREL framework is an important part of the bulwark against financial crises. As discussed in chapter eight, larger banks are required to satisfy their MREL requirement with own funds or debts with lower priority than general unsecured debt. Assuming that banks generally prefer to issue subordinated debt to satisfy such requirements insofar as the own funds they hold for other purposes are insufficient to this end, MREL requirements effectively have implications for priority among bank creditors.

As discussed at 9.2.3, BRRD's approach to determining MREL is one of technocratic fine-tuning. Resolution authorities determine MREL on a case-by-case basis as part of the resolution planning tailored to the specificities of individual banks. If a bank is failing, resolution authorities may intervene and convert to equity the debt instruments issued to satisfy MREL, thereby restoring a failing bank's compliance with capital requirements. Intervention is ideally to occur before problems spread to other banks. By restricting bail-in to the claims held by investors in MREL-eligible debt – ie long-term debt – the framework prevents runs from short-term creditors. As a resolved bank's depositors escape the process unscathed, a resolution need not cause depositors at other banks to doubt whether their funds are at risk.

That is, if all goes according to plan. Technocratic fine-tuning was not the only possible course for post-crisis regulatory reform. Another course would be to opt for more blunt requirements. In the years after the GFC, calls were made in academia for increasing own funds requirements by a substantially higher amount than what ended up being the case.[3] In a similar vein, the Independent Commission on Banking established by the UK government had 'considerable sympathy for arguments in favour of setting much higher minimum equity requirements' than the minimum established by the Basel III framework although certain counterarguments – increased financing costs being passed on to borrowers, the competitiveness of the UK banking sector, and the risk of bank business migrating to unregulated sectors – caused the Commission to opt for less radical proposals.[4]

As discussed at 8.2, the function of MREL could be viewed as equivalent to a higher own funds requirement. In both cases, the idea is that banks should be able to withstand larger losses than they are able to absorb by observing current capital requirements. A recurring issue in capital requirements regulation is whether debt instruments can be loss absorbing and should thus count towards such requirements. The root of the issue lies in a key difference between equity and

[3] A Admati and M Hellwig, *The Banker's New Clothes: What's Wrong with Banking and What to Do about It* (Princeton, Princeton University Press, 2013).

[4] Independent Commission on Banking, 'Final Report: Recommendations' (September 2011) 90–91.

debt instruments: equity instruments do not require the issuer to make payments. When a company suffers losses, its shareholders seamlessly absorb these losses. By contrast, debt must be paid on maturity come what may. This raises the question of why policymakers even bother to design policies where debt may count as loss-absorbing capital. The short answer is likely the view that increases in equity requirements reduce bank lending, which in turn reduces growth.

Requiring banks to issue subordinated debt is essentially a requirement to designate a class of creditors whose claims shall be converted into equity instruments once the bank's debt-load becomes too large, thereby shielding other creditors. In theory, these creditors will upon conversion absorb losses in the same manner as shareholders. However, this outcome requires a mechanism for determining when the debt load is too large, and the subordinated debt accordingly shall convert.

At present, a decision by the resolution authority is necessary for bank debts to convert to equity. Some have argued that the resolution authority might not make a timely decision as the resolution conditions are rather vague and the resolution authority might have an incentive to delay intervention.[5] Others note that once the point of conversion is approaching, persons who stand to benefit from a conversion and those who do not will seek to influence whether conversion occurs.[6] The concern is that this, in turn, could cause panic sales of the shares and convertible instruments issued by other banks.[7]

There are thus theoretical doubts as to the whether MREL requirements will perform as policymakers hope for, that is, make possible the recapitalisation of banks without government funds. What does the experience with the resolution framework so far tell us? The resolution of the Spanish bank Banco Popular is the sole example of resolution under BRRD's framework.[8] In that case, the SRB determined that the conditions for resolution were satisfied. The resolution involved the following steps: First, the SRB used the power to write-down and convert capital instruments to cancel the bank's shares and convert outstanding AT1 and Tier 2 instruments to shares. Thereafter, SRB employed the sale of business tool to transfer the new shares to Banco Santander for a consideration of one euro. The immediate result was that Banco Popular became a subsidiary of Banco Santander, effectively ensuring that creditors other than holders of AT1 and Tier 2 instruments were paid in full.

The resolution of Banco Popular was thus not a resolution involving the use of the bail-in tool to convert debt with priority above own funds to shares. While the resolution appears to be successful, it does not necessarily imply that the resolution

[5] W-G Ringe, 'Bank Bail-in Between Liquidity and Solvency' (2018) 92 *American Bankruptcy Law Journal* 299, 322–26; M Schillig, *Resolution and Insolvency of Banks and Financial Institutions* (Oxford, Oxford University Press, 2016) para 9.14.

[6] Admati and Hellwig (n 3) 188. This point is made in respect of so-called contingent convertible securities but the point would appear to also apply to subordinated MREL debt.

[7] ibid.

[8] Single Resolution Board, Decision of 7 June 2017 SRB/EES/2017/08.

framework will work if used to recapitalise a bank on a stand-alone basis. In other words, uncertainty still attaches to whether MREL requirements will produce the desired results.

What seems clear is this: if resolution authorities in a future crisis prove unwilling to convert MREL-debt to equity, or such conversion has spillover effects on financial stability, the policy response may very possibly be to scrap the idea of MREL and instead increase equity requirements. Were this to occur, the effect would be to reduce the relevance of creditor priority in bank insolvency law.

10.3. Banking Union and the Further Harmonisation of Bank-Specific Priority Rules

10.3.1. The Proposed European Deposit Insurance Scheme and Creditor Priority

In 2015, the Commission made a proposal for the establishment of a European Deposit Insurance Scheme (EDIS). EDIS would establish a pan-European system for deposit insurance within the Banking Union.[9] While national DGSs established in the Banking Union would continue to front the guarantee to depositors of their respective participating banks, the national DGSs would be entitled to claim compensation from a Deposit Insurance Fund.[10] The losses absorbed by the national fund would thus ultimately be covered by the common funds, thereby spreading the losses across national banking sectors. The EDIS proposal would therefore, if adopted, have seen the creation of a common fund that backs the DGSs of states participating in the Banking Union. The scope of protection would generally remain the same in terms of the amount guaranteed and the persons excluded from protection (eg financial institutions and public authorities).

The rationale for a common European deposit insurance scheme is the view that the credibility of such schemes at present derives from the fiscal strength of the scheme's home state, notwithstanding that Member States are under no legal obligation to backstop the scheme. This in turn gives banks whose home state has fiscal strength a competitive advantage vis-à-vis other banks. The underlying logic appears to be the following: Deposits will migrate across borders if depositors believe that: (i) there is a sufficiently grave risk the deposit-taking bank will fail, (ii) the national deposit guarantee scheme will have insufficient funds to make the

[9] Commission, 'Proposal for a Regulation of the European Parliament and of the Council amending Regulation (EU) 806/2014 in order to establish a European Deposit Insurance Scheme' COM (2015) 586 final.

[10] This final phase, termed 'full insurance' in the proposal, would follow a phase of 'reinsurance' and 'co-insurance'. See COM (2015) 586 final, 10–12.

required pay-outs to depositors, and (iii) the bank's home state will fail to act as an ultimate guarantor of the deposits.

The EDIS proposal faced resistance. Wolfgang Schäuble, who was the German minister of finance when the proposal was put forward, opposed it as premature. He argued that there was a need for reducing the risks to which Southern European banks were exposed at the time, and that the creation of EDIS would dull the incentives of their home states to agree to reform.[11] Among the risk reduction reforms called for was the treatment of holdings of government bonds under the capital requirements framework. As remains the case at time of writing, holdings of bonds issued by Member States are assigned a risk-weight of zero per cent under the standardised approach for calculating credit risk and banks may therefore invest in such instruments without having to hold any capital to back the investment.[12] In essence, these rules treat sovereign bonds as if they were risk free. Considering that a write down was forced upon holders of Greek sovereign bonds in 2011, this underlying assumption clearly does not hold.

No quick fix to alleviate these concerns was available. Making investments in sovereign debt subject to more onerous capital requirements would disadvantage Member States who traditionally have relied on their banking sector to purchase significant quantities of their sovereign debt issuances. The requested reform would therefore translate into higher financing costs for these Member States.

Not much progress was made in the years following 2015, but EDIS was not dead. After being elected President of the European Commission, Ursula von der Leyen pledged to work towards agreement on EDIS. Moreover, in a somewhat unexpected turn of events in November 2019, Olaf Scholz, who by then had succeeded Schäuble as the German minister of finance (and would later go on to serve as Chancellor of Germany), published an opinion in the *Financial Times* that held the door open for EDIS.[13]

Scholz' proposal may have disappointed some, however. First, the EDIS envisaged by Scholz would only be a reinsurance scheme. This would likely mean that losses would not be fully shared throughout the Banking Union. Rather, a national guarantee fund paying out funds to depositors would, at best, receive fractional loss coverage from the common fund. By comparison, under the Commission's proposal, reinsurance was intended to only be a transitional arrangement on the road to a fully-fledged common scheme. Secondly, Scholz made clear that EDIS would have to be accompanied by reform of the capital requirements for holding sovereign bonds.

The prospects of EDIS were discussed during the spring of 2022 as the so-called Eurogroup, an informal meeting forum for the finance ministers of Member States

[11] J Brunsden, 'Germany warns on eurozone bank deposit plan' *Financial Times* (8 December 2015).
[12] CRR art 114(4).
[13] O Scholz, 'Germany will consider EU-wide bank deposit reinsurance' *Financial Times* (6 November 2019).

whose currency is the euro, worked on a 'draft work plan to complete the Banking Union'.[14] However, the plan failed to gain sufficient support.[15]

What is the link between the push for the establishment of EDIS and creditor priority in resolution and winding up of banks? It seems clear that a clever fix to the creditor priority framework cannot reconcile the conflicting interests that so far have prevented its establishment. What is of interest in the context of the themes of this book, is that the EDIS proposal implies that policy makers do not entirely trust the elaborate creditor priority system under current EU bank insolvency law to safeguard financial stability. If the priority system works as intended, there should be no risk that depositors covered by national deposit guarantee schemes would stand to lose money. Consider first the case of deposits held with larger banks. As discussed in chapter eight, larger banks will be subject to MREL-requirements and will likely issue debt to comply with such requirements. Given that deposits covered by a DGS have priority over general unsecured debt, debt eligible for MREL may be written down while leaving covered deposits untouched. Moreover, it is not permissible to write down covered deposits through the bail-in tool.[16] While the use of the other resolution tools is not subject to equally strict constraints, the resolution authority is required to impose losses on almost all other unsecured creditors before losses may be imposed on covered depositors.[17] The implication is that if the resolution framework functions as envisaged, and makes possible the recapitalisation of a large failing bank without resorting to support from its home state, the identity of its home state should be irrelevant for covered depositors.

Consider next the case of covered deposits held with a smaller bank. Such banks will often not be subject to MREL requirements that exceed the capital they in any event would hold to satisfy the capital requirements. In such cases, the bank will not necessarily have issued subordinated debt to satisfy MREL. This means that if the bank is liquidated under 'normal insolvency proceedings', which appears to be the most likely scenario, there will not necessarily be a layer of debt between the bank's own funds and its covered deposits. This in turn increases the risk that there will not be a purchaser willing to assume the covered deposits, which would result in the national DGS being required to make payments to depositors. If covered depositors anticipate this outcome, they will have an incentive to ask themselves whether the bank's home state has the fiscal ability to act as the ultimate guarantor of their deposits. If their conclusion is negative, it would be rational to withdraw their deposits at the first sight of trouble.

Where will such depositors transfer their deposits? As argued above, a view implicit in the arguments for the EDIS proposal is that deposits will be transferred to banks in Member States with a strong capacity to back national deposit guarantee

[14] P Donohoe, 'Remarks following the Eurogroup meeting of 23 May 2022' (23 May 2022).
[15] P Tamma, 'Eurozone countries kill banking union plan' (*Politico*, 9 June 2022), at www.politico.eu/article/eurozone-countries-kill-banking-union-plan.
[16] BRRD art 44(2)(a).
[17] See the discussion at 6.4.3.

schemes, hence causing cross-border migration.[18] However, this need not be the case. If we accept the premise that covered deposits are safe in large domestic banks with subordinated debt available for recapitalisation, a small bank's depositors would have little to gain by moving their deposits to banks in other Menber States rather than to a large domestic bank. Accordingly, other national banks with ample amounts of own funds and eligible liabilities could provide a 'safe haven' for a small struggling bank's depositors, thereby mitigating a cross-border flight of deposits. This would solve one of the issues motivating the EDIS proposal.

The efforts to introduce EDIS suggest that the Commission does not subscribe to this logic. This may be a perfectly reasonable position. The above analysis assumes that covered depositors have a clear picture of numerous factors, including the operation of the priority rules. The combined effects of preferential priority and MREL requirements could easily prove hard to grasp for a person with little experience with bank insolvency law. It might thus be unreasonable to expect that an uninformed depositor is able to grasp the combined effects of preferential priority and MREL requirements. By contrast, the concept of a deposit guarantee is straightforward.

10.3.2. The Single Resolution Mechanism and Creditor Priority

In 2021, the Commission launched consultations on the review of the application of the EU's crisis management and deposit insurance framework.[19] The consultation concerned, among other things, whether EU law should harmonise creditor priority in national bank liquidation regimes to eliminate national differences. The Eurogroup has recently agreed to strengthen the 'the common framework for bank crisis management and national deposit guarantee schemes'.[20] Such reform is to include 'harmonisation of targeted features of national bank insolvency laws'.

As noted on several occasions throughout this book, BRRD only partially harmonises bank insolvency law. The directive conceptualises bank insolvency law as consisting of two tracks: resolution, which is to be used when in the public interest, and, in other cases, liquidation under 'normal insolvency proceedings'. While BRRD harmonises national resolution frameworks to a great extent, the directive contains few requirements for national frameworks applicable to the liquidation of insolvent banks whose failure does to not necessitate resolution. For instance, Member States remain free to determine whether the power to open proceedings and appoint a liquidator or administrator should rest with the courts or a public authority.[21]

[18] COM (2015) 586 final 4.

[19] Commission, 'Targeted Consultation: Review of the Crisis Management and Deposit Insurance Framework' (2021).

[20] Eurogroup, 'Statement on the future of the Banking Union of 16 June 2022' (16 June 2022).

[21] See 3.5.

One notable exception discussed at 5.3.1 is that BRRD requires that covered deposits and other deposits held by physical persons and SMEs shall have priority over general unsecured creditors in liquidation.

It is possible that future reform proposals could involve further harmonisation of creditor priority in bank insolvency law as a 'stand-alone' reform measure, that is, without any accompanying amendments to other parts of the framework. The rationale would be that it would level the playing field between banks and ensure that creditors of European banks receive the same treatment. It is debateable whether full harmonisation will bring about significant benefits. While a recent report on national bank insolvency regimes has highlighted that there are discrepancies as to whether covered deposits enjoy priority over all other unsecured debt,[22] the differences seem trivial. The reason is that unsecured debts that typically enjoy priority over general unsecured debt – claims for wages and accrued taxes – in the case of a bank failure will be relatively small compared to the covered deposits owed by the bank. Accordingly, these discrepancies are not of significant importance for the expected recovery of depositors and other commercial creditors. An argument against further harmonisation is that creditor priority is rooted in national traditions and values.[23] This is viewed as an obstacle to harmonisation of the general insolvency law of the Member States.[24]

It is also possible that further harmonisation of creditor priority would form part of a larger reform of EU bank insolvency law. It is conceivable that further harmonisation is deemed a necessary complement to other pieces of reform. There have been discussions in recent years on whether BRRD's two-tracked system should be replaced by with a single framework applicable to all banks.[25]

The creation of a single bank insolvency procedure could take different forms. For instance, a proposal put forward by Schillig is to simply extend the scope of application of BRRD's resolution framework to all banks, meaning that any bank that is failing or likely to fail shall be resolved.[26] Such reform would do away with the current requirement that a bank may only be resolved insofar as this is in the public interest.[27] Moreover, liquidation of banks under national frameworks would no longer be a possibility.

Subjecting all failing banks to a single framework – essentially today's resolution framework without a public interest test – would thus render the concept of

[22] VVA, Grimaldi and Bruegel, 'Study on the differences between bank insolvency laws and on their potential harmonisation: Final report' (November 2019) 31.

[23] European Commission, 'Summary report of the Public and Targeted consultations on the review of the Crisis Management and Deposit Insurance (CMDI) framework' (2021) s 2.2.2.

[24] FM Mucciarelli, 'Not Just Efficiency: Insolvency Law in the EU and Its Political Dimension' (2013) 14 *European Business Organization Law Review* 175, 197–99.

[25] For a summary of current proposals for the future development of EU bank insolvency law, see J-H Binder, 'Failing Banks within the Banking Union at the crossroads: Taking stock and next steps' (2022) EBI Working Paper Series No 115.

[26] M Schillig, 'EU bank insolvency law harmonisation: What next?' (2021) 30 *International Insolvency Review* 239.

[27] See BRRD art 32(1)(c).

'normal insolvency proceedings' devoid of content. This would necessitate some technical adjustments to BRRD. As the directive applies at present, the content of the rules applicable to such proceedings have an indirect effect on how a given Member State is required to implement the directive's resolution framework. For instance, Article 48 provides that a bail-in shall write down claims in accordance with the 'hierarchy of claims in normal insolvency proceedings'. This means, among other things, that if debts owed to public authorities have priority ahead of general unsecured debts in whatever proceedings a Member State employs for liquidating banks, the bail-in must respect this priority: It will not be permissible to write down the claims of the public authorities unless general unsecured claims first have been fully written-down (except for general unsecured debts exempted from bail-in by virtue of BRRD Article 44(2) or (3)). Conversely, where the bank's home state does not accord preferential priority to such claims in normal insolvency proceedings, the resolution authority must subject the claims to bail-in in the same manner as general unsecured debt.

Should 'normal insolvency proceedings' cease to be a feature of national laws, the result would be to impair the operation of BRRD's provisions that reference such proceedings. For instance, the requirement in Article 48 would become devoid of content. Some technical fix to these issues would thus be required.

However, full harmonisation of creditor priority in bank insolvency law would not be the only solution to this technical issue. It would for instance be possible to insert a new provision in the reformed framework providing that a write down shall follow the hierarchy that applies in a liquidation under the general insolvency laws of the bank's home state, subject to the modifications set out in BRRD Article 108. The result would likely be that Member States retain a level of autonomy with respect to creditor priority that resembles that under the current framework.

The creation of a single bank insolvency procedure could involve the SRB being entrusted with its application with respect to all banks established in the Banking Union.[28] Such further centralisation could form part of the reform necessary for reaching political agreement on the establishment of EDIS – which, as discussed above, would comprise all deposits, not only those held with banks currently under the SRB's remit.

Tasking the SRB with responsibility for applying a future unitary bank insolvency framework would give rise to a separate argument for full harmonisation of creditor priority. In essence, the argument is that full harmonisation is necessary to make it easier for the SRB to apply the framework. This is in fact also currently an issue: the interplay between BRRD/SRMR and 'normal insolvency proceedings' means that the SRB currently administers 21 slightly different versions of the resolution framework. Giving the SRB the responsibility for handling every bank failure within the Banking Union would compound this issue.

[28] A Gelpern and N Veron, 'An Effective Regime for Non-viable Banks: US Experience and Considerations for EU Reform' (Brussels, European Parliament: The Economic Governance Support Unit, 2019) 51.

BIBLIOGRAPHY

Adler, BE and Triantis, G, 'Debt Priority and Options in Bankruptcy: A Policy Intervention' (2017) 91 *American Bankruptcy Law Journal* 563.

Admati, A and Hellwig, M, *The Banker's New Clothes: What's Wrong with Banking and What to Do about It* (Princeton, Princeton University Press, 2013).

Admati, AR, DeMarzo, PM, Hellwig, MF and Pfleider, P, 'Fallacies, Irrelevant Facts, and Myths in the Discussion of Capital Regulation: Why Bank Equity is Not Socially Expensive' (2013) Rock Center for Corporate Governance at Stanford University Working Paper No 161.

Ahlborn, C and Piccinin, D, 'The Application of the Principles of Restructuring Aid to Banks during the Financial Crisis' (2010) 9 *European State Aid Law Quarterly* 47.

Aikman, D, Galesic, M, Gigerenzer, G, Kapadia, S, Katsikopoulos, K, Kothiyal, A, Murphy, E and Neumann, T, 'Taking uncertainty seriously: simplicity versus complexity in financial regulation' (2021) 30 *Industrial and Corporate Change* 31.

Alesina, A and Tabellini, G, 'Bureaucrats or Politicians? Part I: A Single Policy Task' (2007) 97 *American Economic Review* 169.

Alexander, K, 'Regulating the Structure of the EU Banking Sector' (2015) 16 *European Business Organization Law Review* 227.

Alexander, K, 'The European Central Bank and Banking Supervision: The Regulatory Limits of the Single Supervisory Mechanism' (2016) 13 *European Company & Financial Law Review* 467.

Allen, F, Carletti, E and Gu, X, 'The Roles of Banks in Financial Systems' in Berger, AN, Molyneux, P and Wilson, JOS (eds), *The Oxford Handbook of Banking*, 2nd edn (Oxford, Oxford University Press, 2014).

Allen, WA and Wood, G, 'Defining and achieving financial stability' (2006) 2 *Journal of Financial Stability* 152.

Amadxarif, Z, Brookes, J, Garbarino, N, Patel, R and Walczak, E, 'The language of rules: textual complexity in banking reforms' (2019) Bank of England Staff Working Paper No 834.

Amorello, L, 'Europe Goes "Countercyclical": A Legal Assessment of the New Countercyclical Dimension of the CRR/CRD IV Package' (2016) 17 *European Business Organization Law Review* 137.

Andenas, M and Chiu, IH-Y, 'Financial stability and legal integration in financial regulation' (2013) 38 *EL Rev* 335.

Andenas, M and Chiu, IH-Y, *The Foundations and Future of Financial Regulation* (London, Routledge, 2014) 102.

Andenæs, MH, *Konkurs* (Oslo, MH Andenæs, 2009).

Anderson, H, 'What is the purpose of insolvency proceedings?' (2016) *Journal of Business Law* 670.

Anderson, H, Cooke, C and Gullifer, L, 'National Report for England' in Faber, D, Vermunt, N, Kilborn, J, Richter, T and Tirado, I (eds), *Ranking and Priority of Creditors* (Oxford, Oxford University Press 2016).

Angeloni, I and Lenihan, N, 'Competition and state aid rules in the time of banking union' in Faia, E, Hackethal, A, Haliassos, M and Langenbucher, K (eds), *Financial Regulation: A Transatlantic Perspective* (Cambridge, Cambridge University Press 2015).

Armour, J, 'The Law and Economics Debate about Secured Lending: Lessons for European Lawmaking' (2008) 5 *European Company and Financial Law Review* 3.

Armour, J and Gordon, JN, 'Systemic Harms and Shareholder Value' (2014) 6 *Journal of Legal Analysis* 35.

Armour, J, Awrey, D, Davies, P, Enriques, L, Gordon, JN, Mayer, C and Payne, J, *Principles of Financial Regulation* (Oxford, Oxford University Press, 2016).

Asimakopoulos, IG, 'The Veneto Banks Resolution: It Shall Be Called "Liquidation"' (2018) 15 *European Company Law* 156.

Avgouleas, E, 'The Global Financial Crisis and the Disclosure Paradigm in European Financial Regulation: The Case of Reform' (2009) 6 *European Company and Financial Law Review* 440.

Awrey, D and Judge, K, 'Why Financial Regulation Keeps Falling Short' (2020) 61 *Boston College Law Review* 2295.

Babis, V, 'The impact of bank crisis prevention, recovery and resolution on shareholder rights' (2012) 6 *Law and Financial Markets Review* 387.

Baldwin, R, Cave, M and Lodge, M, *Understanding Regulation: Theory, Strategy, and Practice*, 2nd edn (Oxford, Oxford University Press, 2012).

Beale, H, Bridge, M, Gullifer, L and Lomnicka, E, *The Law of Security and Title-Based Financing*, 3rd edn (Oxford, Oxford University Press, 2018).

Bebchuk, LA and Fried, JM, 'The Uneasy Case for the Priority of Secured Claims in Bankruptcy' (1996) 105 *Yale Law Journal* 857.

Beck, T, Coyle, D, Dewatripont, M, Freixas, X and Seabright, P, *Bailing out the Banks: Reconciling Stability and Competition* (London, Centre for Economic Policy Research (CEPR), 2010).

Bellamy, R, 'Democracy without democracy? Can the EU's democratic "outputs" be separated from the democratic "inputs" provided by competitive parties and majority rule?' (2010) 17 *Journal of European Public Policy* 2.

Bennett, H, 'Late Floating Charges' in Armour, J and Bennett, H (eds), *Vulnerable Transactions in Corporate Insolvency* (Oxford, Hart Publishing, 2003).

Benoit, S, Colliard, J-E, Hurlin, C and Pérignon, C, 'Where the Risks Lie: A Survey on Systemic Risk' (2017) 21 *Review of Finance* 109.

Benteux, G, Van Gallebaert, C, Bliesener, D, Schneider, H, Wagner, H, Péporté, P, Scheltema, AH, Mercer, C and Black, R, 'Regulated covered bonds: a comparative review' (2009) 4 *Capital Markets Law Journal* 341.

Binder, J-H, 'Ring-Fencing: An Integrated Approach with Many Unknowns' (2015) 16 *European Business Organization Law Review* 97.

Binder, J-H, 'Resolution: Concepts, Requirements, and Tools' in Binder, J-H and Singh, D (eds), *Bank Resolution: The European Regime* (Oxford, Oxford University Press, 2016).

Binder, J-H, 'Resolving a bank – Judicial review with regard to the exercise of resolution powers' in Zilioli, C and Wojcik, K-P (eds), *Judicial Review in the European Banking Union* (Cheltenham, Edward Elgar, 2021).

Binder, J-H, 'Failing Banks within the Banking Union at the crossroads: Taking stock and next steps' (2022) EBI Working Paper Series No 115.

Binder, J-H, Krimminger, M, Nieto, MJ and Singh, D, 'The choice between judicial and administrative sanctioned procedures to manage liquidation of banks: A transatlantic perspective' (2019) 14 *Capital Markets Law Journal* 178.

Black, J, 'Decentring Regulation: Understanding the Role of Regulation and Self-Regulation in a 'Post-Regulatory' World' (2001) 54 *Current Legal Problems* 103.

Black, J, 'Mapping the Contours of Contemporary Financial Services Regulation' (2002) 2 *Journal of Corporate Law Studies* 253.

Black, J, 'Paradoxes and Failures: "New Governance" Techniques and the Financial Crisis' (2012) 75 *Modern Law Review* 1037.

Bliss, R, 'Market Discipline in Financial Markets: Theory, Evidence, and Obstacles' in Berger, AN, Molyneux, P and Wilson, JOS (eds), *The Oxford Handbook of Banking*, 2nd edn (Oxford, Oxford University Press, 2014).

Bork, R, *Einführung in das Insolvenzrecht*, 10th edn (Tübingen, Mohr Siebeck, 2021).

Bork, R and Mangano, R, *European Cross-Border Insolvency Law* (Oxford, Oxford University Press, 2016).

Brunnermeier, M, Crockett, A, Goodhart, C, Persaud, AD and Shin, HS, 'The Fundamental Principles of Financial Regulation' (Geneva Reports on the World Economy, ICMB/CEPR 2009).

Brunnermeier, MK and Oehmke, M, 'Bubbles, Financial Crises, and Systemic Risk' in Constantinides, GM, Harris, M and Stulz, RM (eds), *Handbook of the Economics of Finance*, vol 2B (Amsterdam, Elsevier, 2013).

Busch, D, 'Governance of the European Banking Union's Single Resolution Mechanism' (2017) 28 *European Business Law Review* 447.

Campbell, A and Lastra, RM 'Definition of Bank Insolvency and Types of Bank Insolvency Proceedings' in Lastra, RM (ed), *Cross-Border Bank Insolvency* (Oxford, Oxford University Press, 2011).

Chattopadhyay, R, *Bridge Banks in Deutschland: Abwicklung und Restrukturierung systemrelevanter Banken durch Vermögensübertragung* (Weisbaden, Springer, 2017).

Čihák, M and Nier, E, 'The Need for Special Resolution Regimes for Financial Institutions – The Case of the European Union' (2012) 2 *Harvard Business Law Review* 395.

Colliard, J-E and Georg, C-P, 'Measuring Regulatory Complexity' (2020) CEPR Discussion Paper 14377.

Colomo, PI, 'EU Merger Control Between Law and Discretion: When Is An Impediment to Effective Competition Significant?' (2021) 44 *World Competition* 347.

Conac, P-H, 'Subordinated Debt and Self-placement: Mis-selling of Financial Products' (Brussels, European Parliament: Policy Department A, 2018).

Cooter, R and Ulen, T, *Law & Economics*, 6th edn (Boston, Pearson Addison-Wesley, 2012).

Craig, P, 'Judicial review and judicial deference' in Scholten, M and Brenninkmeijer, A (eds), *Controlling EU Agencies: The Rule of Law in a Multi-jurisdictional Legal Order* (Cheltenham, Edward Elgar, 2020).

Crawford, J, 'Credible Losers: A Regulatory Design for Prudential Market Discipline' (2017) 54 *American Business Law Journal* 107.

Cyndecka, MA, 'The problem of objectives pursued by the state under the application of the Market Economy Investor Principle (MEIP)' (2015) 128 *Tidsskrift for Rettsvitenskap* 263.

Dal Bó, E, 'Regulatory capture: A review' (2006) 22 *Oxford Review of Economic Policy* 203.

Davies, P, 'The Fall and Rise of Debt: Bank Capital Regulation After the Crisis' (2015) 16 *European Business Organization Law Review* 491.

Dawson, M, Maricut-Akbik, A and Bobic, A, 'Reconciling Independence and accountability at the European Central Bank: The false promise of Proceduralism' (2019) 25 *European Law Journal* 75.

de Bandt, O and Hartmann, P, 'Systemic Risk: A Survey' (2000) ECB Working Paper No 35.

de Boer, N and van 't Klooster, J, 'The ECB, the courts and the issue of democratic legitimacy after Weiss' 57 *CML Rev* (2020) 1689.

de Weijs, R, 'Too Big to Fail as a Game of Chicken with the State: What Insolvency Law Theory Has to Say About TBTF and Vice Versa' (2013) 14 *European Business Organization Law Review* 201.

de-Ramon, SJA, Francis, WB and Milonas, K, 'An overview of the UK banking sector since the Basel Accord: insights from a new regulatory database' (2017) Bank of England Staff Working Paper No 652.

Deguée, J-P, 'The Winding Up Directive Finally Establish Uniform Private International Law for Banking Insolvency Proceedings' (2004) 15 *European Business Law Review* 99.

Dewatripont, M and Freixas, X, 'Bank Resolution: Lessons from the Crisis' in Dewatripont, M and Freixas, X (eds), *The Crisis Aftermath: New Regulatory Paradigms* (London, Centre for Economic Policy Research (CEPR), 2012).

Diamond, DW and Dybvig, PH, 'Bank Runs, Deposit Insurance, and Liquidity' (1983) 91 *Journal of Political Economy* 401.

Diamond, DW, 'Financial Intermediation and Delegated Monitoring' (1984) 51 *Review of Economic Studies* 393.

Dragomir, L, *European Prudential Banking Regulation and Supervision: The Legal Dimension* (London, Routledge, 2010).

Drahos, P and Krygier, M, 'Regulation, institutions and networks' in Drahos, P (ed), *Regulatory Theory: Foundations and Applications* (Acton, ANU Press, 2017).

Eidenmüller, H, 'Comparative Corporate Insolvency Law' in Gordon, JN and Ringe, W-G (eds), *The Oxford Handbook of Corporate Law and Governance* (Oxford, Oxford University Press, 2018).

Eidenmüller, H, 'What is an insolvency proceeding?' (2018) 92 *American Bankruptcy Law Journal* 53.

Ellingsæter, SS, 'Creditor Priority and Financial Stability: A study of the emergence and rationales of the creditor hierarchy in EU and EEA bank insolvency law' (PhD thesis, University of Oslo, 2020).
Enriques, L and Gargantini, M, 'The Expanding Boundaries of MiFID's Duty to Act in the Client's Best Interest: The Italian Case' (2017) 3 *Italian Law Journal* 485.
Finch, V and Milman, D, *Corporate Insolvency Law: Perspectives and Principles*, 3rd edn (Cambridge, Cambridge University Press 2017).
Gai, P, Kemp, M, Sánchez Serrano, A and Schnabel, I, 'Regulatory complexity and the quest for robust regulation' (2019) European Systemic Risk Board Reports of the Advisory Scientific Committee No 8.
Ganter, HG, 'Vorbemerkungen vor §§ 49 bis 52' in Kirchhof, H-P, Stürner, R and Eidenmüller, H (eds), *Münchener Kommentar zur Insolvenzordnung*, 4th edn (Munich, CH Beck, 2019).
Gebski, S, 'Competition First? Application of State Aid Rules in the Banking Sector' (2009) 6 *Competition Law Review* 89.
Gelpern, A and Veron, N, 'An Effective Regime for Non-viable Banks: US Experience and Considerations for EU Reform' (Brussels, European Parliament: The Economic Governance Support Unit, 2019).
Gerner-Beuerle, C and Schillig, M, *Comparative Company Law* (Oxford, Oxford University Press, 2019).
Gleeson, S and Guynn, R, *Bank Resolution and Crisis Management: Law and Practice* (Oxford, Oxford University Press, 2016).
Gordon, JN and Ringe, W-G, 'Resolution in the European Banking Union: The Unfinished Agenda of Structural Reform' in Busch, D and Ferrarini, G (eds), *European Banking Union* (Oxford, Oxford University Press, 2015).
Gorton, GB, *Slapped by the Invisible Hand: The Panic of 2007* (Oxford, Oxford University Press, 2010).
Gorton, G and Metrick, A, 'Securitized banking and the run on repo' (2012) 104 *Journal of Financial Economics* 425.
Gorton, G and Winton, A, 'Financial Intermediation' in Constantinides, GM, Harris, M and Stulz, RM (eds), *Handbook of the Economics of Finance*, vol 1A (Amsterdam, Elsevier, 2003).
Grabosky, P, 'Meta-regulation' in Drahos, P (ed), *Regulatory Theory: Foundations and Applications* (Acton, ANU Press, 2017).
Grünewald, SN, *The Resolution of Cross-Border Banking Crises in the European Union* (Alphen aan den Rijn, Kluwer Law International, 2014).
Grünewald, S, 'Judicial Control of Resolution Planning Measures' in Zilioli, C and Wojcik, K-P (eds), *Judicial Review in the European Banking Union* (Cheltenham, Edward Elgar, 2021).
Gullifer, L (ed), *Goode and Gullifer on Legal Problems of Credit and Security*, 6th edn (London, Sweet & Maxwell, 2017).
Gullifer, L and Payne, J, *Corporate Finance Law*, 3rd edn (Oxford, Hart Publishing, 2020).
Hadjiemmanuil, C, 'Special Resolution Regimes for Banking Institutions: Objectives and Limitations' (2013) LSE Law, Society and Economy Working Papers 21/2013.
Haentjens, M (ed), *Financial Collateral: Law and Practice* (Oxford, Oxford University Press, 2020).
Haentjens, M, Wessels, B and Janssen, L, *New Bank Insolvency Law for China and Europe, Volume 2: European Union* (The Hague, Eleven International, 2017).
Haldane, A, 'Constraining Discretion in Bank Regulation' in Goodhart, C, Gabor, D, Vestergaard, J and Ertürk, I (eds), *Central Banking at a Crossroads: Europe and Beyond* (London, Anthem Press, 2014).
Hansmann, H and Kraakman, R, 'Towards Unlimited Shareholder Liability for Corporate Torts' (1991) 100 *The Yale Law Journal* 1879.
Hanson, SG, Kashyap, AK and Stein, JC, 'A Macroprudential Approach to Financial Regulation' (2011) 25 *Journal of Economic Perspectives* 3.
Hardie, I and Macartney, H, 'EU ring-fencing and the defence of too-big-to-fail banks' (2016) 39 *West European Politics* 503.
Harris, SL and Mooney Jr., CW, 'A Property-Based Theory of Security Interests: Taking Debtors' Choices Seriously' (1994) 80 *Virginia Law Review* 2021.

Hellwig, MF, 'Valuation reports in the context of banking resolution: What are the challenges?' (Brussels, European Parliament: The Economic Governance Support Unit, 2018).
Henckel, W, '§ 130' in Henckel, W and Gerhardt, W (eds), *Insolvenzordnung*, vol 4 (Berlin, De Gruyter Recht, 2008).
Huser, K, *Gjeldsforhandling og Konkurs: Omstøtelse*, vol 3 (Bergen, Juristinformasjon, 1992).
Hüpkes, E, 'Allocating Costs of Failure Resolution' in Lastra, RM (ed), *Cross-Border Bank Insolvency* (Oxford, Oxford University Press, 2011).
Iftinchi, V, 'State aid and the financial sector' in Laprévote, F-C, Gray, J and De Cecco, F (eds), *Research Handbook on State Aid in the Banking Sector* (Cheltenham, Edward Elgar, 2017).
Ioannidis, M, 'The Judicial Review of Discretion in the Banking Union: From "Soft" to "Hard(er)" Look?' in Zilioli, C and Wojcik, K-P (eds), *Judicial Review in the European Banking Union* (Cheltenham, Edward Elgar, 2021).
Jackson, TH and Skeel, Jr., DA, 'Dynamic Resolution of Large Financial Institutions' (2012) 2 *Harvard Business Law Review* 435.
Jensen, MC and Meckling, WH, 'Theory of the Firm: Managerial Behavior, Agency Costs and Ownership Structure' (1976) 3 *Journal of Financial Economics* 305.
Kalintiri, A, 'What's in a name? The marginal standard of review of "complex economic assessments" in EU competition enforcement' (2016) 53 *CML Rev* 1283.
Kayser, G and Freudenberg, N, '§ 130' in Kirchhof, H-P, Stürner, R and Eidenmüller, H (eds), *Münchener Kommentar zur Insolvenzordnung*, 3rd edn (Munich, CH Beck, 2013).
Keay, A, Boraine, A and Burdette, D, 'Preferential Debts in Corporate Insolvency: a Comparative Study' (2001) 10 *International Insolvency Review* 167.
Kokkola, T (ed), *The Payment System: Payments, Securities and Derivatives, and the Role of the Eurosystem* (Frankfurt am Main, European Central Bank, 2010).
Kokorin, I, 'The Rise of "Group Solution" in Insolvency Law and Bank Resolution' (2021) 22 *European Business Organization Law Review* 781.
Kraakman, R, Armour, J, Davies, P, Enriques, L, Hansmann, H, Hertig, G, Hopt, K, Kanda, H, Pargendler, M, Ringe, W-G and Rock, E, *The Anatomy of Corporate Law: A Comparative and Functional Approach*, 3rd edn (Oxford, Oxford University Press, 2017).
Krishnamurthy, P, 'Rules, Standards, and Complexity in Capital Regulation' (2014) 43 *The Journal of Legal Studies* S273.
Lamandini, M, Ramos, D and Solana, J, 'The European Central Bank (ECB) Powers As a Catalyst for Change in EU Law. Part 2: SSM, SRM and Fundamental Rights' (2017) 23 *Columbia Journal of European Law* 199.
Laprévote, F-C, 'Selected Issues Raised by Bank Restructuring Plans Under EU State Aid Rules' (2012) 11 *European State Aid Law Quarterly* 93.
Lehmann, M, 'Volcker Rule, Ring-Fencing or Separation of Bank Activities: Comparison of Structural Reform Acts Around the World' (2014) LSE Law, Society and Economy Working Papers 25/2014.
Le Leslé, V and Avramova, S, 'Revisiting Risk-Weighted Assets: Why Do RWAs Differ Across Countries and What Can Be Done About It?' (2012) IMF Working Paper No 12/90.
Lilleholt, L, 'Finansiell trygdgjeving' in Høivik, K, Lunde, T, Truyen, F and Tørum, A (eds), *Håkonarmål 2006* (Bergen, 2006).
Lo Schiavo, G, 'State Aids and Credit Institutions in Europe: What Way Forward?' (2014) 25 *European Business Law Review* 427.
Lo Schiavo, G, *The Role of Financial Stability in EU Law and Policy* (Alphen aan den Rijn, Kluwer Law International, 2017).
Løvold, VI, *Brækhus' Omsetning og Kreditt 1: Tvangsfullbyrdelse, gjeldsforhandling og konkurs* (Oslo, Universitetsforlaget, 2015).
Madaus, S, 'Leaving the Shadows of US Bankruptcy Law: A Proposal to Divide the Realms of Insolvency and Restructuring Law' (2018) 19 *European Business Organization Law Review* 615.
Majone, G, 'The rise of the regulatory state in Europe' (1994) 17 *West European Politics* 77.
Martino, ED, 'Towards an optimal composition of bail-inable debtholders?' (2021) 21 *Journal of Corporate Law Studies* 321.

McCormack, G, *The European Restructuring Directive* (Cheltenham, Edward Elgar, 2021).

McCormack, G, Keay, A and Brown, S, *European Insolvency Law: Reform and Harmonization* (Cheltenham, Edward Elgar, 2017).

McKnight, A, 'Basel 2: the implementation in the UK of its capital requirements for banks' (2007) *Law and Financial Markets Review* 327.

Mevorach, I and Walters, A, 'The Characterization of Pre-insolvency Proceedings in Private International Law' (2020) 21 *European Business Organization Law Review* 855.

Mokal, RJ, *Corporate Insolvency Law: Theory and Application* (Oxford, Oxford University Press, 2005).

Mokal, RJ, 'Liquidity, Systemic Risk, and the Bankruptcy Treatment of Financial Contracts' (2015) 10 *Brooklyn Journal of Corporate, Financial & Commercial Law* 15.

Moloney, N, 'European Banking Union: Assessing its risks and resilience' (2014) 51 *CML Rev* 1609.

Moloney, N, *EU Securities and Financial Markets Regulation*, 3rd edn (Oxford, Oxford University Press, 2014).

Mordhorst, H, 'Verwertung von Kreditsicherheiten im Insolvenzverfahren über das Vermögen des Sicherungsgebers' in Lwowski, H-J, Fischer, G and Gehrlein, M (eds), *Das Recht der Kreditsicherung*, 10th edn (Berlin, Erich Schmidt Verlag, 2018).

Morrison, AD, 'Universal Banking' in Berger, AN, Molyneux, P and Wilson, JOS (eds), *The Oxford Handbook of Banking*, 2nd edn (Oxford, Oxford University Press, 2014).

Morrison, ER, Roe, MJ and Sontchi, CS, 'Rolling back the Repo Safe Harbors' (2014) 69 *The Business Lawyer* 1015.

Mucciarelli, FM, 'Not Just Efficiency: Insolvency Law in the EU and Its Political Dimension' (2013) 14 *European Business Organization Law Review* 175.

Myers, SC, 'Determinants of Corporate Borrowing' (1977) 5 *Journal of Financial Economics* 147.

Myhre, R, 'Må boet lide et tap for å kunne omstøte etter de objektive omstøtelsesregler?' (1992) 105 *Tidsskrift for Rettsvitenskap* 84.

Nier, E and Baumann, U, 'Market discipline, disclosure and moral hazard in banking' (2006) 15 *Journal of Financial Intermediation* 332.

Ojo, M, 'Risk management by the Basel Committee: Evaluating progress made from the 1988 Basel Accord to recent developments' (2010) 18 *Journal of Financial Regulation and Compliance* 305.

Omarova, ST, 'Rethinking the Future of Self-Regulation in the Financial Industry' (2010) 35 *Brooklyn Journal of International Law* 665.

Paech, P, 'The Value of Financial Market Insolvency Safe Harbours' (2016) 36 *OJLS* 855.

Pannen, K, *Krise und Insolvenz bei Kreditinstituten*, 3rd edn (Cologne, Luchterhand, 2010).

Paterson, S, 'Rethinking Corporate Bankruptcy in the Twenty-First Century' (2016) 36 *OJLS* 697.

Paulus, CG and Berberich, M, 'National Report for Germany' in Faber, D, Vermunt, N, Kilborn, J, Richter, T and Tirado, I (eds), *Ranking and Priority of Creditors* (Oxford, Oxford University Press, 2016).

Payne, J, *Schemes of Arrangement*, 2nd edn (Cambridge, Cambridge University Press, 2021).

Payne, J, 'The Role of the Court in Debt Restructuring' (2018) 77 *CLJ* 124.

Pennacchi, G, 'Narrow Banking' (2012) 4 *Annual Review of Financial Economics* 141.

Philippon, T and Salord, A, *Bail-ins and Bank Resolution in Europe: A Progress Report* (Geneva Reports on the World Economy, ICMB/CEPR 2017).

Phillips, M and Tamlyn, L, 'Choice and Initiation of Insolvency Procedure' in Oditah, F (ed), *Insolvency of Banks: Managing the Risks* (London, FT Law & Tax, 1996).

Pohl, M, 'Die Öffnungsklausel der Liquiditätsverordnung – Entwicklung und praktische Umsetzung' (2008) 20 *Zeitschrift für Bankrecht und Bankwirtschaft* 423.

Posner, RA, *Economic Analysis of Law*, 9th edn (New York, Wolters Kluwer Law & Business, 2014).

Ringe, W-G, 'Bank Bail-in Between Liquidity and Solvency' (2018) 92 *American Bankruptcy Law Journal* 299.

Rochet, J-C, 'The Future of Banking Regulation' in Dewatripont, M, Rochet, J-C and Tirole, J, *Balancing the Banks: Global Lessons from the Financial Crisis* (Princeton, Princeton University Press, 2010).

Roe, MJ, 'The Derivatives Market's Payment Priorities as Financial Crisis Accelerator' (2011) 63 *Stanford Law Review* 539.

Rosén, K, *Lov om finansiell sikkerhetsstillelse* (Oslo, Gyldendal, 2011).

Santoro, V and Mecatti, I, 'Write-down and Conversion of Capital Instruments' in Chiti, MP and Santoro, V (eds), *The Palgrave Handbook of European Banking Union Law* (Cham, Palgrave Macmillan, 2019).

Schillig, M, 'Corporate Insolvency Law in the Twenty-First Century: State Imposed or Market Based?' (2014) 14 *Journal of Corporate Law Studies* 1.

Schillig, M, *Resolution and Insolvency of Banks and Financial Institutions* (Oxford, Oxford University Press, 2016).

Schillig, MA, 'The (Il-)Legitimacy of the EU Post-Crisis Bailout System' (2020) 28 *American Bankruptcy Institute Law Review* 135.

Schillig, M, 'EU bank insolvency law harmonisation: What next?' (2021) 30 *International Insolvency Review* 239.

Schinasi, GJ, 'Defining Financial Stability' (2004) IMF Working Paper WP/04/187.

Schmidt, K and Herchen, A, '§ 39' in Schmidt, K (ed), *Insolvenzordnung: InsO mit EuInsVO*, 19th edn (Munich, CH Beck, 2016).

Schoppmeyer, H, 'Anfechtung von Kreditsicherheiten' in Lwowski, H-J, Fischer, G and Gehrlein, M (eds), *Das Recht der Kreditsicherung*, 10th edn (Berlin, Erich Schmidt Verlag, 2018).

Schwarcz, SL, 'The Easy Case for the Priority of Secured Claims in Bankruptcy' (1997) 47 *Duke Law Journal* 425.

Schwarcz, SL, 'Systemic Risk' (2008) 97 *Georgetown Law Journal* 193

Schwarcz, SL, 'The Conundrum of Covered Bonds' (2011) 66 *The Business Lawyer* 561.

Schwarcz, SL, 'Beyond Bankruptcy: Resolution as a Macroprudential Regulatory Tool' (2018) 94 *Notre Dame Law Review* 709.

Schwartz, A, 'Security Interests and Bankruptcy Priorities: A Review of Current Theories' (1981) 10 *Journal of Legal Studies* 1.

Schwartz, A, 'The Continuing Puzzle of Secured Debt' (1984) 37 *Vanderbilt Law Review* 1051.

Segal, N, 'The Effect of Reorganization Proceedings on Security Interests: The Position under English and U.S. Law' (2007) 32 *Brooklyn Journal of International Law* 927.

Shleifer, A and Vishny, R, 'Fire Sales in Finance and Macroeconomics' (2011) 25 *Journal of Economic Perspectives* 29.

Smoleńska, A and van 't Klooster, J, 'A Risky Bet: Climate Change and the EU's Microprudential Framework for Banks' (2022) 8 *Journal of Financial Regulation* 51.

Steinbach, A, 'The Lender of Last Resort in the Eurozone' (2016) 53 *CML Rev* 361.

Tarullo, DK, 'Time-Varying Measures in Financial Regulation' (2020) 83 *Law and Contemporary Problems* 1.

Tirole, J, 'Lessons from the Crisis' in Dewatripont, M, Rochet, J-C and Tirole, J, *Balancing the Banks: Global Lessons from the Financial Crisis* (Princeton, Princeton University Press, 2010).

Tollenaar, NWA, 'The European Commission's Proposal for a Directive on Preventive Restructuring Proceedings' (2017) 30 *Insolvency Intelligence* 65.

Triantis, GG, 'Secured Debt Under Conditions of Imperfect Information' (1992) 21 *Journal of Legal Studies* 225.

Triantis, GG, 'Financial Slack Policy and the Laws of Secured Transactions' (2000) 29 *The Journal of Legal Studies* 35.

Tröger, TH, 'Too Complex to Work: A Critical Assessment of the Bail-in Tool under the European Bank Recovery and Resolution Regime' (2018) 4 *Journal of Financial Regulation* 3.

Tucker, P, *Unelected Power: The Quest for Legitimacy in Central Banking and the Regulatory State* (Princeton, Princeton University Press 2018) 5.

Vale, B, 'The Norwegian banking crisis' in Moe, TG, Solheim, JA and Vale, B (eds), *The Norwegian Banking Crisis* (2004) Norges Bank Occasional Papers No 33.

van der Woude, M, 'Judicial Control in Complex Economic Matters' (2019) 10 *Journal of European Competition Law & Practice* 415.

van Rixtel, A and Gasperini, G, 'Financial crises and bank funding: recent experience in the euro area' (2013) BIS Working Papers No 406.

van Zwieten, K, *Goode on Principles of Corporate Insolvency Law*, 5th edn (London, Sweet & Maxwell, 2018).

VVA, Grimaldi and Bruegel, 'Study on the differences between bank insolvency laws and on their potential harmonisation: Final report' (November 2019).

Waldron, J, 'The Concept and the Rule of Law' (2008) 43 *Georgia Law Review* 1.

Walker, GA, 'Basel III market and regulatory compromise' (2011) 12 *Journal of Banking Regulation* 95.

Warren, E, 'Making Policy with Imperfect Information: The Article 9 Full Priority Debates' (1997) 82 *Cornell Law Review* 137.

Weber, RH and Grünewald, S, 'Settlement Finality and Financial Collateral Directives: ignored but crucial in financial turmoil' (2009) 24 *Butterworths Journal of International Banking and Financial Law* 70.

Wessels, B, 'Commentary on Directive 2001/24/EC on the Reorganisation and Winding Up of Credit Institutions' in Moss, G, Wessels, B and Haentjens, M (eds), *EU Banking and Insurance Insolvency*, 2nd edn (Oxford, Oxford University Press, 2017).

Wetzer, T, 'In two minds: the governance of ring-fenced banks' (2019) 19 Journal of Corporate Law Studies 197.

Yeowart, G, Parsons, R, Murray, E and Patrick, H, *Yeowart and Parsons on the Law of Financial Collateral* (Cheltenham, Edward Elgar, 2016).

INDEX

Ingram Content Group UK Ltd.
Milton Keynes UK
UKHW022354130323
418540UK00004B/189

9 781509 953653